WELLBEING AND POLICY

As wellbeing becomes an increasingly explicit policy goal in countries across the world, the demand for evidence upon which to base intervention is growing. Featuring 41 contributing authors from 18 countries, this book surveys and synthesizes recent developments in wellbeing science and policy to highlight key lessons learned and to offer actionable insights for policy-making.

Opening with a foreword by Roberta Metsola, President of the European Parliament, and an introductory chapter surveying the fundamentals of wellbeing policy, the book reviews the links between wellbeing and various domains, including income, work, health, family, altruism and empathy, ageing, gender, education, housing, environment, crime, democracy, migration, religion, digital technology, and art, culture, and creativity. The book also examines the state of the art on wellbeing policy frameworks in diverse contexts, including developed and developing countries, small and large states, across the world, documenting interventions by governmental, private, or non-governmental organizations. Case studies include Bhutan, New Zealand, Finland, the United Arab Emirates, Canada, Australia, the United Kingdom, Japan, and Malta.

This book is essential reading for anyone interested in progressing towards a wellbeing economy including policy-makers, academics, and students in economics, public policy, public administration, and behavioural and political science.

Marie Briguglio is an Associate Professor at the Department of Economics, University of Malta. She graduated from the Universities of Malta, Stirling, and University College London, has authored over 70 peer-reviewed publications, and has led several collaborative research projects and multi-media works.

Natalia V. Czap is Professor of Economics and the Chair of the Department of Social Sciences at University of Michigan-Dearborn, the United States. Her research interests include behavioural and experimental economics, behavioural public policy, and wellbeing policy.

Kate Laffan is Assistant Professor of Behavioural Science at the Department for Psychological and Behavioural Science at the London School of Economics and Political Science, UK. She researches the reciprocal relationship between human wellbeing and behaviour and works on the application of behavioural science to policy challenges.

WELLBEING AND POLICY

Evidence for Action

Edited by Marie Briguglio, Natalia V. Czap and Kate Laffan

Routledge
Taylor & Francis Group
LONDON AND NEW YORK

Designed cover image: Design idea: co-editors, design elements were sourced from shutterstock.com, design implementation: Marketing, Communications & Alumni Office of the University of Malta.

First published 2025
by Routledge
4 Park Square, Milton Park, Abingdon, Oxon OX14 4RN

and by Routledge
605 Third Avenue, New York, NY 10158

Routledge is an imprint of the Taylor & Francis Group, an informa business

British Library Cataloguing-in-Publication Data
A catalogue record for this book is available from the British Library

ISBN: 978-1-032-46592-0 (hbk)
ISBN: 978-1-032-46591-3 (pbk)
ISBN: 978-1-003-38244-7 (ebk)

DOI: 10.4324/9781003382447

Typeset in Times New Roman
by Apex CoVantage, LLC

We dedicate this book to all those working towards wellbeing – may it serve as a source of information and inspiration.

CONTENTS

FIGURES

TABLES

ABOUT THE EDITORS

Marie Briguglio is an Associate Professor at the Department of Economics, University of Malta. She graduated from the Universities of Malta, Stirling, and University College London, has authored over 70 peer-reviewed publications, and has led several collaborative research projects and multi-media works.

Natalia V. Czap is Professor of Economics and the Chair of the Department of Social Sciences at University of Michigan-Dearborn, the United States. Her research interests include behavioural and experimental economics, behavioural public policy, and wellbeing policy.

Kate Laffan is Assistant Professor of Behavioural Science at the Department for Psychological and Behavioural Science at the London School of Economics and Political Science, UK. She researches the reciprocal relationship between human wellbeing and behaviour and works on the application of behavioural science to policy challenges.

CONTRIBUTORS

Amal AlBlooshi is Director of the National Program for Happiness and Wellbeing at the Ministry of Community Development in the United Arab Emirates. Amal enjoys rich experience in wellbeing from various lenses and governmental perspectives.

Michelle Baddeley is Professor of Economics with UTS Business, University of Technology Sydney, Australia. She holds a bachelor of economics degree (1st class) and B.A. (psychology) from the University of Queensland and M.Phil./Ph.D. in economics from the University of Cambridge.

Leonie Baldacchino is Associate Professor at The Edward de Bono Institute for Creative Thinking and Innovation at the University of Malta and Fellow of the International Society for the Study of Creativity and Innovation.

Kehinde Balogun is a PhD candidate on Emotion and Wellbeing, focusing on Indigenous Knowledge at the Universidade Católica Portuguesa in Portugal. Prior to this, she was a Senior Researcher at the United Nations University Institute for Environment and Human Security (UNU-EHS) in Germany working on Futures and Transformation.

Chris P. Barrington-Leigh is an academic economist jointly appointed at McGill University (Canada) in the Department of Equity, Ethics, and Health and in the Bieler School of Environment.

Dylan Cassar is a resident academic in the Department of Sociology, University of Malta. He holds a Ph.D. in sociology from the University of Edinburgh and has an interest in the sociology and political economy of housing and finance.

Hans Czap is Associate Professor of Economics at the University of Michigan-Dearborn, the United States. His research interests include environmental economics, experimental economics, and wellbeing.

Alfred Michael Dockery is Principal Research Fellow, Bankwest Curtin Economics Centre, Curtin University, Australia. Mike's research focuses on improving the labour market, education, and wellbeing outcomes for marginalized groups, including the benefits of cultural identity for Indigenous Australians.

Teresa García-Muñoz is Professor in the Department of Quantitative Methods, University of Granada, Spain. She specializes in behavioural economics and economics of religion and has publications in reputed journals and has participated in research projects funded by the Spanish government.

Laura M. Giurge is Assistant Professor at the London School of Economics and Political Science, the United Kingdom. She is a leading expert in organizational behaviour, specializing on the role of time and temporality in organizations across various areas, such as employee wellbeing and the future of work.

Maciej Górny, PhD, is a political scientist, lawyer, and practitioner of positive psychology. He is a senior lecturer at the Faculty of Political Science and Journalism at Adam Mickiewicz University, Poland. His research interests focus on subjective wellbeing, the economy of happiness, and social policy.

Daniel Gravino is a resident academic in the Department of Economics at the University of Malta. He is a graduate of the University of Warwick, the University of Loughborough, and the University of Malta, with research interests spanning urban and international economics, including foreign direct investment and the housing market.

Krzysztof Hajder is Professor in the Department of Social and Economic Policy at the Faculty of Political Science and Journalism at Adam Mickiewicz University, Poland. Krzysztof's research interests include unemployment and labour market, public finance, social policy, and Economy 4.0.

Heli Hätönen is a senior ministerial advisor for the Ministry of Social Affairs and Health. She is responsible for health promotion. She has over 20 years of experience in the management, development, and research of social and healthcare

Martijn Hendriks is a senior researcher at the Erasmus Happiness Economics Research Organization (EHERO) of the Erasmus University Rotterdam and an associate professor at the University of Johannesburg. He serves as an associate editor for the *Journal of Happiness Studies* and as an executive board member at the International Society for Quality-of-Life Studies (ISQOLS).

Toshiaki Hiromitsu is a Vising Scholar at the Policy Research Institute, Ministry of Finance, Japan. He specializes in macroeconomics, experimental economics, and political philosophy. His recent book *Resolving Intergenerational Conflicts: An Approach from Philosophy, Economics, and Experiments* (2022 in Japanese; 2024 Springer) was awarded the 66th Nikkei Prize for Excellent Books in Economics Science.

Benjamin Jansen is a PhD student at the Faculty of Business and Economics, University of Basel, Switzerland, where he completed both his master's and bachelor's degrees. His current research interests revolve around affective polarization and economic theories of happiness.

Jaslin Kaur Kalsi is Research Affiliate at Curtin University and Research Advisor at the Minderoo Foundation, Australia. Jaslin's research interests are economic and social wellbeing, gender equality, behavioural economics, political economy, and ecological economics.

Alexandra Kirienko is a PhD candidate in the Department of Psychological and Behavioural Science at the London School of Economics and Political Science. She works at the University of Oxford Wellbeing Research Centre, the United Kingdom. Her research focuses on work wellbeing, hybrid work, and inclusion.

Ingebjørg Kristoffersen is Lecturer in Economics at the University of Western Australia Business School. She is an applied micro-economist working on various topics to do with the causes and consequences of individuals' health, wellbeing, and economic behaviours.

Eva Krulichová is a researcher at the Institute of Sociology of the Czech Academy of Sciences. Her research interests lie in the area of crime, fear of crime, and subjective wellbeing.

Laura Kudrna is Assistant Professor of Health Research Methods in the Department of Applied Health Sciences at the University of Birmingham, the United Kingdom. She researches behaviour change and wellbeing and has specific interests in topics related to workplaces, income, and inequalities.

Ian W. Li is Professor of Economics and Director of Research and Policy at the Australian Centre for Student Equity in Higher Education, at Curtin University. His research interests include determinants of university student and graduate outcomes, including academic performance and graduate employment.

Astghik Mavisakalyan is Professor of Economics at the Bankwest Curtin Economics Centre at Curtin University and Chief Investigator and Curtin University Node Lead of the ARC Centre of Excellence for the Elimination of Violence against Women.

Shoshana Neuman is Professor of Economics, Dean of the Faculty of Economics at Ashkelon Academic College, Israel. Her main fields of research/expertise are labour economics, religion, household economics, and health economics. She has numerous publications in top journals, has served in national/international professional committees, and lectured in universities in Israel and other countries.

Tanner Nichols is a doctoral candidate in the Department of Psychology at the University of Michigan, Ann Arbor, the United States. He studies the effect of incomplete information on decision-making and uses economic games to examine how decision-making varies with socioeconomic status.

Ryusuke Oishi is Professor of Economics at Meikai University, Japan. Ryusuke specializes in finance and researches the gender gaps in Japan.

Riikka Pellikka is a senior advisor for the Ministry of Social Affairs and Health, Finland. Her responsibilities include foresight, strategic development of the branch, and implementation of sustainability thinking. She has extensive experience of cross-governmental development and change management.

Diane Pelly is a Behavioural Economist and company director of Geelon & Co, Ireland. She received her Ph.D. in economics from University College Dublin, Ireland. She provides research, training, and consultancy services to organisations, with a particular focus on applied behavioural science, behaviour change, and worker wellbeing.

Stephanie Preston is Professor of Psychology in Cognition and Cognitive Neuroscience at the University of Michigan, Ann Arbor. She examines real-world behaviours by integrating emotion and decision-making with an evolutionary, neurobiological perspective, including prosocial behaviour, resource decisions, and pro-environmentalism.

Ahmad Samarji is currently Expert and Advisor of Policy & Research at the Community Development Authority (CDA), Government of Dubai, the United Arab Emirates. He is also a visiting scholar at University of Wollongong in Dubai (UOWD). Dr. Samarji has occupied a number of leadership positions in higher education in Australia and Lebanon.

Tobias Schib is a Ph.D. student at the Faculty of Business and Economics, University of Basel, Switzerland. His fields of interest are public choice and public economics, with a special focus on the effects of federal decentralization.

Joanne Smithson is an experienced policy professional, award-winning public health and wellbeing researcher, and a quality improvement specialist. From 2019 to 2024, she worked as Head of Implementation & Learning at the What Works Centre for Wellbeing, the UK's national body for wellbeing evidence, policy, and practice.

Alois Stutzer is Professor of Political Economics at the Faculty of Business and Economics, University of Basel, Switzerland. His research interests are in the areas of public choice, public economics, law and economics, and behavioural economics.

Eriko Teramura is Professor of Economics at Meikai University, Japan. She specializes in human resource management, labour economics, and gender studies. She has co-authored *Perception of Family and Work in Low-Fertility East Asia* (Springer, 2023).

Dan Weijers is Senior Lecturer in Philosophy at the University of Waikato, New Zealand. He edits the *International Journal of Wellbeing* and has advised Treasury and Statistics in New Zealand, the City Government of Dubai, and the United Nations.

Kariuki Weru is Research Associate in the United Nations University Institute for Environment and Human Security (UNU-EHS) in Germany, researching topics ranging from equity, mental health, and climate change with a focus on the wellbeing of people and the planet.

Lili Xia is Assistant Professor in the Department of Sociology, Zhejiang University, China. Her research interests are family and child welfare, mental health and social services development, and social work training education.

ACKNOWLEDGEMENTS

We would like to express our deepest gratitude to everyone who has contributed to the publication of this book.

First and foremost, we extend our heartfelt appreciation to the other 38 contributing authors, whose dedication, expertise, and insights have made this edited volume possible. In addition to writing their chapters, they contributed to the peer review process, offering invaluable feedback that enhanced the quality of the chapters.

We also acknowledge the participants of the two SABE-IAREP conferences in 2023 Nice, France, and in 2024 Dundee, Scotland, for insightful comments and constructive feedback on several chapters included in this volume.

We are very grateful to Scott Sun for his excellent research assistance throughout this project. A special thank you to Lydia Fleming for her assistance with preparing the files for submission.

We are very thankful to our Routledge publisher, Andy Humphries, for the encouragement during the book proposal stage and guidance through the proposal peer review.

Thanks also go to Editorial Assistant Yarisa Wahlang Kharbuli and Project Manager Lakshmi Sriram for their help with manuscript submission and production.

Our universities (University of Malta, University of Michigan-Dearborn, and the London School of Economics and Political Science) have provided a nurturing environment and resources to support this endeavour, for which we are grateful.

We also thank our families, friends, and colleagues for their encouragement and patience.

And last, but certainly not least, we are grateful to each other for the friendship that we formed during this project and for the unwavering support that this collaboration provided us as we were navigating various challenges in our professional and personal lives during its writing. This journey has improved our own wellbeing, and we hope to embark on more journeys together.

With sincere appreciation,

Marie Briguglio
Natalia V. Czap
Kate Laffan

FOREWORD

Roberta Metsola

During my time as President of the European Parliament, I have had the privilege of meeting many political leaders from Europe and around the world. From our discussions, what I can say is that the vision of *all* well-meaning politicians is, without a doubt, to enhance the wellbeing of the people they represent. I would also wager that there are few politicians or policy-makers left in the world who believe that wellbeing is exclusively equated to higher income. Better health, social cohesion, environmental quality, work, and functioning institutions are staple features of political manifestos, government visions, and strategies the world over. Of course, we differ on the priorities and the kind of policies needed to get there, but "improving wellbeing" is a goal many of us share and stand behind.

To date, wellbeing remains unequally distributed both across and within countries. By many global measures of wellbeing, European Union Member States are in the top leagues. These countries are democratic, materially well-off with strong health and educational systems, environmental protection policies, and respect for citizens' rights and personal freedoms, while also providing safety and security for their residents. But averages tend to hide nuances and too many Europeans struggle in terms of their daily wellbeing. The same is true for many people worldwide.

A pivotal question to ask ourselves is whether it is sufficient that our policies implicitly target wellbeing or whether it is time to formally target it, as some countries and regions have done – New Zealand, Scotland, and Iceland come to mind. Should we decide to make wellbeing the long-term stated vision, we would need to consider additional metrics of success that take into account a broader spectrum of conditions, as well as to better understand how people actually think about their lives and feel as they go about living them.

The inclusion of citizens' voices is essential in the crafting of policy objectives and interventions and envisioning goals for our shared future. To embed citizens' voices in policy-making, we – politicians and policy-makers – must do more to listen. That, in fact, was what the 2021–2022 Conference on the Future of Europe was all about: a one-year journey of discussion, debate, and collaboration between politicians and over 700,000 people across all corners of Europe, on a broad range of topics including climate change, digital transformations, and sport. And here, I am proud that the European Parliament, the only directly elected European Institution and the voice of European citizens, was a big supporter and enabler of this exercise. Asking people what matters to them and identifying the circumstances that influence how they feel can help design fairer, more nuanced, and more effective policies that promote wellbeing. Listening can also involve data collection and research inquiring directly and regularly into people's evaluations and experiences of wellbeing.

The potential of the latter, the so-called 'subjective wellbeing approach' to understanding wellbeing and its determinants, is evident from the valuable research and policy insights offered in this book. The volume provides an accessible overview of the research evidence around key factors that explain why some people report high levels of wellbeing and others do not. It explores the links between wellbeing and health, meaningful work, housing, the environment, art, social connections, migration, crime, and many other domains, including democracy itself. It also provides fascinating insights into the progress of countries around the world that are doing the work of embedding subjective wellbeing reports into their policy frameworks.

As politicians and policy-makers, our ultimate goal must always be that of enhancing the wellbeing of our people, including those of generations to come. However, to get there, we need evidence of what works. This book places a heavy emphasis on the key lessons we can learn, building on the work of the many authors who contributed and the many more they cite. It is also upfront about what we do not yet know about wellbeing and in this way provides an agenda for future research. It is an essential resource for politicians, policy-makers, researchers, and citizens who are interested in promoting wellbeing for all.

1

OVERVIEW OF WELLBEING AND POLICY

Evidence for action

Marie Briguglio, Natalia V. Czap, and Kate Laffan

It was exactly one decade after the world celebrated its first International Day of Happiness (United Nations, n.d.) that we decided to embark on writing this book. The United Nations' proclamation on a day for happiness followed its 2011 General Assembly resolution that economic growth should bring happiness and elevated levels of wellbeing (United Nations, 2011).

In the years that followed, the world witnessed a surge of interest in wellbeing in both policy and research. A World Alliance for Wellbeing Economies (WEALL) was founded in 2018 as a ten-year project intended to connect new economic thinkers, activists, and practitioners and to accelerate a transition into a Wellbeing Economy. That same year, the OECD's 6th World Forum paved the way for enhanced cooperation on the measurement of wellbeing among its members (Stiglitz et al., 2018). A year later, the Council of the European Union (EU) asserted that people's wellbeing is a principal aim of the Union, and put forward an agenda for a wellbeing economy, which included reprioritizing investment to account for both wellbeing and growth (Council of the EU, 2019). In 2021, 149 countries agreed on the Geneva Charter for Wellbeing, which set a vision of wellbeing societies, whose indicators of success would guide priorities for public spending (WHO, 2021).

Meanwhile, a growing number of advisory councils, institutes, think tanks, and non-governmental organizations took up the agenda, advocating and championing wellbeing, offering training, providing guidelines for policy-makers, hosting webinars, fora, and summits. At the national level too, several countries around the world established wellbeing measurement frameworks – several predating the UN resolution, some of which are reviewed in this book. Recognizing that it is in governments' best interest to put wellbeing at the heart of policy-making (Frijters et al., 2020), an increasing number of countries recalibrated the goal of policy towards achieving collective wellbeing (Frijters & Krekel, 2021).

DOI: 10.4324/9781003382447-1

In parallel, academic research on wellbeing veritably exploded, with contributions from authors from all over the world and multiple disciplines. This work has yielded wide strides in measuring and understanding wellbeing though many open questions remain (Helliwell et al., 2023). One question that has been hotly debated is the definition of wellbeing (Diener, 2009). Though the literature presents many different takes on what wellbeing is, a good working definition that has withstood the test of time is Ryan and Deci's (2001) *functioning well and feeling good*. This notion of doing well and feeling good is linked to the way wellbeing is now widely measured, namely a combination of objective measures of the multidimensional conditions needed to flourish (measured through a range of indicators) and of the subjective measures of how people evaluate their own lives and their feelings as they go about them (commonly measured by subjective reports in surveys). At the time of writing, a global wellbeing index was yet to be established (UNECE, 2023), although the OECD's Better Life Index (BLI) combining both objective and subjective wellbeing measures served as one of the more diffused indexes in the world.

As part of these efforts, approaches to assessing wellbeing subjectively have flourished. Since Richard Easterlin's pioneering efforts in 1974 (Easterlin, 1974), this second so-called subjective wellbeing (SWB) approach *holds growing sway around the world* (Barrington-Leigh, 2022). Despite the challenges, including the difficulty of cross-country comparisons (Morris, 2012), the science has evolved considerably, with multiple scales used to measure both hedonic and eudaimonic wellbeing (e.g. Adler & Seligman, 2016).

Concurrent with the increased interest in SWB, and the possibility of measuring it, there has been a swell in research on what predicts SWB. The literature is extensive, multidisciplinary, and in some cases still inconclusive about the relationship between SWB and the many factors that affect it. In a Trojan effort to keep track of this literature, a world database of happiness literature consisting of almost 17,000 publications has been compiled by the Erasmus Happiness Economics Research Organization led by Ruut Veenhoven. The literature has emphasized key determinants of SWB including individual-level factors such as employment, health, and social connectedness, as well as more structural ones such as those relating to environmental quality and governance (Layard & De Neve, 2023). The work has highlighted differences in the relative importance of these and other determinants for how people evaluate their lives compared to how they experience them (Dolan et al., 2017). These measures have also been used to investigate psychological phenomena that feed into wellbeing such as adaptation and person–environment fit (Clark et al., 2008; Gander et al., 2020). Other research using SWB measures has investigated how determinants vary in importance across the wellbeing distribution and separately across cultures (Binder & Coad, 2011; Diener et al., 2003). Finally, works which evaluate the impact of life events and policy interventions on wellbeing outcomes have also emerged (Kohler & Mencarini, 2016; d'Addio et al., 2014. This body of work represents a flourishing science of happiness which has garnered the attention of researchers and policy professionals worldwide.

The advances made in defining, measuring, and forecasting wellbeing paved the way for efforts in the design of policy and interventions. Clearly, gearing policy for wellbeing requires a concerted effort (Durand & Exton, 2019), including strategy crafting, assessing impacts, reprioritising investment, and addressing inequalities (Council of the EU, 2021). It involves all the cycles of policy-making from agenda-setting to policy formulation, implementation, monitoring, and evaluation (Exton & Shinwell, 2018). These steps need continuous feedback loops with interconnections between the different steps of policy creation (WEALL, 2021).

It is against this backdrop that the new frontier in wellbeing research emerges: the need to assess the impact of policy interventions – to gather evidence of what works. This has been far less prominent in the literature to date, mainly due to the recency of the initiatives themselves. It is also not straightforward to attribute shifts in wellbeing to specific policies (Wallace & Schmuecker, 2012). Thus, while there is a rich literature that identifies a link between say, environmental quality and wellbeing, there are far fewer examples that document the causal impact of actual environmental interventions on wellbeing. Studies which assess the impact of wellbeing interventions are rare, scattered across disciplines, employing different metrics, methods, and terminologies. Wellbeing policy, more generally, is documented in different languages, and in grey literature.

Indeed, the current book is supported by a whole ecosystem of others which have emerged over the past decade. For instance, in 2014, Allin and Hand (2014) issued the Wellbeing of Nations: Meaning, Motive and Measurement, which focused on the measurement of national wellbeing around the world. In 2016, the *Oxford Handbook of Well-Being and Public Policy* (Adler & Fleurbaey, 2016) went beyond definitions and measurement, to include methodologies for evaluating policy and assessing societal conditions, exploring some of the major challenges involved. In 2018, the *Routledge Handbook of Well-Being* (Galvin, 2018) adopted a multidisciplinary approach to understanding human experiences and endeavours for wellbeing. The *2021 Handbook for Wellbeing Policymaking* (Frijters & Krekel, 2021) examined how wellbeing fits into the political economy, suggesting technical standards for cost-effectiveness analysis based on wellbeing. Meanwhile, the *Wellbeing Economy Alliance Case Studies* (WEAll, n.d.) started to document a growing compendium of case studies online.

Our book looks to build on these important texts by offering an easy-to-consume, evidence-based synthesis of the key findings from the literature and efforts in the field. Our focus was to be neither the conceptual nor theoretical definition of wellbeing, neither its measurement nor the estimation of models to forecast it. Rather we wished to provide an accessible survey of studies and interventions to elicit the lessons learned and, most importantly, actionable points. We wanted to offer the reader a resource to understand what has worked across different policy domains to create an impact on wellbeing, in a cross-disciplinary manner, that also serves to highlight where the evidence has failed to catch up with the rhetoric of wellbeing. It is with this in mind that we ensured that chapters underwent a double-blind peer review.

The book is structured in three main parts. The first part (comprising Chapters 2 to 9) focuses on individual factors that affect wellbeing including demographic, socio-economic, and psychological characteristics. The second part (Chapters 10 to 17) includes social and environmental factors that depend on circumstances that cannot be easily influenced by an individual and which, in many cases, are given by the location where an individual currently lives. In both parts, a distinction is made between correlational, causal, or qualitative evidence as well as documented impacts across demographic groups. The third part (Chapters 18 to 26) focuses on country experiences. Here authors review country-specific wellbeing history, performance, and work, providing key takeaways for others looking to embark on similar initiatives. Because of this comprehensive coverage, chapter contributors were urged to keep their chapters concise, with a focus on transferable findings.

The effects of income, work, and health (Chapters 2–4 in this volume) have been extensively discussed in the literature and arguably occupy a pole position in many policy-makers' agendas. Laura Kurdna discusses the complexity of the relationship between *income* and wellbeing. She notes that higher income does not always lead to higher life satisfaction due to diminishing marginal returns, adaptation, and social comparisons but carefully implemented income interventions can improve wellbeing. Alexandra Kirienko, Kate Laffan, and Laura M. Giurge argue that wellbeing at *work* relates directly to organizational outcomes like performance and retention, as these are influenced by how employees evaluate their work and how they feel doing it. They highlight the predominance of organization-level interventions and identify the focus areas for promoting employee wellbeing. Hans Czap and Marie Briguglio argue that while improvements in *health* often lead to better SWB, policy-makers should take into account the costs and benefits of health interventions, both the direct and indirect effects of health on wellbeing and the potential of bidirectional effect.

Family and social interactions are the focus of the next two chapters. Lili Xia discusses *family* wellbeing as the essential component of individual life satisfaction as well as a key aspect of societal wellbeing. She analyses the case study of the Hong Kong Family Wellbeing Index and its application to public policy development and public service design. Stephanie Preston and Tanner Nichols focus on the phenomenon of *altruism*, noting that this has evolutionary, physiological, and psychological benefits such as genetic propagation, increased cooperation, and improved societal wellbeing. These, they argue, counterbalance the costs of giving. They proceed to call for the framing of wealth redistributive policies to address injustice and to enhance cooperation.

Age, gender, and education are covered in Chapters 7, 8, and 9, respectively. Maciej Górny and Krzysztof Hajder consider the U-shaped relationship between *age* and wellbeing and discuss the challenges associated with aging. They underscore the importance of comprehensive wellbeing policies including those fostering social connections and financial stability. They further note the potential of positive psychology and technology interventions to enhance wellbeing as people age. Jaslin Kaur Kalsi and Astghik Mavisakalyan discuss how *gender* and gendered norms shape women's and men's wellbeing differently throughout their lives, in the context of employment, parenthood, and retirement. They make policy recommendations to address disparities and to support positive societal change. Ingebjørg Kristoffersen, Alfred Michael Dockery, and Ian W. Li underscore that *education* is positively associated with objective measures of quality of life for both individuals and society. However, the relationship between education and subjective wellbeing is complex, as influenced by changing expectations and reference points, diminishing returns, and the development of psychological resilience.

Moving to social and environmental factors, the next cluster of chapters focuses on housing, the environment, and crime (Chapters 10–12). Marie Briguglio, Dylan Cassar, and Daniel Gravino reveal a generally positive association between improved *housing* conditions and housing tenure but a negative impact on the associated financial burden. The authors underscore the context-dependent nature of interventions and suggest incorporating wellbeing assessments into future housing policies. Kate Laffan, Hans Czap, and Natalia V. Czap examine the impact of both *environmental* quality and pro-environmental behaviour on wellbeing. They suggest that interventions should focus on improving environment quality and behaviour for their own sake and because such actions will yield significant wellbeing benefits. Eva Krulichová summarizes the research on how individual experiences with *crime*, fear of crime, and country-level crime factors relate to SWB. She uses the data from the European Social Survey to demonstrate that SWB is influenced less by crime rates and strict criminal policies and more by the public's trust in the police and legal system at least within the European countries.

The effects of democracy, migration, and religion on wellbeing are the focus of Chapters 13 to 15. Alois Stutzer, Benjamin Jansen, and Tobias Schib distinguish between outcome utility derived from the results of *democratic* processes and procedural utility gained from participation in these processes. Their review of empirical studies finds democracy to be vital for wellbeing. Martijn Hendriks explores how different *migration* policies impact the happiness of migrants, host communities, and those remaining in the origin countries. He emphasizes the importance of social cohesion between immigrants and natives, suggesting that well-designed integration policies can create mutual benefits for both. Teresa García-Muñoz and Shoshana Neuman synthesize the evidence from 22 studies over the past two decades on the effect of *religious* and *spiritual* interventions on wellbeing, finding that such interventions are particularly effective in improving wellbeing among those with mental and physical health issues and have potential in patient care and workspaces with high-stress jobs. They also highlight the importance of awareness campaigns to foster tolerance in these domains.

The impact of digital technology and art, culture, and creativity is the focus of Chapters 16 and 17. Diane Pelly acknowledges the widespread concern about the harmful effects of *digital technology* but argues that these may be overstated and heavily dependent on usage patterns. She recommends focusing on positive interventions that leverage technology to enhance wellbeing, tailored to individual differences. Leonie Baldacchino reports that engagement in *art*, *culture*, and creativity enhances wellbeing through mechanisms such as social connection, distraction from suffering, self-expression, skill development, and states of flow, with active engagement yielding the most benefit. She proceeds to recommend interventions for engagement, particularly for marginalized groups and support for artists.

The third part of the book documents the experience of a diverse set of countries which are at different stages of a wellbeing agenda, starting with frontrunners – Bhutan and New Zealand (Chapters 18–19). Kehinde Balogun and Kariuki Weru examine Bhutan's pioneering efforts. Here, the Gross National Happiness policy prioritizes a multidimensional assessment of wellbeing and balance between individual, society, and environmental relationships. The authors advocate for the inclusion of Indigenous Knowledge and relational wellbeing concepts and highlight the importance of inner and cultural poverty alongside traditional income poverty to achieve holistic wellbeing and sustainable development. Dan Weijers provides an overview of how New Zealand became a frontrunner in integrating wellbeing into public policy with the 2011 adoption of the Living Standards Framework and the 2019 adoption of the Wellbeing Budget. He reports on the Wellbeing Data Dashboard and Cost Benefit Analysis tool while making recommendations on environmental concerns and citizens' assemblies on wellbeing.

Chapters 20 and 21 turn to Finland and their Economy of Wellbeing policy approach and the UAE and their National Wellbeing Strategy, respectively. Riikka Pellikka and Heli Hätönen argue that while Finland ranks one of the first in many wellbeing-related indices, it faces challenges in sustaining such high levels for present and future generations. They also note the challenges in ensuring that this framework is apolitical and remains in place regardless of the composition of the government. Ahmad Samarji and Amal AlBlooshi examine the evolution of the UAE' public policy from independent initiatives to a comprehensive UAE's National Wellbeing Strategy 2031. They describe an evidence-based and evolving strategy that balances top–down and bottom–up approaches that can be used as a model of integrating wellbeing into public policy at the regional and global levels.

The experiences of Canada and Australia are documented in Chapters 22 and 23. Chris P. Barrington-Leigh positions Canada as an early adopter of SWB and social connection metrics. He acknowledges the challenging context of the wellbeing agenda but also emphasizes growing efforts to unify wellbeing data, share evidence and experience, and influence policy. Michelle Baddeley reports that despite its high living standards, Australia faces significant wellbeing disparities, particularly among marginalized groups such as Indigenous populations, immigrants, the disabled, and the elderly. Challenges are exacerbated by geographical and climate-related issues, by the recent pandemic and contractionary measures to control inflation, she argues.

Chapters 24 to 26 focus on the experiences of the UK, Japan, and Malta. Joanne Smithson presents the UK's wellbeing measurement framework and the HM Treasury's guidance on integrating wellbeing into the policy evaluation process. The author synthesizes interventions proven to enhance individual and community wellbeing and discusses priority areas, including work, income, society and governance, mental health, relationships, and communities. From Japan, Toshiaki Hiromitsu, Eriko Teramura, and Ryusuke Oishi report efforts to systematically measure citizens' wellbeing since 2010. Noting that recent data revealed significant differences in citizens' wellbeing across the lifespan, the authors highlight the need for public policy to consider population heterogeneity and to focus on work style, remote work, and a four-day workweek. Finally, Marie Briguglio discusses Malta's significant economic progress and potential discrepancies between these achievements and the SWB of its citizens. She notes the challenges in the domains of work, environmental quality, child wellbeing, and government trust. She documents recent interventions in the domain of wellbeing and makes recommendations for advancing a wellbeing agenda.

Together, these 25 chapters offer evidence of the multitude of factors that impact human wellbeing and how public policy can influence these factors, as well as a diverse range of wellbeing policy experiences on a country-by-country basis. Our aspiration is that this book informs governments, political parties, academics, journalists, students, groups, or individuals working in the global quest to move towards better wellbeing for all. Mindful of the constraints of time and attention, we have prepared an appendix to this chapter that summarizes the actionable points emerging from all the chapters in the form of cheat-sheets.

When we embarked on this writing book, we agreed we would seek to achieve gender and geographical balance among the contributors. We have had the privilege of collaborating with academics and practitioners working at universities, governmental agencies, and non-governmental organizations from all continents across the globe, specialized in a wide range of social sciences. We are extremely grateful to them and we hope that, in bringing them together, we have added value to their remarkable work.

References

Adler, A., & Seligman, M. E. P. (2016). Using wellbeing for public policy: Theory, measurement, and recommendations. *International Journal of Wellbeing*, *6*(1), Article 1. https://doi.org/10.5502/ijw.v6i1.429

Adler, M. D., & Fleurbaey, M. (Eds.) (2016). *The Oxford handbook of well-being and public policy*. Oxford University Press. https://doi.org/10.1093/oxfordhb/9780199325818.001.0001

Allin, P., & Hand, D. J. (2014). *The wellbeing of nations: Meaning, motive and measurement*. John Willey and Sons. https://doi.org/10.1002/9781118917046

Barrington-Leigh, C. (2022). Trends in conceptions of progress and well-being. *2022 World Happiness Report, Ch. 3*. https://worldhappiness.report/ed/2022/trends-in-conceptions-of-progress-and-well-being/

Binder, M., & Coad, A. (2011). From Average Joe's happiness to Miserable Jane and Cheerful John: Using quantile regressions to analyze the full subjective well-being distribution. *Journal of Economic Behavior & Organization*, *79*(3), 275–290.

Clark, A. E., Diener, E., Georgellis, Y., & Lucas, R. E. (2008). Lags and leads in life satisfaction: A test of the baseline hypothesis. *The Economic Journal*, *118*(529), F222–F243.

Council of the EU (2019). *Council conclusions on the economy of wellbeing (13432/19)*. https://data.consilium.europa.eu/doc/document/ST-13432-2019-INIT/en/pdf

Council of the EU (2021, April 12). *The economy of wellbeing: Going beyond GDP*. https://www.consilium.europa.eu/en/infographics/economy-wellbeing/

d'Addio, A. C., Chapple, S., Hoherz, A., & Van Landeghem, B. (2014). Using a quasi-natural experiment to identify the effects of birth-related leave policies on subjective well-being in Europe. *OECD Journal: Economic Studies*, *2013*(1), 235–268.

Diener, E. (2009). Subjective well-being. In E. Diener (Ed.), *The science of well-being* (Vol. 37, pp. 11–58). Springer. https://doi.org/10.1007/978-90-481-2350-6_2

Diener, E., Oishi, S., & Lucas, R. E. (2003). Personality, culture, and subjective well-being: Emotional and cognitive evaluations of life. *Annual Review of Psychology*, *54*(1), 403–425.

Dolan, P., Kudrna, L., & Stone, A. (2017). The measure matters: An investigation of evaluative and experience-based measures of wellbeing in time use data. *Social Indicators Research*, *134*, 57–73.

Durand, M., & Exton, C. (2019). Adopting a well-being approach in Central Government: Policy mechanisms and practical tools. In *Global happiness and well-being policy report* (pp. 140–161). Global Council for Happiness and Wellbeing.

Easterlin, R. A. (1974). Does economic growth improve the human lot? Some empirical evidence. *Nations and Households in Economic Growth*, *89*, 89–125. http://dx.doi.org/10.1016/b978-0-12-205050-3.50008-7

Exton, C., & Shinwell, M. (2018). *Policy use of well-being metrics: Describing countries' experiences* (SDD Working Paper No. 94. SDD/DOC(2018)7). OECD Publishing. https://doi.org/10.1787/d98eb8ed-en

Frijters, P., Clark, A. E., Krekel, C., & Layard, R. (2020). A happy choice: Wellbeing as the goal of government. *Behavioural Public Policy*, *4*(2), 126–165. https://doi.org/10.1017/bpp.2019.39

Frijters, P., & Krekel, C. (2021). *A handbook for wellbeing policy-making: History, theory, measurement, implementation, and examples*. Oxford University Press. https://doi.org/10.1093/oso/9780192896803.001.0001

Galvin, K. (2018). *Routledge handbook of well-being*. Routledge: Taylor & Francis Group. www.routledge.com/Routledge-Handbook-of-Well-Being/Galvin/p/book/9780367709648

Gander, F., Hofmann, J., & Ruch, W. (2020). Character strengths: Person–environment fit and relationships with job and life satisfaction. *Frontiers in Psychology*, *11*, 1582.

Helliwell, J. F., Layard, R., Sachs, J. D., De Neve, J.-E., Aknin, L. B., & Wang, S. (Eds.) (2023). *World happiness report 2023* (11th ed.). Sustainable Development Solutions Network. https://worldhappiness.report/ed/2023/

Kohler, H. P., & Mencarini, L. (2016). The parenthood happiness puzzle: An introduction to special issue. *European Journal of Population*, *32*, 327–338.

Layard, R., & De Neve, J. E. (2023). *Wellbeing: Science and policy* (1st ed.). Cambridge University Press. https://doi.org/10.1017/9781009298957

Morris, S. G. (2012). The science of happiness: A cross-cultural perspective. In *Happiness across cultures: Views of happiness and quality of life in non-Western cultures* (pp. 435–450). Springer Science + Business Media. https://doi.org/10.1007/978-94-007-2700-7_29

Ryan, R., & Deci, E. (2001). On happiness and human potentials: A review of research on hedonic and eudaimonic well-being. *Annual Review of Psychology*, *52*, 141–166. http://dx.doi.org/10.1146/annurev.psych.52.1.141

Stiglitz, J., Fitoussi, J., & Durand, M. (2018). *Beyond GDP: Measuring what counts for economic and social performance.* OECD Publishing. https://doi.org/10.1787/9789264307292-en

UNECE (2023). In-depth review of measurement of current well-being: Outcomes of the recent in-depth reviews carried out by the bureau of the conference of European statisticians. *Conference of European Statisticians Seventy-First Plenary Session*, Israel. https://unece.org/statistics/documents/2023/05/working-documents/depth-review-measurement-current-well-being-prepared

United Nations (2011). Happiness: Towards a holistic approach to development. In *General Assembly Resolution 65/309*. United Nations.

United Nations (n.d.). What is the international day of happiness? *United Nations*, United Nations. Retrieved July 27, 2023, from www.un.org/en/observances/happiness-day

Wallace, J., & Schmuecker, K. (2012). *Shifting the dial: From wellbeing measures to policy practice.* Carnegie UK Trust.

WEAll (Wellbeing Economy Alliance) (2021). *Wellbeing economy policy design guide.* https://weall.org/wp-content/uploads/Wellbeing-Economy-Policy-Design-Guide_Mar17_FINAL-1.pdf

WEAll (n.d.) *Case studies.* https://weall.org/case-studies

WHO (World Health Organization) (2021). *Geneva charter for well-being.* https://cdn.who.int/media/docs/default-source/health-promotion/geneva-charter-4-march-2022.pdf

PART I

Wellbeing

Evidence across individual domains

2

INCOME AND WELLBEING

Laura Kudrna

Introduction

Income is one of the most widely studied determinants of wellbeing. It allows people to meet their basic needs for food and housing, access quality healthcare, and satisfy their preferences for goods and services (Angner, 2010). According to some accounts of wellbeing, having income, and opportunities to achieve higher income, equates directly to higher wellbeing. In economics, higher income allows people to buy more of the goods and services they want, which is often assumed to improve their utility. However, higher income is not always associated with higher *subjective* reports of wellbeing, such as how happy or anxious people report feeling and if they are satisfied with their lives (Diener, 1984; Layard et al., 2008).

Measures of subjective wellbeing (SWB) can be used to inform how well individuals and societies are doing, and places like the United Kingdom have adopted indicators of SWB in national statistics (Office for National Statistics, 2022). In this context, it is important to understand if SWB adds anything to what traditional economic indicators tell us about wellbeing. This chapter reviews the evidence, considering the literature on income as a determinant of SWB, and interventions that change income and evaluate subsequent changes in SWB, considering individual, community, and national levels.

Literature on income and wellbeing

The standard finding from studies on individual income, life satisfaction, and overall happiness is that there are diminishing marginal returns to income for SWB. This relationship is shown in Figure 2.1, which indicates that SWB is always increasing in income but more income matters most to those with the least amounts

DOI: 10.4324/9781003382447-3

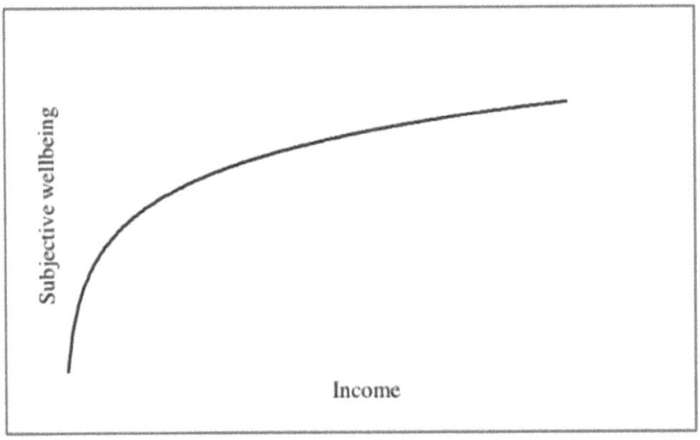

FIGURE 2.1 Stylised graph of the relationship between income and subjective wellbeing for measures of life satisfaction and overall happiness (Kudrna, 2018).

of income because increases are more noticeable, whereas more income matters least to those with the most amounts of income because increases are less noticeable (Layard et al., 2008). However, this standard finding has been challenged. Studies looking at the upper tail of the income distribution document satiation and turning points, whereby higher income is associated with no better or worse SWB, respectively (Jebb et al., 2018), particularly for the least happy people (Killingsworth et al., 2023). But other research has shown a weaker relationship at the upper tail of the SWB distribution, too (Binder & Coad, 2011). The measure of SWB matters. In research using experiential rather than evaluative measures of SWB, there is sometimes a null association between income and positive hedonic feelings like happiness, although associations with negative feelings like sadness remain (Kushlev et al., 2015).

The lack of an association between higher levels of income and some measures of SWB has been criticised on methodological grounds. Methodological critiques include whether the analyses meet the assumptions of the tests conducted, sample representativeness, and whether income is measured and analysed in surveys as a categorical or continuous variable (Kudrna & Kushlev, 2022; Killingsworth et al., 2023). The control variables used in the analyses also change the results, particularly if they reflect mechanisms that explain the relationship between higher income and wellbeing, such as health or education (Easterlin, 2001). It is possible to 'over-control' by adjusting for the benefits that income brings, including goods and services that benefit wellbeing, which could give negative or null impressions of the relationship.

Moving from the individual to community and national levels, the observed relationship between income and wellbeing changes.

At the level of communities, there has been substantial attention to the 'relative income effect' whereby people compare to their neighbours who are doing similarly better over time, and don't feel better themselves as a result (Luttmer, 2005). Studies on the relative income effect find that higher average income in a local geographical area is associated with worse wellbeing, controlling for own income (Graham & Pettinato, 2002; Luttmer, 2005). However, this classic finding has been challenged in studies identifying positive and null effects of relative income on SWB, too (Deaton & Stone, 2013; Kudrna, 2023). Much of the relationship between relative income and wellbeing depends upon the following:

- whether shared resources and public goods like parks and libraries are included in analyses, often with proxies like housing prices;
- the nature of 'reference groups', or those to whom people interact with or compare themselves to (Hyman, 1968; Kudrna, 2023) – age is a relevant reference group (Kudrna, 2023), as are colleagues (Clark & Oswald, 1996), and more local neighbours may have more positive effects (Ifcher et al., 2018);
- if people view others in their reference groups as people they could be like someday or if they have hope that they could be like them in the future (Cheung, 2016; Hirschman & Rothschild, 1973).

The methodological problem of multi-collinearity is an issue in the literature on community effects, too. The signs of coefficients can reverse if absolute and relative income are too similar and qualitative methods may be needed to better disentangle individual and area-level effects (Kudrna, 2023). However, caution needs to be taken when using qualitative methods to assess the relationship between income and wellbeing because people over-estimate the importance of income for their SWB due to 'focussing effects', whereby something is perceived as more important because attention is drawn to it (Kahneman et al., 2006). People also overestimate the importance of future income rises for their wellbeing by underestimating their adaptation rates, contributing to affective forecasting effects (Wilson & Gilbert, 2005).

Looking at country levels, further complicates the picture. In 1974, Richard Easterlin published findings showing that increases in gross domestic product (GDP) over time within a country were not associated with better life evaluations – despite a positive association between income and wellbeing at one point in time (Easterlin, 1974). There are several explanations for this paradox, including the following:

- People adapt to increases in their income and GDP over time (Clark, 2016);
- The aforementioned relative income effect operates at a country level (Luttmer, 2005);
- Income is distributed sub-optimally away from those whose wellbeing would benefit the most from having it – those with the lowest income (Oishi & Kesebir, 2015);
- Decreases in GDP over time have a stronger negative effect on wellbeing compared to comparable increases in GDP (loss aversion) and the changes cancel out the effects on wellbeing over time (de Neve et al., 2018).

The existence of the Easterlin Paradox has been challenged in studies that have included more countries, although the most recent research suggests it is evident when using longitudinal data, at least in Europe (Easterlin & O'Connor, 2022; Sacks et al., 2012; Stevenson & Wolfers, 2013). Most likely, a combination of the above explanations produces the results of studies documenting the paradox, although empirical support for income inequality is mixed. Although income inequality appears to help explain the Easterlin Paradox (Oishi & Kesebir, 2015), income inequality itself is not strongly associated with wellbeing across studies (Ngamaba et al., 2018).

Evidence of interventions

Interventions that re-distribute income are at the heart of many government policies, which collect taxes and provide benefits and subsidies to individuals, organisations, communities, countries, and future generations. When exogenous changes in income occur, the causal effects of income on SWB can be better identified. These changes are important because they help to estimate the effects of income on SWB without potentially confounding factors not always easily captured in research, like motivation or personality. The following examples consider lotteries, cash transfers, taxes and benefits, performance-based financing, and political processes. It is acknowledged, however, that there are many additional ways, such as job creation, that policy-makers can improve wellbeing through income.

For individuals, the classic intervention studies are about winning the lottery. Early research showed winning the lottery did not improve happiness up to one-and-a-half years later (Brickman et al., 1978), perhaps due to adaptation. However, later studies showed more mixed results, with some positive effects of winning the lottery on SWB, too (Lindqvist et al., 2020). Results may depend on factors like the amount won, spending patterns, feelings of luck, time since winning the award, and the amount spent on tickets (Kim et al., 2021). Systematic reviews of causal intervention studies provide the strongest evidence by looking across studies. One review including lottery wins alongside inheritance receipts, changes to social security benefits, and other causal approaches found positive effects of higher income on wellbeing when looking across a range of individuals and contexts (Cooper & Stewart, 2005).

Given that low income is associated with low wellbeing, it might be expected that cash transfers to low-income individuals improve their wellbeing. Randomised evaluations have shown positive effects within low-income countries (McGuire et al., 2022), and cash transfers have greater wellbeing effects on those in lower-income countries than those in high-income countries (Dwyer & Dunn, 2022). Within higher-income countries, some research has shown no effect of cash transfers on wellbeing (Jaroszewicz et al., 2022). Several implementation and process factors could impact if transfers work, including the cash amount transferred and the stigma of being labelled as 'low income'. Moreover, when cash transfers stop, any positive effects could backfire due to issues such as decreased motivation and lack of trust in donors (Maini et al., 2019). There are also broader questions about the effects of redistribution on economic growth over time (Kaiser & Oswald, 2022).

Income is also provided to communities, including local areas, schools, and workplaces. Some reasons for community cash transfers include spending on projects related to economic and social development, windfalls and income shocks, compensation and reparation for historical injustices, performance incentives, and research participation (Reynolds et al., 2015). A randomised trial of monetary incentives provided to UK workplaces for health and wellbeing projects found no effect of the incentives on employee health and wellbeing, although employers provided more wellbeing programming (Thrive at Work Wellbeing Programme Collaboration, 2023). Cash transfers might be combined with community-driven development initiatives, such as in the Uganda Social Action Fund (Golooba-Mutebi & Hickey, 2010). In evaluations of such initiatives, however, the outcomes are rarely SWB and instead focus on factors like health or poverty.

At national levels, political and economic changes can act as interventions to illustrate the effects of income on wellbeing. A classic example of an exogenous change is the reunification of East Germany and West Germany (Frijters et al., 2004). The incomes of those living in East Germany increased for exogenous reasons, which led to gains in life satisfaction even when adjusting for fixed characteristics like place of birth. It is important to go beyond average effects in this literature because certain groups may experience more hardships than others after political and economic changes. In the financial crisis in 2007–08, there was little change in SWB on average in the UK, but people who became unemployed, lost income, or had health problems were worse off (Boyce et al., 2018). There is intersectionality of income with health and other characteristics that affect wellbeing, and looking at the distribution of SWB across groups illustrates opportunities to target resources to improve wellbeing.

Discussion and conclusion

In summary, higher income at individual, community, and national levels does not always appear to translate directly into higher SWB. However, lower income is related to lower SWB. There are methodological issues that need to be addressed before the empirical relationship can be fully clarified, and quantitative empirical studies are important because people overestimate the importance of income for SWB in qualitative research. Interventions that directly improve income levels do not always translate into better wellbeing for individuals and societies, and these need to account for initial income levels, social economic contexts, and the distribution of income within groups and countries.

Given that SWB adds substantially to our understanding of social progress beyond GDP, it should also be used to inform and appraise how public resources are allocated within and across societies (Dolan & Metcalfe, 2012). In policy, SWB valuation methods can be used to supplant or complement more traditional economic valuations of goods and services that use revealed or stated preferences approaches (Fujiwara & Campbell, 2011; HM Treasury, 2021). In brief, SWB valuation method approaches assign a monetary value to the changes in SWB associated with a good or service. The process translates the wellbeing benefits of, for example, clean air or cultural participation, into a price that can inform cost–benefit discussions. Using wellbeing valuation methods moves us towards societies based on true social rather than only economic progress.

Income redistribution with interventions like cash transfers alone may not be enough to improve SWB because, in part, the systems and implementation contexts in which the redistribution occur need to be considered. In public health, systems and implementation research are used to better understand the mechanisms and processes influencing the effectiveness of changes in health prevention, promotion, and service delivery (Damschroder et al., 2022). Systems and implementation considerations are important in this context because programmes focused on cash transfers alone may fail if other aspects of the programme and its delivery context are not working well. The advice and guidance people are given about spending, the fit between spending and needs, and the wider economic climate all affect outcomes (Dwyer & Dunn, 2022; Thrive at Work Wellbeing Programme Collaboration, 2023). SWB intervention studies focusing on income should consider systems and implementation, too.

Actionable points

- Low income is a driver of low SWB and there is good reason to improve low wellbeing by increasing opportunities to raise low incomes.
- Cash transfers should be complemented with efforts to understand and address stigma and trust, considering individual differences and community contexts.
- SWB valuation approaches should be used to determine the costs and benefits of interventions and determine social value.
- Further research is needed to understand how systems-level implementation contexts shape income redistribution initiatives.

References

Angner, E. (2010). Subjective well-being. *The Journal of Socio-Economics*, *39*(3), 361–368.

Binder, M., & Coad, A. (2011). From average Joe's happiness to Miserable Jane and Cheerful John: Using quantile regressions to analyze the full subjective well-being distribution. *Journal of Economic Behavior and Organization*, *79*(3).

Boyce, C. J., Delaney, L., & Wood, A. M. (2018). The great recession and subjective well-being: How did the life satisfaction of people living in the United Kingdom change following the financial crisis? *PLoS One*, *13*(8).

Brickman, P., Coates, D., & Janoff-Bulman, R. (1978). Lottery winners and accident victims: Is happiness relative? *Journal of Personality and Social Psychology*, *36*(8), 917–927.

Cheung, F. (2016). Can income inequality be associated with positive outcomes? Hope mediates the positive inequality–happiness link in rural China. *Social Psychological and Personality Science*, *7*(4), 320–330.
Clark, A. E. (2016). Adaptation and the Easterlin Paradox. In T. Tachibanaki (Ed.), *Advances in happiness research*. Creative Economy. Springer.
Clark, A. E., & Oswald, A. J. (1996). Satisfaction and comparison income. *Journal of Public Economics*, *61*(3), 359–381.
Cooper, K., & Stewart, K. (2005). *Does money in adulthood affect adult outcomes*. Joseph Rowntree Foundation.
Damschroder, L. J., Reardon, C. M., Widerquist, M. A. O., & Lowery, J. (2022). The updated consolidated framework for implementation research based on user feedback. *Implementation Science*, *17*(1), 1–16.
Deaton, A., & Stone, A. A. (2013). Two happiness puzzles. *American Economic Review*, *103*(3), 591–597.
de Neve, J. E., Ward, G., de Keulenaer, F., van Landeghem, B., Kavetsos, G., & Norton, M. I. (2018). The asymmetric experience of positive and negative economic growth: Global evidence using subjective well-being data. *Review of Economics and Statistics*, *100*(2).
Diener, E. (1984). Subjective well-being. *Psychological Bulletin*, *95*(3), 542–575.
Dolan, P., & Metcalfe, R. (2012). Measuring subjective wellbeing: Recommendations on measures for use by national governments. *Journal of Social Policy*, *401*(2).
Dwyer, R. J., & Dunn, E. W. (2022). Wealth redistribution promotes happiness. *Proceedings of the National Academy of Sciences of the United States of America*, *119*(46).
Easterlin, R. A. (1974). Does economic growth improve the human lot? Some empirical evidence. In *Nations and households in economic growth* (pp. 89–125). Academic Press.
Easterlin, R. A. (2001). Income and happiness: Towards a unified theory. *Economic Journal*, *111*(473).
Easterlin, R. A., & O'Connor, K. J. (2022). Explaining happiness trends in Europe. *Proceedings of the National Academy of Sciences of the United States of America*, *119*(37).
Frijters, P., Haisken-DeNew, J. P., & Shields, M. A. (2004). Money does matter! Evidence from increasing real income and life satisfaction in East Germany following reunification. *American Economic Review*, *94*(3), 730–740.
Fujiwara, D., & Campbell, R. (2011). *Valuation techniques for social cost-benefit analysis: Valuation techniques for social cost-benefit analysis*. HM Treasury.
Golooba-Mutebi, F., & Hickey, S. (2010). Governing chronic poverty under inclusive liberalism: The case of the northern Uganda social action fund. *Journal of Development Studies*, *46*(7).
Graham, C., & Pettinato, S. (2002). Frustrated achievers: Winners, losers and subjective well-being in new market economies. *Journal of Development Studies*, *38*(4).
Hirschman, A., & Rothschild, M. (1973). The changing tolerance for income inequality in the course of economic development. *Quarterly Journal of Economics*, *87*(4).
HM Treasury (2021). *Green book supplementary guidance: Wellbeing*. www.gov.uk/government/publications/green-book-supplementary-guidance-wellbeing
Hyman, H. H. (1968). Reference groups. *International Encyclopaedia of the Social Sciences*, *13*, 353–361.
Ifcher, J., Zarghamee, H., & Graham, C. (2018). Local neighbors as positives, regional neighbors as negatives: Competing channels in the relationship between others' income, health, and happiness. *Journal of Health Economics*, *57*, 263–276.
Jaroszewicz, A., Jachimowicz, J., Hauser, O., & Jamison, J. (2022). *How effective is (more) money? Randomizing unconditional cash transfer amounts in the US*. https://doi.org/10.2139/ssrn.4154000
Jebb, A. T., Tay, L., Diener, E., & Oishi, S. (2018). Happiness, income satiation and turning points around the world. *Nature Human Behaviour*, *2*(1), 33–38.
Kahneman, D., Krueger, A. B., Schkade, D., Schwarz, N., & Stone, A. A. (2006). Would you be happier if you were richer? A focusing illusion. *Science*, *312*(5782), 1908–1910.

Kaiser, C., & Oswald, A. J. (2022). Inequality, well-being, and the problem of the unknown reporting function. *Proceedings of the National Academy of Sciences of the United States of America*, *19*(50).
Killingsworth, M. A., Kahneman, D., & Mellers, B. (2023). Income and emotional well-being: A conflict resolved. *Proceedings of the National Academy of Sciences of the United States of America*, *120*(10).
Kim, S., & Oswald, A. (2021). Happy lottery winners and lottery-ticket bias. *Review of Income and Wealth*, *67*(2), 317–333.
Kudrna, L. (2018). *An investigation of the relationships of absolute and relative socio-economic status with subjective wellbeing in the United States and England.* 10.21953/lse.windgi1i2yq7
Kudrna, L. (2024). Reference groups and relative effects on wellbeing. *Review of Income and Wealth*, *70*(3), 581–604. https://doi.org/10.1111/roiw.12656
Kudrna, L., & Kushlev, K. (2022). Money does not always buy happiness, but are richer people less happy in their daily lives? It depends on how you analyze income. *Frontiers in Psychology*, *13*.
Kushlev, K., Dunn, E. W., & Lucas, R. E. (2015). Higher income is associated with less daily sadness but not more daily happiness. *Social Psychological and Personality Science*, *6*(5), 483–489.
Layard, R., Nickell, S., & Mayraz, G. (2008). The marginal utility of income. *Journal of Public Economics*, *92*(8–9).
Lindqvist, E., Östling, R., & Cesarini, D. (2020). Long-run effects of lottery wealth on psychological well-being. *The Review of Economic Studies*, *87*(6), 2703–2726.
Luttmer, E. F. P. (2005). Neighbors as negatives: Relative earnings and well-being. *Quarterly Journal of Economics*, *120*(3), 963–1002.
Maini, R., Lohmann, J., Hotchkiss, D. R., Mounier-Jack, S., & Borghi, J. (2019). What happens when donors pull out? *International Journal of Health Policy and Management*, *8*(11), 646–661.
McGuire, J., Kaiser, C., & Bach-Mortensen, A. M. (2022). A systematic review and meta-analysis of the impact of cash transfers on subjective well-being and mental health in low- and middle-income countries. *Nature Human Behaviour*, *6*(3).
Ngamaba, K. H., Panagioti, M., & Armitage, C. J. (2018). Income inequality and subjective well-being: A systematic review and meta-analysis. *Quality of Life Research*, *27*(3).
Office for National Statistics (2022). *Personal well-being in the UK: April 2021 to March 2022*. https://www.ons.gov.uk/releases/personalwellbeingintheukapril2021tomarch2022
Oishi, S., & Kesebir, S. (2015). Income inequality explains why economic growth does not always translate to an increase in happiness. *Psychological Science*, *26*(10), 1630–1638.
Reynolds, J., Egan, M., Renedo, A., & Petticrew, M. (2015). Conceptualising the "community" as a recipient of money – a critical literature review, and implications for health and inequalities. *Social Science and Medicine*, *143*, 88–97.
Sacks, D. W., Stevenson, B., & Wolfers, J. (2012). The new stylized facts about income and subjective well-being. *Emotion*, *12*(6), 1181–1187.
Stevenson, B., & Wolfers, J. (2013). Subjective well-being and income: Is there any evidence of satiation? *American Economic Review*, *103*(3).
Stiglitz, J., Sen, A., & Fitoussi, J. (2009). *Report by the commission on the measurement of economic performance and social progress.* https://ec.europa.eu/eurostat/documents/8131721/8131772/Stiglitz-Sen-Fitoussi-Commission-report.pdf
Thrive at Work Wellbeing Programme Collaboration (2023). Evaluation of an organisational-level monetary incentive to promote the health and wellbeing of workers in small and medium-sized enterprises. *PLOS Global Public Health*, *3*(7), e0001381.
Wilson, T. D., & Gilbert, D. T. (2005). Affective forecasting. *Current Directions in Psychological Science*, *14*(3), 131.

3

WORK AND WELLBEING

Maximising the wellbeing of tomorrow's workforce

Alexandra Kirienko, Kate Laffan, and Laura M. Giurge

Introduction

People spend between 21% and 40% of their waking hours at work, making it an important domain of life to consider when trying to improve wellbeing (Kantak et al., 1992; Thompson, 2016). In addition to its inherent value to workers themselves, wellbeing is key to organisational success (Nielsen et al., 2017), with research showing that happier employees are more productive (Oswald et al., 2015) and less likely to quit (Pelly, 2023). Employee wellbeing is also positively associated with company profitability and stock market performance (De Neve et al., 2023).

Given its value, wellbeing at work is examined across disciplines, including organisational psychology, management, organisational behaviour, behavioural science, and sociology. Although each scientific discipline has a unique take, most definitions see wellbeing at work as a complex, multi-dimensional concept that captures how employees feel and behave at work. Some scholars speak of happiness as a related concept that broadly captures the joy derived from work (Warr, 2007). In this chapter, we take a subjective wellbeing (SWB) approach and consider how people feel about their work (evaluative SWB) and how they feel while working (experiential SWB). We then highlight some of the factors that impact wellbeing at work and discuss existing evidence on wellbeing at work interventions.

The existing literature looks at evaluative aspects of wellbeing – that is how employees feel about their work. Job satisfaction is one of the most studied variables in organisational behaviour and captures how satisfied employees are with their job (van Saane et al., 2003) or how satisfied employees are with different aspects of their job, such as pay, workplace relationships, or task variety (Judge & Church, 2000).

An alternative approach is looking at the experiential aspects of wellbeing – that is how employees feel at work or when they engage in work-related activities.

DOI: 10.4324/9781003382447-4

Unlike evaluative wellbeing, measuring experiential wellbeing at work is more challenging and requires more complex and time-consuming methods, such as naturalistic monitoring approaches that capture how employees feel throughout the day (Taquet et al., 2016).

A closely related concept in the literature on workplace wellbeing is burnout. Burnout is broadly defined as the feeling of being overextended and depleted physiologically, emotionally, and mentally (Maslach & Leiter, 2008); burnout has been linked to cynicism, inefficacy, sickness, and absenteeism (Barsade & O'Neill, 2014; Lin et al., 2019). Notably, burnout is typically conceptualised and measured not as an outcome but as a determinant of evaluative and experiential wellbeing (Maslach et al., 2012).

Interestingly, the evaluative and experiential approaches to wellbeing can co-exist, such as when capturing meaning at work – that is the extent to which employees experience their work to be both significant and purposeful (Steger et al., 2012). From an evaluative perspective, meaning at work is measured as self-reported judgments of overall job meaningfulness (van Saane et al., 2003). From an experiential perspective, meaning at work is measured by asking employees to indicate how meaningful a particular work activity feels (Dolan & White, 2009). Meaning at work has also been studied as both a wellbeing outcome and a driver of relevant organisational outcomes. For example, meaning at work has been associated with greater engagement and lower absenteeism (Soane et al., 2013).

What is behind wellbeing at work?

The academic literature has produced a wealth of evidence on the positive and negative correlates of wellbeing at work. This research suggests that some of the key factors that determine wellbeing are work–life balance (Hoffmann-Burdzińska & Rutkowska, 2015), working arrangements (Barling et al., 2002), social connection (Inceoglu et al., 2018), and job fit (Lysova et al., 2018). These drivers can be interconnected: for example, more flexible working arrangements can promote or detract from work–life balance (Laine & Rinne, 2015).

Work–life balance is the extent to which people strike a balance between work and non-work responsibilities (Fotiadis et al., 2019). This balance implies space and time for four main areas: self, close ties, distant ties, and career (Hoffmann-Burdzińska & Rutkowska, 2015). Gröpel and Kuhl (2009) show that work–life balance benefits wellbeing because it allows employees to fulfil their personal needs alongside pursuing organisational goals. By contrast, when work–life balance is impaired, employees experience time strain and pressure to multitask (Warren, 2021). A related concept is work–*family* balance, which captures a specific non-work domain that plays a significant role in work–life balance (Clark, 2000). Employees can experience conflict in both directions: work interfering with family and family interfering with work. Notably, the magnitude and direction of conflict can have unique effects on work- and family-related outcomes (see a meta-analysis by Amstad et al., 2011).

Working arrangements capture diversity in employment relationships, work schedules, and work location and are increasingly recognised as an important driver of employee wellbeing (Spreitzer et al., 2017). For example, increased work location flexibility is associated with higher job satisfaction (Possenriede & Plantenga, 2014). Flexible working arrangements positively impact work–life balance, supporting organisations in attracting and retaining talent (Warren, 2021). Although some evidence suggests that work–family conflict can increase when employees work from home (Antino et al., 2022), work location flexibility is becoming a widespread option instead of an exclusive perk (Smite et al., 2022).

Relationship with one's manager can significantly impact employee wellbeing (Gilbreath & Benson, 2004). Employees experience greater wellbeing when they perceive their supervisor as fair and supportive (Sparr & Sonnentag, 2008). By contrast, work–family conflict increases when employees do not align with their manager's normative expectations of work–family boundaries (Hill et al., 2016).

Social relationships can significantly impact both evaluative and experiential wellbeing (Steger et al., 2012). A dominance of negative social connections at work can lead to the development of toxic environments (Rasool et al., 2021), which impedes wellbeing at work. In contrast, feeling included, accepted, and valued at work drives wellbeing (Huong et al., 2016; Pal et al., 2022; Jaiswal & Dyaram, 2019).

Job fit captures the extent to which an individual is suited for the position in terms of alignment between the job requirements and their knowledge, strengths, skills, needs, and preferences (Slemp et al., 2015). Even when there is low job fit, employees can engage in job crafting – that is a self-initiated, proactive approach that employees use to redefine and reimagine their jobs to match their preferences and skills. Both job fit and job crafting have been linked to greater wellbeing at work (Lysova et al., 2018; Wrzesniewski & Dutton, 2001).

A parallel body of literature examines the relationship between voluntary work and wellbeing. Correlational evidence indicates that volunteering is positively associated with wellbeing, particularly among older populations (Becchetti et al., 2018), although there is some evidence of possible reverse causality (Stuart et al., 2020). Volunteering can support physical and mental health during retirement (Filges et al., 2020), can help buttress wellbeing during periods of unemployment (Griep et al., 2015), and can positively impact wellbeing during crises (Dolan et al., 2021). However, findings on the link between volunteering and wellbeing among young people are more mixed (Tanskanen & Danielsbacka, 2016).

Delivering wellbeing at work

With an improved understanding of the benefits and drivers of wellbeing at work, scholars and employers are becoming interested in implementing interventions to promote wellbeing.

To date, most wellbeing-at-work interventions aim to equip employees with resources to address competition demands and workload challenges (Lambert et al., 2022). These interventions typically focus on mindfulness training, work redesign, health behaviour change, or a mix of these approaches (Daniels et al., 2021). Kudesia et al. (2020) found that mindfulness training decreases employees' mental fatigue resulting from multitasking. A randomised control trial spanning 24 weeks found that mindfulness applications can improve wellbeing among law enforcement participants (Fitzhugh et al., 2023). Similarly, a burnout prevention programme consisting of six monthly three-hour sessions used for education and active participation helped reduce burnout among doctors in oncology wards (Le Blanc et al., 2007). Vuori et al. (2011) developed a more comprehensive training model that included a one-week workshop focusing on educating, social modelling, and role-playing to endorse a variety of career and resilience skills. The authors found that this intervention led to a significant decrease in depressive symptoms right after the study and seven months later.

However, other recent research analysing a range of available organisational interventions such as mindfulness training, resilience training, and wellbeing apps found no evidence that these strategies are effective in improving mental health and wellbeing of employees (Fleming, 2023). The 'so-called' workplace wellbeing paradox captures the disconnect between employers' investment in wellbeing at work and experienced wellbeing, highlighting the need for additional research on when, why, and for whom interventions can meaningfully improve wellbeing at work and across organisations (Cunningham, 2023).

Non-peer-reviewed, practitioner research can offer additional insights into wellbeing interventions that work. For example, research into the performance and wellbeing of the National Health Service Trusts in England found that practices that support workers, such as opportunities for development and regular encouragement, led to higher staff job satisfaction (Ogbonnaya & Daniels, 2017). Job-related training was found to improve the wellbeing of workers by an equivalent of a 1% hourly wage increase in some areas of the UK (What Works Wellbeing, 2017b). There is also some evidence that team activities, such as workshops and social events, could improve the social aspects of work that are understood to feed into greater wellbeing (What Works Wellbeing, 2017a).

Although the existing literature provides valuable insights on the effectiveness of some wellbeing interventions, it is still in its infancy. Most existing knowledge base on wellbeing at work is intra-organisational and seldomly evaluated with rigorous experimental methods. Companies conduct internal reviews and roll-out interventions, usually led by HR teams or external consultants, with results rarely shared with the broader community. For example, the for-profit company 2DaysMood helps organisations gather experiential workplace wellbeing data through 15-second surveys that employees receive on their mobile phones (Fehrmann, 2022). However, the data behind these partnerships and intra-organisational interventions are not available to third parties due to anonymity and safety requirements.

Yet another problem is that many organisational policies related to wellbeing are rolled out based on management intuition and with limited empirical evidence of their effectiveness. This prevents any assessment of the successes and failures of these interventions, which could improve our understanding of what promotes or undermines wellbeing at work. Further research and collaboration between organisations and academia (e.g. Fitzhugh et al., 2023) will help develop a stronger knowledge base for creating healthy and inclusive workplaces.

An important success factor for any intervention to achieve the intended improved wellbeing outcome is the continuation of the wellbeing efforts from the organisation post-intervention. Clear governance, strong delivery structures, and continuous learning to supplement interventions such as coaching or workshops can support the intervention implementation but are not themselves sufficient to improve wellbeing (Daniels et al., 2021).

Additionally, many sources of heterogeneity could impact the effectiveness of wellbeing interventions, including gender, age, carer status, socio-economic background, and personality characteristics, yet the evidence is lacking. Further research on the impact of interventions across different types of employees and circumstances is needed to better understand how to create tailored wellbeing interventions that work for all.

Conclusion

Wellbeing at work is a key driver of societal welfare and performance. It is also an important goal in and of itself and should be part of both public and organisational policy. Although there is a substantial body of evidence pointing to the drivers of evaluative aspects of wellbeing at work (e.g. job satisfaction), more research is needed to understand the experiential aspects of wellbeing at work, in terms of both negative (e.g. stress and burnout) and positive experiences (e.g. meaning and happiness). Future research should differentiate between the drivers of wellbeing at work and wellbeing outcomes and use robust, experimental, and longitudinal designs to test interventions that can yield long-lasting and scalable improvements in wellbeing at work.

Actionable points

Some of our recommendations around best practices for wellbeing interventions in organisations include the following:

- Collect evaluative and experiential wellbeing data, as well as objective indicators of wellbeing (e.g. turnover rates, sick days, vacation days), regularly (weekly or at least quarterly) and from everyone in the organisation (employees, leaders, CEOs, etc.). Such a systematic and robust approach can help capture wellbeing trends and discover potential areas for improvement.
- Develop and rigorously test policies that support work–life balance (e.g. limit work-related communication after work hours), flexible working arrangements

(e.g. shift from inputs-based metrics, such as the number of hours worked, to outputs-based metrics, such as quality of work), social connection (e.g. provide employees with time to connect with others within work hours), and job fit (e.g. empower employees to craft different aspects of their job along their strengths).

- Collaborate with academics to develop research-backed interventions and to rigorously measure their impact on employee wellbeing and beyond.
- Share insights on ongoing organisational initiatives and surveys to consolidate the growing knowledge around wellbeing at work.

References

Amstad, F. T., Meier, L. L., Fasel, U., Elfering, A., & Semmer, N. K. (2011). A meta-analysis of work–family conflict and various outcomes with a special emphasis on cross-domain versus matching-domain relations. *Journal of Occupational Health Psychology*, *16*(2), 151–169. https://doi.org/10.1037/a0022170

Antino, M., Ruiz-Zorrilla, P., Sanz-Vergel, A. I., Leon-Perez, J. M., & Rodriguez-Muñoz, A. (2022). The role of job insecurity and work-family conflict on mental health evolution during COVID-19 lockdown. *European Journal of Work and Organizational Psychology*, *31*(5), 1–18. https://doi.org/10.1080/1359432X.2022.2049251

Barling, J., Inness, M., & Gallagher, D. G. (2002). Alternative work arrangements and employee well being. In P. L. Perrewe & D. C. Ganster (Eds.), *Historical and current perspectives on stress and health* (Vol. 2, pp. 183–216). Emerald Group Publishing Limited. https://doi.org/10.1016/S1479-3555(02)02005-X

Barsade, S. G., & O'Neill, O. A. (2014). What's love got to do with it? A longitudinal study of the culture of companionate love and employee and client outcomes in a long-term care setting. *Administrative Science Quarterly*, *59*(4), 551–598.

Becchetti, L., Conzo, P., & Di Febbraro, M. (2018). The monetary-equivalent effect of voluntary work on mental wellbeing in Europe. *Kyklos*, *71*(1), 3–27. https://doi.org/10.1111/kykl.12160

Clark, S. C. (2000). Work/family border theory: A new theory of work/family balance. *Human Relations*, *53*(6), 747–770. https://doi.org/10.1177/0018726700536001

Cunningham, S. (2023, April 26). *How we can tackle the workplace wellbeing paradox – world wellbeing movement*. https://worldwellbeingmovement.org/insights/how-we-can-tackle-the-workplace-wellbeing-paradox/

Daniels, K., Watson, D., Nayani, R., Tregaskis, O., Hogg, M., Etuknwa, A., & Semkina, A. (2021). Implementing practices focused on workplace health and psychological wellbeing: A systematic review. *Social Science & Medicine*, *277*, 113888. https://doi.org/10.1016/j.socscimed.2021.113888

De Neve, J.-E., Kaats, M., & Ward, G. (2023). *Workplace wellbeing and firm performance*. https://ora.ox.ac.uk/objects/uuid:8652ce7e-7bde-449f-a5e7-6b0d0bcc3605

Dolan, P., Krekel, C., Shreedhar, G., Lee, H., Marshall, C., & Smith, A. (2021). Happy to help: The welfare effects of a nationwide micro-volunteering programme. *SSRN Electronic Journal*. https://doi.org/10.2139/ssrn.3865456

Fehrmann, S. (2022). Science of measuring employee happiness success. *2DAYSMOOD*. https://2daysmood.com/us/whitepapers/science-of-measuring-employee-happiness-success/

Filges, T., Siren, A., Fridberg, T., & Nielsen, B. C. V. (2020). Voluntary work for the physical and mental health of older volunteers: A systematic review. *Campbell Systematic Reviews*, *16*(4), e1124. https://doi.org/10.1002/cl2.1124

Fitzhugh, H., Michaelides, G., Daniels, K., Connolly, S., & Nasamu, E. (2023). Mindfulness for performance and wellbeing in the police: Linking individual and organizational outcomes. *Review of Public Personnel Administration*, 0734371X231155794. https://doi.org/10.1177/0734371X231155794

Fleming, W. (2023). *Estimating effects of individual-level workplace mental wellbeing interventions: Cross-sectional evidence from the UK.* https://doi.org/10.5287/ORA-YED9G7YRO

Fotiadis, A., Abdulrahman, K., & Spyridou, A. (2019). The mediating roles of psychological autonomy, competence and relatedness on work-life balance and well-being. *Frontiers in Psychology, 10.* www.frontiersin.org/articles/10.3389/fpsyg.2019.01267

Gilbreath, B., & Benson, P. G. (2004). The contribution of supervisor behaviour to employee psychological well-being. *Work & Stress, 18*(3), 255–266. https://doi.org/10.1080/02678370412331317499

Griep, Y., Hyde, M., Vantilborgh, T., Bidee, J., De Witte, H., & Pepermans, R. (2015). Voluntary work and the relationship with unemployment, health, and well-being: A two-year follow-up study contrasting a materialistic and psychosocial pathway perspective. *Journal of Occupational Health Psychology, 20,* 190–204. https://doi.org/10.1037/a0038342

Gröpel, P., & Kuhl, J. (2009). Work–life balance and subjective well-being: The mediating role of need fulfilment. *British Journal of Psychology, 100*(2), 365–375. https://doi.org/10.1348/000712608X337797

Hill, R. T., Morganson, V. J., Matthews, R. A., & Atkinson, T. P. (2016). LMX, breach perceptions, work-family conflict, and well-being: A mediational model. *The Journal of Psychology, 150*(1), 132–149. https://doi.org/10.1080/00223980.2015.1014307

Hoffmann-Burdzińska, K., & Rutkowska, M. (2015). Work life balance as a factor influencing well-being. *Journal of Positive Management, 6*(4), Article 4. https://doi.org/10.12775/JPM.2015.024

Huong, L., Zheng, C., & Fujimoto, Y. (2016). Inclusion, organisational justice and employee well-being. *International Journal of Manpower, 37*(6), 945–964. https://doi.org/10.1108/IJM-12-2015-0212

Inceoglu, I., Thomas, G., Chu, C., Plans, D., & Gerbasi, A. (2018). Leadership behavior and employee well-being: An integrated review and a future research agenda. *The Leadership Quarterly, 29*(1), 179–202. https://doi.org/10.1016/j.leaqua.2017.12.006

Jaiswal, A., & Dyaram, L. (2019). Perceived diversity and employee well-being: Mediating role of inclusion. *Personnel Review, 49*(5), 1121–1139. https://doi.org/10.1108/PR-12-2018-0511

Judge, T. A., & Church, A. H. (2000). Job satisfaction: Research and practice. In *Industrial and organizational psychology: Linking theory with practice* (pp. 166–198). Blackwell.

Kantak, D. M., Futrell, C. M., & Sager, J. K. (1992). Job satisfaction and life satisfaction in a sales force. *The Journal of Personal Selling and Sales Management, 12*(1), 1–7.

Kudesia, R., Pandey, A., & Reina, C. (2020). Doing more with less: Interactive effects of cognitive resources and mindfulness training in coping with mental fatigue from multitasking. *Journal of Management, 48(2), 410–439.* https://doi.org/10.1177/0149206320964570

Laine, P. A., & Rinne, R. (2015). Developing wellbeing at work: Emerging dilemmas. *International Journal of Wellbeing, 5*(2), Article 2. https://internationaljournalofwellbeing.org/index.php/ijow/article/view/359

Lambert, B., Caza, B. B., Trinh, E., & Ashford, S. (2022). Individual-centered interventions: Identifying what, how, and why interventions work in organizational contexts. *Academy of Management Annals, 16*(2), 508–546. https://doi.org/10.5465/annals.2020.0351

Le Blanc, P. M., Hox, J. J., Schaufeli, W. B., Taris, T. W., & Peeters, M. C. W. (2007). Take care! The evaluation of a team-based burnout intervention program for oncology care providers. *Journal of Applied Psychology, 92*(1), 213. https://doi.org/10.1037/0021-9010.92.1.213

Lin, S.-H. (Joanna), Scott, B. A., & Matta, F. K. (2019). The dark side of transformational leader behaviors for leaders themselves: A conservation of resources perspective. *Academy of Management Journal, 62*(5), 1556–1582. https://doi.org/10.5465/amj.2016.1255

Lysova, E. I., Jansen, P. G. W., Khapova, S. N., Plomp, J., & Tims, M. (2018). Examining calling as a double-edged sword for employability. *Journal of Vocational Behavior, 104,* 261–272. https://doi.org/10.1016/j.jvb.2017.11.006

Maslach, C., & Leiter, M. P. (2008). Early predictors of job burnout and engagement. *Journal of Applied Psychology*, *93*(3), 498–512. https://doi.org/10.1037/0021-9010.93.3.498
Maslach, C., Leiter, M. P., & Jackson, S. E. (2012). Making a significant difference with burnout interventions: Researcher and practitioner collaboration. *Journal of Organizational Behavior*, *33*(2), 296–300. https://doi.org/10.1002/job.784
Nielsen, K., Nielsen, M. B., Ogbonnaya, C., Känsälä, M., Saari, E., & Isaksson, K. (2017). Workplace resources to improve both employee well-being and performance: A systematic review and meta-analysis. *Work & Stress*, *31*(2), 101–120. https://doi.org/10.1080/02678373.2017.1304463
Ogbonnaya, C., & Daniels, K. (2017). *Good work, wellbeing and changes in performance outcomes: Illustrating the effects of good people management practices with an analysis of the National Health Service*. What Works Wellbeing. https://www.whatworkswellbeing.org/product/good-work-wellbeing-and-changes-in-performance-outcomes/
Oswald, A. J., Proto, E., & Sgroi, D. (2015). Happiness and productivity. *Journal of Labor Economics*, *33*(4), 789–822. https://doi.org/10.1086/681096
Pal, I., Galinsky, E., & Kim, S. (2022). Employee health and well-being after a crisis – re-imagining the role of workplace inclusion. *Community, Work & Family*, *25*(1), 30–62. https://doi.org/10.1080/13668803.2021.1987859
Pelly, D. (2023). Worker well-being and quit intentions: Is measuring job satisfaction enough? *Social Indicators Research*, *169*(1), 397–441. https://doi.org/10.1007/s11205-023-03166-x
Possenriede, D. S., & Plantenga, J. (2014). Temporal and locational flexibility of work, working-time fit, and job satisfaction. *SSRN Electronic Journal*. https://doi.org/10.2139/ssrn.2502296
Rasool, S. F., Wang, M., Tang, M., Saeed, A., & Iqbal, J. (2021). How toxic workplace environment effects the employee engagement: The mediating role of organizational support and employee wellbeing. *International Journal of Environmental Research and Public Health*, *18*(5), Article 5. https://doi.org/10.3390/ijerph18052294
Slemp, G. R., Kern, M. L., & Vella-Brodrick, D. A. (2015). Workplace well-being: The role of job crafting and autonomy support. *Psychology of Well-Being*, *5*(1), 7. https://doi.org/10.1186/s13612-015-0034-y
Smite, D., Christensen, E. L., Tell, P., & Russo, D. (2022). The future workplace: Characterizing the spectrum of hybrid work arrangements for software teams. *IEEE Software*, 1–9. https://doi.org/10.1109/MS.2022.3230289
Soane, E., Shantz, A., Alfes, K., Truss, C., Rees, C., & Gatenby, M. (2013). The association of meaningfulness, well-being, and engagement with absenteeism: A moderated mediation model. *Human Resource Management*, *52*(3), 441–456. https://doi.org/10.1002/hrm.21534
Sparr, J. L., & Sonnentag, S. (2008). Fairness perceptions of supervisor feedback, LMX, and employee well-being at work. *European Journal of Work and Organizational Psychology*, *17*(2), 198–225. https://doi.org/10.1080/13594320701743590
Spreitzer, G. M., Cameron, L., & Garrett, L. (2017). Alternative work arrangements: Two images of the new world of work. *Annual Review of Organizational Psychology and Organizational Behavior*, *4*(1), 473–499. https://doi.org/10.1146/annurev-orgpsych-032516-113332
Steger, M. F., Dik, B. J., & Duffy, R. D. (2012). Measuring meaningful work: The work and meaning inventory (WAMI). *Journal of Career Assessment*, *20*(3), 322–337. https://doi.org/10.1177/1069072711436160
Stuart, J., Kamerāde, D., Connolly, D. S., Paine, D. A. E., Nichols, D. G., & Grotz, D. J. (2020). *The impacts of volunteering on the subjective wellbeing of volunteers: A rapid evidence assessment*. What Works Centre for Wellbeing. https://whatworkswellbeing.org/wp-content/uploads/2020/10/Volunteer-wellbeing-technical-report-Oct2020-a.pdf
Tanskanen, A. O., & Danielsbacka, M. (2016). Do volunteering and charity pay off? Well-being benefits of participating in voluntary work and charity for older and younger

adults in Finland. *Research on Ageing and Social Policy*, *4*(2), Article 2. https://doi.org/10.17583/rasp.2016.1640

Taquet, M., Quoidbach, J., de Montjoye, Y.-A., Desseilles, M., & Gross, J. J. (2016). Hedonism and the choice of everyday activities. *Proceedings of the National Academy of Sciences*, *113*(35), 9769–9773. https://doi.org/10.1073/pnas.1519998113

Thompson, A. K. (2016, August 16). What percentage of your life will you spend at work? *ReviseSociology*. https://revisesociology.com/2016/08/16/percentage-life-work/

van Saane, N., Sluiter, J. K., Verbeek, J. H. A. M., & Frings-Dresen, M. H. W. (2003). Reliability and validity of instruments measuring job satisfaction – a systematic review. *Occupational Medicine*, *53*(3), 191–200. https://doi.org/10.1093/occmed/kqg038

Vuori, J., Toppinen-Tanner, S., & Mutanen, P. (2011). Effects of resource-building group intervention on career management and mental health in work organizations: Randomized controlled field trial. *Journal of Applied Psychology*, *97*(2), 273. https://doi.org/10.1037/a0025584

Warr, P. (2007). Searching for happiness at work. *The Psychologist*, *20*, 726–729.

Warren, T. (2021). Work–life balance and gig work: "Where are we now" and "where to next" with the work–life balance agenda? *Journal of Industrial Relations*, *63*(4), 522–545. https://doi.org/10.1177/00221856211007161

What Works Wellbeing (2017a, August). Team working. *What Works Wellbeing*. https://whatworkswellbeing.org/resources/team-working/

What Works Wellbeing (2017b, September). Wellbeing benefits of job-related learning. *What Works Wellbeing*. https://whatworkswellbeing.org/resources/wellbeing-benefits-of-job-related-learning/

Wrzesniewski, A., & Dutton, J. E. (2001). Crafting a job: Revisioning employees as active crafters of their work. *Academy of Management Review*, *26*(2), 179–201. https://doi.org/10.5465/amr.2001.4378011

4

HEALTH AND WELLBEING

Identifying causal effects

Hans Czap and Marie Briguglio

Introduction

Maintaining and improving people's health constitutes one of the United Nations' Sustainable Development Goals, and, in many countries, it is an important public-sector goal accorded hefty budgets (United Nations, n.d.). This chapter questions whether actions or strategies designed to improve or protect health also improve wellbeing, and if so, to what extent.

The OECD's Better Life Index (OECD, n.d.), the European Union's Quality of Life dashboard (Eurostat, n.d.), and wellbeing metrics of various countries (e.g., Canada, New Zealand, and Bhutan) all include indicator/s of health as an intrinsic part of their wellbeing assessment. Such indicators include Life (or Healthy life) expectancy and self-perceived health and others like prevalence of disease, Body Mass Index, and lifestyle habits (e.g., smoking cigarettes, consuming fruit/vegetables, or performing physical activity). If wellbeing is measured by such objective indicators" then changes in health *by definition* lead to changes in wellbeing, *ceteris paribus*. Indeed there is a tendency to use the terms "wellbeing" and "health" interchangeably (Dalingwater, 2019). For instance, the World Health Organization (WHO) defines health as a "state of complete physical, mental and social wellbeing" (WHO, 1946, p. 1). This presents what Bognar (2008) argues is a problem of inseparability; defining health and wellbeing as distinct concepts is an important first step to assessing the impacts of the former on the latter.

It is important to note that there is a vast and established medical literature on health-related quality of life (or HRQoL). These studies are not included in this review as they do not typically assess Subjective Wellbeing (SWB) directly, but rather capture the subjective elements associated with physical conditions (e.g., perceived limits to physical and social functioning, role impairment, pain). Though

DOI: 10.4324/9781003382447-5

there are intuitive reasons to assume that such conditions (together with possible indirect impacts on relationships, one's identity, and finances) may adversely impact SWB, the literature on this, and related interventions (the main focus of this chapter), is less developed. Indeed it is only the past decade or so that healthcare has started to involve psychometric questions about *positive* states of mind (as opposed to, say, common questions about depression), providing the data needed to generate an evidence base (Helliwell, 2019).

Meanwhile, some consensus has emerged on the notion that subjective wellbeing entails three components – evaluative, hedonic, and eudemonic (Steptoe et al., 2015). Assessment of the impact of health-related factors and related interventions on these outcomes presents some challenges: (1) responses on health and wellbeing, typically drawn from surveys, may be transient, strategic, or hard to compare across cultures (Bache et al., 2016); (2) reverse causality makes it challenging to assess effects – health outcomes impact SWB, but SWB itself impacts health outcomes; (3) health impacts education, work, productivity, wealth, and social relations (OECD, n.d.), all of which are determinants of wellbeing in their own right – thus measuring the impact of health on wellbeing with *ceteris paribus* assumptions can result in underestimated impacts, and studies often use the terms "happiness" and "life-satisfaction" interchangeably though the impact of health on these subjective wellbeing outcomes will vary depending on the measure under consideration (Ngamaba et al., 2017).

Evidence of the relationship between health and wellbeing

While numerous studies conclude that health and wellbeing are positively linked, much of the work is correlational. For instance, Shields and Wheatley Price (2005) use cross-sectional data to show that muscular-arthritis-rheumatism, stomach problems, and respiratory system problems are significantly and negatively associated with psychological wellbeing. Lobos et al. (2015) use survey data from Chile to show that the number of unhealthy days is correlated with happiness. Mahon et al. (2005) focus on clinical health among middle school students, finding a positive correlation between happiness and clinical health. Selim (2008) finds a positive correlation between both life satisfaction and happiness and *perceived* health, as opposed to objective measures of health. Using cross-sectional data for Latin America, Graham et al. (2011) note that anxiety and pain have stronger effects on life satisfaction than physical ailments and that the magnitude is large in comparison to income effects. Correlational studies also consistently indicate a significant negative relationship between addictions and wellbeing (e.g., Booker et al., 2015).

A central concern when assessing the impact of health and health interventions on SWB is the possibility of reverse causality. Indeed there is strong evidence that wellbeing is itself associated with many beneficial outcomes – including health (Kansky & Diener, 2017), immune system response, pain tolerance (Howell et al., 2007), recovery and survival in physically ill patients (Lamers et al., 2012), and life expectancy (Diener & Chan, 2011). To account for reverse causality it is necessary to step away from correlational studies to methods such as experiments, randomized control trials (RCTs), and the use of data which is longitudinal.

Binder and Coad (2013) alleviate concerns of causality by using a matching design and panel data from the UK, finding that more hospital days, health appointments, and serious accidents in the prior year consistently had a negative impact on life satisfaction. They note that impacts vary substantially by different conditions, with most physical impairments having a relatively low negative impact on wellbeing. Hegarty et al. (2016) focus on arthritis and fatigue. Using panel data, they establish a causal link going from arthritis to fatigue to happiness and frustration. Dolan (2011) provides some evidence that mental health is a determinant of life satisfaction (and more so than physical health) using a micro two-period fixed effects model. Anxiety, one of the main indicators of mental health, is similarly found to have a strong causal impact on life satisfaction, albeit less important than alcohol and drug abuse (Binder & Coad, 2013). Other studies focus on the relationship between wellbeing and *perceived* health. In an early study, Brief et al. (1993) establish a causal effect by using longitudinal and cross-sectional data. They find no direct effect of objective health on life satisfaction but note that the impact on SWB occurs through the subjective interpretation of health, which, in turn, may depend on personality traits like neuroticism.

Adaptation to new life conditions is one reason why the association between objective physical health (as assessed by a healthcare professional) and wellbeing may be relatively weak (Diener & Seligman, 2004). But evidence on hedonic adaptation is mixed. An early study by Brickman et al. (1978) find strong adaptation of individuals to life-altering accidents, yet Oswald and Powdthavee (2008) find a rate of hedonic adaptation of between 30% and 50%, depending on the degree of disability. Patients with chronic diseases and pain adapt more slowly or not at all (Smith & Wallston, 1992). More recent work by Stöckel et al. (2023) employs fixed effects models to explore longitudinal changes in self-assessed health and life satisfaction around the onset of disability, finding that large decreases in subjective health and quality of life attenuate over time (especially in life satisfaction), but results are heterogeneous. Bussière et al. (2021) estimate panel fixed-effects models, finding that aging increases the importance of health for both eudemonic and experienced wellbeing but the association between health and life satisfaction weakens with age (except for individuals aged 80 and older). On this basis, they caution against the use of the various forms of SWB interchangeably in public policy analysis and economic evaluations of healthcare. In turn, using wellbeing adjusted life years (otherwise known as "WELLBYS") is one way for health policy to take account of health impacts on wellbeing over time (Frijters et al., 2024).

Finally, there is evidence that there is heterogeneity in the impact of health on wellbeing outcomes. For instance, Shields and Wheatley Price (2005) note that the wellbeing of males was most strongly correlated with heart attack or stroke problems, migraine, and epilepsy, while the wellbeing of females was predominantly associated with hypertension and blood pressure problems. Binder and Coad (2013) establish that personality characteristics are important factors to consider. For example extroverts are more negatively affected by anxiety disorders, and neurotic individuals are more strongly affected by disability.

Evidence of the effects of interventions on wellbeing

Public policy can affect public health in a variety of ways, ranging from improved medical access, all the way to safety regulations to reduce the number of life-changing accidents, and environmental policy. To date, there is relatively little research on the effects of health policy and interventions on wellbeing.[1]

One area of intervention pertains to health insurance. In 1995 the Taiwanese government introduced a National Health Insurance that provided healthcare coverage to all citizens. Using a difference-in-difference approach, Liao et al. (2012) find that this significantly increased life satisfaction among the elderly, especially that of elderly women. In 2007, Massachusetts also implemented a healthcare reform that mandated health insurance coverage for all residents, with studies finding that this significantly increased overall life satisfaction (Kim & Koh, 2022). In 2008, Oregon (United States) put in place a lottery that provided Medicaid for low-income adults. This constituted a natural experiment that allowed researchers to establish that healthcare access, health, and wellbeing increased after the first year for those who obtained healthcare through the program (Finkelstein et al., 2012), though research conducted two years later found that the wellbeing gains had disappeared (Baicker et al., 2013). Similarly, research investigating the impact of the Affordable Care Act (2010) paints a mixed picture of the wellbeing effects, resulting in increased accessibility and affordability, but mixed effects on wellbeing. Kim and Koh (2022) see a significant increase in subjective wellbeing among low-income adults in this programme, whereas Kobayashi et al. (2019) find no statistically significant impact.[2]

Another broad area of intervention pertains to expenditure on healthcare services. Kotakorpi and Laamanen (2010) find that increased spending on public healthcare services in Finland leads to higher individual life satisfaction. This impact is heterogeneous across income and political orientation groups, with middle-income individuals deriving higher satisfaction than either low- or high-income individuals and right-wing beliefs being associated with lower benefits from primary healthcare spending but greater benefits from special healthcare.

Psychological interventions are primarily under the purview of medical professionals as part of individual treatment. But governments can play a role by actively promoting wellbeing initiatives. This has been done in Japan as part of the Asia Health and Wellbeing Initiative (AHWIN.org) and in the UK as part of Public Health England's work. A meta-study by van Agteren et al. (2021) finds strong evidence that both mindfulness approaches and interventions based on multiple psychological interventions fare best in clinical and non-clinical populations. The effectiveness of other interventions, such as acceptance and commitment therapy, cognitive behavioural therapy, reminiscence intervention, and positive psychological interventions, depends on the population – reinforcing the need to tailor such therapies to the context and individual.

A promising set of interventions referred to as "social prescribing" involves directing patients to engage in social activities, based on the premise that positive connections can enhance happiness. To date, the emphasis of such interventions has focused on treating illness, but there is also scope for these kinds of interventions to directly target wellbeing among patients (Helliwell, 2019). For instance, the Be-Active-Scheme in Birmingham, UK, focused on increasing gym usage among poor households in the UK by offering Gym membership for free. Both gym visits and wellbeing increased substantially as a result (Rabiee et al., 2015).

It is also important to consider that some health interventions may actually reduce wellbeing outcomes both of the target population and of others. For instance, during the COVID-19 pandemic, public health authorities may well have unduly suppressed wellbeing through strong handed lock-downs, curfews, and other restrictions (Briguglio et al., 2021). In cancer treatment, medical advances have greatly enhanced patient survival rates but at times to the detriment of SWB (Fernando, 2020). SWB varies throughout the treatment experience and measuring it can facilitate service improvements (Lee et al., 2013).

Discussion and conclusion

Improving people's health constitutes an important public-sector goal. While health and wellbeing are closely linked, and while numerous studies have examined the effect on HRQoL, few studies have identified the causal effects (magnitude, direction, and duration) of health interventions and SWB. The studies reviewed in this chapter provide some evidence that health interventions can affect wellbeing positively albeit heterogeneously (depending on the type of health issue, how it is measured, and the type of intervention).

A pertinent question is how policy-makers could act on such evidence. Focusing on SWB offers the potential of bringing this aspect into models of health outcomes and disease monitoring (Crawshaw, 2008), and leading exponents have argued that cost-effectiveness analysis should be reformed with happiness as the outcome of interest, leading to more attention being paid to, for instance, mental health and palliative care (Helliwell, 2019). Yet consensus on government's role in supplying public health services does not automatically extend to consensus on government's role in interventions for wellbeing (Dalingwater, 2019). Policy-makers may need to discuss and weigh the relative importance of SWB compared to health when there are trade-offs involved – as happened during the COVID-19 pandemic.

The following five actionable points emerge:

- The impacts of health interventions on wellbeing over time should be considered as a measurable outcome – distinct from health itself.

- Given the bidirectional relationship between health and subjective wellbeing, isolating the impact of health on wellbeing needs careful design to ensure identification. Mediating and indirect effects of health on wellbeing, as well as adaptation/sensitization over time, should be considered. The various forms of SWB should not be used interchangeably in analysis.
- Policy-makers should consider the relative importance of wellbeing and physical and mental health in cost-effectiveness analysis.
- Government can actively promote effective interventions for wellbeing like health insurance, gym subscriptions, mindfulness approaches, psychological interventions, and social prescribing; SWB responds more strongly to mental health than physical health improvements.
- The impact of interventions is heterogeneous. Interventions need to be tailored to the context and individual needs. Measuring SWB throughout the treatment experience can facilitate improvements and provide the data for an evidence base of what works.

Notes

1 For best practice guidelines for individual practitioners for treating various mental or physical conditions, see for instance Walker et al. (2019) or What Works Wellbeing (n.d.)
2 To identify causal impacts they examine wellbeing before and after Medicaid in states that expanded Medicaid as opposed to those that did not.

References

Asia Health and Wellbeing Initiative (n.d.). www.ahwin.org/

Bache, I., Reardon, L., & Anand, P. (2016). Wellbeing as a wicked problem: Navigating the arguments for the role of government. *Journal of Happiness Studies*, *17*, 893–912. https://doi.org/10.1007/s10902-015-9623-y

Baicker, K., Taubman, S. L., Allen, H. L., Bernstein, M., Gruber, J. H., Newhouse, J. P., Schneider, E. C., Wright, B. J., Zaslavsky, A. M., Finkelstein, A. N., & Oregon Health Study Group (2013). The Oregon experiment – effects of Medicaid on clinical outcomes. *The New England Journal of Medicine*, *368*(18), 1713–1722. https://doi.org/10.1056/NEJMsa1212321

Binder, M., & Coad, A. (2013). "I'm afraid I have bad news for you . . ." Estimating the impact of different health impairments on subjective well-being. *Social Science & Medicine*, *87*, 155–167. https://doi.org/10.1016/j.socscimed.2013.03.025

Bognar, G. (2008). Well-being and health. *Health Care Analysis*, *16*, 97–113. https://doi.org/10.1007/s10728-007-0066-4

Booker, C. L., Skew, A. J., Kelly, Y. J., & Sacker, A. (2015). Media use, sports participation, and well-being in adolescence: Cross-sectional findings from the UK household longitudinal study. *American Journal of Public Health*, *105*, 173–179. https://doi.org/10.2105/AJPH.2013.301783

Brickman, P., Coates, D., & Janoff-Bulman, R. (1978). Lottery winners and accident victims: Is happiness relative? *Journal of Personality and Social Psychology, 36*(8), 917–927. https://doi.org/10.1037/0022-3514.36.8.917

Brief, A. P., Houston Butcher, A., George, J. M., & Link, K. E. (1993). Integrating bottom-up and top-down theories of subjective well-being: The case of health. *Journal of Personality and Social Psychology*, *64*(4), 646–653. https://doi.org/10.1037//0022-3514.64.4.646

Briguglio, M., Caruana, M., & Debono, N. (2021). Well-being disparities during the COVID-19 outbreak: Evidence from Malta. *Traumatology*, *27*(4), 388–398. https://doi.org/10.1037/trm0000323
Bussière, C., Sirven, N., & Tessier, P. (2021). Does ageing alter the contribution of health to subjective well-being? *Social Science & Medicine*, *268*, 113456. https://doi.org/10.1016/j.socscimed.2020.113456
Crawshaw, P. (2008). Whither wellbeing for public health? *Critical Public Health*, *18*(3), 259–261. https://doi.org/10.1080/09581590802351757
Dalingwater, L. (2019). Linking health and wellbeing in public discourse and policy: The case of the UK. *Interventions Economiques*, 6243. https://doi.org/10.4000/interventionseconomiques.6243
Diener, E., & Chan, M. Y. (2011). Happy people live longer: Subjective well-being contributes to health and longevity. *Applied Psychology: Health and Well-Being*, *3*(1), 1–43. https://doi.org/10.1111/j.1758-0854.2010.01045.x
Diener, E., & Seligman, M. E. P. (2004). Beyond money: Toward an economy of well-being. *Psychological Science in the Public Interest*, *5*(1), 1–31. https://doi.org/10.1111/j.0963-7214.2004.00501001.x
Dolan, P. (2011). Using happiness to value health. *Office of Health Economics Report.*
Eurostat (n.d.). https://ec.europa.eu/eurostat/web/quality-of-life/database
Fernando, A. (2020). Mental health and cancer: Why it is time to innovate and integrate-a call to action. *European Urology Focus*, *6*(6), 1165–1167. https://doi.org/10.1016/j.euf.2020.06.025. Epub 2020 Jul 14. PMID: 32680828; PMCID: PMC9972363.
Finkelstein, A. N., Taubman, S. L., Wright, B. J., Bernstein, M., Gruber, J. H., Newhouse, J. P., Allen, H. L., Baicker, K., & Oregon Health Study Group (2012). The Oregon health insurance experiment: Evidence from the first year. *The Quarterly Journal of Economics*, *127*(3), 1057–1106. https://doi.org/10.1093/qje/qjs020
Frijters, P., Krekel, C., Sanchis, R., & Santini, Z. I. (2024). The WELLBY: A new measure of social value and progress. *Humanities and Social Sciences Communications*, *11*(1), 1–12.
Graham, C., Higuera, L., & Lora, E. (2011). Which health conditions cause the most unhappiness? *Health Economics*, *20*, 1431–1447. https://doi.org/10.1002/hec.1682
Hegarty, R. S. M., Treharne, G. J., Stebbings, S., & Conner, T. S. (2016). Fatigue and mood among people with arthritis: Carry-over across the day. *Health Psychology*, *35*(5), 492–499. http://dx.doi.org/10.1037/hea0000321
Helliwell, J. (2019). Determinants of well-being and their implications for health care. *Annals of Nutrition and Metabolism*, *74*(Suppl. 2), 8–14. https://doi.org/10.1159/000499141
Howell, R., Kern, M., & Lyubomirsky, S. (2007). Health benefits: Meta-analytically determining the impact of well-being on objective health outcomes. *Health Psychology Review*, *1*(1), 83–136. https://doi.org/10.1080/17437190701492486
Kansky, J., & Diener, E. (2017). Benefits of well-being: Health, social relationships, work, and resilience. *Journal of Positive Psychology and Wellbeing*, *1*(2), 129–169.
Kim, S., & Koh, K. (2022). Health insurance and subjective well-being: Evidence from two healthcare reforms in the United States. *Health Economics*, *31*, 233–249. https://doi.org/10.1002/hec.4448
Kobayashi, L. C., Altindag, O., Truskinovsky, Y., & Berkman, L. F. (2019). Effects of the Affordable Care Act Medicaid expansion on subjective well-being in the US adult population, 2010–2016. *American Journal of Public Health – Open Themed Research*, *109*, 1236–1242. https://doi.org/10.2105/AJPH.2019.305164
Kotakorpi, K., & Laamanen, J. P. (2010). Welfare state and life satisfaction: Evidence from public health care. *Economica*, *77*(307), 565–583. https://doi.org/10.1111/j.1468-0335.2008.00769.x
Lamers, S. M. A., Bolier, L., Westerhof, G. J. (2012). The impact of emotional well-being on long-term recovery and survival in physical illness: A meta-analysis. *Journal of Behavioral Medicine*, *35*, 538–547. https://doi.org/10.1007/s10865-011-9379-8

Lee, H., Vlaev, I., King, D., Mayer, E., Darzi, A., & Dolan, P. (2013). Subjective well-being and the measurement of quality in healthcare. *Social Science & Medicine*, *99*, 27–34. https://doi.org/10.1016/j.socscimed.2013.09.027.

Liao, P. A., Chang, H. H., & Sun, L. C. (2012). National Health Insurance program and life satisfaction of the elderly. *Aging & Mental Health*, *16*(8), 983–992. http://dx.doi.org/10.1080/13607863.2012.692765

Lobos, G., Mora, M., del Carmen Lapo, M., Caligari, C., & Schnettler, B. (2015). Happiness and health and food-related factors: Evidence for different age groups in Chile. *Suma Psicológica*, *22*, 120–128. https://doi.org/10.1016/j.sumpsi.2015.09.002

Mahon, N. E., Yarcheski, A., & Yarcheski, T. J. (2005). Happiness as related to gender and health in early adolescents. *Clinical Nursing Research*, *14*(2), 175–190. https://doi.org/10.1177/1054773804271936

Ngamaba, K., Panagioti, M., & Armitage, C. (2017). How strongly related are health status and subjective well-being? Systematic review and meta-analysis. *European Journal of Public Health*, *27*(5), 879–885. https://doi.org/10.1093/eurpub/ckx081

Organization for Economic Cooperation and Development (OECD) (n.d.). *Better life index: Health*. www.oecdbetterlifeindex.org/topics/health/

Oswald, A. J., & Powdthavee, N. (2008). Does happiness adapt? A longitudinal study of disability with implications for economists and judges. *Journal of Public Economics*, *92*, 1061–1077. https://doi.org/10.1016/j.jpubeco.2008.01.002.

Rabiee, F., Robbins, A., & Khan, M. (2015). Gym for free: The short-term impact of an innovative public health policy on the health and wellbeing of residents in a deprived constituency in Birmingham, UK. *Health Education Journal*, *74*(6), 691–704. https://doi.org/10.1177/0017896914553957

Selim, S. (2008). Life satisfaction and happiness in Turkey. *Social Indicators Research*, *88*, 531–562. https://doi.org/10.1007/s11205-007-9218-z

Shields, M. A., & Wheatley Price, S. (2005). Exploring the economic and social determinants of psychological well-being and perceived social support in England. *Journal of the Royal Statistical Society*, *Series A*, *168*(3), 513–537. https://doi.org/10.1111/j.1467-985X.2005.00361.x

Smith, C. A., & Wallston, K. A. (1992). Adaptation in patients with chronic rheumatoid arthritis: Application of a general model. *Health Psychology*, *11*(3), 151–162. https://doi.org/10.1037/0278-6133.11.3.151

Steptoe, A., Deaton, A., & Stone, A. A. (2015, February 14). Subjective wellbeing, health, and ageing. *Lancet*, *385*(9968), 640–648. https://doi.org/10.1016/S0140-6736(13)61489-0.

Stöckel, J., van Exel, J., & Brouwer, W. B. (2023). Adaptation in life satisfaction and self-assessed health to disability-evidence from the UK. *Social Science & Medicine*, *328*, 115996. https://doi.org/10.1016/j.socscimed.2023.115996

United Nations (UN) (n.d.). *Goal 3: Ensure healthy lives and promote well-being for all at all ages*. www.un.org/sustainabledevelopment/health/

van Agteren, J., Iasiello, M., Lo, L., Bartholomaeus, J., Kopsaftis, Z., Carey, M., & Kyrios, M. (2021). A systematic review and meta-analysis of psychological interventions to improve mental wellbeing. *Nature Human Behavior*, *5*, 631–652. https://doi.org/10.1038/s41562-021-01093-w

Walker, I. F., Stansfield, J., Makurah, L., Garnham, H., Robson, C., Lugton, C., Hey, N., & Henderson, G. (2019). Delivering national public mental health – experience from England. *Journal of Public Mental Health*, *18*(2), 112–123. https://doi.org/10.1108/JPMH-06-2018-0032

What Works Wellbeing (n.d.). *What works wellbeing: Resources*. https://whatworkswellbeing.org/

World Health Organization (1946). *Constitution of the World Health Organization*. https://apps.who.int/gb/bd/PDF/bd47/EN/constitution-en.pdf?ua=1

5

FAMILY AND WELLBEING

The emerging importance of family wellbeing studies for social policies and services

Lili Xia

Introduction

Family has long been recognized as an important dimension having an immediate influence on an individual's wellbeing by both economists and sociologists (Dolan et al., 2008; Layard, 2005; Sanchez-Sanchez, 2017). A family cares for and supports its members physically, emotionally, and socially, affecting an individual's developmental outcomes throughout their lifespan (La Placa et al., 2013; McKeown & Sweeney, 2001; Newland, 2015). Family is an intermediate system that bridges the interaction between individuals and society, so its characteristics and wellbeing are important for social development. For instance, family structural characteristics such as family size, marriage and divorce rates, and the fertility rate of married couples are used as indicators of social stability and sustainability (Jones, 2012). At the managerial level, there is evidence that having a family to support could boost one's job absorption, motivation, and performance (Dumas & Perry-Smith, 2018; Menges et al., 2017). A four-country comparison study conducted by Krys et al. (2021) revealed that people from diverse sociocultural backgrounds value family wellbeing over individual wellbeing.

Consequently, family wellbeing has gradually emerged as not only an essential aspect of individual wellbeing but also an important indicator of social development that can inform public policy-making and social services planning (Wollny et al., 2010; Zimmerman, 2013).

Conceptualizing family wellbeing

"Family wellbeing" has emerged as a prominent topic of interest in recent decades among scholars, policy-makers, and helping professionals. There has been a growing recognition of the uniqueness of the wellbeing of family as a unit, leading to

DOI: 10.4324/9781003382447-6

a shift toward a family-centered approach in research and practice. It is a multi-dimensional concept that poses challenges in terms of philosophical, theoretical, and conceptual clarity and agreement. In policy documents and research articles, family wellbeing has been referred to as "individual and family wellbeing," "family life satisfaction," "quality of family relationships (i.e., marital, parent–child relationship)," "family quality of life," "family functioning," or a combination of these terms (McGregor, 2020; Summers et al., 2005).

According to the comprehensive reviews by Wollny et al. (2010), Zimmerman (2013), and McGregor (2020), four approaches to conceptualizing and studying family wellbeing could be identified. First, the family systems theory views the family as an organized system comprising interdependent members, having multiple functions, and differentiating and interacting with the external environment. Family wellbeing was measured based on the family's ability to fulfil its various functions. Second, ecological systems theory emphasizes the interaction and interdependence between family wellbeing and the environment, suggesting that physical, economic, political, and cultural contexts be included while evaluating family wellbeing. Third, family stress and resource theory assesses family wellbeing by considering the balance between stressors affecting a family and the coping resources available to it. Fourth, there are also non-theoretical approaches: the family functioning approach (focuses on family communication end execution), data-driven and domain-based frameworks (explore the qualities of a happy/functioning family), and frameworks with special focuses (i.e., child welfare, parenting, positive family behaviors) (Karakas et al., 2004; McKeown et al., 2003; Yaxley et al., 2012).

As approaches overlap, many studies incorporate two or more models. For instance, studies of the Family Wellbeing Index (FWI) adopted an inclusive definition of family wellbeing as "the state of the family in performing its various functions to satisfy the diverse needs of family members through interactions with the environment" (Noor et al., 2014; Wong et al., 2022). The measurements encompass dimensions such as financial security and stability, relational wellbeing, group dynamics and cohesion, family autonomy, collective health, community connections and belonging, spiritual health, and ecological wellbeing (McGregor, 2020). Though there is a generally agreed framework, the components of the FWI developed by different countries (or for different ethnic groups) are not the same, because of the socially, culturally, and historically specific nature of family life and family wellbeing (Maulana et al., 2018; Wollny et al., 2010). For example, the religion/spiritual dimension was included in the Malaysian and a Canadian FWI, but not in that for Chinese people in Hong Kong (Wong et al., 2022).

Some prominent examples of the growing trend toward studying family wellbeing include the development of indexes in the United States (Martinez et al., 2003), Malaysia (Noor et al., 2014), and Hong Kong (Hong Kong Family Welfare Society & Hong Kong Public Opinion Research Institute, 2022); the long-term tracking of family wellbeing in Australia (McCalman et al., 2018), New Zealand

(Social Policy Evaluation and Research Unit, 2018), and Indonesia (Sujarwoto, 2017); and the special-focus study of the wellbeing of low-income families in Ireland (Sword et al., 2013).

Methodologically, quantitative approaches have been commonly adopted in the development of FWIs. Data are usually collected through surveys from a large representative sample of individuals or through a household-survey approach (i.e., Malaysia, Australia) (Noor et al., 2014; Webster et al., 2008). These studies calculate the FWI score and provide an overview of the wellbeing of families in a particular region. They also identify specific population characteristics that require additional attention and support, uncover influential factors and mechanisms impacting family wellbeing, and generate evidence for public policy-making and service planning aimed at promoting family wellbeing.

Wellbeing interventions case study: tracking family wellbeing in Hong Kong

Hong Kong is an important metropolis that embodies a fusion of Eastern and Western cultures and beliefs. It adopts a laissez-faire approach to social welfare, but is developing a well-structured and highly professionalized social services system at the same time (Xia & Ma, 2019). At the beginning of the 21st century, the Hong Kong government began to recognize the importance of the family perspective in formulating social policy, resulting in increasing support for family services, policy, and related studies accordingly.

In 2000 the Hong Kong government commissioned a research team under the family services review to examine the strength and problems within existing family services. Out of that a new service mode – the Integrated Family Service Centre (IFSC) – was proposed and then gradually implemented. This subvention "child-centered, family-focused and community-based" service model has been assessed as effective in adhering to the guiding principles of service (i.e., accessibility, early identification, integration, and partnership) and in serving specific vulnerable groups (Tsang & Team, 2010). A family-oriented perspective and a family-centered approach have now been widely promoted for use by Hong Kong's social services (Lau, 2020).

Since 2007, with the establishment of the Family Council, a family-centered perspective has been officially embraced for family policy design. In 2013, an assessment of the policy impact on family was mandated for all policy papers and Legislative Council briefs, with the impact on family core values and on family structure and functions being the gauging parameters. To enhance the implementation of Family Impact Assessments (FIA), in 2016 the government initiated a study to develop a comprehensive checklist tool and a procedure manual for conducting FIAs (Department of Social Work and Social Administration, The University of Hong Kong, 2018). Starting in 2018, all policies were required to undergo a thorough assessment to evaluate their potential influences on family responsibility, stability, relationships, and engagement.

The Hong Kong government has also made both direct and indirect investments in family research. In 2018, the Family Council initiated a review of over 4000 Hong Kong family studies done between 2000 and 2017 to create a comprehensive account of these studies' methodologies, findings, theoretical perspectives, funding sources, dissemination, characteristics, and deficiencies. As a result, an accessible electronic database was developed (Wong et al., 2019). The analysis revealed that more than one-third of the studies reviewed were directly funded by various units of Hong Kong's government, indicating the government's commitment.

However, the research that specifically focuses on directly measuring and monitoring family wellbeing among the Hong Kong population has only emerged in recent years. Notably, the initiative for such research has primarily been led by a non-governmental service agency, the Hong Kong Family Welfare Society. In 2017 and 2018, the agency supported two Hong Kong family wellbeing surveys using adapted scales. In 2019, the agency commissioned a research team to develop a measurement tool that would be socially relevant, culturally appropriate, and psychometrically robust for assessing family wellbeing in Hong Kong.

A tailor-made measurement – the Hong Kong Family Wellbeing Index (HKFWI) – was developed based on an integrated approach to conceptualizing family wellbeing, and done through a 5-step mixed-methods research procedure (Wong et al., 2020). The HKFWI contains six domains (family solidarity, family resources, family health, social involvement, social resources, and work–life balance), 23 indicators, and 26 questions. It incorporates both subjective and objective dimensions of family life, and respondents rate their family wellbeing on a Likert scale ranging from 0 to 10. The overall family wellbeing status was categorized into four levels: good (≥7.5), average (6 to <7.5), below average (5 to <6), and poor (<5), according to the percentiles of the HKFWI scores obtained from the sample used in this study and with reference to other relevant measurements (Wong et al., 2020).

The results of a region-wide survey provided comprehensive knowledge about the status quo of the family wellbeing of people with different demographic and family structural characteristics and revealed the influential factors affecting family wellbeing (Wong et al., 2020). For example, the 2019 survey found the following: (1) significant gender and age differences in the perception of family wellbeing among Hong Kong individuals; (2) the positive association of education levels, family income, and hiring a domestic helper with family wellbeing; (3) that the impacts of economic activity status, family size, and the burden of caring for young children on family wellbeing were insignificant (Xia et al., 2023). The results serve as valuable references for the various stakeholders when formulating policies and services.

The development of the HKFWI made depicting, tracking, and monitoring the family wellbeing of Hong Kong people possible. Since 2019, the region-wide survey, collected every two years, aims at tracking family wellbeing in Hong Kong over time and examining the impacts of societal factors on it. The second survey completed in January 2022 revealed two important findings: (1) the overall family wellbeing score has dropped to a worrying level, indicating the negative impact of the pandemic on families, particularly those with low incomes; (2) the varying degrees of impact in the six domains highlighted the complex nature of family wellbeing and the family resilience (Hong Kong Family Welfare Society & Hong Kong Public Opinion Research Institute, 2022). These findings provide valuable insight for developing strategies to promote family recovery and resilience in the face of challenging circumstances. A third survey was carried out in early 2024 for the purpose of examining the potential long-lasting impacts of the pandemic on families and also evaluating the effectiveness of various policies implemented for economic recovery and family enhancement. The results revealed the continuation of the negative impact of the pandemic on family wellbeing and that most aspects of family wellbeing did not recover immediately after the "ending of the pandemic period." Though the resource aspect of family wellbeing recovered immediately, worsened family health and social connection continued deterioration, suggesting the usefulness of the economic recovery measurements and but even more complicated challenges for health and social connection related efforts.

In addition to its implications for macro-level policy-making, the HKFWI measurement has also been adopted and promoted as a useful assessment tool. It aids in identifying the needs of service users, developing service plans, and evaluating service efficacy. For instance, the Hong Kong Family Welfare Society has integrated the completion of the HKFWI questionnaire as a mandatory step in the case-intake and case-closing procedures for their service users. In addition, a self-assessment of family wellbeing has been made available online, enabling individuals to gain a general understanding of their family's wellbeing and to identify areas that may require attention or improvement.

Last, the standard measurement and comprehensive theoretical framework of the HKFWI facilitates the cross-national and regional comparison of family wellbeing. Being the first study of its kind in China and the second in Asia, it also serves as an exemplar for other countries with similar intentions. In line with this, the author of this chapter is adapting the HKFWI approach to conducting a family wellbeing survey in mainland China. which offers different social, economic, and political contexts.

Discussion and conclusion

This review highlights the holistic, comprehensive, and dynamic nature of family wellbeing, which goes beyond the summation of the individuals' wellbeing within the family (McGregor, 2020; La Placa et al., 2013). Family wellbeing is usually measured via self-assessment that evaluates both the objective and subjective dimensions of family life and that reflects the characteristics of social context. However, there still exists a gap in evaluating family wellbeing holistically because the majority of the current studies adopted an intrapersonal instead of a household approach to data collection (Xia et al., 2023).

We should be cautious in generalizing the potentially biased conceptualization and the measurement of family wellbeing, as the majority of existing studies of family wellbeing were conducted in Western and economically developed societies (Krys et al., 2021). There is a need for further research to develop a comprehensive understanding of family wellbeing, especially in non-Western and developing societies. Though family structure and family life have become similar because of industrialization and globalization, the meaning and components of family wellbeing, as well as the hierarchy and weighting of the dimensions, may still differ across different societies and contexts (Sanchez-Sanchez, 2017). Therefore, culturally specific frameworks and measurement tools should be developed to capture the unique aspects of family wellbeing within different cultural contexts. Additionally, the influence of intelligent technology on family wellbeing should also be considered, as it plays an increasingly important role in human life.

In recent years family wellbeing has gained prominent relevance and has become of practical importance to family policy and social services due to its direct connection to human development. Design of the evidence-informed family policies and services is impossible without a robust measure of family wellbeing that is tracked, monitored, and compared internationally and over time. To make this possible, the government should allocate resources to support relevant research and commit to implementing policies and service initiatives aimed at improving family wellbeing.

Actionable points

This chapter outlines the differences and connectedness of individual wellbeing and family wellbeing and points to the special importance of family wellbeing for policy-making and social service planning in the pursuit of human development and social progress. It calls for the development of a comprehensive measurement for family wellbeing that is theoretically sound, socially adapted, and culturally specific. We offer the following actionable points for scholars and policy-makers:

- Conceptualize family wellbeing according to the local sociocultural context.
- Develop an index that comprehensively measures family wellbeing.
- Launch cross-sectional and longitudinal studies that track, monitor, and analyze family wellbeing and its determinants.
- Embed the family wellbeing measurement in assessments of the effects of policies and social services that affect families.
- Conduct international comparative studies to identify the universal and context-specific dimensions and mechanisms of family wellbeing.

References

Department of Social Work and Social Administration, The University of Hong Kong (2018). A study of family impact assessment in Hong Kong: A checklist approach – final report. *Family Council*. www.familycouncil.gov.hk/sc/files/research/Study%20of%20Family%20Impact%20Assessment.pdf

Dolan, P., Peasgood, T., & White, M. (2008). Do we really know what makes us happy? A review of the economic literature on the factors associated with subjective well-being. *Journal of Economic Psychology*, *29*(1), 94–122.
Dumas, T. L., & Perry-Smith, J. E. (2018). The paradox of family structure and plans after work: Why single childless employees may be the least absorbed at work. *Academy of Management Journal*, *61*(4), 1231–1252.
Hong Kong Family Welfare Society, & Hong Kong Public Opinion Research Institute (2022). *Hong Kong family wellbeing index 2022*. Hong Kong Family Welfare Society.
Jones, G. W. (2012). Changing family sizes, structures and functions in Asia. *Asia-Pacific Population Journal*, *27*(1), 83–102.
Karakas, F., Dean Lee, M., & MacDermid, S. M. (2004). A qualitative investigation into the meaning of family well-being from the perspective of part-time professionals. *Equal Opportunities International*, *23*(1/2), 57–77.
Krys, K., Capaldi, C. A., Zelenski, J. M., Park, J., Nader, M., Kocimska-Zych, A., Kwiatkowska, A., Michalski, P., & Uchida, Y. (2021). Family well-being is valued more than personal well-being: A four-country study. *Current Psychology*, *40*(7), 3332–3343.
La Placa, V., McNaught, A., & Knight, A. (2013). Discourse on wellbeing in research and practice. *International Journal of Wellbeing*, *3*(1), 116–125.
Lau, Y. K. (2020). A critical review of school social work in Hong Kong. In J. Gao, R. Baikady, L. Govindappa, & S. L. Cheng (Eds.), *Social welfare in India and China: A comparative perspective* (pp. 101–117). Palgrave Macmillan.
Layard, R. (2005). *Happiness: Lessons from a new science*. Penguin Press.
Martinez, J., Mehesy, C., & Seeley, K. (2003). *What counts: Measuring indicators of family well-being – executive summary report*. Office of Justice Programs, U.S. Department of Justice.
Maulana, H., Obst, T., & Khawaja, N. (2018). Indonesian perspective of wellbeing: A qualitative study. *Qualitative Report*, *23*(12), 3136–3152.
McCalman, J., Bainbridge, R., Brown, C., Tsey, K., & Clarke, A. (2018). The aboriginal Australian family wellbeing program: A historical analysis of the conditions that enabled its spread. *Frontiers in Public Health*, *6*, Article 26. https://doi.org/10.3389/fpubh.2018.00026
McGregor, S. L. T. (2020). *Conceptualizing family well-being*. McGregor Consulting Group.
McKeown, K., Pratschke, J., & Haase, T. (2003). *Family well-being: What makes a difference? Study based on a representative sample of parents and children in Ireland*. The Céifin Centre.
McKeown, K., & Sweeney, J. (2001). *Family well-being and family policy: A review of research on benefits and costs*. Kaieran McKeown Limited. http://hdl.handle.net/10147/46302
Menges, J. I., Tussing, D. V., Wihler, A., & Grant, A. M. (2017). When job performance is all relative: How family motivation energizes effort and compensates for intrinsic motivation. *Academy of Management Journal*, *60*(2), 695–671.
Newland, L. A. (2015). Family wellbeing, parenting, and child wellbeing: Pathways to healthy adjustment. *Clinical Psychologists*, *19*(1), 3–14.
Noor, N. M., Gandhi, A. D., Ishak, I., & Wok, S. (2014). Development of indicators for family well-being in Malaysia. *Social Indicators Research*, *115*(1), 279–318.
Sanchez-Sanchez, C. (2017). Moving towards a general definition of public happiness: A grounded theory approach to the recent academic research on well-being. *International Journal of Social, Behavioral, Educational, Economic, Business and Industrial Engineering*, *11*(7), 1624–1639.
Social Policy Evaluation and Research Unit (2018). Families and Whānau status report 2018. *Social Policy Evaluation and Research Unit*.
Sujarwoto, S. (2017). Small family norms and family well-being in Indonesia, 2006–2014. *Journal of Biosocial Science*, *49*(1), 96–115.
Summers, J. A., Poston, D. J., Turnbull, A. P., Marquis, J., Hoffman, L., Mannan, H., & Wang, M. (2005). Conceptualizing and measuring family quality of life. *Journal of Intellectual Disability Research*, *49*(10), 777–783.

Swords, L., Merriman, B., & O'Donnell, M. (2013). *Family wellbeing on a limited income: A study of families living at risk of poverty in Ireland*. Children's Research Centre, Trinity College Dublin.
Tsang, S. K. M., & Team, C. (2010). *Building effective family services: Review on the implementation of the integrated family service centre service mode*. Commissioned by the Social Welfare Department, Hong Kong SAR Government.
Webster, A., Bode, G., & Posselt, H. (2008). *Measuring wellbeing: The Australian Bureau of Statistics framework for social statistics*. United Nations Statistics Division, United Nations.
Wollny, I., Apps, J., & Henricson, C. (2010). *Can government measure family wellbeing? A literature review*. Family and Parenting Institute.
Wong, M. C., Ma, J. L., Xia, L. L., & Hui, J. K. (2019). *A study on family research in Hong Kong: A critical review and annotated bibliography*. Family Council of HKSAR Government.
Wong, M. M., Ma, J. L., Wan, P. S., Xia, L. L., & Fok, M. H. (2020). *Research report on a study on family wellbeing index in Hong Kong*. Hong Kong Family Welfare Society.
Wong, M. M., Ma, J. L., Wan, P. S., Xia, L. L., & Fok, M. H. (2022). The development and validation of a family wellbeing index for Hong Kong Chinese families. *Journal of Child and Family Studies*, *31*(6), 1683–1697.
Xia, L. L., & Ma, J. L. (2019). Childcare policies and services in Hong Kong after the handover: Beyond a feminist critique. *Asian Social Work and Policy Review*, *13*(3), 295–306.
Xia, L. L., Wong, M. C., Ma, J. L., & Wan, P. S. (2023). The family-structural and socioeconomic characteristics of the family wellbeing of Hong Kong people. *International Journal of Social Welfare*. https://doi.org/10.1111/ijsw.12627
Yaxley, V., Gill, V., & McManus, S. (2012). *Family wellbeing: Measuring what matters, identifying and validating domains*. NatCen Social Research.
Zimmerman, S. L. (2013). Conceptualizing family wellbeing. In A. M. Mínguez (Ed.), *Family wellbeing: European perspectives* (pp. 9–25). Springer.

6

ALTRUISM, EMPATHY, AND WELLBEING

Improving lives through policy that aligns with our better angels

Stephanie Preston and Tanner Nichols

Introduction

Contrary to early theorizing about homo economicus (Mill, 1824), humans and many other species feel empathy for others and help, even when it costs them in the short term; this is known as altruism (Hamilton, 1964; Preston, 2013; Trivers, 1971). People give their time (Binder & Freytag, 2013; Hui et al., 2020; Thoits & Hewitt, 2001), money (Aknin et al., 2013; Gray et al., 2014; Kustov, 2021), and even vital organs (Brethel-Haurwitz & Marsh, 2014) to help others.

Empathy and altruism benefit humans at multiple levels of analysis. Evolutionarily, these "prosocial" phenomena improve the success of genes that givers share with recipients (Hamilton, 1964) while increasing reciprocation to givers or their family (Trivers, 1971). Such aid also increases cooperation and inhibits defection, improving the success of social groups (Nowak, 2006). Psychologically, prosocial phenomena bring people closer and elicit positive feelings that further promote future altruism (Algoe et al., 2020; Andreoni, 1990; Collins et al., 2022). Thus, the short-term costs of prosociality are offset by benefits to givers or their genes in the long run.

Humans are characterized by their social nature and the aid they extend to offspring (Preston, 2013, 2022). These features of social life fostered a capacity to feel into others' emotions, through implicit, neurophysiological, perception-action processes (Preston & de Waal, 2002). Empathy motivates aid by helping us understand others' experiences and generating the motivation to help through empathic concern (Batson, 2010) and the drive to relieve our own empathic suffering (Cialdini et al., 1997). Based on our neurobiological inheritance, people feel an "altruistic urge" to help in the face of an infant-like victim who is vulnerable, is in distress, and needs urgent aid that we can provide; in contrast people fail to help when they feel distant from a victim, when the suffering is unclear or we do not know what

DOI: 10.4324/9781003382447-7

to do (Preston, 2013, 2022). People also help because they can predict that it will feel good, that they will impress others or will elicit reciprocation (Preston, 2022). Interventions to increase empathy or altruism, with the aim of improving our general health and wellbeing, should rely upon these natural predispositions.

Prosocial behaviour thus benefits our genes, feelings, and health, which can be captured through measures of "wellbeing," or an overall sense of contentment, physical capability, and quality of life; this assessment includes subjective (e.g., perceived quality of life, psychological wellbeing, etc.) and objective (e.g., positive environment, behavioural competence) components (Lawton, 1983). Wellbeing can also be divided into emotional (positive outlook, self-respect, life satisfaction) and physical (safety and physical competence) aspects (Hui et al., 2020). Importantly, empathy, altruism, and wellbeing are dynamic processes that mutually enhance one another while bolstering social support, health, and longevity.

We review research on how empathy, altruism, and wellbeing facilitate one another and, in turn, benefit health and society. Nations thrive when people report higher wellbeing; thus, if we know how to promote wellbeing and the urge to care for one another, we can achieve the benefits to human health and happiness. We end with suggestions for how to integrate this research into policy suggestions to motivate people to help in ways that enhance general health and wellbeing, to the benefit of society.

Literature on empathy, altruism, and wellbeing

Empathy and altruism are linked to positive feelings and wellbeing in a variety of ways. At the most basic level, empathy promotes altruism. For example, participants who imagined a friend, family member, and stranger in unpleasant or dangerous scenarios felt more connection and empathy towards them and offered more help (Cialdini et al., 1997).

Altruism also fosters positive feelings in helpers that motivate future acts, such as the "warm glow of giving" (Andreoni, 1990). In one study, bank employees were happier and more satisfied with their jobs when their bonuses were donated in their name compared to a direct bonus (Anik et al., 2013). Participants also reported being happier after spending a coffee gift card on a friend than on themselves, especially after observing the friend's enjoyment (Aknin et al., 2013). Thus, altruism can increase positive emotions that feedback to encourage future acts.

Altruism also increases positive feelings through elicited gratitude, defined as a positive emotion "triggered by the perception that one is the beneficiary of another's intentionally-provided benefit" (Algoe & Haidt, 2009, p. 106). Gratitude is instrumental in forming and maintaining social bonds (Algoe et al., 2020). For example, participants who witnessed even a written "thank you" for correcting typos in a movie review were then more helpful towards the author on the task and wanted to be closer to the recipient of gratitude (Algoe et al., 2020).

The increased social bonds that come with altruism and gratitude also increase wellbeing. A sample from the United States, China, Russia, India, Mexico, and

South Africa found that individual-level social interaction predicted overall wellbeing (Collins et al., 2022). Social connections across facets of life (e.g., relationships at work, the neighbourhood, family) increased wellbeing even more. Thus, empathy can promote altruism, which produces good feelings and gratitude that foster social bonds – all of which motivate good deeds.

The specific effects of altruistic behaviour on wellbeing vary by age, sex, and type of altruism. A recent meta-analysis of 126 studies and 201 independent samples noted that behaviours such as volunteering and charitable giving had a greater effect on non-physical than physical wellbeing in young adults, but the reverse was true for older adults. This analysis also found that eudaimonic wellbeing (feelings of accomplishment and self-worth) was more correlated with altruism in females and younger adults. Finally, altruism like planned volunteering was less correlated with wellbeing than informal altruism, such as spontaneous volunteering or unplanned donations (Hui et al., 2020). While the specific relationship varied by sample, consistent correlations across studies were found between altruism and overall wellbeing.

Wellbeing also feeds back to promote altruism. For example, Gallup Daily Tracking found that the number of kidney donations per US state from 1999 to 2010 positively correlated with the state's mean self-reported wellbeing (Brethel-Haurwitz & Marsh, 2014). Moreover, participants with higher wellbeing on an initial survey performed more prosocial behaviour by the second survey three years later (Thoits & Hewitt, 2001). Prosocial behaviour and wellbeing are thus mutually reinforcing.

Taken together, empathy can promote altruism, which can elicit gratitude – all of which enhance wellbeing and social connection and reinforce future altruism. However, there are gaps in the literature, such as whether the relationship between altruism and wellbeing is linear. One study of older Australian adults found that a moderate amount of volunteer work per year was linked to increased wellbeing, but people who volunteered over 800 hours reported similar wellbeing to non-volunteers (Windsor et al., 2008). Research could also investigate how socioeconomic status (SES) moderates the link between altruistic action and wellbeing, because SES impacts wellbeing (Tan et al., 2020) and the amount of time and resources one can commit.

Interventions to promote altruistic behaviour

At the individual level, experimenters increase altruism by giving participants gifts before the choice, akin to the "pay it forward" effect (Fredrickson, 2001). For example, participants who received aid with a computer malfunction helped someone more on a subsequent lengthy survey (Bartlett & DeSteno, 2006). Participants were also more generous as dictators if they had received a generous amount from another dictator (Gray et al., 2014). A meta-analysis of 91 studies across 65 papers found that participants who recently benefitted from prosocial behaviour (e.g., receiving money in an economic game or a positive message) were more prosocial later (e.g., donating money or writing a positive message) and reported wanting to help in the future (Ma et al., 2017). Thus, observing and experiencing altruism fosters the motivation to help, as in indirect or "strong reciprocity" theories (Fehr & Fischbacher, 2003).

Even people who are forced to be altruistic report increased wellbeing. Participants instructed to spend money on themselves, another person, or a charity reported greater increased subjective wellbeing after spending on others (Dunn et al., 2008). One half of a high school class that was randomly assigned to volunteer for the semester had a lower body mass index and fewer cardiovascular risk factors than the non-volunteers (Schreier et al., 2013). Results of such interventions suggest a causal link between altruism and wellbeing, even when the altruism is dictated by an intervention or policy.

Nationally, hardship can also promote in-group giving. A meta-analysis of national prosocial behaviour found that communities who had experienced war in the prior 13 years were more likely to cooperate with one another in economic games and to volunteer in the community (Bauer et al., 2016). People who left Egypt, Jordan, Morocco, Pakistan, or Tunisia for work sent more money home when their nation's agricultural revenue fell (Bouhga-Hagbe, 2006). Our evolution as a caregiving and social species ensures that people help their in-group during times of suffering when they can.

Our evolved social ties lead to aversion to inequality or unfairness and even sacrifices to correct it (Fehr & Fischbacher, 2003). For example, European countries with more income inequality support wealth redistribution more (Dimick et al., 2017). Americans also support wealth redistribution more if they live in a wealthier than in a poorer state (Dimick et al., 2017). Swiss voters who support wealth redistribution reported being motivated by altruism and an aversion to wealth inequality (Fehr et al., 2021). People do not require things to be totally fair because some inequity is natural (Kiatpongsan & Norton, 2014) and unfairness may drive the aversion more than inequality per se (Starmans et al., 2017). In sum, people with more resources support wealth redistribution to re-balance a very unfair system.

Policy that promotes altruism also increases wellbeing. Across 42 European nations, income redistribution policies reduced disparities in mental and physical health and social spending in each nation increased their overall health (Jutz, 2015). Western Europeans who had to give more of their income for redistribution reported an increase in life satisfaction (Cheung, 2018). Finally, increased taxation for redistribution in each of 29 European countries increased that nation's individual subjective wellbeing (Hajdu & Hajdu, 2014).

Even if data support a link between altruistic policies that help fellow citizens in need and wellbeing, voters do not always support such policies. Failed support often occurs when people fail to comprehend others' plight and the degree of inequity. For example, Western, democratic countries with higher national SES inequality report lower subjective wellbeing (Kelley & Evans, 2017), but voters still often reject social welfare policies to address inequality (Davidai & Gilovich,

2015). People grossly underestimate the degree of inequality and structural barriers to socioeconomic mobility (Hauser & Norton, 2017). Citizens in the United States (Cansunar, 2016) and United Kingdom (UK) (Hauser & Norton, 2017) vastly underestimated their nation's income inequality. In 2012, mean CEO compensation for a US S&P 500 company was 354 times that of an unskilled labourer, but survey respondents estimated the gap to be around 30 times – less than a tenth of the real number (Kiatpongsan & Norton, 2014). Americans also overestimate their socioeconomic mobility (Davidai & Gilovich, 2015). In line with the theory of altruism, however, people who accurately perceive inequality do support wealth redistribution more (Cansunar, 2016) and make more charitable donations to alleviate poverty (Derin & Uler, 2009). People are motivated to help when they perceive the hardships of poverty, gross inequality, and unfair systems, but accurate perceptions are lacking.

Discussion and conclusion

People evolved to want to help when those they feel connected to are suffering physically or from injustice, assuming they have the means to help. Such responses benefit caregiving and cooperation by rendering suffering and injustice to be highly aversive and altruism to be pleasurable – feeding back to increase prosociality over time.

Because of this evolution, people also fail to help when conditions prevent the natural cycle, such as when others' suffering or unfair treatment is opaque, distant, or associated with out-group members. Knowing this, politicians obscure or justify unfair systems, and cast the victims as out-groups who are irrelevant or even opposing us. For example, Americans are united as a nation, but divided by state, race, religion, or partisanship (Fischer & Mattson, 2009).

The main limitation of this research is that most of it is experimental. Many intervention studies suggest a causal pathway, but usually in a limited domain rather than for a nation-wide policy change. For instance, different messages (varying by country or state) to support wealth redistribution are likely to be effective in showing that redistribution will improve wellbeing.

Based on our review we propose the following actionable points to improve wellbeing through policy aimed at enhancing altruism:

- Voters must press politicians and policy-makers into action on thorny issues by tying their votes to policies that improve altruism (Mermelstein & Preston, 2023).
- Policy-makers must make clear the scale of and associated suffering from unfairness and inequality (e.g., see Morath, 2022), and cast those in need as part of our interconnected group.
- Appeals for altruistic action should highlight the strong positive feelings that people derive from helping others and from receiving gratitude and reciprocation.
- Policy framing should focus on what we gain and not on what we lose (e.g., the rewards of a strong interconnected group, wellbeing, gratitude versus financial costs; see Caruso et al., 2013; Kustov, 2021).

- Policies should be designed in a way to make it obvious to voters that a plan will work. People do not behave altruistically when they believe that their efforts will fail (Preston, 2022).

References

Aknin, L. B., Dunn, E. W., Sandstrom, G. M., & Norton, M. I. (2013). Does social connection turn good deeds into good feelings? On the value of putting the "social" in prosocial spending. *International Journal of Happiness and Development*, *1*(2), 155. https://doi.org/10.1504/IJHD.2013.055643

Algoe, S. B., Dwyer, P. C., Younge, A., & Oveis, C. (2020). A new perspective on the social functions of emotions: Gratitude and the witnessing effect. *Journal of Personality and Social Psychology*, *119*(1), 40–74. https://doi.org/10.1037/pspi0000202

Algoe, S. B., & Haidt, J. (2009). Witnessing excellence in action: The "other-praising" emotions of elevation, gratitude, and admiration. *The Journal of Positive Psychology*, *4*(2), 105–127. https://doi.org/10.1080/17439760802650519

Andreoni, J. (1990). Impure altruism and donations to public goods: A theory of warm-glow giving. *The Economic Journal*, *100*(401), 464. https://doi.org/10.2307/2234133

Anik, L., Aknin, L. B., Norton, M. I., Dunn, E. W., & Quoidbach, J. (2013). Prosocial bonuses increase employee satisfaction and team performance. *PLoS One*, *8*(9), e75509. https://doi.org/10.1371/journal.pone.0075509

Bartlett, M. Y., & DeSteno, D. (2006). Gratitude and prosocial behavior: Helping when it costs you. *Psychological Science*, *17*(4), 319–325. https://doi.org/10.1111/j.1467-9280.2006.01705.x

Batson, C. D. (2010). *Altruism in humans*. Oxford University Press.

Bauer, M., Blattman, C., Chytilová, J., Henrich, J., Miguel, E., & Mitts, T. (2016). Can war foster cooperation? *Journal of Economic Perspectives*, *30*(3), 249–274. https://doi.org/10.1257/jep.30.3.249

Binder, M., & Freytag, A. (2013). Volunteering, subjective well-being and public policy. *Journal of Economic Psychology*, *34*, 97–119. https://doi.org/10.1016/j.joep.2012.11.008

Bouhga-Hagbe, J. (2006). Altruism and workers' remittances: Evidence from selected countries in the Middle East and Central Asia. *IMF Working Papers*, *6*(130), 1. https://doi.org/10.5089/9781451863901.001

Brethel-Haurwitz, K. M., & Marsh, A. A. (2014). Geographical differences in subjective well-being predict extraordinary altruism. *Psychological Science*, *25*(3), 762–771. https://doi.org/10.1177/0956797613516148

Cansunar, A. (2016). Calculating with the unknown: The effects of (mis) perceptions of inequality between income groups on tax preferences. *Duke University Archives*. https://sites.duke.edu/preferencesoverredistribution/files/2016/04/Cansunar-inequality-misperceptions.pdf

Caruso, E. M., Vohs, K. D., Baxter, B., & Waytz, A. (2013). Mere exposure to money increases endorsement of free-market systems and social inequality. *Journal of Experimental Psychology: General*, *142*(2), 301–306. https://doi.org/10.1037/a0029288

Cheung, F. (2018). Income redistribution predicts greater life satisfaction across individual, national, and cultural characteristics. *Journal of Personality and Social Psychology*, *115*(5), 867–882. https://doi.org/10.1037/pspp0000164.supp

Cialdini, R. B., Brown, S. L., Lewis, B. P., Luce, C., & Neuberg, S. L. (1997). Reinterpreting the empathy–altruism relationship: When one into one equals oneness. *Journal of Personality and Social Psychology*, *73*(3), 481–494. https://doi.org/10.1037/0022-3514.73.3.481

Collins, H. K., Hagerty, S. F., Quoidbach, J., Norton, M. I., & Brooks, A. W. (2022). Relational diversity in social portfolios predicts well-being. *Proceedings of the National Academy of Sciences*, *119*(43), e2120668119. https://doi.org/10.1073/pnas.2120668119

Davidai, S., & Gilovich, T. (2015). Building a more mobile America – one income quintile at a time. *Perspectives on Psychological Science*, *10*(1), 60–71. https://doi.org/10.1177/1745691614562005

Derin, P., & Uler, N. (2009). The relationship between charitable giving and inequality aversion. *academia.edu*.

Dimick, M., Rueda, D., & Stegmueller, D. (2017). *Models of other-regarding preferences and redistribution* (SSRN Scholarly Paper 3072652). https://papers.ssrn.com/abstract=3072652

Dunn, E. W., Aknin, L. B., & Norton, M. I. (2008). Spending money on others promotes happiness. *Science*, *319*(5870), 1687–1688. https://doi.org/10.1126/science.1150952

Fehr, E., Epper, T., & Senn, J. (2021). Other-regarding preferences and redistributive politics. *Working Paper*, University of Zurich, Department of Economics. https://doi.org/10.5167/UZH-183052

Fehr, E., & Fischbacher, U. (2003). The nature of human altruism. *Nature*, *425*(6960), 785–791. https://doi.org/10.1038/nature02043

Fischer, C. S., & Mattson, G. (2009). Is America fragmenting? *Annual Review of Sociology*, *35*(1), 435–455. https://doi.org/10.1146/annurev-soc-070308-115909

Fredrickson, B. L. (2001). The role of positive emotions in positive psychology: The broaden-and-build theory of positive emotions. *American Psychologist*, *56*(3), 218–226. https://doi.org/10.1037/0003-066X.56.3.218

Gray, K., Ward, A. F., & Norton, M. I. (2014). Paying it forward: Generalized reciprocity and the limits of generosity. *Journal of Experimental Psychology: General*, *143*(1), 247–254. https://doi.org/10.1037/a0031047

Hajdu, T., & Hajdu, G. (2014). Reduction of income inequality and subjective well-being in Europe. *Economics*, *8*(1), 1–29A.

Hamilton, W. D. (1964). The genetical evolution of social behaviour. I. *Journal of Theoretical Biology*, *7*(1), 1–16. https://doi.org/10.1016/0022-5193(64)90038-4

Hauser, O. P., & Norton, M. I. (2017). (Mis)perceptions of inequality. *Current Opinion in Psychology*, *18*, 21–25. https://doi.org/10.1016/j.copsyc.2017.07.024

Hui, B. P. H., Ng, J. C. K., Berzaghi, E., Cunningham-Amos, L. A., & Kogan, A. (2020). Rewards of kindness? A meta-analysis of the link between prosociality and well-being. *Psychological Bulletin*, *146*(12), 1084–1116. https://doi.org/10.1037/bul0000298

Jutz, R. (2015). The role of income inequality and social policies on income-related health inequalities in Europe. *International Journal for Equity in Health*, *14*(1), 117. https://doi.org/10.1186/s12939-015-0247-y

Kelley, J., & Evans, M. D. R. (2017). Societal inequality and individual subjective well-being: Results from 68 societies and over 200,000 individuals, 1981–2008. *Social Science Research*, *62*, 1–23. https://doi.org/10.1016/j.ssresearch.2016.04.020

Kiatpongsan, S., & Norton, M. I. (2014). How much (more) should CEOs make? A universal desire for more equal pay. *Perspectives on Psychological Science*, *9*(6), 587–593. https://doi.org/10.1177/1745691614549773

Kustov, A. (2021). Borders of compassion: Immigration preferences and parochial altruism. *Comparative Political Studies*, *54*(3–4), 445–481. https://doi.org/10.1177/0010414020938087

Lawton, M. P. (1983). The varieties of wellbeing. *Experimental Aging Research*, *9*(2), 65–72. https://doi.org/10.1080/03610738308258427

Ma, L. K., Tunney, R. J., & Ferguson, E. (2017). Does gratitude enhance prosociality?: A meta-analytic review. *Psychological Bulletin*, *143*(6), 601–635. https://doi.org/10.1037/bul0000103

Mermelstein, I. J., & Preston, S. D. (2023). Using effective psychological techniques to subvert a US socio-political context. *Brain and Behavior Science*, In press.

Mill, J. S. (1824). The collected works of John Stuart Mill, volume IV – essays on economics and society part I | online library of liberty. *Collected Works of John Stuart Mill, in 33 Vols*. https://oll.libertyfund.org/title/mill-the-collected-works-of-john-stuart-mill-volume-iv-essays-on-economics-and-society-part-i

Morath, S. J. (2022, February 24). Plastic pollution is a global problem – here's how to design an effective treaty to curb it. *The Conversation*. http://theconversation.com/plastic-pollution-is-a-global-problem-heres-how-to-design-an-effective-treaty-to-curb-it-176226

Nowak, M. A. (2006). Five rules for the evolution of cooperation. *Science*, *314*(5805), 1560–1563. https://doi.org/10.1126/science.1133755

Preston, S. D. (2013). The origins of altruism in offspring care. *Psychological Bulletin*, *139*(6), 1305–1341. https://doi.org/10.1037/a0031755

Preston, S. D. (2022). The altruistic urge: Why we're driven to help others. In *The altruistic urge*. Columbia University Press. www.degruyter.com/document/doi/10.7312/pres20440/html?lang=de

Preston, S. D., & De Waal, F. B. M. (2002). Empathy: Its ultimate and proximate bases. *Behavioral and Brain Sciences*, *25*(1), 1–20. https://doi.org/10.1017/S0140525X02000018

Schreier, H. M. C., Schonert-Reichl, K. A., & Chen, E. (2013). Effect of volunteering on risk factors for cardiovascular disease in adolescents: A randomized controlled trial. *JAMA Pediatrics*, *167*(4), 327–332. https://doi.org/10.1001/jamapediatrics.2013.1100

Starmans, C., Sheskin, M., & Bloom, P. (2017). Why people prefer unequal societies. *Nature Human Behaviour*, *1*(4), 0082. https://doi.org/10.1038/s41562-017-0082

Tan, J. J. X., Kraus, M. W., Carpenter, N. C., & Adler, N. E. (2020). The association between objective and subjective socioeconomic status and subjective well-being: A meta-analytic review. *Psychological Bulletin*, *146*(11), 970–1020. https://doi.org/10.1037/bul0000258

Thoits, P. A., & Hewitt, L. N. (2001). Volunteer work and well-being. *Journal of Health and Social Behavior*, *42*(2), 115–131. https://doi.org/10.2307/3090173

Trivers, R. L. (1971). The evolution of reciprocal altruism. *The Quarterly Review of Biology*, *46*(1), 35–57. https://doi.org/10.1086/406755

Windsor, T. D., Anstey, K. J., & Rodgers, B. (2008). Volunteering and psychological well-being among young-old adults: How much is too much? *The Gerontologist*, *48*(1), 59–70. https://doi.org/10.1093/geront/48.1.59

7

AGEING AND WELLBEING

The potential of senior policy to support seniors' subjective wellbeing

Maciej Górny and Krzysztof Hajder

Introduction

According to the United Nations, people aged 60 and over represent 13% of the world's population with this group growing at a rate of about 3% per year (United Nations General Assembly, 2021; Yuan et al., 2021, p. 727). In Europe, in 2060, seniors are expected to constitute as much as 30% of its inhabitants (Grossi et al., 2019). The current trends in ageing in developed societies are often referred to as a "silver tsunami", and are explained by a combination of the extension of human life and the low fertility rate in the countries with high GDP per capita (United Nations, 2022). This phenomenon is expected to have wide-ranging consequences for future social and economic life (Górny & Lorek, 2021, p. 41).

Research in the subjective wellbeing (SWB) literature generally points to later years in life as being more satisfied than in middle age but equivalent to young age, reflecting a so-called U-shape in the wellbeing–age relationship on average (Blanchflower, 2021; Becker & Trautmann, 2022). At the same time, work examining SWB as experiences of positive and negative affect, as well as life satisfaction, indicates that there is significant diversity in people's wellbeing trajectories in older years – with a significant minority of people suffering from a decline in SWB across all three measures (Moreno-Agostino et al., 2020). This finding, along with the trends in ageing occurring throughout the developed world, raises the important question of how to ensure people age well. This is important not only for the seniors themselves but also because high levels of SWB act as a protective factor against many diseases and therefore have knock-on benefits for health systems and societies more broadly (Helliwell, 2011; Steptoe et al., 2014; Swift et al., 2014).

In the current work, we investigate some of the key risk and protective factors identified in work on seniors' subjective wellbeing and examine the potential for senior policy to safeguard the wellbeing of people as they age.

DOI: 10.4324/9781003382447-8

The determinants of wellbeing among the elderly

Douma and colleagues (2017) examine older peoples' conceptions of wellbeing and distinguish 15 higher-order domains: social life, activities (e.g., reading), physical and mental health, space and place (e.g., living environment), independence, mobility, financial situation, societal criticism (e.g., environmental pollution), political situation, personal characteristics (e.g., being positive), way of life, other (e.g., weather), religion, healthcare and support, and personal development. Many of these perceived determinants map directly onto those identified by the SWB literature (Lukaschek et al., 2017). In what follows we discuss three determinants that have been particularly well evidenced.

Social relationships have been identified as being positively predictive of subjective wellbeing in older age, as have social capital and support (Shankar et al., 2015; Nyqvist et al., 2013). In line with this, other research indicates that loneliness and social isolation are among the most important risk factors for wellbeing in older age. Infrequent social interaction has also been shown to increase the risk of dementia by 60% and the likelihood of dying by 30% (Ibarra et al., 2020). Seniors, often due to lack of work and erosion of family ties, need new forms of social activity and connection (Cosco et al., 2017). In short, staying socially and emotionally active seems crucial for the wellbeing of seniors (Hasan & Linger, 2016).

Retirement is often associated with a reduction in the standard of living as well as other social and health consequences (Silva et al., 2023; Moffatt & Heaven, 2017). A sudden change in the daily agenda can cause a blurring of the sense of time and lower self-esteem (Wiebke & Schwaba, 2018; Boniwell & Osin, 2015, p. 87; Wang & Shultz, 2010). Research which has examined the impacts of retirement on life satisfaction, as well as satisfaction with different domains of life, indicates that while retirement does not seem to greatly impact overall satisfaction, this can be explained by balancing out increased satisfaction with leisure time and a decreased satisfaction with income (Bonsang & Klein, 2012; Abramowska-Kmon & Łątkowski, 2021). Interestingly, the impact of retirement itself on subjective wellbeing depends to a large extent on the sense of control in the process, with involuntary retired faring worse than those who choose to retire (Calvo et al., 2009; Bonsang & Klein, 2012). Relatedly, other work has found that while overall wellbeing either remains constant or improves with retirement, for a subset of those who have to retire early due to job loss or health issues, the associated drop in income results in marked declines in SWB (Barrett & Kecmanovic, 2013).

Psychological resilience has been highlighted as an important protective factor for wellbeing in old age. People's later years often involve negative life events and challenges, including, for example, disease diagnoses and bereavement. For example, evidence indicates that when diagnosed with conditions such as diabetes, heart disease, stroke, or kidney disease, seniors are at greater risk of experiencing depression (Steptoe et al., 2014). The loss of a spouse is among the most stressful life events identified in the SWB literature (Spahni et al., 2015). Older people with higher levels of resilience in the face of such adversities have better wellbeing in later life (Cosco et al., 2017) and research comparing a wide range of psychological variables with wellbeing in an older population found resilience to be the most important protective factor examined, followed by perceived social support (Carandang et al., 2020). Research into how to foster resilience emphasises the importance of social and environmental resources to enable older adults to build psychological reserves that can help them maintain their wellbeing in the face of the challenges of ageing (Cosco et al., 2017). Other work indicates that psychological resilience plays a mediating role between a sense of meaning in life and satisfaction with life, suggesting meaningful activities likely help to build resilience too (Sikorska et al., 2019).

While research in the various domains often sheds light on differences experienced by age, further in-depth research on the determinants of seniors' happiness in different countries around the world and across different measures of SWB is needed.

Senior policy to improve wellbeing

Social capital and economic security are crucial as they influence the SWB and minimise the occurrence of mental illnesses such as depression (Park, 2017; Sibai et al., 2017). To improve the functioning and wellbeing of seniors and contribute to better ageing, it is important to strengthen healthcare systems to ensure access to specialised tests, modern treatment methods, and necessary rehabilitation services (Krug & Cieza, 2017). Developing support for organising free time activities, such as senior tourism, is also necessary. Moreover, public authorities should consider social realities, like housing and the level of social benefits, in their policies. Improving financial wellbeing generally leads to increased satisfaction with financial conditions, a heightened sense of security, and an overall better quality of life among older people (Cresswell-Smith et al., 2022; Pak, 2019; Daniel et al., 2018). Additionally, involving older people in productive activities like part-time work (e.g., homemaking, handicrafts), caregiving (e.g., for grandchildren or orphanage children), and various forms of volunteering can be beneficial. This may improve social relations, maintain individual mobility and economic security, and partially offset the fiscal burden resulting from the care of seniors (Gonzales et al., 2015).

A comprehensive and friendly senior policy is crucial for older people who require various forms of state assistance and benefits (Kalseth et al., 2022). Though of crucial importance, the goals of senior policy should not be limited to quality health policy, care services, and welfare transfers. In what follows, we highlight two key areas from the wellbeing intervention literature that go beyond these more traditional public policy domains and have demonstrated promise: positive psychology and positive technology interventions.

Positive psychology practices have been highlighted as fostering resilience and fortifying the psychological wellbeing of the elderly through enhancing their positive outlook (Sikorska et al., 2019). Marks (2021) underscores the significance of cultivating a positive attitude, emphasising that irrespective of age and health conditions, actively engaging in positive actions can profoundly impact an ageing adult's ability to achieve optimal health, maintain high energy levels, and experience overall satisfaction and motivation. This is supported by more general empirical research which emphasises the positive effects of positivity, including transforming thinking patterns, countering negativity, boosting self-esteem, enhancing resilience to stress, sparking creativity, and even positively influencing the functioning of the immune system (Fredrickson, 2011). Senior policies targeting the care of the elderly could stand to benefit from the integration of positive psychology practices (Ho, 2015). Such practices focus on fostering gratitude, forgiveness, and mindfulness and could be incorporated into care practices, preventative health activities, and other services (Proyer et al., 2015; Ramírez et al., 2014).

Technologies, particularly information and communications technology, are increasingly recognised for their potential to enhance the wellbeing of seniors, marking the emergence of a new scientific paradigm known as "positive technology" (Grossi et al., 2019, p. 1). The ageing process often brings inherent challenges such as mobility limitations, loneliness, and loss of motivation (Baez et al., 2019). The application of positive technologies in the elderly spans crucial areas which address these challenges, such as social care, healthcare, stimulation of social and civic participation, as well as social connection, education, and entertainment. The versatility and cost-effectiveness of modern technologies contribute to their increased use in ageing societies, potentially reducing expenses related to hospitalisation and long-term care by qualified personnel (Zapędowska-Kling, 2015; Hajder et al., 2022). While positive technologies offer substantial promise in helping older people navigate the challenges of ageing, difficulties in handling technology often hinder seniors' capacity to leverage this potential. Positive technologies should be tailored to seniors in various living arrangements, including those who are independent, in nursing homes, or receiving other forms of support to help them overcome these difficulties (Cahill et al., 2018; Khosravi et al., 2016).

While both positive psychology and positive technology interventions hold promise as ways to help to support people in ageing well, more research is needed into delivery pathways and forms of support to maximise their potential.

Discussion and actionable points

Trends in increased average life expectancy beg the question of how to ensure elderly people live their lives happily. While reports of life satisfaction tend on average to be higher in older compared to middle age, evidence suggests that the changes and challenges involved in ageing can put older people's wellbeing at risk. In particular, sensitive live events, including role transitions like retirement, diagnosis with health problems, and bereavement present challenges. On the other hand, external factors like social connection, as well as internal ones like psychological resilience, can help protect people's wellbeing in their later years even in the face of adversity. While more traditional interventions to support ageing well including economic and health and care supports are vital for people in their later years, other interventions including those which leverage positive psychology practices and positive technologies offer promise and may also prove effective given their links to important determinants of wellbeing in later life.

Based on our review on ageing and wellbeing, we propose the following actionable points for researchers and policy-makers:

- Conduct further research on the determinants of wellbeing that considers wellbeing distributions as well as averages and examines heterogeneity across different countries, population subgroups, and measures of wellbeing.
- Support initiatives which can help foster social connectedness and mitigate loneliness.
- Emphasise and look to mitigate the risks to the wellbeing of those facing lower-than-expected income and involuntary retirement in older age.
- Consider how positive psychology practices aimed at building psychological resilience and promoting positive emotions can be integrated into existing services delivered for seniors, as well as whether new services could be offered.
- Support the development and testing of positive technologies aimed at seniors, which range in function from entertainment to social connection to helping to address health issues.
- Engage seniors in identifying needs and designing solutions to the challenges of ageing.
- Evaluate senior policy efforts in terms of their impacts on wellbeing.

References

Abramowska-Kmon, A., & Łątkowski, W. (2021). The impact of retirement on happiness and loneliness in Poland – evidence from panel data. *International Journal of Environmental Research and Public Health*, *18*(18). https://doi.org/10.3390/ijerph18189875

Baez, M., Nielek, R., Casati, F., & Wierzbicki, A. (2019). Technologies for promoting social participation in later life. In B. Neves & F. Vetere (Eds.), *Ageing and digital technology*. Springer.

Barrett, F., & Kecmanovic, M. (2013). Changes in subjective well-being with retirement: Assessing savings adequacy. *Applied Economics*, *45*(35). https://doi.org/10.1080/00036846.2013.806786

Becker, C. K., & Trautmann, S. T. (2022). Does happiness increase in old age? Longitudinal evidence from 20 European countries. *Journal of Happiness Studies*, *23*(7). https://doi.org/10.1007/s10902-022-00569-4

Blanchflower, D. G. (2021). Is happiness U-shaped everywhere? Age and subjective well-being in 145 countries. *Journal of Population Economics*, *34*. https://doi.org/10.1007/s00148-020-00797-z

Boniwell, I., & Osin, E. (2015). Beyond time management: Time use, performance and well-being. *Organizational Psychology*, *5*(3).

Bonsang, E., & Klein, T. J. (2012). Retirement and subjective well-being. *Journal of Economic Behavior & Organization*, *83*(3). https://doi.org/10.1016/j.jebo.2012.06.002

Cahill, J., McLoughlin, S., & Wetherall, S. (2018). The design of new technology supporting wellbeing, independence and social participation, for older adults domiciled in

residential homes and/or assisted living communities. *Technologies*, *6*(18). https://doi.org/10.3390/technologies6010018
Calvo, E., Haverstick, K., & Sass, S. A. (2009). Gradual retirement, sense of control, and retirees' happiness. *Research on Aging*, *31*(1). https://doi.org/10.1177/0164027508324704
Carandang, R. R., Shibanuma, A., Asis, E., Chavez, D. C., Tuliao, M. T., & Jimba, M. (2020). Are Filipinos aging well?": Determinants of subjective well-being among senior citizens of the community-based ENGAGE study. *International Journal of Environmental Research and Public Health*, *17*(20). https://doi.org/10.3390/ijerph17207636
Cosco, T. D., Howse, K., & Brayne, C. (2017). Healthy ageing, resilience and well-being. *Epidemiology and Psychiatric Sciences*, *26*.
Cresswell-Smith, J., Wahlbeck, K., & Kalseth, J. (2022). Life conditions as mediators of welfare state effect on mental wellbeing among oldest old in Europe. *International Journal of Environmental Research and Public Health*, *19*. https://doi.org/10.3390/ijerph19074363
Daniel, H., Bornstein, S. S., & Kane, G. C. (2018). Addressing social determinants to improve patient care and promote health equity: An American college of physicians position paper. *Annals of Internal Medicine*, *168*(8). https://doi.org/10.7326/M17-2441
Douma, L., Steverink, N., Hutter, I., & Meijering, L. (2017). Exploring subjective well-being in older age by using participant-generated word clouds. *The Gerontologist*, *57*(2). https://doi.org/10.1093/geront/gnv119
Fredrickson, B. L. (2011). *Pozytywność*. Wydawnictwo Zysk i S-ka. ISBN: 9788381162029.
Gonzales, E., Matz-Costa, C., & Morrow-Howell, N. (2015). Increasing opportunities for the productive engagement of older adults: A response to population aging. *The Gerontologist*, *55*(2). https://doi.org/10.1093/geront/gnu176
Górny, M., & Lorek, A. M. (2021). Czy szczęście przyjmuje kształt litery U? Polityka senioralna a dobrostan osób starszych. *Polityka i Społeczeństwo*, *4*(19). https://doi.org/10.15584/polispol.2021.4.3
Grossi, G., Lanzarotti, R., Napoletano, P., Noceti, N., & Odone, F. (2019). Positive technology for elderly well-being: A review. *Pattern Recognition Letters*, *137*. https://doi.org/10.1016/j.patrec.2019.03.016
Hajder, K., Kacperska, M., & Górny, M. (2022). Nowe technologie a dobrostan seniorów w świetle deinstytucjonalizacji usług społecznych. In J. Babiak & M. Kacperska (Eds.), *Dylematy polityki senioralnej miasta Poznania*. Wydawnictwo Miejskie Posnania. ISBN: 978-83-7768-325-5.
Hasan, H., & Linger, H. (2016). Enhancing the well-being of the elderly: Social use of digital technologies in aged care. *Education Gerontology*. https://doi.org/10.1080/03601277.2016.1205425
Helliwell, F. J. (2011). *How can subjective well-being be improved?* Retrieved April 10, 2023, from www.researchgate.net/publication/233401595_How_Can_Subjective_Well-being_Be_Improved
Ho, H.-C. (2015). Elderly volunteering and psychological well-being. *International Social Work*, *60*(4), 1028–1038. https://doi.org/10.1177/0020872815595111
Ibarra, F., Baez, M., Cernuzzi, L., & Casati, F. (2020). A systematic review on technology-supported interventions to improve old-age social well-being: Loneliness, social isolation and connectedness. *Journal of Healthcare Engineering*, *2020*, 1–14. https://doi.org/10.1155/2020/2036842
Kalseth, J., Donisi, V., Miret, M., Forsman, A. K., & Cresswell-Smith, J. (2022). Exploring the association between welfare state and mental wellbeing in Europe: Does age matter? *International Journal of Environmental Research and Public Health*. https://doi.org/10.3390/ijerph191710985
Khosravi, P., Rezvani, A., & Wiewiora, A. (2016). The impact of technology on older adults' social isolation. *Computers in Human Behavior*, *63*. https://doi.org/10.1016/j.chb.2016.05.092

Krug, E., & Cieza, A. (2017). Strengthening health systems to provide rehabilitation services. *European Journal of Physical and Rehabilitation Medicine*. https://doi.org/10.23736/S1973-9087.17.04728-1

Lukaschek, K., Vanajan, A., Johar, H., Weiland, N., & Ladwig, K. H. (2017). "In the mood for ageing": Determinants of subjective well-being in older men and women of the population-based KORA-age study. *BMC Geriatrics*, *17*(1). https://10.1186/s12877-017-0513-5

Marks, R. (2021). Ageing and positive psychology. *Journal of Ageing Research and Healthcare*, *4*(1). Retrieved April 10, 2023, from https://openaccesspub.org/jarh/article/1705

Moffatt, S., & Heaven, B. (2017). "Planning for uncertainty": Narratives on retirement transition experiences. *Ageing and Society*, *37*(5). https://10.1017/S0144686X15001476

Moreno-Agostino, D., de la Torre-Luque, A., de la Fuente, J., Lara, E., Martin-Maria, N., Moneta, M. V., Bayes, I., Olaya, B., Haro, J. M., Miret, M., & Ayuso-Mateos, J. L. (2020). Determinants of subjective wellbeing trajectories in older adults: A growth mixture modeling approach. *Journal of Happiness Studies*, *22*. https://doi.org/10.1007/s10902-020-00248-2

Nyqvist, F., Forsman, A. K., Giuntoli, G., & Cattan, M. (2013). Social capital as a resource for mental well-being in older people: A systematic review. *Aging & Mental Health*, *17*(4). https://doi.org/10.1080/13607863.2012.742490

Pak, T.-Y. (2019). Social protection for happiness? The impact of social pension reform on subjective well-being of the Korean elderly. *Journal of Policy Modeling*, *42*(2). https://doi.org/10.1016/j.jpolmod.2019.12.001

Park, M.-J. (2017). Impact of social capital on depression trajectories of older women in Korea. *Aging & Mental Health*, *21*(4). https://doi.org/10.1080/13607863.2015.1088511

Proyer, R. T., Gander, F., Wellenzohn, S., & Ruch, W. (2015). Strengths-based positive psychology interventions: A randomized placebo-controlled online trial on long-term effects for a signature strengths- vs. a lesser strengths-intervention. *Frontiers in Psychology*, *22*(6). https://doi.org/10.3389/fpsyg.2015.00456

Ramírez, E., Ortega, A. R., Chamorro, A., & Colmenero, J. M. (2014). A program of positive intervention in the elderly: Memories, gratitude and forgiveness. *Aging & Mental Health*, *18*(4). https://doi.org/10.1080/13607863.2013.856858

Shankar, A., Rafnsson, S. B., & Steptoe, A. (2015). Longitudinal associations between social connections and subjective wellbeing in the English longitudinal study of ageing. *Psychology & Health*, *30*(6). https://doi.org/10.1080/08870446.2014.979823

Sibai, A. M., Rizk, A., & Chemaitelly, H. (2017). Self-rated health disparities among disadvantaged older adults in ethnically diverse urban neighborhoods in a Middle Eastern country. *Ethnicity & Health*, *22*(5). https://doi.org/10.1080/13557858.2016.1244736

Sikorska, I., Lipp, N., Stadtmuller, K., & Mostowik, J. (2019). Szczęśliwe życie w okresie późnej dorosłości. Znaczenie motywu indywidualnego. *Psychologia Rozwojowa*, *24*(1).

Silva, I. G. P., Marquete, V. F., Lino, I. G. T., Batista, V. C., Magnabosco, G., Haddad, M. D. C. F. L., & Marcon, S. S. (2023). Factors associated with quality of life in retirement: A systematic review. *Revista Brasileira de Medicina do Trabalho*, *20*(4). https://doi.org/10.47626/1679-4435-2022-876

Spahni, S., Morselli, D., Perrig-Chiello, P., & Bennett, K. M. (2015). Patterns of psychological adaptation to spousal bereavement in old age. *Gerontology*, *61*(5). https://doi.org/10.1159/000371444

Steptoe, A., Deaton, A., & Stone, A. A. (2014). Subjective wellbeing, health, and ageing. *Lancet*, *385*(9968). https://doi.org/10.1016/S0140-6736(13)61489-0

Swift, H. J., Vauclair, C.-M., Abrams, D., Bratt, C., Marques, S., & Lima, M.-L. (2014). Revisiting the paradox of well-being: The importance of national context. *Journals of Gerontology, Series B: Psychological Sciences and Social Sciences*, *69*(6), 920–929.

United Nations (2022). *Day of eight billion*. Retrieved April 10, 2023, from www.un.org/en/dayof8billion#:~:text=Day%20of%20Eight%20Billion,a%20milestone%20in%20human%20development

United Nations General Assembly (2021). *United nations decade of healthy ageing (2021–2030)*. Retrieved April 10, 2023, from https://bit.ly/3pyINiA

Wang, M., & Shultz, K. S. (2010). Employee retirement: A review and recommendations for future investigation. *Journal of Management*, *36*(1). https://doi.org/10.1177/0149206309347957

Wiebke, B., & Schwaba, T. (2018). Retirement is associated with change in self-esteem. *Psychology and Ageing*, *33*(4). https://doi.org/10.1037/pag0000253

Yuan, Z., Zheng, X., & Hui, E. C. M. (2021). Happiness under one roof? The integrational co-residence and subjective well-being of elders in China. *Journal of Happiness Studies*, *22*. https://doi.org/10.1007/s10902-020-00249-1

Zapędowska-Kling, K. (2015). Nowe technologie w służbie seniorom. *Acta Universitatis Lodziensis, Folia Oeconomica*, *4*(315). https://doi.org/10.18778/0208-6018.315.14

8

GENDER AND WELLBEING

Key stages of the life course

Jaslin Kaur Kalsi and Astghik Mavisakalyan

Introduction

According to the World Health Organization (WHO, 2025) gender refers to "the characteristics of women, men, girls and boys that are socially constructed". This includes social and cultural roles, behaviours, and expectations that are associated with being a woman, man, girl, or boy. Expectations can vary widely across different cultures and communities and may influence everything from personal relationships to professional opportunities. Based on these gender norms and resulting socioeconomic outcomes, men and women may be impacted differently by events over the life course resulting in substantial gendered implications for wellbeing.[1]

The large advances in the theoretical analysis of gendered wellbeing issues over recent decades have been matched by a growing body of empirical research. However, a key challenge has been the approach to the measurement of "wellbeing". Earlier studies tend to exploit income or consumption as direct proxies for wellbeing. However, several scholars have identified problems with equating larger resources to increased wellbeing. Sen (1990, p. 462) observed that what matters for wellbeing is not simply resources, but also one's ability to transform resources into "functionings" (or "doings and beings") and one's ability to choose between alternative sets of functionings. Therefore, in more recent studies on gender and wellbeing, scholars have more commonly used measures of subjective wellbeing (SWB) as a more direct way of assessing an individual's wellbeing.

However, SWB measures are not without their limitations. Most importantly, the interpretation of SWB can be questioned if individuals assess their own situation using endogenously determined standards of social comparisons. This goes to Sen's (1980, p. 218) point that people can become habituated to their existing set of circumstances. For example, women who face systematically inferior positions

DOI: 10.4324/9781003382447-9

may adapt to their poor conditions and inequality, taking pleasure in small mercies. Notwithstanding their limitations, measures of SWB are likely to still provide partial insights. Indeed, Sen (2009, p. 26) clarified that happiness (a form of SWB) is extremely important and that "the capability to be happy is a major aspect of the freedom that we have good reason to treasure. The perspective of happiness illuminates one critically important element of human living". He also emphasised that negative emotions such as frustration would relate to failure to achieve one's objectives. As such, this felt wellbeing can be thought of as evidential in checking whether people are succeeding or not in getting what they value and have reason to value (Sen, 2009, p. 27). Thus, although the process of habituation makes it important to be cautious when using SWB measures, they still contain some useful information on individuals' lives.

As such, this chapter provides a comprehensive assessment of SWB of men and women at key stages of the life course including during employment, parenthood, and retirement. We then review the policy frameworks and interventions around the world which have been designed to promote more gender-equal increases in wellbeing.

Gender and wellbeing

Employment

The long-standing interest in estimating the extent of gender pay gaps across the world has led to a growing body of research on the implications of gendered patterns of employment for SWB. Some studies have analysed the implication of types of positions and occupational levels. For example, using Eurostat's EU-SILC survey data from over 28 European countries, Navarro and Salverda (2019) find no relation between SWB and type of occupation for women; however, men in elementary occupations report higher SWB. Instead, the results from Navarro and Salverda's (2019) study demonstrated that when factors such as working hours and time spent on domestic tasks are considered, women prefer to advance their careers rather than adhering to traditional gender roles that emphasise housework (Navarro & Salverda, 2019).

Interestingly, many studies have found that women tend to report higher SWB in relation to their jobs than men. Davison (2014) explains this as the "paradox of the contented female worker" given obstacles such as the gender wage gap and cultural norms that favour men in high-paying positions and make it difficult to achieve equal earnings distribution between genders. This is because the job characteristics valued by men and women differ. Several studies have demonstrated that higher earnings add more to the SWB of men than women (Sloane & Williams, 2000; Donohue & Heywood, 2004; OECD, 2013). However, women are more likely than men to prioritise flexibility in work schedule, positive social interactions at work, and the meaningfulness of the work itself when considering SWB (Bender et al., 2005; Skalli et al., 2008).

On the other hand, women report higher SWB if they make a significant contribution to their household's income. For example, in a study using data from the Household, Income, and Labour Dynamics in Australia survey, men's and women's financial contributions were found to be an important predictor of financial satisfaction (Kalsi et al., 2022). The study also found that within Australian households, the changes in the man's employment is more likely to influence his SWB compared to changes in the woman's employment. Similar findings are presented in other country contexts including the UK (De Henau & Himmelweit, 2013), Germany (Elsas, 2016), and the Czech Republic (Mysíková, 2016). These findings suggest that wellbeing achieved through employment is still commonly influenced by male breadwinner ideologies. Furthermore, Artz et al. (2022) find that women who take on more "traditional" roles report substantially more job-related burnout compared to more "progressive" women.

Parenthood

During the 2010s, several studies analysed the impacts of parenthood on SWB following the impacts of the global financial crisis on the rising costs of raising children (see, e.g., Cooper, 2014). In addition, increased women's workforce participation and changing social norms also motivated studies of parental wellbeing. Many studies have found that parenthood doesn't lead to significant effects on men's and women's SWB (Nelson et al., 2014; Powdthavee et al., 2015; Nomaguchi & Milkie, 2020). However, a handful of studies which analyse the gendered effects of parenthood on SWB demonstrate that the impact of parenthood varies across country contexts. For example, in Australia, studies have found negative effects of parenthood on the SWB of both men and women (Shields & Wooden, 2003; Dockery, 2010). On the other hand, Mikucka (2016) finds that in Russia, on average, there are positive effects on SWB upon the arrival of a first child. The positive effects are even stronger on the birth of a second child, and highly significant for women but not for men. Other studies have demonstrated that parenthood has mixed implications for SWB. For example, using US data from the National Survey of Families and Household, Nomaguchi and Milkie (2003) found that having children has both disadvantageous and self-fulfillment implications for the wellbeing of men and women.

Some studies have analysed the transient impacts of parenthood. These studies often demonstrate that the effects of a newborn on mother's and father's SWB is short lived. For example, using data from the German Socio-Economic Panel Study, Clark et al. (2008) find that following the birth of a child women's SWB increases significantly while there are no significant changes to men's SWB; however, in the year following the birth of a child the effects on SWB are negative for both men and women although these changes are short lived and mothers and fathers tend to return to their baseline level of SWB. Similar results have been found in the United Kingdom (Clark & Georgellis, 2013) and Australia (Frijters et al., 2011; Matysiak et al., 2016).

Many of these studies focus on unidimensional SWB measures such as life satisfaction. Studies which focus on specific mental health outcomes such as depression, stress, or fulfillment suggest that parenthood has positive and negative effects, with these effects often being gendered. For example, most recently, Metzger and Gracia (2023) find evidence that parenthood leads to fluctuating mental health, consistent with the *costs and rewards* approach to parenthood. The fluctuations, however, are larger among women than men. During the transition into parenthood approximately 9% to 21% of women report lowered mental SWB (McLeish & Redshaw, 2017). These gendered effects on SWB become larger with the number of children present. For example, Austen et al. (2023) find that the negative consequences of having more than one child appear to be more pronounced for women compared to men and that the gendered effect is likely due to relatively large time conflicts experienced by mothers as demonstrated through lower free time satisfaction. Moreover, Giusta et al. (2011) find that childcare affects women's SWB negatively, while the effects are statistically insignificant for men.

Some interesting findings have been presented within the SWB domain of financial satisfaction. Evidence from Denmark (Andersson et al., 2014), Norway (Hart, 2015), Finland (Vikat, 2004), and Australia (Austen et al., 2023) suggests that higher financial wellbeing is a prerequisite in fertility decisions for women, but not men. Given that parenthood is often associated with the "motherhood penalty", women may opt to only have children once a certain level of career maturity (and financial security) is reached (Andersson et al., 2014).

Retirement

Many empirical studies tended to focus on the effects of retirement on men's wellbeing given the historical low labour force participation of women. A common finding is that retirement is associated with lower SWB (Atchley, 1976). However, some studies have found that retired men report relatively low levels of stress and depression (Jackson et al., 1993; Midanik et al., 1995). Later, based on an analysis of a sample of both men and women from the US Health and Retirement Study, Bender (2004) explained that individuals who were forced to retire reported on average lower levels of SWB compared to those who retired voluntarily, although male retirees reported lower SWB compared to female retirees. Relatedly, Bonsang and Klein (2012) used data from the German Socio-Economic Panel and found that generally retirement led to negligible effects on life satisfaction, although involuntary retirement had a negative impact on SWB.

Panis (2003) and Rohwedder (2006) found that retirement generally increases the SWB of both men and women. However, the degree of this increase is based on individual characteristics such as health status and financial resources (Panis, 2003; Rohwedder, 2006). Notably, individuals' wellbeing during retirement is likely to be influenced by several factors including the circumstances within which they are retiring, past labour-market opportunities, and their accumulated wealth. An individual's wealth position at retirement is likely to closely reflect their employment history. As discussed earlier, employment experiences are often gendered with women more likely to take on part-time work, earn lower wages and face more career interruptions due to parenthood than men.

Studies which focus on other domains of SWB demonstrate these disparities. For example, Austen et al. (2022) demonstrate patterns of financial satisfaction within Australian households that suggest women's financial preferences may not be reflected in decisions about household spending during retirement. Women are more likely to run out of retirement savings and social security, especially because older women are more likely to outlive older men. Empirical studies continue to emphasise that social norms which require women to be primary carers earlier on in life raise their poverty risks later by intensifying the negative effects of retirement as seen through declining women's wellbeing (Wakabayashi & Donato, 2006; Gonçalves et al., 2021)

Interventions on gender and wellbeing

Evidence on the gendered implications for SWB suggests that despite the substantial changes in women's workforce participation that have been underway over recent decades, gendered norms and breadwinner ideologies persist. Accordingly, there is a key role to be played by policies to support the breakdown of these norms, encourage women's labour force participation, and account for the gendered nature of care work.

One such intervention can be seen through the evolution of maternity and paternity leave policies across the world. The design of these policies is integral to influencing the share of care and women's opportunity to return to work. An analysis of 35 countries by DeRose et al. (2019) demonstrated that countries with more generous parental leave provisions did not necessarily achieve a more equal division of household labour, but that countries with paid leave reserved for fathers did. Nordic countries are particularly known for their father-friendly policies. The promotion of gender equality has been on the political agenda for many decades, and their policies are designed to encourage men to take up a more active role in care. For example, in Norway the introduction of a four-week "dad quota" meant parents exposed to the policy were 50% more likely to share household tasks equally (Kotsadam & Finseraas, 2011). Empirical evidence also suggests that the expansion of dad leave was associated with a faster average return to work for Norwegian mothers (Rønsen & Kitterød, 2015).

Moreover, as our review of the literature shows, workplace flexibility is an important factor of women's wellbeing and policies that allow for such flexibility are likely to lead to wellbeing gains for women. Additionally, as recent evidence from Australia shows, what drives significant improvements in gender equity outcomes is a suite of policies including pay equity strategies, recruitment and retention, and other policies and actions aimed at driving progress, such as parental leave, family and caregiving, and sex-based harassment (Duncan et al., 2023). Based on this research, gender diversity in leadership and boards is a key driver of organisational change. Unfortunately, the prevalence of some policies, including those preventing sex-based harassment, appears to be low (Duncan et al., 2022). Yet women's safety at work is a key consideration in women's choices of whether or not to work, and the type of employment. Evidence from Sweden indicates that the risk of sexual harassment influences women's career choices, leading them to self-select into female-dominated fields, which are often lower-paid (Folke & Rickne, 2022).

According to the World Bank (2023), women receive pensions that are between 25% and 30% lower than those of men. The pension gap is fully intertwined with the gender pay gap, the motherhood penalty, and the uneven distribution of care work. Securing wellbeing in retirement requires a multi-faceted approach such as progressive redistribution of pension systems. This may include separate targeted retirement-income programs which pay a higher benefit to poorer retirees. Chile has one of the longest running private retirement savings systems in the world and often serves as an example for other countries. Joubert and Todd (2022) explain the three design features that have reduced the gender pension gaps and old-age poverty in Chile: expanding minimum pension benefit eligibility, providing a per-child pension bonus, and increasing women's retirement age to be equal to men's. Overall, gender inequality in wellbeing is a complex issue that requires comprehensive and multi-faceted policy interventions.

Conclusion and actionable points

This chapter discussed the gendered experiences of wellbeing with reference to the key stages of the life course including employment, parenting, and retirement. Based on a review of existing studies, we highlight the gender differences in wellbeing associated with employment, parenting, and retirement. Our analysis suggests that the experiences of men and women at key stages of the life course are intertwined, and the presence of gender-biased social norms often means wellbeing costs associated with key life events carry through over the life course. Actionable points to improve wellbeing outcomes include the following:

- Promote policy interventions by both governments and organisations that support the breakdown of such gendered norms and breadwinner ideologies.
- Enact evidence-based parental leave and retirement policies that are equitably designed to promote wellbeing increase in both men and women.
- Implement organisational policies around pay equity, recruitment, and retention as well as other policies and actions aimed at driving progress, such as parental leave, family and caregiving, and elimination of sex-based harassment.

These policies have a strong potential to close the gender gaps in outcomes in various dimensions of life and contribute to the increase in women's wellbeing.

Acknowledgement

Astghik Mavisakalyan receives funding from the Australian Government through the Australian Research Council Centre of Excellence for the Elimination of Violence Against Women (project number CE230100004).

Note

1 In this chapter we focus on individuals who identify as a man or a woman given the lack of substantial evidence/data on individuals with other gender identities.

References

Andersson, G., Kreyenfeld, M., & Mika, T. (2014). Welfare state context, female labour-market attachment and childbearing in Germany and Denmark. *Journal of Population Research*, *31*, 287–316.

Artz, B., Kaya, I., & Kaya, O. (2022). Gender role perspectives and job burnout. *Review of Economics of the Household*, *20*(2), 447–470.

Atchley, R. C. (1976). *The sociology of retirement*. Halsted Press.

Austen, S., Kalsi, J. K., & Mavisakalyan, A. (2022). Retirement and the distribution of intra-household wellbeing. *The Journal of the Economics of Ageing*, *23*, 100404.

Austen, S., Kalsi, J., & Mavisakalyan, A. (2023). Parenthood and the distribution of intra-household inequalities in wellbeing. *The Journal of Economic Inequality*, *21*(2), 405–440.

Bender, K. A. (2004). *The well-being of retirees: Evidence using subjective data* (Working Papers), Centre for Retirement Research, Boston College.

Bender, K. A., Donohue, S. M., & Heywood, J. S. (2005). Job satisfaction and gender segregation. *Oxford Economic Papers*, *57*, 479–496.

Bonsang, E., & Klein, T. (2012). Retirement and subjective well-being. *Journal of Economic Behaviour and Organization*, *83*(3), 311–329.

Clark, A. E., Diener, E., Georgellis, Y., & Lucas, R. E. (2008). Lags and leads in life satisfaction: A test of the baseline hypothesis. *Economic Journal*, *118*(529), 222–243.

Clark, A. E., & Georgellis, Y. (2013). Back to baseline in Britain: Adaptation in the British Household Panel Survey. *Economica*, *80*(319), 496–512.

Cooper, M. (2014). *Cut adrift: Families in insecure times*. University of California Press.

Davison, H. K. (2014). The paradox of the contented female worker: Why are women satisfied with lower pay? *Employee Responsibilities and Rights Journal*, *26*, 195–216.

De Henau, J., & Himmelweit, S. (2013). Unpacking within-household gender differences in partners' subjective benefits from household income. *Journal of Marriage and Family*, *75*(3), 611–624.

De Rose, L., Goldscheider, F., Brito, J., Salazar-Arango, A., Corcuera, P., Corcuera, P. J., & Gas Aixendri, M. (2019). Are children barriers to the gender revolution? International comparisons. *European Journal of Population*, *35*, 987–1021.

Della Giusta, M., Jewell, S. L., & Kambhampati, U. S. (2011). Gender and life satisfaction in the UK. *Feminist Economics*, *17*(3), 1–34.

Dockery, A. M. (2010). *Happiness, life satisfaction and the role of work: Evidence from two Australian surveys (School of Economics and Finance working paper no. 3)*. Curtin Business School.

Donohue, S., & Heywood, J. (2004). Job satisfaction, comparison income and gender: Evidence from the NLSY. *International Journal of Manpower*, *25*, 211–234.

Duncan, A., Kalsi, J., & Mavisakalyan, A. (2022). *Towards a healthy and safe workplace in the mining industry: A review and mapping of current practice*. Bankwest Curtin Economics Centre.

Duncan, A., Mavisakalyan, A., & Vu, L. (2023, September). *Gender equity insights 2023: Accelerating the pace of change*, BCEC|WGEA Gender Equity Series, Issue #8.
Elsas, S. (2016). Income sharing within households: Evidence from data on financial satisfaction. *Social Sciences*, *5*(3), 1–16.
Folke, O., & Rickne, J. (2022). Sexual harassment and gender inequality in the labor market. *The Quarterly Journal of Economics*, *137*(4), 2163–2212.
Frijters, P., Johnston, D., & Shields, M. (2011). Life satisfaction dynamics with quarterly life event data. *The Scandinavian Journal of Economics*, *113*(1), 190–211.
Gonçalves, V. N., Ponchio, M. C., & Basílio, R. G. (2021). Women's financial well-being: A systematic literature review and directions for future research. *International Journal of Consumer Studies*, *45*(4), 824–843.
Hart, R. K. (2015). Earnings and first birth probability among Norwegian men and women 1995–2010. *Demographic Research*, *33*(38), 1067–1104.
Jackson, J. S., Chatters, L. M., & Taylor, R. J. (1993). *Aging in black America*. Sage.
Joubert, C., & Todd, P. E. (2022). Gender pension gaps in a private retirement accounts system: A dynamic model of household labor supply and savings. *Journal of Econometrics*, *243*(1–2), 105337.
Kalsi, J. K., Austen, S., & Mavisakalyan, A. (2022). Employment and the distribution of intra-household financial satisfaction. *The Economic and Labour Relations Review*, *33*(2), 329–350.
Kotsadam, A., & Finseraas, H. (2011). The state intervenes in the battle of the sexes: Causal effects of paternity leave. *Social Science Research*, *40*(6), 1611–1622.
Matysiak, A., Mencarini, L., & Vignoli, D. (2016). Work–family conflict moderates the relationship between childbearing and subjective wellbeing. *European Journal of Population*, *32*, 355–379.
McLeish, J., & Redshaw, M. (2017). Mothers' accounts of the impact on emotional wellbeing of organised peer support in pregnancy and early parenthood: A qualitative study. *BMC Pregnancy and Childbirth*, *17*(1), 1–14.
Metzger, S., & Gracia, P. (2023). Gender differences in mental health following the transition into parenthood: Longitudinal evidence from the UK. *Advances in Life Course Research*, *56*, 100550.
Midanik, L. T., Soghikian, K., Ransom, L. J., & Tekawa, I. S. (1995). The effect of retirement on mental health and health behaviours: The Kaiser Permanente Retirement Study. *Journals of Gerontology, Series B: Psychological Sciences & Social Sciences*, *50B*(1), 59–61.
Mikucka, M. (2016). How does parenthood affect life satisfaction in Russia? *Advances in Life-Course Research, 30*, 16–29.
Mysíková, M. (2016). Within-couple financial satisfaction in the Czech Republic: A test of income pooling hypothesis. *Ekonomický časopis/Journal of Economics*, *64*(4), 301–316.
Navarro, M., & Salverda, W. (2019). Earner position and job and life satisfaction: Do contributions to the household income have the same effect by gender and occupations? *Journal of Happiness Studies*, *20*, 2227–2250.
Nelson, S. K., Kushlev, K., & Lyubomirsky, S. (2014). The pains and pleasures of parenting: When, why, and how is parenthood associated with more or less well-being? *Psychological Bulletin*, *140*(3), 846–895.
Nomaguchi, K. M., & Milkie, M. A. (2003). Costs and rewards of children: The effects of becoming a parent on adults' lives. *Journal of Marriage and Family*, *65*(2), 356–374.
Nomaguchi, K., & Milkie, M. A. (2020). Parenthood and well-being: A decade in review. *Journal of Marriage and Family*, *82*(1), 198–223.
OECD (2013). *How's life? 2013: Measuring well-being*. OECD Publishing.
Panis, C. (2003). *Annuities and retirement satisfaction* (RAND Labor and Population Program Working Paper 03–17, DRU-30212), RAND.

Powdthavee, N., Lekfuangfu, W. N., & Wooden, M. (2015). What's the good of education on our overall quality of life? A simultaneous equation model of education and life satisfaction for Australia. *Journal of Behavioural and Experimental Economics*, *54*, 10–21.

Rohwedder, S. (2006). *Self-assessed retirement outcomes: Determinants and pathways* (IDEAS Working Paper Series from RePEc), Michigan Retirement Research Centre.

Rønsen, M., & Kitterød, R. (2015). Gender-equalizing family policies and mothers' entry into paid work: Recent evidence from Norway. *Feminist Economics*, *21*(1), 59–89.

Sen, A. (1980). Equality of what? In S. McMurrin (Ed.), *The tanner lectures on human values (197–220)*. Cambridge University Press.

Sen, A. (1990). Gender and cooperative conflicts. In I. Tinker (Ed.), *Persistent inequalities* (pp. 123–149). Oxford University Press.

Sen, A. (2009). The economics of happiness and capability. In L. Bruni, F. Comim & M. Pugno (Eds.), *Capability and happiness* (pp. 16–27). Oxford University Press.

Shields, M., & Wooden, M. (2003). Marriage, children and subjective well-being. *8th Australian Institute of Family Studies Conference*, Australia.

Skalli, A., Theodossiou, I., & Vasileiou, E. (2008). Jobs as Lancaster goods: Facets of job satisfaction and overall job satisfaction. *The Journal of Socio-Economics*, *37*, 1906–1920.

Sloane, P. J., & Williams, H. (2000). Job satisfaction, comparison earnings and gender. *Labour*, *14*, 473–502.

Vikat, A. (2004). Women's labor-force attachment and childbearing in Finland. *Demographic Research Special Collection*, *3*(8), 177–212.

Wakabayashi, C., & Donato, K. M. (2006). Does caregiving increase poverty among women in later life? Evidence from the Health and Retirement Survey. *Journal of Health and Social Behavior*, *47*(3), 258–274.

WHO (2025). *Gender and health*. www.who.int/health-topics/gender

World Bank (2023). *The gender pension gap: What does it tell us and what should be done about it?* https://blogs.worldbank.org/

9

EDUCATION AND WELLBEING

Ingebjørg Kristoffersen, Alfred Michael Dockery, and Ian W. Li

Introduction: the education-happiness paradox

There is overwhelming evidence of a positive association between education and objective quality-of-life measures, demonstrating both monetary and non-monetary returns to individuals, and both private and external economic benefits to societies. However, early research failed to produce consistent evidence that education translates into higher subjective wellbeing. The search for possible explanations has revealed patterns suggesting that the association between education and subjective wellbeing is far more nuanced and complex than was previously assumed and encompasses a range of direct and indirect dynamics.

This chapter aims to provide an overview of this body of research, the current state of play, implications for policy, and areas requiring further research. These considerations have implications for policy settings relating to the level of education that should be mandated and publicly supported, and for individuals' decisions to invest in further years of education. In most advanced economies, key educational outcomes relate to the completion of high school and the subsequent choice to pursue vocational training or a university/college degree and, potentially, post-graduate qualifications. This is reflected in relevant research, and so also this review.

Education, objective life circumstances, and wellbeing

Education is an investment in human capital

One of the most studied relationships in economics is that between education and earnings, which is most commonly understood in terms of Human Capital Theory (Becker, 1964). In this view, education enhances productive capacity, leading to

DOI: 10.4324/9781003382447-10

better employment prospects, higher earnings, and other positive labour market outcomes. At the societal level, a more agile and productive workforce implies higher tax receipts, lower social welfare expenses, more consumption and private health investment, less poverty and despair, and – consequently – happier lives for more people. The main alternative view, in line with screening or queuing models of the labour market (Layard & Psacharopoulos, 1974; Thurow, 1975; Spence, 1973), is that education acts as a signal of workers' abilities, thereby improving their position in the job queue. A critical point of difference is that 'signalling' does not rely on productivity enhancements, and the association between education and labour market outcomes is attributable to pre-existing characteristics or to 'selection bias' (see, e.g., Heckman et al., 2018). Others have suggested education is (partly) a positional good, which mitigates the value of investment at the societal level (we return to this point later).

Increased education has also been associated with positive outcomes beyond the labour market. These include better health and longevity (Leigh, 1983)[1]; lower engagement in risky behaviours such as smoking, substance abuse, criminal activity and unplanned pregnancies; and improved marriage prospects (Hartog & Oosterbeek, 1998; Oreopoulos & Salvanes, 2011; Wolfe & Haveman, 2002). Some detrimental associations have also been suggested, such as more educated people feeling more stressed in their jobs and pressed for time (Oreopoulos & Salvanes, 2011).

Education has consequences for time-use

Education, through higher productivity, raises the opportunity cost of leisure – though scarcity of leisure also increases its value. People with more education tend to work more. Australian research on mismatch between actual and preferred hours of work has found that overemployment dominates underemployment, and that mismatch has a substantial negative effect on subjective wellbeing (Wooden et al., 2009). Others have found that preferred working hours fall with higher education (Stier & Lewin-Epstein, 2003). Hence, education may affect wellbeing negatively due to overwork, either because people overestimate the realised utility of income relative to leisure or because they have limited control over working hours.

The type of education may matter

The literature mostly considers formal education, typically distinguishing between compulsory (primary), secondary, vocational, and tertiary schooling. Research suggests there are high monetary and non-monetary returns to completion of secondary school (Heckman et al., 2018), after which returns to further education are more varied. To our knowledge, no research has investigated the effect of education on wellbeing conditional on the degree of vocational orientation. However, Dockery (2010) reports that Australian high-school students entering university are initially happier than those who enter vocational training, with a strong subsequent reversal in following years. We will return to this point later, when considering the effect of education over the life-course.

Cognitive and non-cognitive skills

There is increasing focus in the economic literature on the distinction between cognitive and non-cognitive skills. Endowments of both appear important for educational attainment and for monetary and non-monetary outcomes. As Oreopoulos and Salvanes (2011) note, evidence that positive effects of education extend beyond the labour market has implications for competing views on how education affects outcomes. Clearly, signalling effects of higher educational attainments should not apply to non-market outcomes, except perhaps with regard to partnering. Psychology research suggests education may have a positive effect on subjective wellbeing via improved agency (Kitayama & Markus, 2000) and resilience (Desjardins, 2008). Reduced risky behaviours are indicative of less myopic behaviour, suggesting education may lengthen individuals' decision-making horizons. Relatedly, Oreopoulos and Salvanes (2011) note two alternative models formulated by Grossman (2006) that potentially link education to non-pecuniary outcomes: a 'productive efficiency model' where more educated people generate better outcomes for any given input, such as time and money; and an 'allocative efficiency' model where better resource-allocation choices are made.

In the personality trait literature, academic achievement has been linked with conscientiousness. Conscientiousness is associated with higher earnings through higher productivity and propensity to work longer hours, but also greater suffering during unemployment spells (Wood & Tarrier, 2010). Openness to experience, which captures creativity and has been alternatively known as 'intellect', is associated with moderately higher levels of positive affect and mental health, but is shown to be unrelated to subjective wellbeing because people who exhibit high levels of conscientiousness are more moderate in their evaluations of their own wellbeing (Steel et al., 2008). No link is identified between intelligence and subjective wellbeing (Frey & Stutzer, 2002).

Observed differences in skills across individuals with different levels of education are of obvious interest and importance. However, without more robust causal evidence, it is unclear whether these associations reflect pre-determined traits or are attributed to educational transitions. This is therefore an important area for future research.

Education, subjective evaluation of circumstances, and wellbeing

The evidence discussed here concerns associations between education and economic circumstances and other objective life outcomes. The following section considers psychological processes, which affect the ways in which observed objective circumstances translate into subjective evaluations of these circumstances, in which education may play a role.

Education is associated with different aspects of wellbeing in different ways

The early literature on subjective wellbeing focused on broad single-item measures, such as life satisfaction. More recent work explores how education may affect different aspects of wellbeing in different ways. Firstly, there is a recognition that education influences various life domains differently, implying trade-offs between these. For example, positive associations have been observed with satisfaction with finances, work, and health (Ferrante, 2017; Kristoffersen, 2018), though negative associations are reported with satisfaction with the amount of leisure time (Kristoffersen, 2018). This implied trade-off may provide one possible explanation for the education-happiness paradox.

Secondly, recent work has examined whether education may be motivated by, and have specific consequences for, different *qualities* of wellbeing. Contemporary stated objectives of higher education tend to focus on the attainment of job-relevant skills and associated labour market rewards. This may be interpreted as associated with hedonic wellbeing: the balance of positive over negative conscious experiences (Moore, 2019).[2] However, the cognitive skills gained through education may also promote eudaimonic wellbeing via improved meaning, purpose, authenticity, and self-actualisation (Kallova, 2021; Nikolaev, 2018; Schinkel et al., 2016). The discomfort associated with learning and personal growth implies a likely trade-off between eudaimonic and hedonic wellbeing, and education may nurture the skills necessary to make welfare-enhancing decisions concerning these choices (Kallova, 2021; Roberts, 2016; Schinkel et al., 2016).

Recent studies examine the evidence for whether education is associated specifically with eudaimonic wellbeing, often contrasted against hedonic wellbeing (Nikolaev, 2018; Jongbloed, 2018; Kallova, 2021; Ferrante, 2017). Unfortunately, this emerging part of the literature is marred by definitional inconsistencies, rendering meaningful conclusions challenging.[3] However, this line of inquiry is important, given the common emphasis on 'customer' satisfaction in higher education institutions competing for student tuition fees. Reliable (causal) evidence demonstrating the ability of educational institutions to build these capacities could be highly impactful for education providers, students, and policy-makers and should be prioritised.

Education is likely to affect the way we evaluate our objective circumstances

Education can affect self-evaluation and shift aspirations and expectations, and thereby the way in which objective circumstances translate into subjective evaluations of those circumstances (Clark et al., 2008; Easterlin, 2001; Frey & Stutzer, 2002; Ferrante, 2009, 2017; McBride, 2010). Consequently, education may improve wellbeing if expectations are exceeded, but decrease wellbeing if they are not met. While it's difficult to observe expectations directly using survey data, existing empirical evidence supports this hypothesis. Using Japanese survey data with specific information about aspirations, Clark et al. (2015) show that much of the effect of education on subjective wellbeing is cancelled out by increases in aspirations. Similarly, evidence presented by Kristoffersen (2018), based on Australian panel data, suggests that people with higher levels of education tend to have higher expectations of life circumstances but are not systematically different in terms of their ability to meet expectations. Similar evidence is reported by Powdthavee et al. (2015). These accord with the literature on the effects of overeducation, where individuals are educated in excess of their job requirements. Overeducation has been shown to result in adverse outcomes, including lower earnings, reduced job satisfaction (Fleming & Kler, 2014), life satisfaction (Piper, 2015), and other measures of subjective wellbeing (Ilieva-Trichkova & Boyadjieva, 2021). Reduced job satisfaction is attributed to being unchallenged at work, while lower life satisfaction arises due to raised but unmet expectations and dissatisfaction when comparing oneself with lower educated peers in similar positions at work.

Other patterns emerge when considering satisfaction within specific life domains. Kristoffersen (2018) reports no such mitigating dynamics in financial, health and job, satisfaction. However, expectations appear to differ with respect to leisure, as people with higher levels of education appear to expect (or desire) less work and more leisure, yet the opposite occurs. This produces a very strong negative association with satisfaction with leisure time once relative circumstances (particularly the amount of leisure time) are accounted for. Higher incomes appear to compensate marginally for losses in leisure. This evidence points to significant 'costs' of unfulfilled expectations around work and leisure for the more highly educated.

Finally, if education is considered a positional good, and subjective wellbeing is a function of relative rather than absolute circumstances, raising the education (and circumstances) of all will deliver no net gain, and even reduce subjective wellbeing if positional gains are neutralised by those of everyone else. Nikolaev (2016) reports evidence in support of this. Using Australian data, he shows that having a lower education level is associated with lower levels of life satisfaction. Interestingly, he also reports that the better educated appear less affected by social comparison. Araki (2022) provides additional evidence that skills diffusion (share of respondents with high skills) weakens the positive overall association between educational attainment and subjective wellbeing, using cross-national individual-level European data. This appears to imply that 'in highly skilled societies, educated individuals face the diminishing economic value of their high credentials, and consequently it becomes difficult to maintain relatively higher levels of life satisfaction as compared to less educated counterparts' (p. 608).

Education may affect the trajectory of subjective wellbeing across the lifespan

The existence of a U-shape in subjective wellbeing across the lifespan is widely documented in survey data internationally. Nikolaev and Rusakov (2016) and

Ferrante (2017) present evidence that people with different levels of education exhibit different subjective wellbeing trajectories across the lifespan. Ferrante (2017) examines Italian cross-sectional survey data and reports a stronger U-shape (a lower minimum, though at roughly the same age) for individuals with vocational qualifications than for those with secondary and tertiary education. This, combined with a greater prevalence of under- and overeducation and skill mismatch for younger respondents, leads the author to propose that those with higher education experience wide mismatches in their aspirations and expectations with respect to labour market outcomes early in their adult lives, but are able to adjust to these mismatches to enjoy the rewards of their investment in education later in life. This is undoubtedly important evidence, though the reliance on cross-sectional variation is a key methodological drawback, and hence the reported patterns may reflect cohort effects rather than life-cycle dynamics. However, consistent evidence is reported by Nikolaev and Rusakov (2016), who examined within-individual variation in a panel study. Their results show those with higher levels of education exhibit increasing subjective wellbeing after around age 40 (consistent with general patterns in the literature), while those with less education (high school or below) exhibit higher wellbeing earlier in life, but lower wellbeing from their mid-30s.

Discussion and actionable points

This literature spans various fields of study, and can appear unclear, complex, and inconsistent, and thus difficult to reconcile. That an educated population benefits society as a whole and individuals benefit from being educated is not at question. However, investing in education is costly, and subject to diminishing returns at both the individual and social levels. We need to recognise that education has the capacity to change not only our objective circumstances but also our subjective evaluations of these same circumstances. Ferrante (2017, p. 749) offers a useful approach to understanding how education affects wellbeing:

> First, human capital improves decision-making skills in a variety of life domains. Second, it improves the skills and knowledge associated with doing things and enjoying life: that is, it improves productivity in various life domains. Third, human capital shapes identity and personality traits and, fourth, by doing so, it shapes aspirations in different life domains. The first two effects are expected to improve people's performance and subjective well being in diverse life domains. More ambiguous is the joint impact of human capital through people's identity and aspirations.

Ideally, research on the relationship between educational attainment and subjective wellbeing would help to inform the formulation of education policy and individuals' choices on optimal investment in education. Yet the 'education-happiness paradox' raises critical questions. In our view, the theoretical and empirical literature surrounding the paradox is not sufficiently developed to offer concrete implications, save perhaps for a need for improved career information to better align expectations associated with educational investments with likely outcomes. The benefits of education will differ across individuals, different types of education will have differential effects, and education has different impacts on the separate domains of subjective wellbeing. Along with the confounding role of education on expectations, aspirations, and reference points, not enough is known about these relationships warranting more research on these.

Actionable points

- Wellbeing is a complex concept, with different meanings attributed to it across different contexts. While designing and evaluating public policies, it is crucial to distinguish between objective circumstances and subjective evaluations of these.
- Education is a big investment made early in life, often under considerable uncertainty. It brings diverse and enduring costs and rewards across the lifecycle. Educational policies need to recognise the high opportunity cost of leisure, and therefore often 'time-poverty' during active working years. So policy-makers should highlight all rewards, including not just better pay and working conditions, but also highly valuable psychological skills, perspectives, and resilience.
- Most of the research conducted on the costs and rewards of investment in education is correlational, and at best likely to reflect some degree of selection and pre-determined individual differences. Reliable causal evidence is scarce, so policy-makers should be careful not to overestimate the consequences of encouraging the pursuit of additional education for individuals and societies.

Notes

1 Leigh (1983) distinguishes between indirect and direct effects of education on health, finding that the indirect effects are larger than previously thought and that these dominate over direct effects.
2 Hedonic wellbeing is associated with the pursuit and experience of pleasure and the avoidance of pain (Nikolaev, 2018). In contrast, eudaimonic wellbeing is related to the pursuit of meaning, purpose, and self-realisation.
3 Nikolaev measures eudaimonic wellbeing based on four of the ten items included in the Kessler Scale of Psychological Distress (K10): feeling worthless, hopeless, tired for no reason, and feeling that everything is an effort. Five other items from the K10 are used to capture hedonic wellbeing (feelings of sadness, restlessness, nervousness, inability to sit still, and inability to calm down). Nikolaev reports positive associations with education for both measures, also after controlling for income. Jongbloed takes a very different approach to measuring eudaimonic wellbeing, combining responses to 11 survey items to construct an index for 'flourishing', among which conventional life satisfaction is one. These are grouped into three different composite measures using principal component analysis, including psychological wellbeing (competence, engagement, meaning, optimism, and self-esteem), emotional wellbeing (positive emotion, positive relationships,

and satisfaction with life), and mental wellbeing (emotional stability, resilience, and vitality). The evidence presented shows weak positive associations across these measures, controlling for unemployment and occupation, but not income.

References

Araki, S. (2022). Does education make people happy? Spotlighting the overlooked societal condition. *Journal of Happiness Studies*, *23*, 587–629.
Becker, G. (1964). *Human capital: A theoretical and empirical analysis, with special reference to education*. University of Chicago Press (for NBER).
Clark, A. E., Frijters, P., & Shields, M. A. (2008). Relative income, happiness, and utility: An explanation for the Easterlin paradox and other puzzles. *Journal of Economic Literature*, *46*(1), 95–144.
Clark, A. E., Kamesaka, A., & Tamura, T. (2015). Rising aspirations dampen satisfaction. *Education Economics*, *23*(5), 515–531.
Desjardins, R. (2008). Researching the links between education and well-being. *European Journal of Education, 43*, 23–35.
Dockery, A. M. (2010). *Education and happiness in the school-to-work transition*. National Centre for Vocational Education Research.
Easterlin, R. A. (2001). Income and happiness: Towards a unified theory. *The Economic Journal*, *111*, 463–484.
Ferrante, F. (2009). Education, aspirations and life satisfaction. *Kyklos*, *62*(4), 542–562.
Ferrante, F. (2017). Great expectations: The unintended consequences of educational choices. *Social Indicators Research*, *131*, 745–767.
Fleming, C. M., & Kler, P. (2014). Female overeducation, job satisfaction and the impact of children at home in Australia. *Economic Analysis and Policy*, *44*(2), 143–155.
Frey, B. S., & Stutzer, A. (2002). *Happiness and economics*. Princeton University Press.
Grossman, M. (2006). Education and nonmarket outcomes. In E. Hanushek & F. Welch (Eds.), *Handbook of the economics of education* (Vol. 1), Chapter 10. Elsevier.
Hartog, J., & Oosterbeek, H. (1998). Health, wealth and happiness: Why pursue a higher education? *Economics of Education Review*, *17*(3), 245–256.
Heckman, J., Humphries, J., & Veramendi, G. (2018). Returns to education: The causal effects of education on earnings, health, and smoking. *Journal of Political Economy*, *126*(Suppl 1), S197–S246.
Ilieva-Trichkova, P., & Boyadjieva, P. (2021). The fragile axes of life: A capability approach perspective towards graduates' education–job mismatches and subjective well-being. *Social Sciences*, *10*(7), 262.
Jongbloed, J. (2018). Higher education for happiness? Investigating the impact of education on the hedonic and eudaimonic wellbeing of Europeans. *European Educational Research Journal*, *17*(5), 733–754.
Kallova, N. (2021). Happiness as an aim of education. *Human Affairs*, *31*, 165–174.
Kitayama, S., & Markus, H. R. (2000). The pursuit of happiness and the realization of sympathy'. In E. Diener & E. M. Suh (Eds.), *Culture and subjective well-being* (pp. 113–161). MIT Press.
Kristoffersen, I. (2018). Great expectations: Education and subjective wellbeing. *Journal of Economic Psychology*, *66*, 64–78.
Layard, R., & Psacharopoulos, P. (1974). The screening hypothesis and the returns to education. *Journal of Political Economy*, *82*(5), 985–998.
Leigh, J. P. (1983). Direct and indirect effects of education on health. *Social Science and Medicine, 17*(4), 227–234.
McBride, M. (2010). Money, happiness and aspirations: An experimental study. *Journal of Economic Behaviour & Organization*, *74*, 262–276.

Moore, A. (2019). Hedonism. In E. N. Zalta & U. Nodelman (Eds.), *The Stanford encyclopedia of philosophy.* Metaphysics Research Lab, Stanford University.
Nikolaev, B. (2016). Does other people's education make us less happy? *Economics of Education Review*, *52*(2), 176–191.
Nikolaev, B. (2018). Does higher education increase hedonic and eudaimonic happiness? *Journal of Happiness Studies*, *19*(2), 483–504.
Nikolaev, B., & Rusakov, P. (2016). Education and happiness: An alternative hypothesis. *Applied Economics Letters*, *23*(12), 827–830.
Oreopoulos, P., & Salvanes, K. G. (2011). Priceless: The nonpecuniary benefits of schooling. *Journal of Economic Perspectives*, *25*(1), 159–184.
Piper, A. (2015). Heaven knows I'm miserable now: Overeducation and reduced life satisfaction. *Education Economics*, *23*(6), 677–692.
Powdthavee, N., Lekfangfu, W. N., & Wooden, M. (2015). What's the good of education on our overall quality of life? A simultaneous equation model of education and life satisfaction for Australia. *Journal of Behavioral and Experimental Economics*, *54*, 10–21.
Roberts, P. (2016). *Happiness, hope, and despair: Rethinking the role of education.* Peter Lang Publishing.
Schinkel, A., Ruyter, D., & Aviram, A. (2016). Education and life's meaning. *Journal of Philosophy of Education*, *50*(3), 398–418.
Spence, M. (1973). Job market signaling. *The Quarterly Journal of Economics*, *87*(3), 355–374.
Steel, P., Schmidt, J., & Shultz, J. (2008). Refining the relationship between personality and subjective well-being. *Psychological Bulletin*, *134*(1), 138–161.
Stier, H., & Lewin-Epstein, N. (2003). Time to work: A comparative analysis of preferences for working hours. *Work and Occupations*, *30*(3), 302–326.
Thurow, L. C. (1975). *Generating inequality.* Basic Books.
Wolfe, B. L., & Haveman, R. H. (2002, June). Social and nonmarket benefits from education in an advanced economy. In Y. Kodrzycki (Ed.), *Education in the 21st century: Meeting the challenges of a changing world, 47th economic conference [Proceedings]* (pp. pp. 97–142). Federal Reserve Bank of Boston.
Wood, A. M., & Tarrier, N. (2010). Positive clinical psychology: A new vision and strategy for integrated research and practice. *Clinical Psychology Review*, *30*(7), 819–829.
Wooden, M., Warren, D., & Drago, R. (2009). Working time mismatch and subjective well-being. *British Journal of Industrial Relations*, *47*(1), 147–179.

PART II

Wellbeing

Evidence across social and environmental domains

10

HOUSING, NEIGHBOURHOODS, AND WELLBEING

Marie Briguglio, Dylan Cassar, and Daniel Gravino

Introduction

Adequate housing is a basic human right (United Nations [UN], 1948), but one out of four people in the world are estimated to live in informal settlements or inadequate housing (UN Statistics Division, 2022). The relevance of housing to wellbeing is underscored by the inclusion of housing indicators in several composite indices and dashboards of wellbeing. In the OECD's Better Life Index, housing is 1 of 11 topics, in turn measured by three equally weighted indicators: (1) dwellings without basic facilities, (2) rooms per person, and (3) housing expenditure (OECD, 2023). The index also includes an indicator on neighbourhood, measuring whether people feel safe walking alone at night. Eurostat's Quality of Life dashboard reports the number of over- and under-occupied dwellings, dwellings with a leaking roof, damp walls, floors or foundation, or rot in window frames or floor as well as crime, violence or vandalism in the area (Eurostat, 2023). Similar aspects of housing also feature in several well-developed national indices such as the Canadian Index of wellbeing (University of Waterloo, 2016), Bhutan's Gross National Happiness (Ura et al., 2012), and the New Zealand Living Standards Framework Dashboard (New Zealand Treasury, 2022).

Later we review some empirical evidence on the relationship between housing and wellbeing, as well as insights from housing-related interventions to inform future policy interventions. The chapter is not intended as an exhaustive review, but draws more heavily from studies that establish a causal relationship.

Housing and neighbourhoods – impacts on wellbeing

Housing and neighbourhoods directly and indirectly provide the context for several wellbeing determinants. For instance, home is the place where personal relationships

DOI: 10.4324/9781003382447-12

and families are nurtured (Thornock et al., 2019). Inadequate housing may also negatively affect physical health, particularly if it is linked to inadequate water and sewage supply and damp and mouldy conditions (World Health Organization, 2009). Post-COVID-19, home is increasingly the place of work and housing conditions can also impact working experience (Eurofound, 2022). One's home can also be the place which hinders or facilitates certain lifestyle choices, such as having pets, engaging in creative or physical activities, and gardening, which are associated with higher levels of SWB (Briguglio, 2019). Neighbourhoods can afford residents diverse levels of social interaction or isolation, environmental quality or pollution, transport links to lifestyle activities, and safety. Moreover, housing often represents the largest expenditure for many households when mortgage/rent, heating/cooling, water, furniture, repairs are considered (OECD, 2022), impacting disposable income and leading to longer work hours to the potential detriment of wellbeing.

Several empirical studies examine the direct effects of housing on wellbeing focusing on housing tenure, the dwelling's physical condition, and the neighbourhood environment. For example, Zheng et al. (2020) study the effect of tenure on wellbeing using the 2011 and 2013 waves of the Chinese Household Finance Survey. Controlling for wealth, house value and other variables, Cheng et al. (2016) find a positive relationship between home ownership and SWB, a negative effect from informal home loans. By comparing the SWB of households that transitioned from rental to homeownership to that of households that continued to rent, they find that homeownership has a positive impact on SWB and that this outcome is unaffected by the financial constraints faced by new homeowners. Similarly, using data from the German Socio-Economic Panel Study for 1992–2009, Zumbro (2013) finds a positive relationship between home ownership and life satisfaction. Taking individual fixed effects and controlling for a wide range of personal characteristics, he finds that the association between homeownership and SWB is positive if the dwelling is in good physical condition. Zumbro (2013) also shows that homeownership is particularly important for low-income households and that its association with SWB may turn negative if there is a high financial burden of homeownership.

The importance of the house's physical characteristics is noted in Herbers and Mulder (2017). Using data on older adults from the 2012 Survey of Health, Ageing and Retirement in Europe, they find that having a large house is positively associated with SWB, though the effect is more pronounced in countries with lower housing quality. Overcrowded housing conditions (a measure of quality) may have various deleterious effects on wellbeing, particularly for children (Solari & Mare, 2012). A positive association has been found between wellbeing and the quality of the neighbourhood. Using cross-sectional data for residents in deprived areas in Glasgow, Scotland, Bond et al. (2012) also find that the quality and aesthetics of neighbourhoods is associated with mental wellbeing. Environmental incivilities in the local neighbourhood (e.g., vandalism), the quality of local amenities (e.g., play areas; schools; health centre), and the attractiveness of the buildings were considered.

Housing and neighbourhood interventions – impacts on wellbeing

Housing-related interventions take many shapes, from home-specific to urban and neighbourhood regeneration programmes, and from social-housing programmes to fiscal interventions for homeownership. In the domain of physical interventions, Cattaneo et al. (2009) examine the wellbeing effect of a large-scale Mexican government program, Piso Firme, which replaced dirt floors with cement floors. The authors take advantage of the geographic variability in the implementation of the program by comparing beneficiaries with their socio-economic counterparts in neighbouring cities that did not implement the program yet. On the basis of this quasi-experimental set-up, the improvements in physical health and satisfaction with housing and quality of life were attributed to improved quality housing.

Broader in scope, a city-wide regeneration housing programme in 2003 by the Glasgow Housing Association in Scotland aimed to refurbish homes on a home-by-home basis, to build new socially rented and private sector housing, to regenerate neighbourhoods, and to engage the community through different initiatives. This programme was followed by a longitudinal research and learning programme, GoWell, investigating the impact of housing and neighbourhood interventions on the health and wellbeing of the targeted population (Egan et al., 2010). Using the GoWell survey and a quasi-experimental design, Curl et al. (2015) find evidence that installing secure front doors enhances feelings of safety in the short term, especially in contexts where crime and antisocial behaviour is common. These changes were also indirectly associated with psychosocial benefits, such as feelings of control and status (GoWell, 2010). Mental health improved due to warmer housing and an aesthetically pleasing environment. Exploiting the same data with different estimation methods and controlling for health and socio demographic factors, Bond et al. (2012) find that improvements in the aesthetic quality of the home and especially neighbourhood were also positively associated with mental wellbeing.

Housing interventions may also involve the rehousing or relocation of residents to newly built housing. Based on a meta-review, Gibson et al. (2011) conclude that such interventions lead to improvements in mental health and wellbeing, particularly for disadvantaged groups. One example is Communities Scotland's programme of newly built social housing between 2001 and 2008. Using mixed methods, Petticrew et al. (2009) find significant improvements in reported neighbourhood satisfaction and psychosocial benefits. Gibson et al.'s (2011) qualitative work finds that improvements in a range of psychosocial outcomes, such as control, privacy and sociability derived from having a private entrance, private garden, and outdoor recreational space, have a positive impact on mental wellbeing and quality of life. An earlier intervention is that of the United States' Department of Housing and Urban Development Moving to Opportunity (MTO) program. Between 1994 and 1998, via random lottery, the MTO offered vouchers to relocate to a less-distressed neighbourhood to only some families. This randomization enabled Ludwig et al.

(2012) to attribute differences in post-relocation SWB between voucher recipients and non-recipients to differences in neighbourhood conditions across otherwise comparable groups. Interviewing the families periodically, they found that moving from a high-poverty to a low-poverty neighbourhood led to short- and long-term (10–15 years) improvements in SWB. New Zealand's Social Investment Agency (NZSIA) assessed a social housing project over 2008 to 2014 and its impact on three dimensions of wellbeing: life satisfaction, non-market domains of wellbeing such as health and social connections, and market outcomes such as income (NZSIA, 2018). Using a before-and-after method, the study finds that physical conditions improved as people were moved into social housing. However, while life satisfaction improved, feelings of safety deteriorated persistently over time.

However, not all studies assessing interventions find a positive effect. For instance, Thomas et al.'s (2005) quasi-experimental study of a 1999 housing regeneration initiative in Manchester shows evidence of a worsening mental health, as the target group reported higher stress levels due to the additional environmental nuisance of regeneration-related activity. A more recent study also finds no impact on mental wellbeing from living in large-scale regeneration areas when the redevelopment remained incomplete (Kearns et al., 2020). There is also evidence that the *process* of the intervention matters. Baba et al. (2017) using GoWell survey data showed that when residents feel they have a *choice* during the intervention (as opposed to forced relocation), when they are treated as stakeholders, they tend to feel more satisfied with its outcomes, possibly due to psychosocial processes such as control (GoWell, 2011; Kearns et al., 2011). Rogers et al. (2008) study the impacts of a regeneration programme in South Manchester and show that when respondents see the intervention as implementing cosmetic changes, rather than tackling their needs, they are less likely to judge it positively, with negative implications on their mental health.

Discussion and conclusion

The literature surveyed here employs a range of measures for wellbeing – an observation also noted in a review by Clapham et al. (2018). While some studies adopted a self-reported subjective wellbeing variable (e.g. Cattaneo et al., 2009; Cheng et al., 2016; Herbers & Mulder, 2017), many measured mental health/wellbeing (e.g. Curl et al., 2015; Kearns et al., 2020). Two of the studies employed the *Warwick-Edinburgh Mental Wellbeing Scales*, capturing feelings and functioning (Bond et al., 2012; Baba et al., 2017) despite recent criticism (Kearns et al., 2020) that it has barely moved over a decade. Thus, the measure of wellbeing may affect the estimated impact of housing and housing interventions on wellbeing. As wellbeing acquires more importance in the public policy agenda we anticipate more research to target wellbeing alongside public-health variables.

The diversity of the interventions, the target groups, and the context (such as institutional frameworks) render the measurement of intervention effects particularly challenging (Egan et al., 2010). Institutional contexts include legislative and regulatory frameworks as well as norms. For example, renting is negatively associated with SWB, but the effect is smaller in accessible and well-regulated markets (Herbers & Mulder, 2017). The relationship also varies along income distribution. While entry to homeownership is generally seen to be positively related to life satisfaction, the relationship is especially strong for low-income households. However, if homeownership entails an onerous financial burden, the relationship turns negative, suggesting that financial security is an important intermediary factor, which is bound to be more material for low-income households (Zumbro, 2013). Satisfaction with housing and neighbourhood is found to be related to age. For instance, physical conditions (doorsteps, flooring) impact older people's quality of life to a larger extent than others (WHO, 2007). Older people develop a keener sense of place as they spend more time in their homes and neighbourhood (Oswald et al., 2011). Residing in deprived neighbourhoods and low-quality housing is linked to lower social participation and overall wellbeing for older people (Tomaszewski, 2013; Scharf et al., 2005). Children's wellbeing deteriorates in overcrowded housing conditions, as they experience limited space and privacy as well as difficulties studying and sleeping, which impacts their social mobility and wellbeing in adulthood (Solari & Mare, 2012). Housing instability is linked to low wellbeing in children, though this is also linked to the family circumstances (like unemployment and family breakdown) that trigger moving house (Beck et al., 2016).

Relatedly, the mediating qualitative factors, which are often glossed over (Clapham et al., 2018), are a possible source of non-universal translatability. Housing tenure may be related to wellbeing because homeownership may enhance an individual's sense of autonomy, personal control, and ontological security (Dupuis & Thorns, 1998). Owning a home lowers the risk of being driven out by a landlord, which may incentivise individuals to invest in their home, thus leading to improved housing conditions (Clapham et al., 2018). Physical housing conditions may be related to wellbeing because poor conditions lower feelings of safety and security. Housing may also heighten or constrain identity and self-esteem, which may also depend on the level of social capital (Clapham, 2010). Importantly, the impact of housing on wellbeing may also be contingent on the housing conditions of a reference group in any given society, implying that social status is a powerful mediating factor (Clapham et al., 2018).

Many studies offer correlational evidence, running the risk that associations between housing quality and wellbeing are driven by a masked yet correlated variable. We limited our analysis to those studies that controlled for confounding factors by running multivariate regressions, by employing fixed effects (to control for any unobserved heterogeneity), or by employing an experimental or quasi-experimental approach. Studies that offer robust causal evidence to guide policy-makers remain scarce. While experimental studies with interventions rolled out by lottery can offer such evidence, they are harder to implement due to financial, logistical, and ethical challenges. Incorporating impact assessments within the intervention, both short term and long terms, would generate more evidence in diverse contexts, allowing us to assess interaction effects and mediating channels, to be responsive to outcomes, and to tailor future interventions to socio-economic realities.

Actionable points

On the basis of this review, we propose the following:

- Housing and neighbourhoods should feature strongly in the public sector agenda given that they can directly boost or suppress several of the key determinants of wellbeing including family life and social interaction, work, physical activity and other life-style choices, and internal and external environmental quality and safety.
- Policy-makers should be aware that housing tenure, housing quality, and neighbourhood quality all have a positive impact on wellbeing, although a high financial burden may have a negative effect.
- The effect of interventions on wellbeing is generally but not always positive. The means and not just the ends of the intervention should be given careful consideration, for instance by involving the targeted population in the design and implementation of the intervention.
- Given the gaps identified, more studies are needed on the wellbeing effects of different housing and neighbourhood interventions, in diverse contexts, which examine interaction effects (e.g. income, age, gender), as well as the channels by which housing impacts wellbeing.
- Incorporating wellbeing impact assessments within the intervention, in a manner that allows causality to be inferred, can yield useful evidence for the design of future intervention.

References

Baba, C., Kearns, A., McIntosh, E., Tannahill, C., & Lewsey, J. (2017). Is empowerment a route to improving mental health and wellbeing in an urban regeneration (UR) context? *Urban Studies*, *54*(7), 1619–1637. https://doi.org/10.1177/0042098016632435

Beck, B., Buttaro Jr., A., & Lennon, M. C. (2016). Home moves and child wellbeing in the first five years of life in the United States. *Longitudinal and Life Course Studies: International Journal*, *7*(3), 240–264. https://doi.org/10.14301/llcs.v7i3.374

Bond, L., Kearns, A., Mason, P., Tannahill, C., Egan, M., & Whitley, E. (2012). Exploring the relationships between housing, neighbourhoods and mental wellbeing for residents of deprived areas. *BMC Public Health*, *12*(48). https://doi.org/10.1186/1471-2458-12-48

Briguglio, M. (2019). Wellbeing: An economics perspective. In S. Vella, R. Falzon, & A. Azzopardi (Eds.), *Perspectives on wellbeing* (pp. 145–157). Brill Sense.

Cattaneo, M. D., Galiani, S., Gertler, P. J., Martinez, S., & Titiunik, R. (2009). Housing, health, and happiness. *American Economic Journal: Economic Policy*, *1*(1), 75–105. https://doi.org/10.1257/pol.1.1.75

Cheng, Z., King, P. S., Smyth, R., & Wang, H. (2016). Housing property rights and subjective wellbeing in urban China. *European Journal of Political Economy*, *45*, 160–174. https://doi.org/10.1016/j.ejpoleco.2016.08.002

Clapham, D. (2010). Happiness, well-being and housing policy. *Policy and Politics*, *38*(2), 253–267. https://doi.org/10.1332/030557310X488457
Clapham, D., Foye, C., & Christian, C. (2018). The concept of subjective well-being in housing research. *Housing, Theory and Society*, *35*(3), 261–280. https://doi.org/0.1080/14036096.2017.1348391
Curl, A., Kearns, A., Mason, P., Egan, M., Tannahill, C., & Ellaway, A. (2015). Physical and mental health outcomes following housing improvements: Evidence from the GoWell study. *Journal of Epidemiology and Community Health*, *69*(1), 12–19. https://doi.org/10.1136/jech-2014-204064
Dupuis, A., & Thorns, D. C. (1998). Home, home ownership and the search for ontological security. *The Sociological Review*, *46*(1), 24–47. https://doi.org/10.1111/1467-954X.00
Egan, M., Kearns, A., Mason, P., Tannahill, C., Bond, L., Coyle, J., . . . & the GoWell Team (2010). Protocol for a mixed methods study investigating the impact of investment in housing, regeneration and neighbourhood renewal on the health and wellbeing of residents: The GoWell programme. *BMC Medical Research Methodology*, *10*, 41. https://doi.org/10.1186/1471-2288-10-41
Eurofound (2022). *The rise in telework: Impact on working conditions and regulations*. Publications Office of the European Union.
Eurostat (2023). *Quality of life*. https://ec.europa.eu/eurostat/cache/infographs/qol/index_en.html
Gibson, M., Thomson, H., Kearns, A., & Petticrew, M. (2011). Understanding the psychosocial impacts of housing type: Qualitative evidence from a housing and regeneration intervention. *Housing Studies*, *26*(4), 555–573. https://doi.org/10.1080/02673037.2011.559724
GoWell (2010). *Progress for people and places: Monitoring change in Glasgow's communities, evidence from the GoWell surveys 2006 and 2008*. Glasgow Centre for Population Health.
GoWell (2011). *Moving out, moving on? Short to medium term outcomes from relocation through regeneration in Glasgow*. Glasgow Centre for Population Health.
Herbers, D. J., & Mulder, C. H. (2017). Housing and subjective well-being of older adults in Europe. *Journal of Housing and the Built Environment*, *32*(3), 533–558. https://doi.org/10.1007/s10901-016-9526-1
Kearns, A., Ghosh, S., Mason, P., & Egan, M. (2020). Urban regeneration and mental health: Investigating the effects of an area-based intervention using a modified intention to treat analysis with alternative outcome measures. *Health & Place*, *61*, 102262. https://doi.org/10.1016/j.healthplace.2019.102262
Kearns, A., Whitley, E., Mason, P., Petticrew, M., & Hoy, C. (2011). Material and meaningful homes: Mental health impacts and psychosocial benefits of rehousing to new dwellings. *International Journal of Public Health*, *56*(6), 597–607. https://doi.org/10.1007/s00038-011-0275-3
Ludwig, J., Duncan, G. J., Gennetian, L. A., Katz, L. F., Kessler, R. C., Kling, J. R., & Sanbonmatsu, L. (2012). Neighborhood effects on the long-term well-being of low-income adults. *Science*, *337*(6101), 1505–1510. https://doi.org/10.1126/science.1224648
New Zealand Social Investment Agency (2018). *Measuring the wellbeing impacts of public policy: Social housing*, Wellington, New Zealand.
New Zealand Treasury (2022, April 12). *The living standards framework dashboard*, New Zealand Government.
Organisation for Economic Co-operation and Development (2022). *HC1.2. Housing costs over income, affordable housing*, OECD.
Organisation for Economic Co-operation and Development (2023). *Better life index*. www.oecdbetterlifeindex.org/
Oswald, F., Jopp, D., Rott, C., & Wahl, H. (2011). Is aging in place a resource for or risk to life satisfaction? *The Gerontologist*, *51*(2), 238–250. https://doi.org/10.1093/geront/gnq096
Petticrew, M., Kearns, A., Mason, P., & Hoy, C. (2009). The SHARP study: A quantitative and qualitative evaluation of the short-term outcomes of housing and neighbourhood renewal. *BMC Public Health*, *9*(415), 1–14. https://doi.org/10.1186/1471-2458-9-415

Rogers, A., Huxley, P., Evans, S., & Gately, C. (2008). More than jobs and houses: Mental health, quality of life and the perceptions of locality in an area undergoing urban regeneration. *Social Psychiatry and Psychiatric Epidemiology*, *43*(5), 364–372. https://doi.org/10.1007/s00127-008-0316-2

Scharf, T., Phillipson, C., & Smith, A. E. (2005). Social exclusion of older people in deprived urban communities of England. *European Journal of Ageing*, *2*(2), 76–87. https://doi.org/10.1007/s10433-005-0025-6

Solari, C. D., & Mare, R. D. (2012). Housing crowding effects on children's wellbeing. *Social Science Research*, *41*(2), 464–476. https://doi.org/10.1016/j.ssresearch.2011.09.012

Thomas, R., Evans, S., Huxley, P., Gately, C., & Rogers, A. (2005). Housing improvement and self-reported mental distress among council estate residents. *Social Science & Medicine*, *60*(12), 2773–2783. https://doi.org/10.1016/j.socscimed.2004.11.015

Thornock, C., Nelson, L., Porter, C., & Evans-Stout, C. (2019). There's no place like home: The associations between residential attributes and family functioning. *Journal of Environmental Psychology*, *64*, 39–47. https://doi.org/10.1016/j.jenvp.2019.04.011

Tomaszewski, W. (2013). Living environment, social participation and wellbeing in older age: The relevance of housing and local area disadvantage. *Population Ageing*, *6*, 119–156. https://doi.org/10.1007/s12062-012-9077-5

United Nations (1948). *Article 25 of the universal declaration of human rights*. www.un.org/en/documents/udhr/

United Nations Statistics Division (2022). *SDG report goal 11*. https://unstats.un.org/sdgs/report/2022/goal-11/

University of Waterloo (2016). How are Canadians really doing? *The 2016 CIW National Report*.

Ura, K., Alkire, S., Zangmo, T., & Wangdi, K. (2012). *An extensive analysis of GNH index*. Centre for Bhutan Studies. ISBN 978-99936-14-67-8.

World Health Organization (2007). *Global age-friendly cities: A guide*. WHO. https://apps.who.int/iris/handle/10665/43755

World Health Organization (2009). *Guidelines for indoor air quality: Dampness and mould*. www.who.int/publications/i/item/9789289041683

Zheng, X., Yuana, Z., & Zhang, X. (2020). Does happiness dwell in an owner-occupied house? Homeownership and subjective well-being in urban China. *Cities*, *96*, 102404. https://doi.org/10.1016/j.cities.2019.102404

Zumbro, T. (2013). The relationship between homeownership and life satisfaction in Germany. *Housing Studies*, *29*(3), 319–338. https://doi.org/10.1080/02673037.2013.773583

11

ENVIRONMENT AND WELLBEING

Assessing the impact of environmental quality and pro-environmental behavior on wellbeing

Kate Laffan, Hans Czap, and Natalia V. Czap

Introduction

It has long been recognized that human wellbeing is inextricably linked with the natural world (Neller & Neller, 2009). Attention restoration theory (Kaplan, 1995) posits that time in nature reduces mental fatigue and restores the ability to focus, process information, and solve problems. Stress reduction theory (Ulrich et al., 1991) argues that nature facilitates recovery from stress. Biophilia hypothesis (Kellert & Wilson, 1995) suggests that humans have an innate need to seek connection with nature. In addition, the natural environment is recognized as an important factor of wellbeing by OECD's Better Life Index, Happy Planet Index, and Social Progress Index, among other frameworks.

In what follows, we review the evidence of the impact of pro-environmental action and environmental quality on wellbeing. While we recognize the importance of the built environment for wellbeing, in the interest of space, the current work focuses on natural environments.

Environment and wellbeing

Pro-environmental attitudes, behaviour, and information

A growing body of research explores the relationships between subjective wellbeing (SWB) and pro-environmental behavior (PEB) (see the meta-analysis by Zawadzki et al., 2020). Several studies also examine links between SWB and nature connectedness, pro-environmental attitudes and identity (Welsch & Kühling, 2018), and environmental concern and climate anxiety (Ogunbode et al., 2022).

DOI: 10.4324/9781003382447-13

The PEB/SWB literature focuses on whether PEB represents a sacrifice or a benefit too. Across three dimensions of SWB (evaluative, affective, and eudemonic), there exists evidence of positive associations with pro-environmental action, though the strength of these associations varies (Laffan, 2020). More specifically, PEBs are most closely related to eudemonic measures of SWB, which capture the purposefulness and meaningfulness of their activities (Zawadzki et al., 2020). Positive PEB/SWB associations are documented in both individualistic and more collectivist cultures (Capstick et al., 2022), albeit stronger ones are seen in the latter.

The relationships with particular behaviors vary according to the costs involved, the conscious/habitual nature of the behaviour, and the extent to which it is social and/or visible. Schmitt et al. (2018) find that those behaviors that are more costly in terms of money, time, or effort are those most closely linked to SWB, possibly because of more conscious engagement (Zawadzki et al., 2020), or greater perceived impact. Many public PEBs, like campaigning or volunteering, lead to connection with others (an important determinant of wellbeing) and thus result in higher SWB than actions done alone (Capstick et al., 2022).

Binder and Blankenberg (2017) find evidence that green identity is a better predictor of life satisfaction than PEB. Relatedly, Welsch and Kühling (2018) discover that pro-environmental self-image positively predicts life satisfaction. While a meta-analysis by Capaldi et al. (2014) showed the positive association between SWB and people's connectedness to nature, concern over the environment may detract from SWB. Environment-related distress, including negative emotions like fear, worry, guilt, and hopelessness, is encompassed in the terms eco and climate anxiety. The evidence on how to treat people with these conditions is in its infancy (see the review by Baudon & Jachens, 2021).

Several limitations apply to the existing literature. The work to date has been largely cross-sectional (Zawadzki et al., 2020), precluding a clear causal picture of the relationship between PEB and other variables of interest on one side and SWB on the other. Where longitudinal work has been carried out, the evidence indicates that there is likely a bi-directional relationship between PEB and SWB, with higher-SWB people being more likely to engage in PEB and PEB enhancing people's SWB (Prati et al., 2017). Further longitudinal and experimental work is needed to establish whether and under what conditions PEB and attitudes cause wellbeing.

Environmental quality and wellbeing

Environmental conditions are important predictors of SWB and other wellbeing outcomes. Local *noise pollution* is negatively associated with SWB (Van Praag & Baarsma, 2005), and it negatively impacts wellbeing through cardiovascular disease, cognitive impairment in children, sleep disturbance, tinnitus, and annoyance (World Health Organization, 2011).

Similar to noise pollution, high *air pollution* is associated with decreased SWB (MacKerron & Mourato, 2009). High air pollution also leads to more high-risk pregnancies, fetal malformations and infant mortality (Currie & Neidell, 2005), and cardiorespiratory diseases (Fan et al., 2020). It causes anxiety (Power et al., 2015), depression (Lamers et al., 2011), and increases suicide risk (Kim et al., 2010). Poor air quality reduces outside leisure activities (Laffan, 2018), which removes a possible stress release (Chang et al., 2019) and reduces cognitive performance, which can lead to lower socioeconomic outcomes (Ebenstein et al., 2016). Modest air pollution levels, however, have relatively little impact on SWB (Li et al., 2019). While air quality is often not known, information disclosure of air pollution leads to decreased life satisfaction through cognitive (realization that pollution is a problem), avoidance (changed spending and behavior), and envy effects (toward other regions) (Zhu & Lin, 2022). At the same time, increased government transparency is associated with increased public satisfaction (Ma, 2017) and reduced pollution by firms (Wang et al., 2021).

Proximity to *green and blue spaces* lessens the negative impact of environmental stressors on wellbeing (Day, 2007; Welsch, 2006), facilitates behaviors positively linked to wellbeing such as physical exercise and social interaction (see the multi-study analysis by Barton & Pretty, 2010), improves health (De Vries et al., 2003), and decreases mortality from circulatory diseases (Mitchell & Popham, 2008). The wellbeing benefits of green and blue spaces are greater when places are perceived as safe and natural (Fisher et al., 2021) and more biodiverse (Wolf et al., 2017).

The perception of accessibility and biodiversity matters more for wellbeing than the objective quality of the space (Ruckelshauß, 2020). That relationship is also sensitive to what aspect of SWB is measured. For instance, the ease of access to blue space is more strongly associated with the reduction of negative outcomes (mental distress) than with a boost in positive ones (feeling of happiness) (White et al., 2013). Furthermore, the relationship depends on the time spent and whether the space is used for physical activity or social interaction (Carrus et al., 2015).

Water quality affects humans through multiple channels, from health and survival (e.g., drinking water in developing countries) to recreational activities (e.g., swimming and boating) and commerce (e.g., fisheries) (Keeler et al., 2012). Research on developing countries is focused on the adverse effects of poor water quality and scarcity that threatens health and survival. Those who are dissatisfied with their water quality rate their lives more poorly (Rzepa & Pugliese, 2012), because of adverse health effects, negative economic implications (Pinto et al., 2020), and food insecurity (Cullen-Unsworth et al., 2014). Water insecurity affects mental wellbeing (Maxfield, 2020). *Water scarcity* also impacts wellbeing indirectly through reduced female employment and school attendance (Arceo-Gómez et al., 2020). The research on water and wellbeing in developed countries focuses more on the blue spaces discussed earlier. It shows that subjective water quality can be more important for wellbeing than objective measures (Gunko et al., 2022), and learning about water management increases wellbeing (Lehtoranta & Louhi, 2021).

Heterogeneity of environmental quality impact on wellbeing

The impact of environmental quality on SWB is often heterogeneous. For instance, people with more education and older individuals are affected more by noise (Yang et al., 2022). The impact also depends on mitigating factors, including the signal-to-background ratio, the preference for outdoor activities, the perceived lack of compensating benefits, and proclivities for opening windows (Lercher & Kofler, 1996).

Along the same lines, studies demonstrated that single parents and the less educated (Ambrey & Fleming, 2014), older residents and males (Krekel et al., 2016), and single residents (Bertram & Rehdanz, 2015) benefit more from green space. Welfare damages of invasive species are more pronounced for individuals in poor health and communities with a high share of racial and ethnic minorities (Jones, 2020). On the other hand, other research finds no difference by income, age, gender (Bertram & Rehdanz, 2015), and parental status (Krekel et al., 2016).

The impact of water on wellbeing differs in developed and developing countries. In high-income countries it was demonstrated that water quality is a less important determinant of life quality at the lower income level (Gunko et al., 2022), while water scarcity has generally not been a subject of investigation. In low-income countries, where water insecurity is a big issue, parents report more severe scarcity than their children, but girls report slightly worse water insecurity than fathers (Maxfield, 2020).

Nature-based interventions

The impact of environmental interventions on wellbeing is represented by nature-based interventions. Closely related concepts are Green Care and Ecotherapy; see Steigen et al. (2016) and Roberts et al. (2020) respectively for a literature review. These interventions can be categorized into approaches that alter the lived environment (parks and gardens) and those that affect behaviors (activities in nature) (Shanahan et al., 2019). Others classify these therapies into wilderness therapy, adventure therapy, horticulture therapy, forest rehabilitation therapy, and animal-assisted therapy (Lewis et al., 2022).

The evidence is generally supportive of the effectiveness of these approaches for improved mental and physical health and general wellbeing (see, e.g., reviews by Maller et al. (2005) and Lewis et al. (2022)). However, at this point, results have to be interpreted with caution, as there are many methodological issues with existing studies, ranging from selection bias, relatively small sample sizes, and lack of control groups to confounders (Lewis et al., 2022; Roberts et al., 2020).

Discussion and actionable points

PEB is positively associated with life satisfaction, positive affect, and eudemonic measures of wellbeing and thus benefits both the individuals and the environment. However, concerns over environmental problems like climate change and biodiversity loss may reduce wellbeing. This will likely worsen with the intensifying environmental crises.

Both environmental goods (e.g., greenspace and proximity to the coast) and environmental bads (e.g. noise, pollution, invasive species) affect wellbeing. The impact is heterogenous: disadvantaged individuals and communities with racial and ethnic minorities have the least access to goods, while being affected the most by the bads. Environmental bads also impact wellbeing indirectly through physical and mental health, food insecurity, and low outdoor recreation and exercise. While SWB is affected by objective environmental quality, subjective evaluation, which is sometimes inaccurate, is often more important.

Drawing on the research linking wellbeing with environmental quality, behaviors, and concerns, we offer the following actionable points:

- Policy-makers should emphasize the wellbeing benefits of pro-environmental action, rather than presenting it as a sacrifice.
- Experts need to develop evidence-based guidance for interventions to treat eco-anxiety.
- Researchers and policy-makers have to recognize that the impact of environmental quality on wellbeing extends beyond its indirect impacts through health.
- Policy-makers need to prioritize combating environmental injustice given that disadvantaged communities have less resources to improve environmental quality yet would benefit the most from it.
- Policy-makers need to communicate good environmental conditions clearly and highlight the work done to improve these.
- Given the interdependencies between wellbeing and nature, enhancing environmental quality and encouraging sustainable behavior are urgent policy imperatives.

References

Ambrey, C., & Fleming, C. (2014). Public greenspace and life satisfaction in urban Australia. *Urban Studies*, *51*(6), 1290–1321.

Arceo-Gómez, E. O., Hernández-Cortés, D., & López-Feldman, A. (2020). Droughts and rural households' wellbeing: Evidence from Mexico. *Climatic Change*, *162*(3), 1197–1212.

Barton, J., & Pretty, J. (2010). What is the best dose of nature and green exercise for improving mental health? A multi-study analysis. *Environmental Science & Technology*, *44*(10), 3947–3955.

Baudon, P., & Jachens, L. (2021). A scoping review of interventions for the treatment of eco-anxiety. *International Journal of Environmental Research and Public Health*, *18*(18), 9636.

Bertram, C., & Rehdanz, K. (2015). The role of urban green space for human well-being. *Ecological Economics*, *120*, 139–152.

Binder, M., & Blankenberg, A.-K. (2017). Green lifestyles and subjective well-being: More about self-image than actual behavior? *Journal of Economic Behavior & Organization*, *137*, 304–323.

Capaldi, C. A., Dopko, R. L., & Zelenski, J. M. (2014). The relationship between nature connectedness and happiness: A meta-analysis. *Frontiers in Psychology*, 976.

Capstick, S., Nash, N., Whitmarsh, L., Poortinga, W., Haggar, P., & Brügger, A. (2022). The connection between subjective wellbeing and pro-environmental behaviour: Individual and cross-national characteristics in a seven-country study. *Environmental Science & Policy*, *133*, 63–73.

Carrus, G., Scopelliti, M., Lafortezza, R., Colangelo, G., Ferrini, F., Salbitano, F., Agrimi, M., Portoghesi, L., Semenzato, P., & Sanesi, G. (2015). Go greener, feel better? The positive effects of biodiversity on the well-being of individuals visiting urban and peri-urban green areas. *Landscape and Urban Planning*, *134*, 221–228.

Chang, P.-J., Song, R., & Lin, Y. (2019). Air pollution as a moderator in the association between leisure activities and well-being in urban China. *Journal of Happiness Studies*, *20*, 2401–2430.

Cullen-Unsworth, L. C., Nordlund, L. M., Paddock, J., Baker, S., McKenzie, L. J., & Unsworth, R. K. (2014). Seagrass meadows globally as a coupled social–ecological system: Implications for human wellbeing. *Marine Pollution Bulletin*, *83*(2), 387–397.

Currie, J., & Neidell, M. (2005). Air pollution and infant health: What can we learn from California's recent experience? *The Quarterly Journal of Economics*, *120*(3), 1003–1030.

Day, R. (2007). Place and the experience of air quality. *Health & Place*, *13*(1), 249–260.

De Vries, S., Verheij, R. A., Groenewegen, P. P., & Spreeuwenberg, P. (2003). Natural environments – healthy environments? An exploratory analysis of the relationship between greenspace and health. *Environment and Planning A*, *35*(10), 1717–1731.

Ebenstein, A., Lavy, V., & Roth, S. (2016). The long-run economic consequences of high-stakes examinations: Evidence from transitory variation in pollution. *American Economic Journal: Applied Economics*, *8*(4), 36–65.

Fan, M., He, G., & Zhou, M. (2020). The winter choke: Coal-fired heating, air pollution, and mortality in China. *Journal of Health Economics*, *71*, 102316.

Fisher, J. C., Irvine, K. N., Bicknell, J. E., Hayes, W. M., Fernandes, D., Mistry, J., & Davies, Z. G. (2021). Perceived biodiversity, sound, naturalness and safety enhance the restorative quality and wellbeing benefits of green and blue space in a neotropical city. *Science of the Total Environment*, *755*, 143095.

Gunko, R., Rapeli, L., Vuorisalo, T., Scheinin, M., & Karell, P. (2022). Does water quality matter for life quality? A study of the impact of water quality on well-being in a coastal community. *Environmental Management*, *70*(3), 464–474.

Jones, B. A. (2020). Happiness and forest-attacking invasive alien species. In *Handbook on wellbeing, happiness and the environment* (pp. 144–163). Edward Elgar Publishing.

Kaplan, S. (1995). The restorative benefits of nature: Toward an integrative framework. *Journal of Environmental Psychology*, *15*(3), 169–182.

Keeler, B. L., Polasky, S., Brauman, K. A., Johnson, K. A., Finlay, J. C., O'Neill, A., Kovacs, K., & Dalzell, B. (2012). Linking water quality and well-being for improved assessment and valuation of ecosystem services. *Proceedings of the National Academy of Sciences*, *109*(45), 18619–18624.

Kellert, S. R., & Wilson, E. O. (1995). *The biophilia hypothesis*. Island press.

Kim, C., Jung, S. H., Kang, D. R., Kim, H. C., Moon, K. T., Hur, N. W., Shin, D. C., & Suh, I. (2010). Ambient particulate matter as a risk factor for suicide. *American Journal of Psychiatry*, *167*(9), 1100–1107.

Krekel, C., Kolbe, J., & Wüstemann, H. (2016). The greener, the happier? The effect of urban land use on residential well-being. *Ecological Economics*, *121*, 117–127.

Laffan, K. (2018). Every breath you take, every move you make: Visits to the outdoors and physical activity help to explain the relationship between air pollution and subjective wellbeing. *Ecological Economics*, *147*, 96–113.

Laffan, K. (2020). Green with satisfaction: The relationship between pro-environmental behaviours and subjective wellbeing. In *Handbook on wellbeing, happiness and the environment* (pp. 329–348). Edward Elgar Publishing.

Lamers, F., van Oppen, P., Comijs, H. C., Smit, J. H., Spinhoven, P., van Balkom, A. J., Nolen, W. A., Zitman, F. G., Beekman, A. T., & Penninx, B. W. (2011). Comorbidity patterns of anxiety and depressive disorders in a large cohort study: The Netherlands Study of Depression and Anxiety (NESDA). *The Journal of Clinical Psychiatry*, *72*(3), 3397.

Lehtoranta, V., & Louhi, P. (2021). Does conservation in Natura 2000 areas promote water quality improvement? Findings from a contingent valuation study on environmental benefits and residents' preferences. *Environmental Science & Policy*, *124*, 226–234.

Lercher, P., & Kofler, W. W. (1996). Behavioral and health responses associated with road traffic noise exposure along alpine through-traffic routes. *Science of the Total Environment*, *189*, 85–89.

Lewis, O., Ohrt, J., Toomey, T. M., Linich, K., Wymer, B., & Newton, T. (2022). A systematic review of nature-based counseling interventions to promote mental health and wellness. *Journal of Mental Health Counseling*, *44*(3), 191–208. https://doi.org/10.17744/mehc.44.3.01

Li, Y., Guan, D., Yu, Y., Westland, S., Wang, D., Meng, J., Wang, X., He, K., & Tao, S. (2019). A psychophysical measurement on subjective well-being and air pollution. *Nature Communications*, *10*(1), 5473.

Ma, L. (2017). Performance management and citizen satisfaction with the government: Evidence from Chinese municipalities. *Public Administration*, *95*(1), 39–59.

MacKerron, G., & Mourato, S. (2009). Life satisfaction and air quality in London. *Ecological Economics*, *68*(5), 1441–1453.

Maller, C., Townsend, M., Pryor, A., Brown, P., & St Leger, L. (2005). Healthy nature healthy people: "Contact with nature" as an upstream health promotion intervention for populations. *Health Promotion International*, *21*(1), 45–54. https://doi.org/10.1093/heapro/dai032

Maxfield, A. (2020). Testing the theoretical similarities between food and water insecurity: Buffering hypothesis and effects on mental wellbeing. *Social Science & Medicine*, *244*, 112412.

Mitchell, R., & Popham, F. (2008). Effect of exposure to natural environment on health inequalities: An observational population study. *The Lancet*, *372*(9650), 1655–1660.

Neller, A. H., & Neller, R. J. (2009). Environment well-being and human well-being. *Institutional Issues Involving Ethics and Justice*, *2*, 137.

Ogunbode, C. A., Doran, R., Hanss, D., Ojala, M., Salmela-Aro, K., van den Broek, K. L., Bhullar, N., Aquino, S. D., Marot, T., Schermer, J. A., Wlodarczyk, A., Lu, S., Jiang, F., Maran, D. A., Yadav, R., Ardi, R., Chegeni, R., Ghanbarian, E., Zand, S., . . . Karasu, M. (2022). Climate anxiety, wellbeing and pro-environmental action: Correlates of negative emotional responses to climate change in 32 countries. *Journal of Environmental Psychology*, *84*, 101887. https://doi.org/10.1016/j.jenvp.2022.101887

Pinto, U., Thoradeniya, B., & Maheshwari, B. (2020). Water quality and chronic kidney disease of unknown aetiology (CKDu) in the dry zone region of Sri Lanka: Impacts on well-being of village communities and the way forward. *Environmental Science and Pollution Research*, *27*, 3892–3907.

Power, M. C., Kioumourtzoglou, M.-A., Hart, J. E., Okereke, O. I., Laden, F., & Weisskopf, M. G. (2015). The relation between past exposure to fine particulate air pollution and prevalent anxiety: Observational cohort study. *BMJ*, *350*.

Prati, G., Albanesi, C., & Pietrantoni, L. (2017). The interplay among environmental attitudes, pro-environmental behavior, social identity, and pro-environmental institutional climate. A longitudinal study. *Environmental Education Research*, *23*(2), 176–191.

Roberts, A., Hinds, J., & Camic, P. M. (2020). Nature activities and wellbeing in children and young people: A systematic literature review. *Journal of Adventure Education and Outdoor Learning*, *20*(4), 298–318. https://doi.org/10.1080/14729679.2019.1660195

Ruckelshauß, T. (2020). The effect of green areas on life satisfaction: A comparison of subjective and objective measures. In *Handbook on wellbeing, happiness and the environment* (pp. 245–265). Edward Elgar Publishing.

Rzepa, A., & Pugliese, A. (2012). Water quality linked to well-being in Sub-Saharan Africa. *Gallup News*, December 6, from https://news.gallup.com/poll/159086/water-quality-linked-wellbeing-sub-saharan-africa.aspx.

Schmitt, M. T., Aknin, L. B., Axsen, J., & Shwom, R. L. (2018). Unpacking the relationships between pro-environmental behavior, life satisfaction, and perceived ecological threat. *Ecological Economics*, *143*, 130–140.

Shanahan, D. F., Astell–Burt, T., Barber, E. A., Brymer, E., Cox, D. T. C., Dean, J., Depledge, M., Fuller, R. A., Hartig, T., Irvine, K. N., Jones, A., Kikillus, H., Lovell, R., Mitchell, R., Niemelä, J., Nieuwenhuijsen, M., Pretty, L., Townsend, M., van Heezik, Y., Warber, S., & Gaston, K. J. (2019). Nature–based interventions for improving health and wellbeing: The purpose, the people and the outcomes. *Sports*, *7*(141), 1–20. https://doi.org/10.3390/sports7060141

Steigen, A. M., Kogstad, R., & Hummelvoll, J. K. (2016). Green care services in the Nordic countries: An integrative literature review. *European Journal of Social Work*, *19*(5), 692–715. https://doi.org/10.1080/13691457.2015.1082983

Ulrich, R. S., Simons, R. F., Losito, B. D., Fiorito, E., Miles, M. A., & Zelson, M. (1991). Stress recovery during exposure to natural and urban environments. *Journal of Environmental Psychology*, *11*(3), 201–230.

Van Praag, B. M., & Baarsma, B. E. (2005). Using happiness surveys to value intangibles: The case of airport noise. *The Economic Journal*, *115*(500), 224–246.

Wang, J., Wang, Y., Sun, C., & Chen, X. (2021). Does mandatory air quality information disclosure raise happiness? Evidence from China. *Energy Economics*, *94*, 105094.

Welsch, H. (2006). Environment and happiness: Valuation of air pollution using life satisfaction data. *Ecological Economics*, *58*(4), 801–813.

Welsch, H., & Kühling, J. (2018). How green self image is related to subjective well-being: Pro-environmental values as a social norm. *Ecological Economics*, *149*, 105–119.

White, M. P., Alcock, I., Wheeler, B. W., & Depledge, M. H. (2013). Would you be happier living in a greener urban area? A fixed-effects analysis of panel data. *Psychological Science*, *24*(6), 920–928.

Wolf, L. J., Zu Ermgassen, S., Balmford, A., White, M., & Weinstein, N. (2017). Is variety the spice of life? An experimental investigation into the effects of species richness on self-reported mental well-being. *PLoS One*, *12*(1), e0170225.

World Health Organization (2011). *Burden of disease from environmental noise – Quantification of healthy life years lost in Europe*. www.euro.who.int/__data/assets/pdf_file/0008/136466/e94888.pdf

Yang, D., Liu, X., Ren, Z., & Li, M. (2022). Relation between noise pollution and life satisfaction based on the 2019 Chinese social survey. *International Journal of Environmental Research and Public Health*, *19*(12), 7015.

Zawadzki, S. J., Steg, L., & Bouman, T. (2020). Meta-analytic evidence for a robust and positive association between individuals' pro-environmental behaviors and their subjective wellbeing. *Environmental Research Letters*, *15*(12), 123007.

Zhu, P., & Lin, B. (2022). Vanishing happiness: How does pollution information disclosure affect life satisfaction? *International Journal of Environmental Research and Public Health*, *19*(15), 9530.

12

(FEAR OF) CRIME AND WELLBEING

The role of individual and country-level determinants

Eva Krulichová

Introduction

Scientists have been looking for an answer to the question of how to increase people's quality of life and wellbeing for several decades. This is not an easy task, since both phenomena are known to be influenced by a number of individual factors ranging from unemployment, job satisfaction, and income to personal relationships and health (Hamplová, 2015). At a country level, determinants such as income inequality, economic performance, and unemployment rate have also been widely discussed (Di Tella & MacCulloch, 2008; Vauclair & Bratanova, 2016; Večerník & Mysíková, 2015). However, recent research has begun to focus more intently on factors associated with crime.

Initially, the consequences of crime for quality of life were mostly addressed by economists investigating the pecuniary costs of victimization,[1] such as loss of earnings and increased socioeconomic disadvantage. Nevertheless, more and more studies have gradually shifted their attention to the effect of crime on subjective wellbeing (SWB), as it has been found that victims of crime often suffer depression, anxiety and fear, and consequently, a decreased quality of life (Powdthavee, 2005).

In this chapter, we review existing evidence on the relationship between SWB, commonly measured as an individual's evaluation of life satisfaction and happiness, and crime-related phenomena, while paying special attention to both individual- and country-level determinants of SWB. Throughout the text, data from the European Social Survey Round 9 (ESS 9) complemented with country-level data from Eurostat and World Prison Brief are used to support existing findings and derive evidence-based interventions.

DOI: 10.4324/9781003382447-14

SWB and crime-related factors

The role of individual victimization experience, fear of crime, and its joint effect on SWB is well documented, as it has been confirmed in both cross-sectional (Hanslmaier, 2013; Michalos & Zumbo, 2000; Staubli et al., 2014) and longitudinal (Cornaglia et al., 2014; Dustmann & Fasani, 2016; Frijters et al., 2011) research. Victimization experience is also known to intensify fear of crime (e.g., Krulichová, 2018), which makes people more vulnerable to losses of physical, social, and economic resources (Killias & Clerici, 2000), and consequently lowers their SWB.

On the other hand, country-level determinants such as crime and prison population rates have generally been overlooked. This can partly be attributed to the fact that comparisons of official crime statistics across different countries and thus different justice systems are not without their shortcomings (Aebi, 2010). Nevertheless, studies addressing crime at a neighborhood level (e.g., Hanslmaier, 2013) suggest that crime is only weakly and often indirectly associated with SWB. Therefore, other crime-related factors and its association with SWB need to be further explored.

SWB, victimization experience, and perceived unsafety

Although some studies point to the relatively strong relationship between SWB and victimization, the findings remain mixed, especially with respect to the type of crime. Specifically, Sulemana (2015) found that both theft and physical assault influence SWB, while a study by Cohen (2008) only revealed an effect in the case of burglary (cf. Kuroki, 2013). Staubli et al. (2014) studied the effect of a wide range of victimization experiences and demonstrated life satisfaction to be negatively associated with theft, attempted burglary, and consumer fraud, as well as crimes against persons. Conversely, the effect of completed burglary and credit/debit card and identity fraud remained negligible. In addition, Michalos and Zumbo (2000) found that victimization contributes very little to explaining life satisfaction once other neighborhood characteristics were taken into account, and Møller (2005) confirmed the effect of victimization on SWB to be limited and easily replaceable by indicators of crime perception.

Accordingly, existing evidence proves more consistent with respect to fear of crime, perceived unsafety, and its association with SWB. The research repeatedly shows that those who fear crime or feel unsafe in their environment declare lower SWB (Franc et al., 2012; Hanslmaier, 2013; Medina & Tamayo, 2012). The association between perceived unsafety and happiness was also confirmed by Moore (2006), who, at the same time, reported no relationship between victimization and SWB, though this is likely due to crowding out via perceived unsafety (Hanslmaier, 2013). Indeed, support for the mediating effect of perceived unsafety and fear of crime in the victimization–SWB link has been found in a number of studies, suggesting that victims of crime report higher fear and unsafety, which is in turn associated with lower SWB (Brenig & Proeger, 2018; Johnston et al., 2018;

Krulichová, 2018). In other words, perceived unsafety seems to be one of the key mechanisms through which crime victimization affects SWB (Møller, 2005).

To illustrate the relationship between SWB, perceived unsafety, and victimization experience, we use data from the ESS 9.[2] Table 12.1 reports descriptive statistics of SWB as well as its correlation with the aforementioned factors.[3] The data suggest that the level of SWB significantly varies across European countries. The highest SWB is reported by residents of Northern countries and Switzerland. On the other end of the spectrum, we find Bulgaria, Hungary, and Slovakia.

In line with existing evidence, the relationship between perceived unsafety and SWB proved consistent across almost all analyzed European countries in the ESS. In these

TABLE 12.1 SWB, victimization, and perceived unsafety across Europe

		SWB		*Perceived unsafety*		*Victimization*	
		N	*Mean*	*Mean*	r_s	*Mean*	r_s
DK	Denmark	1572	8.40	1.54	−0.11***	0.22	0.03
IS	Island	861	8.18	1.46	−0.10**	0.14	−0.20***
CH	Switzerland	1542	8.16	1.62	−0.13***	0.17	−0.02
FI	Finland	1755	8.07	1.63	−0.15***	0.24	−0.04
NL	Netherlands	1673	7.95	1.92	−0.17***	0.15	−0.02
AT	Austria	2499	7.91	1.74	−0.18***	0.07	−0.01
NO	Norway	1406	7.90	1.47	−0.07**	0.15	−0.02
SE	Sweden	1539	7.84	1.71	−0.11***	0.21	−0.03
DE	Germany	2358	7.67	2.04	−0.17***	0.12	−0.06**
BE	Belgium	1767	7.64	1.97	−0.16***	0.23	−0.13***
ME	Montenegro	1200	7.62	1.69	−0.15***	0.08	0.00
ES	Spain	1668	7.56	1.99	−0.08***	0.27	−0.05*
IE	Ireland	2216	7.47	1.94	−0.11***	0.15	−0.06**
SI	Slovenia	1318	7.47	1.65	−0.18***	0.11	−0.06*
GB	Great Britain	2204	7.44	2.00	−0.13***	0.17	−0.13***
HR	Croatia	1810	7.27	1.66	−0.19***	0.04	−0.01
CY	Cyprus	781	7.26	1.96	−0.05	0.16	−0.06
EE	Estonia	1904	7.22	1.90	−0.14***	0.14	−0.04
PT	Portugal	1055	7.19	1.89	−0.23***	0.18	0.00
PL	Poland	1500	7.15	1.81	−0.15***	0.06	−0.04
CZ	Czechia	2398	7.05	2.07	−0.19***	0.09	−0.04
LV	Lithuania	1835	7.00	2.01	−0.11***	0.15	−0.03
IT	Italy	2745	6.95	2.22	−0.16***	0.14	0.02
FR	France	2010	6.94	1.93	−0.21***	0.21	−0.05*
LT	Latvia	918	6.70	2.22	−0.26***	0.09	−0.02
RS	Serbia	2043	6.68	1.93	−0.13***	0.12	0.01
SK	Slovakia	1083	6.57	2.05	−0.23***	0.05	0.00
HU	Hungary	1661	6.47	2.13	−0.16***	0.03	−0.05
BG	Bulgaria	2198	5.42	2.59	−0.27***	0.09	−0.05*

Source: ESS 9; $*p < 0.05$, $**p < 0.01$, $***p < 0.001$.

Note: SWB (0 = low SWB, 10 = high SWB), perceived unsafety (1 = very safe, 4 = very unsafe), victimization (0 = no, 1 = yes).

countries, with the exception of Cyprus, people who feel unsafe in their environment declare lower SWB than those who feel rather safe. On the other hand, the relationship between SWB and victimization experience is not unequivocal, as being victimized by crime is only associated with lower SWB in a select few of the analysed countries.

SWB, crime, and trust in criminal justice institutions

Although there is a wide range of studies that address the effect of individual victimization and perceived unsafety on SWB, there is a paucity of evidence on the role of crime in a given country. To our knowledge, one exception is a study by Di Tella and MacCulloch (2008), which revealed that the violent crime rate, measured by the number of serious assaults per 100,000 residents, decreased life satisfaction in 12 OECD nations. However, the relationship proved rather weak when considered in multiple regression models.

There are also studies that assess crime as a predictor of SWB at a neighbourhood level. For example, a study by Medina and Tamayo (2012) revealed a negative relationship between homicide rate and life satisfaction, while a higher arrest rate, defined as the ratio of arrests to homicides, was associated with an increase in life satisfaction. Hanslmaier (2013) also showed that county-level street crime, which captures different categories of sexual, violent, and property crimes committed on the street or in the public sphere, has a negative effect on life satisfaction (cf. Powdthavee, 2005), though the effect is crowded out by individual victimization and fear of crime. In a similar vein, Cohen (2008) found that violent crime rate turned insignificant once factors associated with neighbourhood safety were considered.

Given the limited effect of official crime on SWB, it is necessary to consider the possible effect of other crime-related determinants. A promising pathway is to examine the relationship between SWB and the level of trust at a national level, as higher levels of crime as well as fear of crime and perceived unsafety are likely to be reflected in both generalized and institutional distrust (Jang et al., 2010; Singer et al., 2019). Indeed, a study by Algan (2018) confirmed that higher life satisfaction in European countries is associated with higher trust in other people as well as in the judicial system (cf. Helliwell et al., 2016). Nevertheless, this area of research remains surprisingly unexplored.

Figure 12.1 demonstrates the bivariate relationships between SWB and four country-level factors: homicide (Eurostat, 2023) and prison population (World Prison Brief, 2023) rates and trust in the police and legal system, both calculated as mean values of individual trust in the ESS data. SWB is significantly associated with all country-level characteristics. People declare that they are happier and more satisfied with their lives in countries with less homicide and, surprisingly, lower prison population rates. Nevertheless, the effect of homicide rate is relatively weak. Conversely, factors other than official crime levels seem to exhibit an even stronger association with SWB, as the higher the trust in the police and legal system, the higher the SWB in European countries.

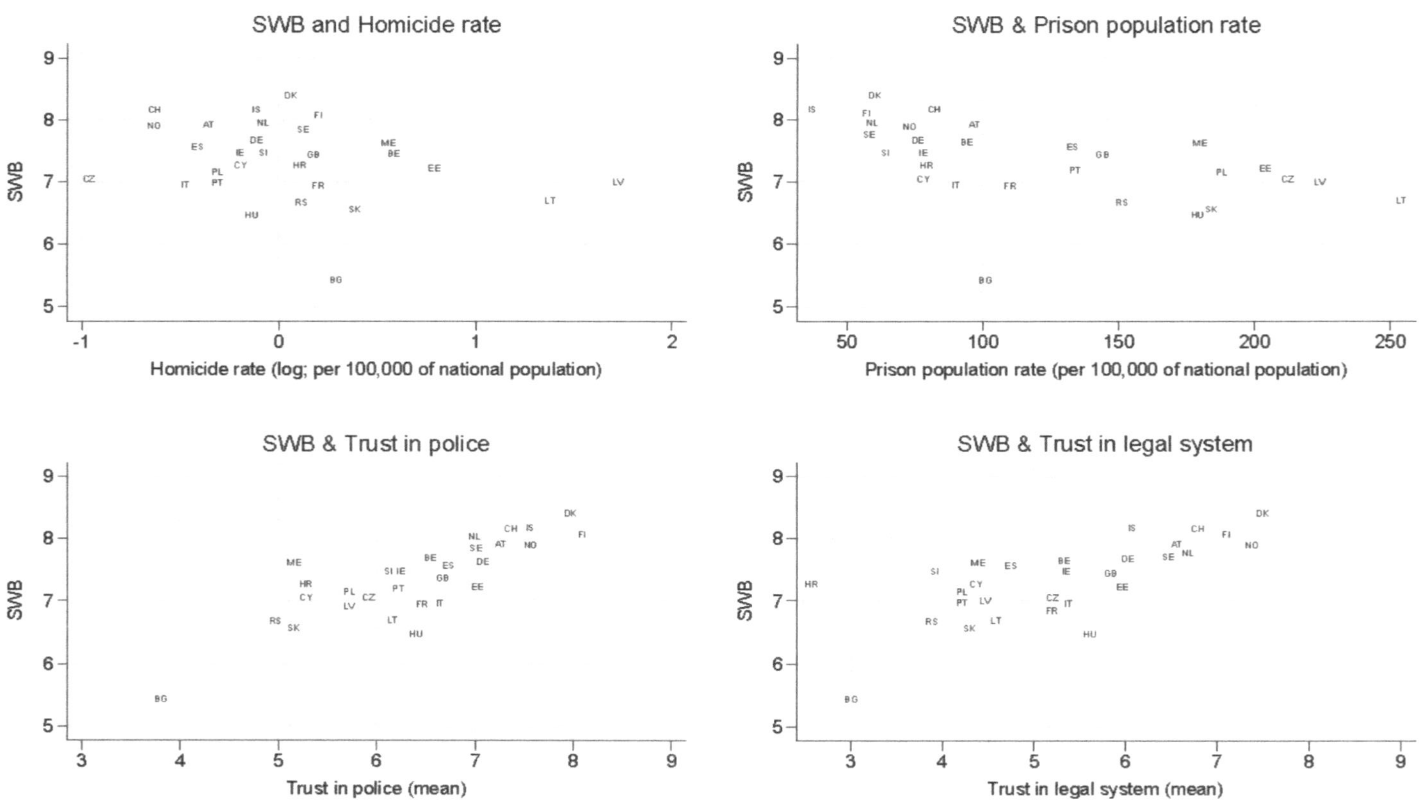

FIGURE 12.1 SWB, crime, and trust in criminal justice institutions across Europe.

Source: ESS 9, World Prison Brief (Prison population rate), Eurostat (Homicide rate).

Note: $r_{s(\text{Homicide rate (log)})} = -0.225$; $r_{s(\text{Prison population rate})} = -0.688$; $r_{s(\text{Trust in police})} = 0.776$; $r_{s(\text{Trust in legal system})} = 0.735$.

Discussion and conclusion

There are several lessons to be learned from this chapter. The relationship between fear of crime, perceived unsafety, and SWB is relatively strong and consistent, as respondents who feel unsafe report lower SWB compared to their counterparts. Conversely, a direct association between SWB and victimization highly depends on the type of crime in question (e.g., Staubli et al., 2014) and generally remains relatively weak or even non-existent. Nevertheless, the indirect effect of victimization on SWB through higher unsafety and fear has been well documented (Brenig & Proeger, 2018; Hanslmaier, 2013). Similar to individual victimization, the effect of official crime rates remains limited. Neither a lower number of homicides nor crime prevention, including incarceration level, necessarily translates into higher SWB. Conversely, a relatively strong association was found between SWB and institutional trust, as countries whose residents report relatively high trust in the police and the country´s legal system experience higher SWB than countries on the other end of the trust spectrum.

In line with the systematic review by Lorenc et al. (2012), we can conclude that there is limited evidence regarding the effects of crime reduction on wellbeing. Consequently, it remains difficult to assess the extent to which narrowly focused interventions on crime prevention can result in an improved quality of life. Some authors suggest that a promising avenue for enhancing wellbeing could be through interventions aimed at reducing fear of crime and perceived unsafety, both at an individual level and within the broader context of community life (Lorenc et al., 2013; Møller, 2005).

In their reflections on interventions and strategies to enhance the feeling of safety, Donder et al. (2010) identify three key actors: individuals, police, and the government. First, individuals themselves should adopt protective measures such as securing their homes by installing alarms, locks, and lights (e.g., Lorenc et al., 2013). At this point, however, we should bear in mind that the possibilities of responsibilization have their limits depending on the individual's social and economic vulnerability, which is also often the result of life in disadvantaged neighbourhoods that struggle with higher crime rates and social incivilities (Skogan & Maxfield, 1981). In this respect, neighbourhood initiatives vying for increased social cohesion and the improvement of informal social control within the neighbourhood play a crucial role in fear of crime reduction. Next, the police should focus on active community policing and providing information about crime and crime prevention strategies. More importantly, however, the police should make a concerted effort to enhance people´s feeling of safety in their environment. This can be achieved, for example, by establishing fair and respectful cooperation with members of the community and thus strengthening peoples′ confidence in this institution and criminal justice in general (Jackson & Bradford, 2010; Jackson et al., 2009). Finally, the government both directly and indirectly influences the living conditions of neighbourhoods and their inhabitants. As Donder et al. (2010) put forth, for decades, safety has only been understood in terms of crime prevention. However, existing evidence suggests that in addition to tackling crime and improving the built environment (Lorenc et al., 2012), attention needs to be paid to broader policies, such as those targeting social and economic vulnerability, as well as the reinforcement of social capital and social networks, including the level of trust in society (Jackson, 2009; Lorenc et al., 2014).

Actionable points

- Higher SWB can be accomplished through individual and neighbourhood initiatives aimed at enhancing security systems within a community and improving the quality of the built environment (e.g., community surveillance systems, access control measures, lighting, and environmental design). Further, it is important to foster cooperation between the police and community members and support neighbourhood cohesion and informal social control by encouraging community engagement and volunteerism.
- The government/policy-makers should focus on reducing social and economic vulnerability (e.g., through implementing social safety nets, expanding access to quality healthcare and education, and creating job training and employment programs for populations at risk). Additionally, efforts should be directed toward promoting social capital by investing in programs that enhance social cohesion and a sense of belonging and strengthening institutional trust in society. This can be achieved by promoting transparency and accountability in government operations, ensuring fair and impartial law enforcement and justice systems, and implementing policies that combat corruption and promote ethical behaviour in public institutions.
- Policy-makers should refrain from implementing repressive interventions and stringent anti-crime measures leading to higher imprisonment rates, as people report higher SWB in countries with less punitive criminal justice systems. Instead, they should focus on alternative methods like rehabilitation, community-based initiatives, and restorative justice programs that are more likely to promote subjective wellbeing.

Notes

1 Victimization is the act of causing someone to become a victim, often through harm, injury, or negative experiences resulting from crime or mistreatment.
2 ESS Round 9: European Social Survey Round 9 Data (2018). Data file edition 3.1. Sikt – Norwegian Agency for Shared Services in Education and Research, Norway – Data Archive and distributor of ESS data for ESS ERIC. doi:10.21338/NSD-ESS9-2018.
3 SWB was measured as an index constructed from the respondents' answers to questions about their life satisfaction and happiness on a 10-point scale, where 10 = high SWB. Perceived unsafety was measured by asking respondents how safe they feel walking alone in their neighbourhood after dark on a 4-point scale, where 4 = very unsafe, and victimization experience was constructed as a binary variable to identify individuals who were directly or indirectly (household) victimized by burglary or physical assault over the previous 5 years.

References

Aebi, M. F. (2010). Methodological issues in the comparison of police-recorded crime rates. In *International handbook of criminology* (pp. 237–254). Routledge. https://doi.org/10.1201/9781420085525-16

Algan, Y. (2018). Trust and social capital. In J. E. Stiglitz, J.-P. Fitoussi, & M. Durand (Eds.), *For good measure: Advancing research on well-being metrics beyond GDP* (pp. 283–320). OECD. https://doi.org/10.1787/9789264307278-12-en

Brenig, M., & Proeger, T. (2018). Putting a price tag on security: Subjective well-being and willingness-to-pay for crime reduction in Europe. *Journal of Happiness Studies*, *19*(1), 145–166. https://doi.org/10.1007/s10902-016-9814-1

Cohen, M. A. (2008). The effect of crime on life satisfaction. *The Journal of Legal Studies*, *37*(S2), 325–353. https://doi.org/10.1086/588220

Cornaglia, F., Feldman, N. E., & Leigh, A. (2014). Crime and mental well-being. *Journal of Human Resources*, *49*(1), 110–140. https://doi.org/10.3368/jhr.49.1.110

Di Tella, R., & MacCulloch, R. (2008). Gross national happiness as an answer to the Easterlin Paradox? *Journal of Development Economics*, *86*(1), 22–42. https://doi.org/10.1016/J.JDEVECO.2007.06.008

Donder, L. D., Verte, D., Witte, N. D., Buffel, T., & Dury, S. (2010). Reflections about interventions and strategies on increasing feelings of safety in later life. *International Journal of Social Sciences and Humanity Studies*, *2*(1), 83–89.

Dustmann, C., & Fasani, F. (2016). The effect of local area crime on mental health. *The Economic Journal*, *126*(593), 978–1017. https://doi.org/10.1111/ecoj.12205

Eurostat (2023, April 23). *Intentional homicide and sexual offences by legal status and sex of the person involved – Number and rate for the relevant sex group*. https://ec.europa.eu/eurostat/databrowser/view/crim_hom_soff/default/table?lang=en

Franc, R., Prizmic-Larsen, Z., & Lipovčan, L. K. (2012). Personal security and fear of crime as predictors of subjective well-being. In D. Webb & E. Wills-Herrera (Eds.), *Subjective well-being and security* (pp. 45–67). Springer. https://doi.org/10.1007/978-94-007-2278-1_4

Frijters, P., Johnston, D. W., & Shields, M. A. (2011). Life satisfaction dynamics with quarterly life event data. *Scandinavian Journal of Economics*, *113*(1), 190–211. https://doi.org/10.1111/j.1467-9442.2010.01638.x

Hamplová, D. (2015). *Proč potřebujeme rodinu, práci a přátele – Štěstí ze sociologické perspektivy*. Fortuna Libri.

Hanslmaier, M. (2013). Crime, fear and subjective well-being: How victimization and street crime affect fear and life satisfaction. *European Journal of Criminology*, *10*(5), 515–533. https://doi.org/10.1177/1477370812474545

Helliwell, J. F., Huang, H., & Wang, S. (2016). *New evidence on trust and well-being* (Working Paper 22450). Cambridge. https://doi.org/10.3386/w22450

Jackson, J. (2009). A psychological perspective on vulnerability in the fear of crime. *Psychology, Crime & Law*, *15*(4), 365–390. https://doi.org/10.1080/10683160802275797

Jackson, J., & Bradford, B. (2010). What is trust and confidence in the police? *Policing*, *4*(3), 241–248. https://doi.org/10.1093/police/paq020

Jackson, J., Bradford, B., Hohl, K., & Farrall, S. (2009). Does the fear of crime erode public confidence in policing? *Policing*, *3*(1), 100–111. https://doi.org/10.1093/police/pan079

Jang, H., Joo, H.-J., & Zhao, J. (Solomon) (2010). Determinants of public confidence in police: An international perspective. *Journal of Criminal Justice*, *38*(1), 57–68. https://doi.org/10.1016/J.JCRIMJUS.2009.11.008

Johnston, D. W., Shields, M. A., & Suziedelyte, A. (2018). Victimisation, well-being and compensation: Using panel data to estimate the costs of violent crime. *The Economic Journal*, *128*(611), 1545–1569. https://doi.org/10.1111/ecoj.12478

Killias, M., & Clerici, C. (2000). Different measures of vulnerability in their relation to different dimensions of fear of crime. *British Journal of Criminology*, *40*(3), 437–450. https://doi.org/10.1093/bjc/40.3.437

Krulichová, E. (2018). Life satisfaction and happiness: Discussing the impact of fear of crime and victimization. *Acta Universitatis Carolinae Philosophica et Historica*, *24*(2), 23–37.

Kuroki, M. (2013). Crime victimization and subjective well-being: Evidence from happiness data. *Journal of Happiness Studies*, *14*(3), 783–794. https://doi.org/10.1007/s10902-012-9355-1

Lorenc, T., Clayton, S., Neary, D., Whitehead, M., Petticrew, M., Thomson, H., Cummins, S., Sowden, A., & Renton, A. (2012). Crime, fear of crime, environment, and mental health and wellbeing: Mapping review of theories and causal pathways. *Health & Place*, *18*(4), 757–765. https://doi.org/10.1016/j.healthplace.2012.04.001

Lorenc, T., Petticrew, M., Whitehead, M., Neary, D., Clayton, S., Wright, K., Thomson, H., Cummins, S., Sowden, A., & Renton, A. (2013). Environmental interventions to reduce fear of crime: Systematic review of effectiveness. *Systematic Reviews*, *2*(1), 30. https://doi.org/10.1186/2046-4053-2-30

Lorenc, T., Petticrew, M., Whitehead, M., Neary, D., Clayton, S., Wright, K., Thomson, H., Cummins, S., Sowden, A., & Renton, A. (2014). Crime, fear of crime and mental health: Synthesis of theory and systematic reviews of interventions and qualitative evidence. *Public Health Research*, *2*(2), 1–398.

Medina, C., & Tamayo, J. A. (2012). An assessment of how urban crime and victimization affects life satisfaction. In D. Webb & E. Wills-Herrera (Eds.), *Subjective well-being and security* (pp. 91–147). Springer. https://doi.org/10.1007/978-94-007-2278-1_6

Michalos, A. C., & Zumbo, B. D. (2000). Criminal victimization and the quality of life. *Social Indicators Research*, *50*(3), 245–295. https://doi.org/10.1023/A:1006930019814

Møller, V. (2005). Resilient or resigned? Criminal victimisation and quality of life in South Africa. *Social Indicators Research*, *72*(3), 263–317. https://doi.org/10.1007/s11205-004-5584-y

Moore, S. C. (2006). The value of reducing fear: An analysis using the European social survey. *Applied Economics*, *38*(1), 115–117. https://doi.org/10.1080/00036840500368094

Powdthavee, N. (2005). Unhappiness and crime: Evidence from South Africa. *Economica*, *72*(287), 531–547. https://doi.org/10.1111/j.0013-0427.2005.00429.x

Singer, A. J., Chouhy, C., Lehmann, P. S., Walzak, J. N., Gertz, M., & Biglin, S. (2019). Victimization, fear of crime, and trust in criminal justice institutions: A cross-national analysis. *Crime & Delinquency*, *65*(6), 822–844. https://doi.org/10.1177/0011128718787513

Skogan, W. G., & Maxfield, M. G. (1981). *Coping with crime: Individual and neighborhood reactions*. Sage.

Staubli, S., Killias, M., & Frey, B. S. (2014). Happiness and victimization: An empirical study for Switzerland. *European Journal of Criminology*, *11*(1), 57–72. https://doi.org/10.1177/1477370813486866

Sulemana, I. (2015). The effect of fear of crime and crime victimization on subjective well-being in Africa. *Social Indicators Research*, *121*(3), 849–872. https://doi.org/10.1007/s11205-014-0660-4

Vauclair, C.-M., & Bratanova, B. (2016). Income inequality and fear of crime across the European region. *European Journal of Criminology*. https://doi.org/10.1177/1477370816648993

Večerník, J., & Mysíková, M. (2015). GDP and life satisfaction in European countries – Focus on transition. *Post-Communist Economies*, *27*(2), 170–187. https://doi.org/10.1080/14631377.2015.1026687

World Prison Brief (2023, April 23). *World prison brief data*. www.prisonstudies.org/world-prison-brief-data

13

DEMOCRACY AND WELLBEING

Alois Stutzer, Benjamin Jansen, and Tobias Schib

Introduction

The overarching goal of democracy as one of the most fundamental social inventions of humankind is to provide an institutional framework for people to pursue their ideas of the good life in areas where collective action is required. However, whether this expectation can be fulfilled might depend very much on the design of the democratic rules. In fact, political economic theory has developed many propositions about the behavior of different actors in different democratic settings and its consequences for people's welfare. Measuring the actual effects of democratic norms and behaviors on subjective wellbeing (SWB) helps to assess these theoretical claims (see, e.g., Frey & Stutzer, 2019). This chapter focuses on links between different aspects of democracy and SWB. Related reviews provide important findings about many more institutional aspects like the influence of corruption control, legal equality, property rights, monetary policy, economic liberties, the rule of law, or social norms (see, e.g., Berggren & Bjørnskov, 2020; Rode, 2013) and about various public policy topics (Odermatt & Stutzer, 2018). We consider it topical and of high societal value to better understand the mechanisms that connect democratic institutions to people's perceived life satisfaction. Insights might ideally help to counter political alienation and rising support for political leaders who are openly trying to undermine horizontal, vertical, and temporal separations of powers.

To start with, we briefly clarify our understanding of democracy. We then provide a short introduction to two conceptionally distinguishable sources of utility that can be derived from democracy, that is, outcome-based and procedural utility. Against this background, we summarize empirical findings on how different forms of democracy are associated with individuals' wellbeing.

DOI: 10.4324/9781003382447-15

The concept of democracy

Democracy comes in many forms, ranging from participatory to illiberal democracy. The concept of democracy should thus be understood in a multidimensional way, with dimensions accounting for graduations rather than binary features. Accordingly, the catalog of the relevant dimensions of democracy differs depending on the context and the school of thought. The most commonly used conceptualizations, though, coincide on three main aspects that best capture the fundamental core of democracy (for a detailed review, see Boese et al., 2022). The first two of these dimensions refer to political contestation and popular participation. Whereas the aspect of political contestation sometimes gets subsumed under the more tangible criterion of open and fair elections, the aspect of popular participation is more complex, involving concepts like inclusion, suffrage extensiveness, or self-government. The third aspect captures the existence of constitutional constraints to executive power. It is less of a main pillar of democracy itself but can be understood as a dimension that refers to what restrictions are in place to ensure that decision-making authorities cannot abuse their power to manipulate the political process in a way that undermines the basic aspects of political contestation and popular participation.

With regard to the question of how different aspects of democracy affect people's wellbeing, the mentioned dimensions are well suited for discussing the propositions from traditional political and economic theory that mainly emphasize an outcome-based perspective as well as the ideas in theories of participatory democracy that also consider more direct procedural effects.

Outcome-based versus procedural utility

Political economic theory provides a clear hypothesis on how democratic institutions affect people's wellbeing. Constitutionally assured competitive elections and different kinds of separation of powers, like the personnel division between judicial, executive, and legislative authorities, or a federal structure that assures a minimum of local autonomy, break the political elites' monopoly so that the people in charge of governmental decision-making are more likely to respond to the preferences of at least a critical mass of "the people". Democratic decision-making is expected to lead to an allocation and distribution of (governmental) resources that increase welfare compared to a situation with an authoritarian ruler in place. This effect refers to a channel on how democracy affects individuals' wellbeing that focuses on what can be described as *outcome-based utility*. While the examples here are manyfold, one could easily think of differences in the provision of services in the areas of public healthcare, public security and education, or social transfers. Government activities in these areas typically account for large shares of governmental spending in Western democracies.

A complementary source of utility is procedural utility. The idea is that people not only value the consequences of a specific decision-making process but also the process itself. People gain wellbeing from living and acting under institutionalized processes, as this contributes to a positive sense of self by addressing their innate needs for autonomy, relatedness, and competence (for an introductory review, see Frey et al., 2004). In the context of politics, Lane (1988) refers to procedural goods of democracy when people feel respected and treated with dignity and perceive some personal control, understanding, and public resonance.

Forms of democracy and their effects on wellbeing

Composite indicators of democracy

To empirically illuminate the most general relations between democracy and wellbeing, correlational analyses build on composite indicators that can account for the multidimensionality of democracy. These indicators typically consist of several submeasures, ideally capturing distinct (but mostly not fully independent) dimensions of democracy aggregated in one way or another. In the following, we draw on the widely used Variety of Democracy indices from the V-Dem Institute (2023). Its five core indices attempt to capture each of five different "high principle components" where the first resulting index – namely, the one measuring the presence of fair and extensive elections (polyarchy index) – is incorporated within each of the other four indices since it clearly represents a necessary condition for the concept of democracy (Coppedge et al., 2023).

Figure 13.1 shows a scatter plot setting the extent of democracy according to the V-Dem democracy indices[1] in perspective to the mean life satisfaction in a country.

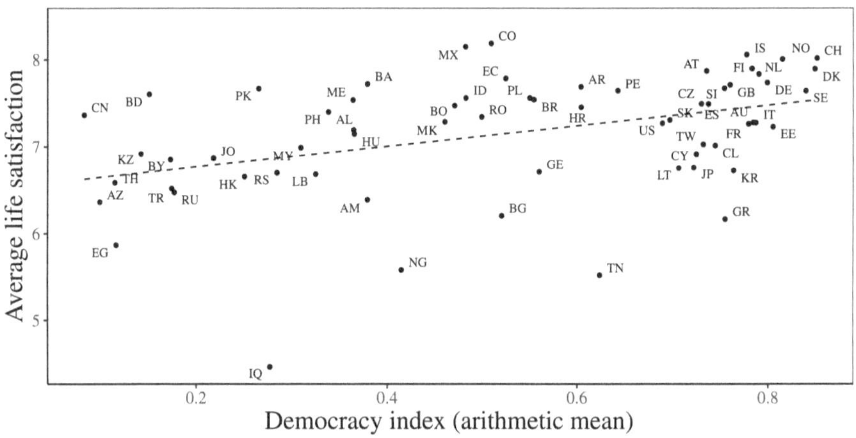

FIGURE 13.1 Democracy and wellbeing across nations in 2017–19.

Sources: EVS/WVS (2022); V-Dem Institute (2023).

Notes: The y-axis shows the average life satisfaction on a scale from 1 to 10 computed using the most recent wave of the World Values Survey jointly with the European Values Study taking survey weights into account. The x-axis shows the arithmetic mean of the five high-level V-Dem democracy indices, ranging from 0 to 1. Data points by country refer to the most recent survey year available before 2020.

Data on reported life satisfaction on a scale from 1 "completely dissatisfied" to 10 "completely satisfied" for 64 countries is taken from the most recent wave of the World Values Survey (2017–2022). Overall, a clear positive correlation is observed.

The related existing literature, however, suggests that the relationship between democracy and SWB is less clear. In the survey on institutions and life satisfaction by Berggren and Bjørnskov (2020), a significant number of studies find no robust relationship between democracy and life satisfaction. Others find a positive relationship. The mixed empirical evidence might be attributed to various reasons. Berggren and Bjørnskov (2020) point out that a certain level of prosperity might be necessary for democratic rights to contribute to greater life satisfaction, emphasizing complementarities between country characteristics and basic institutions. We argue that there are two other potentially important reasons. First, there is a high risk of incorporating "bad controls" when empirically looking at the relationship between democracy and SWB. Several cross-country studies control for factors such as economic prosperity or inequality, both of which are potentially a consequence of democratic transition. Second, it is both theoretically and empirically unclear how quickly the effects of democratization materialize into higher wellbeing, as there are no studies that examine the dynamic aspects of this relationship.

Table 13.1 provides an illustration of the two arguments. Specification (1) captures the strong positive correlation between the extent of democracy and average

TABLE 13.1 Democracy and life satisfaction across countries in 2017–2019

Dependent variable: Life satisfaction (avg.)	(1)	(2)	(3)	(4)
Democracy	1.2041***	0.9091**	0.7075	
	(0.3091)	(0.4335)	(0.4358)	
Human development		1.1071		
		(1.6203)		
Government effectiveness			0.2050	
			(0.1740)	
Democracy_{1985}				1.3132***
				(0.3188)
$\Delta\ \text{Democracy}_{t-1985}$				0.7342**
				(0.3661)
Constant	6.5269***	5.7636***	6.6825***	6.5760***
	(0.2002)	(1.2368)	(0.1716)	(0.1975)
R-squared	0.1682	0.1809	0.2016	0.1986
Observations	63	63	63	63

Sources: EVS/WVS (2022); V-Dem Institute (2023); HDI (2022); WGI (2022).

Notes: Standard errors are heteroscedasticity robust in all specifications. In contrast to data in Figure 13.1, Taiwan is not included due to missing information on the HDI. Significance levels: ** $0.05 \geq p > 0.01$, *** $0.01 \geq p$.

life satisfaction shown in Figure 13.1. For a difference in the level of democracy of 0.6 units of the composite V-Dem index – reflecting roughly the difference between the United Kingdom and Russia – a 0.72-point higher life satisfaction is reported, on average. The size of the estimated coefficient decreases significantly when either the UN's human development index or the World Bank's government effectiveness indicator is included in Specifications (2) and (3). In the latter case, the index for democracy is no longer statistically significantly associated with life satisfaction. However, it is important to note that the interpretation of the coefficient for democracy changes when control variables that could be an outcome of democratic transition are included. For example, when a measure of government effectiveness is included, many of the positive outcomes of democracy are captured (and statistically accounted for) by the additional covariate. As a result, the V-Dem coefficient no longer represents the potential overall wellbeing effect of democratic institutions. Specification (4) demonstrates the idea of potential dynamic effects of democratic transition by examining the relationship between the current level of life satisfaction in a country with the degree of democracy in 1985 (i.e., before the collapse of the Soviet Union and Yugoslavia) and the change in democracy from 1985 to today. The results suggest that a stock of democracy or a democratic heritage is positively associated with life satisfaction. In a country with a current high level of democracy (0.8 on the index) that builds on an equally high level in 1985, people, on average, report a 0.79-unit higher life satisfaction when compared to people in an autocracy (0.2 on the index now and in 1985). However, if democratization was recent and the situation in 1985 was non-democratic (0.2 on the index), the difference to people in a country that remained autocratic is estimated to be only 0.44 units. This finding suggests that the formation of formal and informal democratic institutions since 1985, for example, in countries like Poland or the Czech Republic, may require more time to fully manifest in enhanced wellbeing.

Electoral system

Two constitutional choices that fundamentally shape the form and functioning of democracies refer to (1) the checks and balances between the legislative and the executive branch when selecting either a presidential or a parliamentary system and (2) the electoral process when choosing either a proportional or a majoritarian voting system. These design choices for democracy have several consequences, including how the public's preferences are translated into political representation and the incentives that the representatives have in policy-making, both of which may shape citizens' wellbeing. Altman et al. (2017) examined the impact of the institutionalization of democracy on SWB in a cross-country study of 21 OECD countries, using national samples from the World Values Survey covering the period from 1981 to 2008. They find that life satisfaction is higher in parliamentarian systems and under proportional representation, which may indicate that political gridlocks (in presidential systems) and poor representation of the citizenry (under majoritarian voting) decrease wellbeing.

However, the empirical analysis relied on a cross-sectional design so that many (unobservable) country characteristics could not be taken into account.

Direct democracy

The use of direct democratic institutions for major policy and constitutional choices has been a subject of heated debate and controversy, not least since the Brexit vote in the UK in 2016. In evaluating direct democracy, Frey and Stutzer (2000) introduced two initial arguments for why it could benefit individual wellbeing. Their first argument is outcome based and considers direct democracy to be associated with policies more closely aligned with citizens' preferences, either directly through citizen initiatives or indirectly through improved monitoring and control of policy-makers through referendums. Their second argument is that citizens value the procedural aspect of direct democratic rights per se. Based on cross-sectional survey data from roughly 6,000 individuals in 1992–1994, they provide empirical evidence of higher average life satisfaction in Swiss cantons with more direct democratic rights. Moreover, the positive partial correlation turned out larger for Swiss citizens than for foreigners. Given that both groups benefit from the same improvements in the provision of public goods and services, the differential effect is attributed to the procedural benefits of direct democracy. While the positive correlation for the initial data set was replicated, the size of the positive correlation turned out sensitive to the inclusion of variables capturing cultural differences across Switzerland (with estimates close to zero for two data sets covering the years 2000–2002 and 2006) (Dorn et al., 2008; Stadelmann-Steffen & Vatter, 2012).

While the main focus of the research for Switzerland is on the rules-in-form (formal legal rules), a study for the United States emphasizes the rules-in-use (working rules). In their work studying data from the DDB Life Style Survey 1985–1998, Radcliff and Shufeldt (2016) find a positive relationship between the cumulative number of initiatives in US states and people's reported satisfaction with life. Interestingly, this positive correlation is most pronounced for low-income people.

Finally, in the development context, Olken (2010) evaluates different democratic processes based on a field experiment. Before development projects were chosen in 49 Indonesian villages, responsibility for the decisions was randomly assigned either to delegated representatives or to all villagers deciding in direct ballot voting. While there was little difference in the projects chosen, villagers who had a direct say in the project selection reported a much higher level of satisfaction with their choice, expected to benefit more, and were more likely to consider the proposal fair.

Federalism

The allocation of decision-making, financing, and spending powers in a multi-layered state organization is a fundamental constitutional issue in democratic systems. The economic theory of federalism suggests that decentralization may contribute to increased wellbeing among individuals due to a more effective and efficient provision of public goods and services. However, it is also argued that centralization would secure economies of scale, with differences in preferences for local public goods being minor, and prevent a race to the bottom in public service delivery as well as an expansion of corruption and the shadow economy (see Martínez-Vázquez et al., 2017 for a review of these arguments). Notwithstanding which indirect mechanism dominates, citizens may additionally derive direct benefits from local autonomy in a decentralized system in the form of procedural utility, for example, through empowerment, a sense of community, and involvement in local politics.

Empirical research on this nexus has evolved over time, starting with cross-sectional studies. Based on data from the early 1990s across Swiss cantons, Frey and Stutzer (2000) document a positive correlation between local autonomy (i.e., the independence of a municipality from its cantonal authority) and people's life satisfaction. Turning to cross-country evidence, Bjørnskov et al. (2008) do not find a systematic relationship across 66 countries between subnational autonomy and life satisfaction using data from the World Values Survey. Based on repeated cross-sectional data from the European Social Survey and a fixed effects estimation strategy, Diaz-Serrano and Rodríguez-Pose (2012) find a positive correlation between regional self-rule and individuals' life satisfaction. The most methodologically advanced study on the relationship between decentralization and wellbeing to date is from Flèche (2021), who used a difference-in-differences design to examine the welfare effects of staggered centralization reforms in Swiss cantons between 2001 and 2012. The study finds that exposure to centralization is associated with an average decrease in life satisfaction equivalent to 4.36% of a standard deviation.

Discussion

Research on democracy and wellbeing has taken at least two different paths. One tries to capture the interaction of different aspects of democratic systems and link them to people's SWB in cross-country studies. This approach makes it possible to measure and study the net effects of various democratic processes in several countries. However, it is difficult to draw conclusions about the importance of individual democratic institutions. The other approach attempts to do just that and focuses on individual aspects of democratic constitutions. While the interaction of these aspects with other institutions is challenging to study, it opens up the possibility of using methodologically more rigorous approaches to get closer to the causal effects of democratic institutions on wellbeing.

The empirical challenges in this research loom large. While the action perspective is concerned with the consequences of democracy, empirical regularities might also reflect reverse causality. For example, Inglehart and Klingemann (2000) prominently argue that satisfied people would foster and sustain democracy. Thus, the researcher of human wellbeing has to deal with self-reinforcing interrelations and potentially long time lags between institutional change and reactions in empirical proxies of individual welfare. As data with longer time series become available for more countries in the coming years, it should become possible to study more aspects of democratic institutions in combined longitudinal cross-sectional analyses. Many empirical tests from the literature should then be replicated carefully dealing with the inclusion of possible control variables to avoid a "bad controls problem".

Actionable points

Democratic reform is one of the most demanding undertakings. However, the potential benefits of suitable democratic rules for people's wellbeing can barely be overrated. It is the form of democracy that largely shapes collective action. And it is the democratic processes that give citizens a sense of agency, counteracting political alienation and helplessness. Obviously, however, there is no blueprint for democratic reforms. The existing work on democracy and wellbeing rather points to the importance of a continuous search for better institutions when designing a plan for wellbeing. The future search could go in the following directions.

- Gather additional evidence on which form of democracy is best for people across a wide range of contexts.
- Specifically, further investigate proportional representation, direct democratic participation, and decentralized decision-making powers in federal systems as promising candidates for good rules.
- Explore additional institutional features that enable the inclusion and representation of the preferences of broad segments of the population that have particular potential for ensuring sustained high levels of wellbeing.

Acknowledgment

We are grateful to Marc Pouget for his excellent research assistance.

Note

1 Here, not one specific index is used; the arithmetic mean of all five core indices is considered.

References

Altman, D., Flavin, P., & Radcliff, B. (2017). Democratic institutions and subjective well-being. *Political Studies*, *65*(3), 685–704. https://doi.org/10.1177/0032321716683203

Berggren, N., & Bjørnskov, C. (2020). Institutions and life satisfaction. In K. F. Zimmermann (Ed.), *Handbook of labor, human resources and population economics* (pp. 1–48). Springer. https://doi.org/10.1007/978-3-319-57365-6_192-1

Bjørnskov, C., Dreher, A., & Fischer, J. A. V. (2008). On decentralization and life satisfaction. *Economics Letters*, *99*(1), 147–151. https://doi.org/10.1016/j.econlet.2007.06.016

Boese, V. A., Gates, S., Knutsen, C. H., Nygård, H. M., & Strand, H. (2022). Patterns of democracy over space and time. *International Studies Quarterly*, *66*(3). https://doi.org/10.1093/isq/sqac041

Coppedge, M., Gerring, J., Knutsen, C. H., Lindberg, S. I., Teorell, J., Marquardt, K. L., Medzihorsky, J., Pemstein, D., Gastaldi, L., Grahn, S., Pernes, J., Rydén, O., von Römer, J., Tzelgov, E., Wang, Y.-t., & Wilson, S. (2023). *"V-Dem methodology v13" varieties of democracy (V-Dem) project*. www.v-dem.net/documents/26/methodology_v13.pdf

Diaz-Serrano, L., & Rodríguez-Pose, A. (2012). Decentralization, subjective well-being, and the perception of institutions. *Kyklos*, *65*(2), 179–193. https://doi.org/10.1111/j.1467-6435.2012.00533.x

Dorn, D., Fischer, J. A., Kirchgässner, G., & Sousa-Poza, A. (2008). Direct democracy and life satisfaction revisited: New evidence for Switzerland. *Journal of Happiness Studies*, *9*(2), 227–255. https://doi.org/10.1007/s10902-007-9050-9

EVS/WVS (2022). European values study and World Values Survey: Joint EVS/WVS 2017–2022 dataset (Joint EVS/WVS). *JD Systems Institute & WVSA*. Dataset Version 4.0.0. https://doi.org/10.14281/18241.21

Flèche, S. (2021). The welfare consequences of centralization: Evidence from a quasinatural experiment in Switzerland. *Review of Economics and Statistics*, *103*(4), 621–635. https://doi.org/10.1162/rest_a_00894

Frey, B. S., Benz, M., & Stutzer, A. (2004). Introducing procedural utility: Not only what, but also how matters. *Journal of Institutional and Theoretical Economics*, *160*(3), 377–401. www.jstor.org/stable/40752468

Frey, B. S., & Stutzer, A. (2000). Happiness, economy and institutions. *Economic Journal*, *110*(466), 918–938. https://doi.org/10.1111/1468-0297.00570

Frey, B. S., & Stutzer, A. (2019). Public choice and happiness. In R. D. Congleton, B. G. Grofman, & S. Voigt (Eds.), *The Oxford handbook of public choice* (Vol. 1, pp. 779–795). Oxford University Press. https://doi.org/10.1093/oxfordhb/9780190469733.013.40

HDI (2022). Trends in the human development index 1990–2021 dataset. *Human Development Reports, United Nations Development Programme*. https://hdr.undp.org/data-center/documentation-and-downloads

Inglehart, R., & Klingemann, H.-D. (2000). Genes, culture, democracy, and happiness. In E. Diener & E. M. Suh (Eds.), *Culture and subjective well-being* (pp. 165–183). MIT Press. https://doi.org/10.7551/mitpress/2242.003.0012

Lane, R. E. (1988). Procedural goods in a democracy: How one is treated versus what one gets. *Social Justice Research*, *2*(3), 177–192. https://doi.org/10.1007/BF01054555

Martínez-Vázquez, J., Lago-Peñas, S., & Sacchi, A. (2017). The impact of fiscal decentralization: A survey. *Journal of Economic Surveys*, *31*(4), 1095–1129. https://doi.org/10.1111/joes.12182

Odermatt, R., & Stutzer, A. (2018). Subjective well-being and public policy. In E. Diener, S. Oishi, & L. Tay (Eds.), *Handbook of well-being* (pp. 954–968). DEF Publishers. www.nobascholar.com/chapters/7

Olken, B. A. (2010). Direct democracy and local public goods: Evidence from a field experiment in Indonesia. *American Political Science Review*, *104*(2), 243–267. https://doi.org/10.1017/S0003055410000079

Radcliff, B., & Shufeldt, G. (2016). Direct democracy and subjective well-being: The initiative and life satisfaction in the American states. *Social Indicators Research*, *128*(3), 1405–1423. https://doi.org/10.1007/s11205-015-1085-4

Rode, M. (2013). Do good institutions make citizens happy, or do happy citizens build better institutions? *Journal of Happiness Studies*, *14*(5), 1479–1505. https://doi.org/10.1007/s10902-012-9391-x

Stadelmann-Steffen, I., & Vatter, A. (2012). Does satisfaction with democracy really increase happiness? Direct democracy and individual satisfaction in Switzerland. *Political Behavior*, *34*(3), 535–559. https://doi.org/10.1007/s11109-011-9164-y

V-Dem Institute (2023). V-dem [country-year/country-date] dataset v13. *Varieties of Democracy (V-Dem) Project*. https://v-dem.net/data/the-v-dem-dataset/

WGI (2022). Worldwide governance indicators 1996–2021 dataset. *World Bank Group*. https://datacatalog.worldbank.org/search/dataset/0038026/Worldwide-Governance-Indicators

14

MIGRATION AND WELLBEING

A policy review

Martijn Hendriks

Introduction

The purpose of this chapter is to provide an overview of key findings from the literature on the relationship between migration policy and subjective wellbeing. It will help elicit the lessons learned and actionable points for policy-makers and anyone interested in evidence on what migration policies benefit subjective wellbeing (SWB). The chapter covers international migration from a global perspective and considers the outcomes of both the migrants and hosting communities in relation to admission and integration policies/interventions.

In the migration literature, the SWB angle has emerged as an important new frontier to advance the understanding of migration (Hendriks, 2015). SWB, colloquially often referred to as happiness and used interchangeably in this chapter, is a person's subjective experience of his or her quality of life. It includes people's affective experiences (the frequency of experiencing positive and negative emotions and moods) and life evaluations (contentment or life satisfaction).

An important reason for the emerging SWB angle is the growing evidence that people's choice behavior in important life decisions, including migration decisions, is strongly driven by ambitions of improving their quality of life or happiness when basic survival needs are met (Benjamin et al., 2014). This reflects the notion that virtually all people yearn for a happy life. A second reason relates to the core strengths of SWB measures. The literature discussed in this chapter makes use of SWB measures based on self-reported information, with experienced affect being gauged by survey questions asking people how often they experience certain emotions and moods (e.g., the PANAS scale) and life evaluations being gauged by survey questions about life satisfaction such as "How satisfied are you with your life, all things considered?" or by the Cantril ladder-of-life question in

DOI: 10.4324/9781003382447-16

which respondents rate their life on a scale from 0 (worst possible life) to 10 (best possible life). While measurement biases lead SWB measures to be less precise than objective measures of wellbeing such as income and educational outcomes, they capture in an integrated manner what people hope to ultimately gain from life by allowing individuals to evaluate their own outcomes while considering their own preferences and hedonic adaptation mechanisms (Hendriks & Bartram, 2019; OECD, 2013).

Literature on migration and wellbeing

An emerging literature has considered the impact of immigration and ethnic diversity on the happiness of hosting populations in developed countries. The literature, reviewed in Hendriks and Burger (2021), documents mixed and context-dependent effects, with most studies highlighting that the observed effects are of a very small magnitude, such that only large immigrant flows have a substantial positive or negative impact on the happiness of natives. Yet some heterogeneity in outcomes exists. In some contexts, older people and those with lower socio-economic status benefit less (or are hurt more) by ethnic diversity and immigration, possibly due to perceived labor market competition and socio-cultural preferences (Howley et al., 2020). Yet the effects remain small and much smaller than could be expected based on the worries of many natives about the negative consequences of migration for their wellbeing (O' Connor, 2020). Objective macroeconomic gains or losses are not found to be major channels driving positive or negative effects of immigration on the SWB of natives (e.g., O' Connor, 2020). However, Howley et al. (2020) provide suggestive evidence that perceived (not actual) labour market competition and social identity are relevant channels for a negative impact of immigration on the happiness of some natives in the United Kingdom. Possible non-economic channels such as congestion, social cohesion, and perceived safety have remained unexplored.

Another stream of literature has examined to what extent, and under what conditions, migrants themselves become happier through migration. Given the scarcity of longitudinal or experimental data covering pre-migration and post-migration periods, most studies have resorted to comparing migrants to stayers with similar characteristics in the home country ("matched stayers") or stayers who intend to move ("matched potential migrants"). The evidence shows that most, but not all, international migrants gain happiness from migration and that their happiness levels converge closely to the happiness levels of the host country's native populations (Hendriks et al., 2018; Helliwell et al., 2018). The largest gains are achieved by those moving to happier and more developed countries, while neutral or negative effects are commonly experienced by those moving in the opposite direction. Happiness gains are achieved in the first years after migration, after which happiness does not further increase with the length of stay because of shifting reference points that cause rising expectations and aspirations (Hendriks & Burger, 2020). The stagnant happiness level is consistent with hedonic adaptation theory (Diener et al.,

2006) and occurs despite migrants' objectively improving life conditions. Shifting reference points can also explain why the second generation is generally not happier than their immigrant parents (Hendriks & Burger, 2020).

Many migrants leave family members and significant others behind. The most common reason is to support, via remittances, the wellbeing of family members and others who remain in the less developed place of origin. Household members staying behind generally experience a positive impact on evaluative wellbeing but not emotional wellbeing (Hendriks et al., 2018; Ivlevs et al., 2019). Specifically, those left behind tend to experience both more positive affect (e.g., enjoyment) and negative affect (e.g., worry and sadness). Left-behind household members experience stronger happiness gains when receiving remittances and when the migrant moved from a developing to a developed country. The influence of emigration on overall happiness in home countries has not been thoroughly investigated.

The literature on the causes of migration has consistently documented that those aspiring or intending to move abroad tend to have relatively high objective success (wealthy and well-educated) but relatively low happiness. This may occur for two reasons. The first reason is that many prospective migrants are so-called "frustrated achievers," meaning that their unhappiness is driven by the striving for still greater success, which they cannot obtain in their current location (Graham & Markowitz, 2011). The second reason is that unhappy people stand to gain the most from migration, while wealthier people can better bear the financial costs of migration. Indeed, in contrast to middle- and high-income countries, unhappier people in low-income countries act less often on their migration aspirations because they lack the financial resources to cover the costs of migration and face greater legal barriers to move abroad (Migali & Scipioni, 2019). Therefore, a "happiness drain" may occur in low-income but not middle- or high-income countries. The importance of happiness is also evident in return decisions—migrants have stronger return intentions when having less positive happiness trajectories or when the happiness difference between the host and home country decreases (Shamsuddin & Katsaiti, 2020). Taken together, happiness dynamics capture important underlying quality-of-life related reasons for migration that are not captured by standard migration models.

The literature has convincingly documented that the determinants of migrants' happiness go well beyond achieving the concrete motives for migration, such as economic gains for economic migrants (Paloma et al., 2021). For instance, while economic gains typically improve happiness, the social costs of migration can partly, or sometimes fully, offset these gains. On the one hand, migrants and natives have many core determinants of happiness in common, with primary domains being health, social relationships, economic factors, personal values and goals, adaptation and resilience, and societal/institutional conditions. On the other hand, migrants' happiness functions differ from those of natives, with major additional determinants being ethnic discrimination, integration, and language barriers, amongst other factors (Safi, 2010). In this regard, a policy-pertinent and well-documented finding is that migrants maximize happiness when successfully acculturating to the mainstream society, while simultaneously maintaining their heritage culture (Nguyen & Benet-Martínez, 2013). These findings highlight the need for specialized happiness policies for migrants and that there are many channels and domains through which public policy can increase immigrants' happiness.

Evidence of interventions

While there is ample evidence on the determinants of migrants' and natives' SWB, there is scant evidence on how specific policies, programs, and interventions related to migration and integration affect SWB. I provide here an overview of the current evidence on SWB outcomes.

There is as yet sparse evidence on how immigrant admission policies affect natives' SWB. This can be explained by the marginal impact of immigrant flows on natives' SWB, which holds across subgroups of immigrants (O' Connor, 2020). Consequently, changes in admission policies targeted at certain migrant groups (refugees, high-skilled migrants, etc.) will have marginal impacts. For instance, Ivlevs and Veliziotis (2018) find no main effect of inflows of Eastern European immigrants in local areas on natives' life satisfaction following the 2004 enlargement that resulted in an unprecedented wave of Eastern European workers relocating to the UK—even if some subgroups experienced small positive or negative effects (linked to the Brexit vote). Only very severe policy changes will have a substantial positive or negative impact on natives' SWB.

A leading index to evaluate and monitor national integration policies is the Migrant Integration Policy Index (MIPEX). Inclusive integration policies (i.e., higher MIPEX scores) are associated with higher SWB of non-European Union (EU) immigrants (Heizmann & Böhnke, 2019) and natives (Tatarko et al., 2021), with a smaller SWB gap between immigrants and natives (Sand & Gruber, 2018). However, it is not associated with higher SWB of EU immigrants (Heizmann & Böhnke, 2019). The Multiculturalism Policies Index, which focuses more on recognising and appreciating cultural diversity, is not associated with immigrants' SWB (Heizmann & Böhnke, 2019).

Given that a wide range of determinants affect migrants' SWB, many programmes or policies could be beneficial. Policies providing language courses, permanent residence permits, and labour market access to migrants, such as The Migration Act (2000/2005) and the EU Blue Card programme (2012) in Germany, have proven effective in increasing migrants' SWB through greater societal participation (Giovanis et al., 2021; Giovanis, 2023). This finding corresponds with the literature showing the importance of having work (Paloma et al., 2021) and support in second language use for SWB (Hendriks & Birnberg, 2023). However, not every integration policy is effective. For instance, Granderath et al. (2021) found no impact of adult education on the SWB of immigrants and natives. In addition, Kóczán (2016) showed that changes in the German citizenship law did not affect the SWB of those obtaining citizenship through these reforms, which is in line with the broader finding that citizenship is not a main determinant of immigrant happiness.

Discussion and conclusion

For many people, international migration is a powerful instrument to improve their lives. More lenient national admission policies could benefit the SWB of immigrants, while having marginal and mixed impacts on hosting populations and unknown effects on immigrants' origin countries.

The prevalent and vast concerns in immigrant-receiving countries about migration make sense from a psychological perspective; abundant research on integrated threat theory shows that ingroup members are likely to have negative attitudes toward outgroup members, such as immigrants, if they perceive them as a threat. Yet these concerns are not in line with the marginal (and often nonnegative) effects of immigration on societal happiness, even if some natives do experience negative effects.

Similarly, some policy-makers are hesitant to invest in immigrant wellbeing out of fear of attracting more immigrants or giving natives the impression that they are disadvantaged or not prioritized. Yet the targeted investment in policies that contribute to migrant happiness can create a win–win situation for both immigrants and natives. Increasing the happiness of immigrants can be a fruitful way to enhance the benefits of immigration for the host society, since happiness has proven to be a key driver of economic, social, and health advantages, such as greater productivity, more openness toward other cultures, and greater integration (De Neve et al., 2013; Li et al., 2018). Moreover, the fear of attracting more immigrants is a negligible concern from a SWB perspective given the marginal impact of immigration inflows.

There are many potentially effective migrant-focused policies and interventions for which the impact on SWB has not yet been tested. Given that SWB depends on numerous factors, single interventions will have a small impact on immigrants, but comprehensive policies addressing multiple crucial SWB determinants can lead to substantial increases in SWB. I will highlight three domains that could be particularly fruitful in improving immigrants' SWB due to their strong relationship with immigrant happiness and whose effect merits further investigation:

1. Policies that facilitate the formation of social connections through community centers, support groups, and mentorship programs can be particularly effective for immigrants' happiness. Fostering inclusive communities can help immigrants feel welcomed and valued and reduce the high levels of loneliness among asylum seekers, thereby positively impacting their SWB;
2. Implementing and enforcing laws that protect immigrants from discrimination and ensure their equal rights and opportunities may be effective. This includes measures to combat xenophobia, racism, and prejudice in various domains, such as employment, housing, and public services.
3. Encouraging immigrants' participation in cultural and recreational activities can enhance their SWB and sense of belonging. Policies that promote multicultural events, festivals, and opportunities for cultural exchange can foster a sense of pride in heritage while facilitating interactions with the wider community.

Yet it is important to note that the impact of integration policies on subjective wellbeing can vary depending on individual factors such as socioeconomic status, cultural background, and personal experiences. Moreover, the specific design and implementation of integration policies in each country also influence their effectiveness.

Actionable points

I highlight five actionable points aimed at maximizing the SWB benefits of international migration.

- First, it is important to take the marginal impact of migration on SWB into account when making policy decisions and in policy debates to avoid needlessly fueling anti-immigrant sentiments that themselves can negatively affect the SWB of both natives and immigrants.
- Second, investing more in integration policies can transform the neutral impact of immigrant inflows into a positive effect and thereby create a win–win situation for immigrants and natives. There is a wide array of potentially effective policy intervention domains, notably facilitating migrants' acculturation to the mainstream society while allowing them to also maintain their heritage culture.
- Third, the information provided by the migration and SWB literature does not fully meet the needs of policy-makers. While most studies provide policy implications based on correlational or longitudinal evidence, direct impact evaluations of new policies, policy reforms, and training programs related to migration/integration are rare. This is one reason for the hesitancy of policy-makers to invest in immigrant integration. To promote evidence-based policy-making, more cooperation is needed between policy-makers and academics to test such impacts using experimental designs.
- Fourth, public policies on immigration should be directed toward not only immigrants but also natives. Given that anti-immigrant sentiments strongly impair immigrants' happiness, policies aimed at improving social cohesion between immigrants and natives can help make the most out of migration.
- Fifth, the documented relevance of happiness as a determinant of migration suggests that policy-makers aiming to reduce outmigration, and particularly a "happiness drain" in developing countries, should target improving not only the objective wellbeing of citizens but also their subjective wellbeing.

References

Benjamin, D. J., Heffetz, O., Kimball, M. S., & Rees-Jones, A. (2014). Can marginal rates of substitution be inferred from happiness data? Evidence from residency choices. *The American Economic Review*, *104*(11), 3498–3528. http://doi.org/10.1257/aer.104.11.3498

De Neve, J.-E., Diener, E., Tay, L. et al. (2013). The objective benefits of subjective wellbeing. In J. F. Helliwell, R. Layard, & J. Sachs (Eds.), *World happiness report 2013* (pp. 54–74). UN SDSN.

Diener, E., Lucas, R. E., & Scollon, C. N. (2006). Beyond the hedonic treadmill: Revising the adaptation theory of well-being. *American Psychologist*, *61*(4), 305–314. https://doi.org/10.1037/0003-066X.61.4.305

Giovanis, E. (2023). Impact of migration policies on socio-cultural participation and well-being: Evidence from the Migration Act of 2000 in Germany. *Journal of Economic and Administrative Sciences*, In press.

Giovanis, E., Akdede, S. H., & Ozdamar, O. (2021). Impact of the EU Blue Card programme on cultural participation and subjective well-being of migrants in Germany. *PLoS One*, *16*(7), e0253952. https://doi.org/10.1371/journal.pone.0253952

Graham, C., & Markowitz, J. (2011). Aspirations and happiness of potential Latin American immigrants. *Journal of Social Research & Policy*, *2*(2), 9.

Granderath, J. S., Martin, A., & Froehlich, L. (2021). The effect of participation in adult education on life satisfaction of immigrants and natives: A longitudinal analysis. *Journal of Happiness Studies*, *22*(7), 3043–3067. https://doi.org/10.1007/s10902-020-00340-7

Heizmann, B., & Böhnke, P. (2019). Immigrant life satisfaction in Europe: The role of social and symbolic boundaries. *Journal of Ethnic and Migration Studies*, *45*(7), 1027–1050. https://doi.org/10.1080/1369183X.2018.1438252

Hendriks, M. (2015). The happiness of international migrants: A review of research findings. *Migration Studies*, *3*(3), 343–369. https://doi.org/10.1093/migration/mnu053

Hendriks, M., & Bartram, D. (2019). Bringing happiness into the study of migration and its consequences: What, why, and how? *Journal of Immigrant & Refugee Studies*, *17*(3), 279–298. https://doi.org/10.1080/15562948.2018.1458169

Hendriks, M., & Birnberg, R. (2023). Happiness in the daily socio-cultural integration process: A day reconstruction study among American immigrants in Germany. *International Migration Review*. https://doi.org/10.1177/01979183221149022

Hendriks, M., & Burger, M. J. (2020). Unsuccessful subjective well-being assimilation among immigrants: The role of faltering perceptions of the host society. *Journal of Happiness Studies*, *21*(6), 1985–2006. https://doi.org/10.1007/s10902-019-00164-0

Hendriks, M., & Burger, M. J. (2021). Happiness and migration. In K. F. Zimmermann (Ed.), *Handbook of labor, human resources and population economics*. Springer. https://doi.org/10.1007/978-3-319-57365-6_178-1

Hendriks, M., Burger, M., Ray, J., & Esipova, N. (2018). Do international migrants increase their happiness and that of their families by migrating. In J. F. Helliwell, R. Layard, & J. Sachs (Eds.), *World happiness report 2018* (pp. 44–65). UN SDSN.

Helliwell, J. F., Huang, H., Wang, S., & Shiplett, H. (2018). International migration and world happiness. In J. F. Helliwell, R. Layard, & J. Sachs (Eds.), *World happiness report 2018* (pp. 13–44). UN SDSN.

Howley, P., Waqas, M., Moro, M., Delaney, L., & Heron, T. (2020). It's not all about the economy stupid! Immigration and subjective well-being in England. *Work, Employment and Society*, *34*(5), 919–936. https://doi.org/10.1177/0950017019866643

Ivlevs, A., Nikolova, M., & Graham, C. (2019). Emigration, remittances, and the subjective well-being of those staying behind. *Journal of Population Economics*, *32*, 113–151. https://doi.org/10.1007/s00148-018-0718-8

Ivlevs, A., & Veliziotis, M. (2018). Local-level immigration and life satisfaction: The EU enlargement experience in England and Wales. *Environment and Planning A: Economy and Space*, *50*(1), 175–193. https://doi.org/10.1177/0308518X1774089

Kóczán, Z. (2016). (Why) are immigrants unhappy? *IZA Journal of Migration*, *5*(1), 1–25. https://doi.org/10.1186/s40176-016-0052-4

Li, T. C., Chu, C. C., Meng, F. C., Li, Q., Mo, D., Li, B., & Tsai, S. B. (2018). Will happiness improve the psychological integration of migrant workers? *International Journal of Environmental Research and Public Health*, *15*(5), 900. https://doi.org/10.3390/ijerph15050900

Migali, S., & Scipioni, M. (2019). Who's about to leave? A global survey of aspirations and intentions to migrate. *International Migration*, *57*(5), 181–200. https://doi.org/10.1111/imig.12617

Nguyen, A. M. D., & Benet-Martínez, V. (2013). Biculturalism and adjustment: A meta-analysis. *Journal of Cross-Cultural Psychology*, *44*(1), 122–159. https://doi.org/10.1093/esr/jcp013

O'Connor, K. J. (2020). The effect of immigration on natives' well-being in the European Union. *Journal of Economic Behavior & Organization*, *180*, 257–274. https://doi.org/10.1016/j.jebo.2020.10.006

OECD (2013). *OECD guidelines on measuring subjective well-being*. OECD Publishing. https://doi.org/10.1787/9789264191655-en

Paloma, V., Escobar-Ballesta, M., Galván-Vega, B., Díaz-Bautista, J. D., & Benítez, I. (2021). Determinants of life satisfaction of economic migrants coming from developing countries to countries with very high human development: A systematic review. *Applied Research in Quality of Life*, *16*, 435–455. https://doi.org/10.1007/s11482-020-09832-3

Safi, M. (2010). Immigrants' life satisfaction in Europe: Between assimilation and discrimination. *European Sociological Review*, *26*(2), 159–176. https://doi.org/10.1093/esr/jcp013

Sand, G., & Gruber, S. (2018). Differences in subjective well-being between older migrants and natives in Europe. *Journal of Immigrant and Minority Health*, *20*(1), 83–90. https://doi.org/10.1007/s10903-016-0537-5

Shamsuddin, M., & Katsaiti, M. S. (2020). Migration and happiness: Evidence from Germany. *Journal of Happiness Studies*, *21*(8), 2931–2955. https://doi.org/10.1007/s10902-019-00207-6

Tatarko, A., Jurcik, T., & Hadjar, A. (2021). How migration policy shapes the subjective well-being of the non-immigrant population in European countries. *Journal of Cross-Cultural Psychology*, *52*(3), 316–333. https://doi.org/10.1177/00220221211001531

15

RELIGION, SPIRITUALITY AND WELLBEING

Can spiritual/religious practice improve individuals' wellbeing?

Teresa García-Muñoz and Shoshana Neuman

Introduction

This chapter focuses on effects of religious/spiritual (RS) interventions on individual wellbeing. Specifically, our research question is whether the use of tools based on stimulation of religious and/or spiritual feelings can enhance individual wellbeing. A positive and evidence-based response to RS interventions could drive improvements in peoples' lives. This study conducts a meta-analysis of publications that employed randomized controlled trials (RCTs) focusing on the impact of RS interventions on wellbeing. The articles selected employ measures of wellbeing that capture the individual's subjective experience of life as a whole. Trials that relied on objective measures, such as medical outcomes, were excluded from the analysis. The literature relates to spirituality and religiosity as two distinct but interrelated concepts. Religion is defined as the set of beliefs, practices, ceremonies, and rituals that are normally acquired by tradition within a group or community (Koening et al., 2001). Driver et al. (1996, p. 5) define spirituality as '*interaction and relationship to something other and greater than oneself*'. While Hill and Pargament (2003, p. 65) argue that many people experience spirituality within organized religions, Roof (1993) identifies individuals who consider themselves spiritual, but in no way religious. Our meta-analysis combines and synthesizes studies referring to RS interventions, that is, interventions which incorporate (as a central component) spiritual and/or religious dimensions.

Literature on religiosity/spirituality and wellbeing

Over the past half century, an extensive literature has explored the relationship between religiosity/spirituality and attitudes/behaviour, spanning a wide range of spheres

DOI: 10.4324/9781003382447-17

including wellbeing. Different measures of religiosity, spirituality, and of wellbeing have been employed in empirical studies. For instance, religiosity/spirituality has been measured by frequency of church attendance and/or by participation in religious activities (Briguglio et al., 2020), and practice of meditation, among others. Wellbeing has been proxied by positive measures like life satisfaction, quality of life, and happiness.

Extensive research has consistently demonstrated a positive association between spirituality/religiosity and wellbeing (Sawatzky et al., 2005). Participation in RS sessions and rituals provides comfort and a strong social support network (fostering a sense of community and belonging, while reducing feelings of isolation and depression) and generally act as 'balm for the soul' (Connor, 2012, p. 130). However, findings differ across research studies due to variations in the methods used to measure these complex concepts (Kim-Prieto & Miller, 2018).

While evidence indicates that individuals with extensive religious and/or spiritual involvement tend to be more positive about their lives, a related question is whether RS interventions have an impact on wellbeing. Numerous studies have examined the efficacy of the RS interventions for individuals with chronic or life-threatening diseases (Casuso-Holgado et al., 2022), as well as those with mental health problems (Marques et al., 2022). Most of these studies measure potential improvements in terms of medical and physical outcomes and symptom improvement. In this chapter we focus on measuring the impact of RS interventions on the subjective wellbeing of individuals.

Evidence of interventions

Study selection

RCTs qualified for this study if they investigated the impact of interventions incorporating religious/spiritual elements on wellbeing outcomes. RS interventions were defined as strategies that prioritize the inclusion of RS components as key elements of the intervention, with the objective of enhancing wellbeing. The inclusion criteria were as follows: (1) participants had to be 18 years of age or older; (2) studies had to be published in peer-reviewed journals and written in English; and (3) studies needed to measure wellbeing, life satisfaction, or quality of life through subjective ratings provided by the participants themselves, assessed at post-treatment, and capture an individual's subjective experience related to life as a whole. To avoid redundancy with existing meta-analyses, trials involving patients with cancer were not included, as previous studies have already demonstrated the positive impact of RS interventions on the quality of life of cancer patients (Xing et al., 2018; Bauereiß et al., 2018).

Search method and result of the search

The literature was screened using three databases: PubMed, Scopus, and Web of Science. The search text consisted of the following Boolean expressions: (spiritu* OR relig*) AND ('wellbeing' OR 'wellbeing' OR 'life satisfaction' OR 'quality of

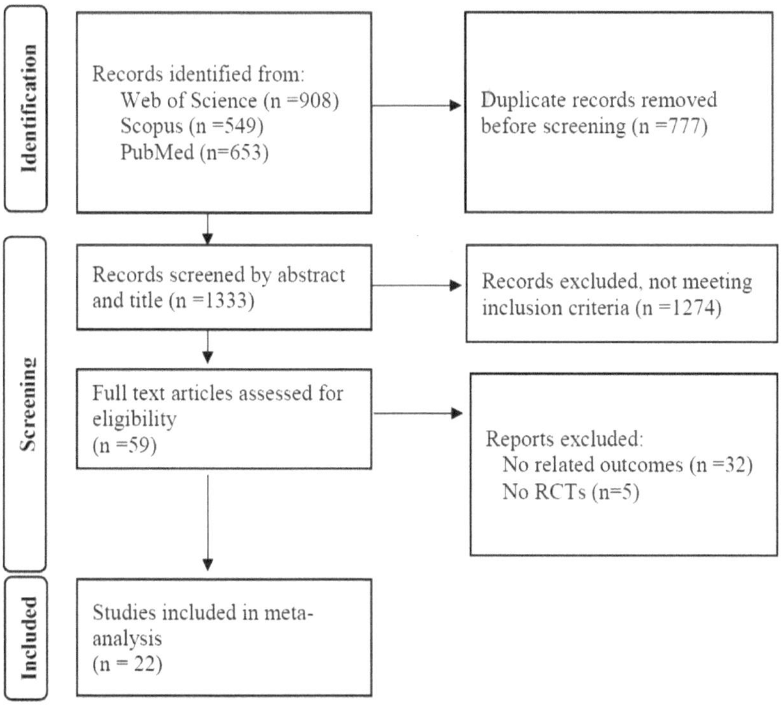

FIGURE 15.1 Study flow diagram.

life') AND (assistance OR intervention OR treatment OR therapy OR assessment OR group) AND (clinical trial OR meta-analysis OR Randomized Controlled Trial OR controlled clinical trial). The search was run in February 2023. We identified 2,110 records and ultimately recruited 22 studies (see Figure 15.1).

Study characteristics

The studies, conducted between 2006 and 2020, encompassed a total of 1,337 participants, with 664 individuals assigned to the intervention groups and 673 to the control groups. The samples consisted of individuals diagnosed with health-related physical problems (40.9%) and mental health problems (27.3%), as well as samples comprising older individuals (13.6%), participants employed in stressful occupations (police officers, health professionals, nurses), and individuals facing stressful situations (mothers of premature babies) (18.2%).

The RS interventions encompassed various approaches, such as mindfulness, meditation, yoga, mantra repetition, as well as specific programs targeting specific aspects like trust, resilience, patience, altruism, forgiveness, active listening, supportive presence, arousing hope, and engaging in prayer or reading sacred texts, among others.

The characteristics of the recruited studies are presented in Table 15.1.

TABLE 15.1 Characteristics of the included studies

Study	*Country*	*Participants*	*N*	*I*	*Measure*	*Effect*
Abdi et al. (2019)	Iran	Elderly people with heart failure	93	RS	LS questionnaire of LSI-Z	+
Armento et al. (2012)	United States	Depressed undergraduate students	50	RS	QOL Inventory	=
Ayyari et al. (2020)	Iran	Elderly females in nursing home	38	RS	Oxford Happiness Questionnaire	+
Binaei et al. (2016)	Iran	Patients with heart failure	46	R	Quality-of-life index	+
Bormann et al. (2006)	United States	HIV-infected adults	93	S	Q-LESQ	=
Bormann et al. (2018)	United States	Veterans with military-related PTSD	141	S	WHOQOL	=
Caponnetto et al. (2019)	Italy	Patients with schizophrenia	30	S	EQ Visual Analogue Scale	=
Ghandi et al. (2018)	Iran	Patients diagnosed with IBS	16	S	IBS-QOL	=
Mackenzie et al. (2006)	Canada	Nurses	30	S	LS scale	=
McCarthy et al. (2017)	United States	Elderly females in senior community centres	20	S	LS index for the third age	=
Moeini et al. (2016)	Iran	Elderly patients with hypertension	52	RS	LS scale	+
Mohamadi et al. (2019)	Iran	Patients diagnosed with IBS	40	S	IBS-QOL	=
Oman et al. (2006)	United States	Health professionals	58	S	LS scale	=
Pramesona and Taneepanichskul (2018)	Indonesia	Elderly residents in nursing home	60	R	WHOQOL	+
Sekhavatpour et al. (2020)	Iran	Mothers of premature infants	60	RS	WHOQOL	+
Trombka et al. (2021)	Brazil	Police officers	128	S	WHOQOL	+
Tulbure et al. (2017)	Romania	Depressed individuals	31	R	QOL Inventory	+
Vermandere et al. (2015)	The Netherland	Palliative patients in home care	49	S	Palliative Specific QOL Questionnaire	=
Wachholtz and Pargament (2008)	United States	People with migraine headaches	42	S	Migraine Specific QOL Scale	=

(*Continued*)

TABLE 15.1 (Continued)

Study	*Country*	*Participants*	*N*	*I*	*Measure*	*Effect*
Wu and Koo (2016)	Taiwan	Elderly people with mild or moderate dementia	103	S	LS Scale	+
Yaghubi et al. (2019)	Iran	Methadone-treated patients	67	RS	WHOQOL	+
Zernicke et al. (2013)	Canada	Patients diagnosed with IBS	90	S	IBS-QOL	+

IBS, irritable bowel syndrome; I, intervention; LS, life-satisfaction; N, sample size; PTSD, posttraumatic stress disorder; QOL, quality of life; Q-LESQ, Quality-of-Life Enjoyment and Satisfaction Questionnaire; R, religious; S, spiritual; WHOQOL, World Health Organization Quality-of-Life; =, no significant difference; +, positive difference.

Methodology

Means and standard deviations were extracted from the articles, and because of the different scales used in the studies, effect sizes for the meta-analysis were calculated using standardized mean differences (SMDs) between treatment and control groups with 95% confidence intervals (CI). Caution should be exercised in two respects. First, differences in intervention approaches and patient settings may contribute to some of the variability in effects, potentially biasing the SMD results. Second, pooling data for a meta-analysis from different instruments may obscure substantial heterogeneity between studies, even if they appear to assess similar constructs.

To account for substantial heterogeneity among studies, a random effects model was used to pool the data and calculate the weight of each study. Variability between studies was assessed using the I^2 statistic, which quantifies the percentage of the total variability in effect size estimates that is due to heterogeneity. I^2 ranges from 0% (indicating that all heterogeneity is due to sampling error) to 100% (indicating true heterogeneity between studies) but should be interpreted with caution when a meta-analysis has few studies, as in our case.

To reduce heterogeneity, we performed two types of decomposition. First, we decomposed the studies according to the type of intervention: spiritual, religious, and joint (with both spiritual and religious components) (see Table 15.1). Second, we decomposed the studies into four groups, based on the recorded health status of the participants, distinguishing between participants with physical health problems, people with mental health problems, elderly people living in nursing homes, and people with no recorded health problems but engaged in stressful occupations and situations.

We present the results in forest plots, graphical representations that provide a visual summary of the estimated effects, their associated confidence intervals, and the weight of each study. Studies with a more precise estimate of the population effect size (a low variance) carry more weight.

Results

The three types of interventions all have positive effects on wellbeing (see Figure 15.2) with statistically significant SMDs of 0.27 for spiritual interventions, 1.37 for religious interventions, and 3.11 for religious/spiritual interventions. If we exclude the two articles with very high mean differences (Sekhavatpour et al., 2020; Yaghubi et al., 2019), the effect of joint interventions decreases to 1.40, although it is still statistically significant and positive.

Distinction by type of participant (see Figure 15.3) indicates that three subgroups seem to benefit from RS interventions: individuals diagnosed with mental health symptoms (SMD = 1.32), people diagnosed with health-related physical problems (SMD = 0.48), and those characterized by employment in stressful occupations (health professionals, nurses, police officers) and situations (mothers of premature babies) (SMD = 1.82). The positive effects found for people in stressful occupations/situations disappear when studies with very large mean differences are removed. No significant effects were found for samples consisting of older people. Overall, we conclude that RS interventions led to an improvement in wellbeing of 0.6 (SMD) at the 95% CI = 0.31, 0.89, which increases to 1.04 (SMD) when two studies with large mean differences are included 95% CI = 0.60, 1.48.

Conclusion

RS interventions resulted in an improvement in wellbeing, and the extent of improvement varies across subgroups of interventions and participants. The most substantial effects were observed among participants receiving religious and joint religious/spiritual interventions, compared to those receiving solely spiritual interventions. One possible explanation is that most interventions classified as spiritual are designed with a single activity (e.g. yoga, meditation). Another plausible explanation is that, given the absence of a one-size-fits-all solution applicable to all individuals or situations, interventions involving several activity types may better cater to individual needs. More research is clearly needed to identify the precise characteristics of interventions that have the largest impact on wellbeing.

Distinguishing by type of participant, we found improvements in individual wellbeing among participants with mental and physical problems. These are most likely due to the balancing and comforting influence of RS interventions, which lead to improved mood and provide a sense of meaning, purpose, or hope. All in all, the final outcome is an improvement in emotional wellbeing and resilience, which helps to cope with difficult experiences of illness and disability. An interesting finding relates to older individuals. Samples consisting of older people yielded no significant results. This may stem from the location and environment of older people in our samples. The studies involving the elderly have been conducted in residential care homes and centres. These community centres provide a strong social support network, offering opportunities for connection, belonging,

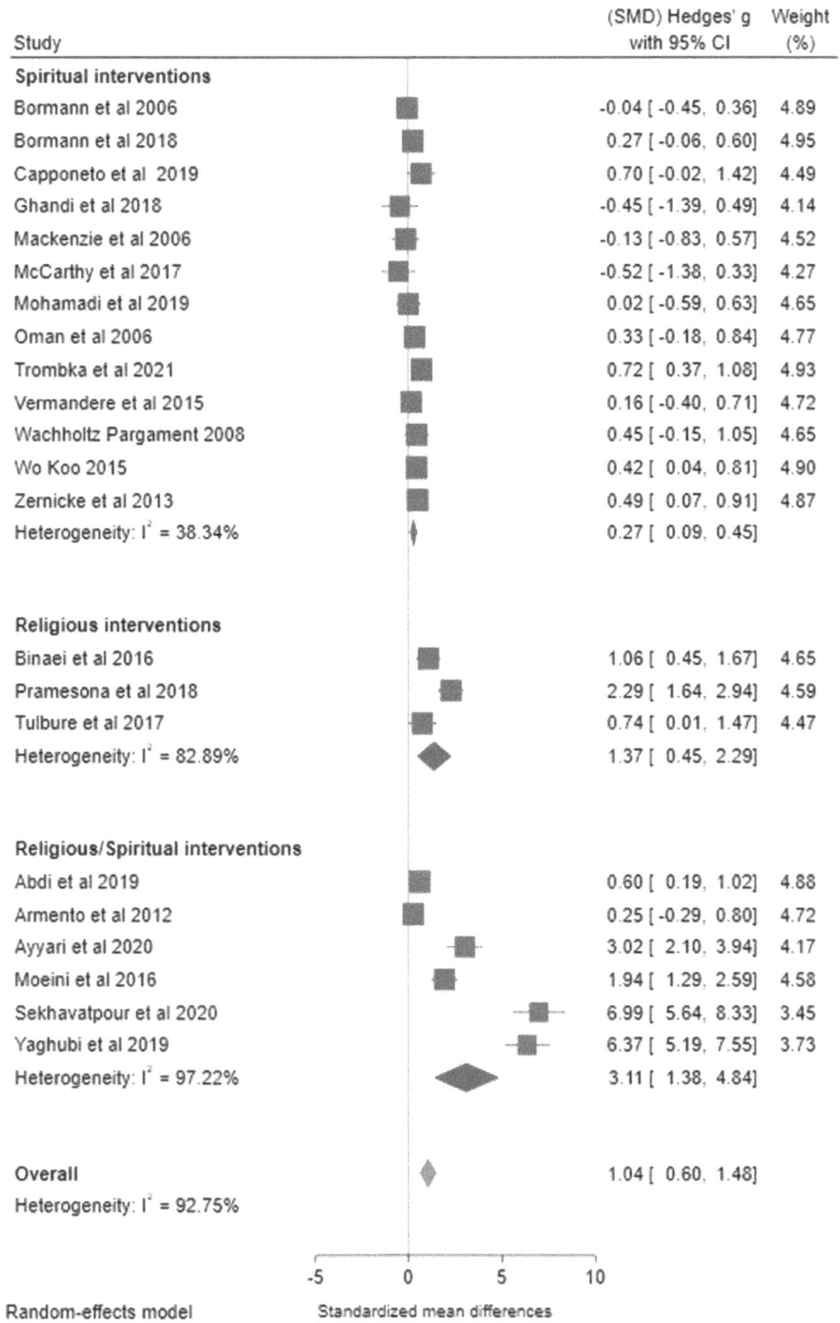

FIGURE 15.2 Forest plot of effect sizes by type of intervention.

SMD, standardized mean difference; CI, confidence interval.

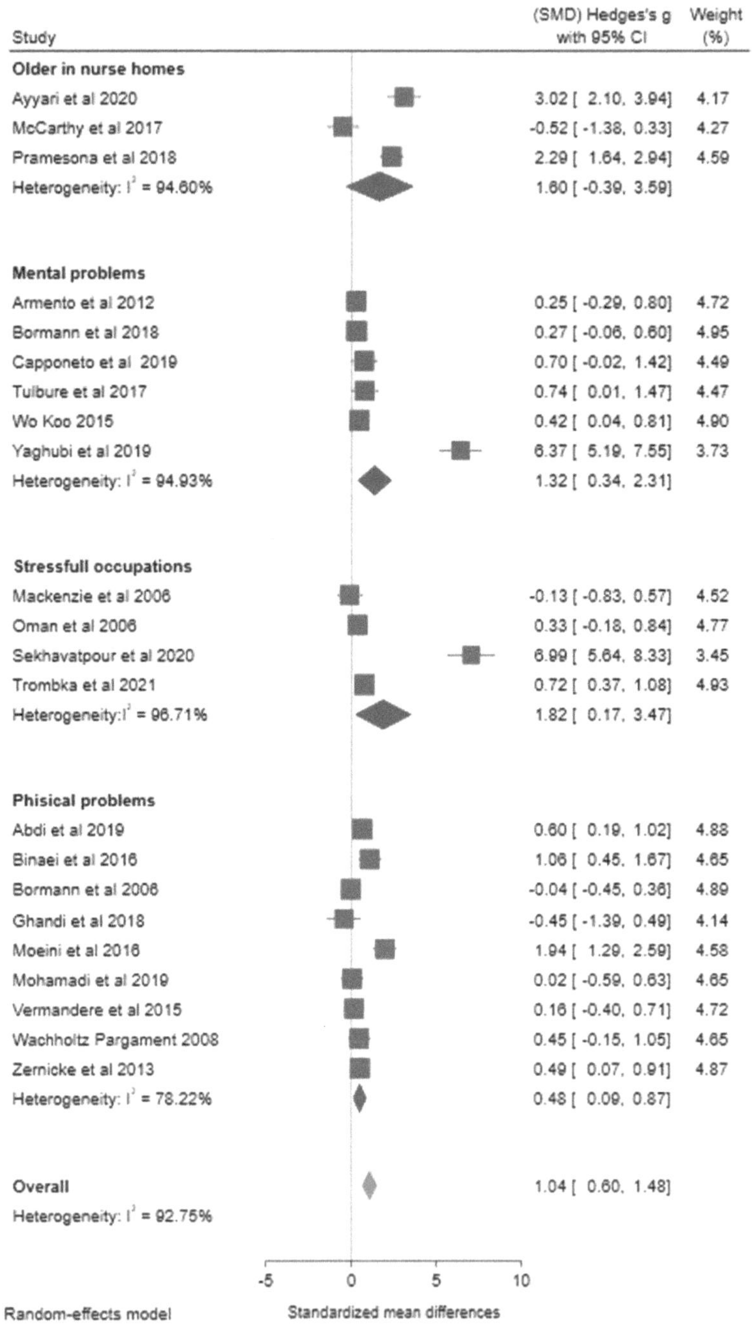

FIGURE 15.3 Forest plot of effect sizes by type of individual characteristics. CI, confidence interval; SMD, standardized mean difference.

and social interaction, reducing feelings of isolation, loneliness, and depression. Therefore, RS interventions have low/insignificant added effects on wellbeing.

While this review provides valuable evidence, the results and interpretations should be treated with some caution, given the heterogeneity in the types of interventions and wellbeing measures. As noted earlier, further research would be needed to identify the precise characteristics of interventions that have the largest impact on wellbeing and the types of participants who would benefit most from them. The reported effects are averages across all participants, and the effects may vary between individuals. Some people may even experience a negative impact of RS interventions on their wellbeing, for example if they experience conflicts with their personal beliefs.

Actionable points

- Train professionals in the healthcare sector to sensitively address and accommodate patients' spiritual and religious needs and practices.
- Design and offer joint spiritual/religious interventions for interested patients.
- Design and offer spiritual/religious intervention sessions, for interested employees, at work places of stressful occupations, as part of the welfare envelope of the workplace.
- Design education programs and awareness campaigns in order to contribute to a more inclusive and tolerant society and reduce discrimination based on religious/spiritual beliefs.
- Target RS interventions where connection, belonging, and social interaction are missing for significant added effects on wellbeing.

The specific policy recommendations may vary based on the cultural and religious frameworks of different countries or regions.

References

Abdi, A., Soufinia, A., Borji, M., & Tarjoman, A. (2019). The effect of religion intervention on life satisfaction and depression in elderly with heart failure. *Journal of Religion and Health*, *58*(3), 823–832. https://doi.org/10.1007/s10943-018-0727-7

Armento, M. E. A., McNulty, J. K., & Hopko, D. R. (2012). Behavioral Activation of Religious Behaviors (BARB): Randomized trial with depressed college students. *Psychology of Religion and Spirituality*, *4*(3), 206–222. https://doi.org/10.1037/a0026405

Ayyari, T., Salehabadi, R., Rastaghi, S., & Rad, M. (2020). Effects of spiritual interventions on happiness level of the female elderly residing in nursing home. *Evidence Based Care Journal*, *10*(1), 36–43. https://doi.org/10.22038/ebcj.2020.44422.2205

Bauereiß, N., Obermaier, S., Özünal, S. E., & Baumeister, H. (2018). Effects of existential interventions on spiritual, psychological, and physical well-being in adult patients with cancer: Systematic review and meta-analysis of randomized controlled trials. *Psycho-Oncology*, *27*(11), 2531–2545. https://doi.org/10.1002/pon.4829

Binaei, N., Moeini, M., Sadeghi, M., Najafi, M., & Mohagheghian, Z. (2016). Effects of hope promoting interventions based on religious beliefs on quality of life of patients with congestive heart failure and their families. *Iranian Journal of Nursing and Midwifery Research*, *21*(1), 77. https://doi.org/10.4103/1735-9066.174755

Bormann, J. E., Gifford, A. L., Shively, M., Smith, T. L., Redwine, L., Kelly, A., Becker, S., Gershwin, M., Bone, P., & Belding, W. (2006). Effects of spiritual mantram repetition on HIV outcomes: A randomized controlled trial. *Journal of Behavioral Medicine*, *29*(4), 359–376. https://doi.org/10.1007/s10865-006-9063-6

Bormann, J. E., Thorp, S. R., Smith, E., Glickman, M., Beck, D., Plumb, D., Zhao, S., Ackland, P. E., Rodgers, C. S., Heppner, P., Herz, L. R., & Elwy, A. R. (2018). Individual treatment of posttraumatic stress disorder using mantram repetition: A randomized clinical trial. *American Journal of Psychiatry*, *175*(10), 979–988. https://doi.org/10.1176/appi.ajp.2018.17060611

Briguglio, M., Garcia-Muñoz, T., & Neuman, S. (2020). Environmental engagement, religion and spirituality in the context of secularization. *Environmental Research Letters*, *15*(10), 104098.

Caponnetto, P., Auditore, R., Maglia, M., Pipitone, S., & Inguscio, L. (2019). Psychological wellness, yoga and quality of life in patients affected by schizophrenia spectrum disorders: A pilot study. *Mental Illness*, *11*(1). https://doi.org/10.4081/mi.2019.8003

Casuso-Holgado, M. J., Heredia-Rizo, A. M., González-García, P., Muñoz-Fernández, M. A., & Martinez-Calderon, J. (2022). Mind–body practices for cancer-related symptoms management: An overview of systematic reviews including one hundred twenty-nine meta-analyses. *Support Care Cancer*, *30*(12), 10335–10357. https://doi.org/10.1007/s00520-022-07426-3

Connor, P. (2012). Balm for the soul: Immigrant religion and emotional well-being. *International Migration*, *50*(2), 130–157.

Driver, B. I., Dustin, D., Baltic, T., Elsner, G., & Peterson, G. (1996). *Nature and the human spirit: Toward an expanded land management ethic*. Venture Publishing.

Ghandi, F., Sadeghi, A., Bakhtyari, M., Imani, S., Abdi, S., & Banihashem, S. S. (2018). Comparing the efficacy of mindfulness-based stress reduction therapy with emotion regulation treatment on quality of life and symptoms of irritable bowel syndrome. *Iranian Journal of Psychiatry*, *3*(3), 175–183.

Hill, P. C., & Pargament, K. I. (2003). Advances in the conceptualization and measurement of religion and spirituality: Implications for physical and mental health research. *American Psychologist*, *58*(1), 64–74. https://doi.org/10.1037/0003-066x.58.1.64

Kim-Prieto, C., & Miller, L. (2018). Intersection of religion and subjective well-being in Handbook of well-being. In E. Diener, O. Oishi, & L. Tay (Eds.), *Handbook of well-being* (pp. 1–9). DEF Publishers.

Koening, H. G., McCullough, M. E., & Larson, D. B. (2001). *Handbook of religion and health*. Oxford University Press.

Mackenzie, C. S., Poulin, P. A., & Seidman-Carlson, R. (2006). A brief mindfulness-based stress reduction intervention for nurses and nurse aides. *Applied Nursing Research*, *19*(2), 105–109. https://doi.org/10.1016/j.apnr.2005.08.002

Marques, A., Ihle, A., Souza, A., Peralta, M., & de Matos, M. G. (2022). Religious-based interventions for depression: A systematic review and meta-analysis of experimental studies. *Journal of Affective Disorders*, *309*, 289–296. https://doi.org/10.1016/j.jad.2022.04.126

McCarthy, V. L., Hall, L. A., Crawford, T. N., & Connelly, J. (2017). Facilitating self-transcendence: An intervention to enhance well-being in late life. *Western Journal of Nursing Research*, *40*(6), 854–873. https://doi.org/10.1177/0193945917690731

Moeini, M., Sharifi, S., & Zandiyeh, Z. (2016). Does Islamic spiritual program lead to successful aging? A randomized clinical trial. *Journal of Education and Health Promotion*, *5*(1), 2. https://doi.org/10.4103/2277-9531.184561

Mohamadi, J., Ghazanfari, F., & Drikvand, F. M. (2019). Comparison of the effect of dialectical behavior therapy, mindfulness based cognitive therapy and positive psychotherapy on perceived stress and quality of life in patients with irritable bowel syndrome: A pilot randomized controlled trial. *Psychiatric Quarterly*, *90*(3), 565–578. https://doi.org/10.1007/s11126-019-09643-2

Oman, D., Hedberg, J., & Thoresen, C. E. (2006). Passage meditation reduces perceived stress in health professionals: A randomized, controlled trial. *Journal of Consulting and Clinical Psychology*, *74*(4), 714–719. https://doi.org/10.1037/0022-006x.74.4.714

Pramesona, B. A., & Taneepanichskul, S. (2018). The effect of religious intervention on depressive symptoms and quality of life among Indonesian elderly in nursing homes: A quasi-experimental study. *Clinical Interventions in Aging*, *13*, 473–483. https://doi.org/10.2147/cia.s162946

Roof, W. C. (1993). *A generation of seekers: The spiritual journeys of the baby boom generation*. Harper-Collins.

Sawatzky, R., Ratner, P. A., & Chiu, L. (2005). A meta-analysis of the relationship between spirituality and quality of life. *Social Indicators Research*, *72*(2), 153–188. https://doi.org/10.1007/s11205-004-5577-x

Sekhavatpour, Z., Reyhani, T., Heidarzade, M., Moosavi, S. M., Mazlom, S. R., Dastoorpoor, M., Karimollahi, M., & Khanjani, N. (2020). The effect of spiritual self-care training on the quality of life of mothers of preterm infants: A randomized controlled trial. *Journal of Religion and Health*, *59*(2), 714–724. https://doi.org/10.1007/s10943-018-0620-4

Trombka, M., Demarzo, M., Campos, D., Antonio, S. B., Cicuto, K., Walcher, A. L., García-Campayo, J., Schuman-Olivier, Z., & Rocha, N. S. (2021). Mindfulness training improves quality of life and reduces depression and anxiety symptoms among police officers: Results from the POLICE study – A multicenter randomized controlled trial. *Frontiers in Psychiatry*, *12*. https://doi.org/10.3389/fpsyt.2021.624876

Tulbure, B. T., Andersson, G., Sălăgean, N., Pearce, M., & Koenig, H. G. (2017). Religious versus conventional internet-based cognitive behavioral therapy for depression. *Journal of Religion and Health*, *57*(5), 1634–1648. https://doi.org/10.1007/s10943-017-0503-0

Vermandere, M., Warmenhoven, F., Van Severen, E., De Lepeleire, J., & Aertgeerts, B. (2015). Spiritual history taking in palliative home care: A cluster randomized controlled trial. *Palliative Medicine*, *30*(4), 338–350. https://doi.org/10.1177/0269216315601953

Wachholtz, A. B., & Pargament, K. I. (2008). Migraines and meditation: Does spirituality matter? *Journal of Behavioral Medicine*, *31*(4), 351–366. https://doi.org/10.1007/s10865-008-9159-2

Wu, L.-F., & Koo, M. (2016). Randomized controlled trial of a six-week spiritual reminiscence intervention on hope, life satisfaction, and spiritual well-being in elderly with mild and moderate dementia. *International Journal of Geriatric Psychiatry*, *31*(2), 120–127. https://doi.org/10.1002/gps.4300

Xing, L., Guo, X., Bai, L., Qian, J., & Chen, J. (2018). Are spiritual interventions beneficial to patients with cancer? *Medicine*, *97*(35), e11948. https://doi.org/10.1097/md.0000000000011948

Yaghubi, M., Abdekhoda, M., & Khani, S. (2019). Effectiveness of religious-spiritual group therapy on spiritual health and quality of life in methadone-treated patients: A randomized clinical trial. *Addict Health*, *11*(3), 156–164. https://doi.org/10.22122/ahj.v11i3.238

Zernicke, K. A., Campbell, T. S., Blustein, P. K., Fung, T. S., Johnson, J. A., Bacon, S. L., & Carlson, L. E. (2013). Mindfulness-based stress reduction for the treatment of irritable bowel syndrome symptoms: A randomized wait-list controlled trial. *International Journal of Behavioral Medicine*, *20*(3), 385–396. https://doi.org/10.1007/s12529-012-9241-6

16

DIGITAL TECHNOLOGY AND WELLBEING

Moving beyond the hype

Diane Pelly

Introduction

Digital technology (DT) permeates every facet of our lives: 67.1% of the global population (5.3 billion) use mobile phones and 62.5% (4.95 billion) are Internet users, spending 6.5 hours online daily. Social media (SM) is the fastest growing sector, with 4.6 billion active users and 1 million new users on average per day (DataReportal, 2022). One in three Internet users are children (Livingstone et al., 2015). Due to its ubiquity, interest in the wellbeing consequences of DT has exploded over the past 15 years. While the data is inconclusive, negative media coverage and growing concerns about DT over-use (Büchi et al., 2019) has propelled problematic social media use, or "compulsive use that leads to impaired daily functioning in terms of productivity, social relationships, physical health, or emotional wellbeing" (Horwood & Anglim, 2019, p. 45), into the public health firing line.

In this chapter, I follow standard convention and use "DT" as an umbrella term which includes the Internet, smartphones/apps, wearables, social media platforms and so forth. While acknowledging that DT has many functions, as evidenced by the emergent literature on digital wellbeing (e.g., Vanden Abeele and Nguyen, 2022), I mirror the broader literature and focus on social media usage (SMU) given its policy relevance and empirical dominance (77% of studies reviewed by Schønning et al., 2020 examine SMU). SM are defined as Internet-based applications which facilitate the creation and dissemination of user-generated content (Brooks, 2015) and allow users to interact through computer-mediated communication (texts, etc.). They include social networking sites (e.g., Facebook) and interpersonal SM (e.g., WhatsApp).

While most studies on the welfare effects of DT employ mental health indicators, my focus is on wellbeing outcomes. In line with extant research, this includes

DOI: 10.4324/9781003382447-18

subjective wellbeing (SWB), namely individuals' cognitive evaluations of (life satisfaction) and emotional responses to (positive and negative affect) their daily lives (Diener et al., 2018). However, given that "feeling better" and "doing better" are not synonymous (Martela & Sheldon, 2019), in contrast to most of the extant research, I expand the definition of wellbeing to include eudaimonic wellbeing (EWB). EWB involves functioning optimally and living a life which is rich in meaning, purpose and authenticity and characterised by self-acceptance, personal growth and self-actualization (Huta & Waterman, 2014). It occurs when basic psychological needs for autonomy (agency and coherence), relatedness (meaningful social connections) and competence (self-efficacy and self-esteem) are met (Deci & Ryan, 2008). In summary, I define wellbeing (WB) as "feeling good and functioning well" (Huppert & So, 2013, p. 839).

The current state of knowledge

Multiple psychological mechanisms have been proposed for explaining hypothesised links between DT and WB. Exposure to curated SM profiles is purported to trigger upward social comparison, provoking unfavourable comparisons and negative emotions (Verduyn et al., 2017). SM features linked to social approval (e.g. likes) may also directly activate emotions such as elation or despondence (Steinert & Dennis, 2022). SMU may also facilitate emotion regulation (Wadley et al., 2020). The influential displacement hypothesis (Neuman, 1988) argues that DT is harmful if it (1) distracts users from performing more beneficial activities (like work) or (2) reduces relatedness by motivating users to substitute in-person socialising with poorer quality online social relationships and/or solitary activities (like scrolling). SMU may also provoke guilt (Labban & Bizzi, 2022). Conversely, the augmentation hypothesis argues that DT can boost WB when used for capital-enhancing purposes (networking, accessing resources Kearns & Whitley, 2019). Apps like BeReal may also potentially enrich off-line friendships by facilitating more authentic self-disclosure (Luo & Hancock, 2020).

The dominance of the displacement hypothesis has produced a negatively biased research agenda which mainly targets one question: are the (adverse) WB effects of DT directly proportional to exposure? Kross et al. (2021) outline three generations of screen time research. The first (2005–2011) comprises self-report/cross-sectional studies which yield very mixed findings (see Stoycheff et al.'s, 2017 review). The second (post-2010) generation employs more sophisticated methods (longitudinal studies, Experience Sampling Methods) but the results are also inconclusive. While some studies find positive links between increased SMU and negative affect (Twigg et al., 2020), others report null, conflicting, moderated or nonlinear results. For example, Przybylski and Weinstein (2017) show that moderate SMU increases (a hybrid measure of) WB, whereas low/high SMU reduces it – the "Goldilocks hypothesis". Directionality notwithstanding, effect sizes are small. Since 2015 a few third-generation experiments have revealed small but significant negative effects of SMU on life satisfaction and/or happiness (Tromholt et al., 2015), a pattern supported by systematic reviews (Dienlin & Johannes, 2022). However, small effect sizes ($r = -0.05$ to -0.15) undermine their practical significance (Orben, 2020). While SMU is moderately positively associated with social capital (Hancock et al., 2022), the relationship between SMU and life satisfaction is inconsistent, with Webster et al. (2021) reporting a negative association for 15 studies and a positive association for 9. Meta-analytic evidence on the impact of DT on affect and/or EWB is sparse (Meier & Reinecke, 2021b).

The most important finding to emerge from the early research is that all screen time is not equal in terms of WB effects. Researchers typically distinguish between active SMU (direct exchanges between SM users such as public posts and private messages which provide social support) and passive SMU (inactive consumption of content like lurking and scrolling) (Verduyn et al., 2017). There is however increasing evidence that social structures like age, gender, socioeconomic status (Twigg et al., 2020; Twenge & Martin, 2020) and prior beliefs may mediate the link between SMU and WB. For example Pouwels et al. (2022) find larger SMU social capital benefits for socially poor than socially rich adolescents, and Donoso et al. (2021) show that high intensity Internet use only reduces the WB (satisfaction) of students who perceive it as problematic. Further research is required to uncover factors which may exacerbate existing inequalities and explain heterogeneity in DT–WB effects. Person-specific approaches hold promise as they produce individual-level effect sizes which may expose heterogeneity otherwise masked by small average effect sizes. Qualitative idiographic studies, although rarely used (6% of studies reviewed by Schønning et al., 2020), also offer potential in terms of exploring individual differences in lived experiences of DT.

The lack of a concrete conclusion as to the net impact of DT on WB reflects the complexity of the relationship in which positive and negative outcomes often occur simultaneously (Büchi et al., 2019). However, it has also been linked to poor research quality, in particular to an over-reliance on cross-sectional studies and the so-called "jingle jangle problem" which occurs when different terms are used interchangeably or when the same term refers to different constructs (Kross et al., 2021). The lack of a common approach or lexicon stymies generalisable conclusions. Similarly, the common practices of collapsing all DT behaviours into a single predictor, arbitrarily combining conceptually distinct concepts such as stress and life satisfaction into aggregated WB measures and mis-labelling WB constructs (for instance categorising LS as EWB), erode precision and hamper interpretability (Valkenburg, 2022). Other challenges include reverse causality and reciprocal relationships. For example Wang et al. (2018) find that passive SMU predicts lower WB and low WB predicts passive SMU. Recommendations to bridge knowledge gaps and increase validity include incorporating EWB outcomes; more diverse sampling; shifting the focus from SMU to other DT; more person-centred qualitative studies and more accurate usage tracking.

High-quality field experiments will also play a crucial role in disentangling the causal DT–WB chain.

Interventions

Over the past five years there has been a notable increase in government regulation of DT. With regard to harm mitigation, policy initiatives generally mirror the literature and focus heavily on screen-time reduction. Interventions include (1) limiting access to DT (Utah recently mandated age verification and parental consent for U-18 SMU); (2) issuing expert recommendations (American Academy of Paediatrics screen-time guidelines); (3) encouraging abstention (The British Royal Society for Public Health's annual "Scroll-free September") and (4) digital literacy initiatives targeted at children, parents and teachers. Very little, if any, evaluation of these initiatives has occurred to date.

Market interventions can be categorised as follows: (1) parental control/surveillance tools (see Anderson, 2016); (2) digital detox self-help books/websites (e.g. digitaldetox.org) and (3) nudges (behavioural prods informed by behavioural economics). While Radtke et al. (2022) report moderate treatment effects on smartphone use for a variety of digital detox interventions, the WB effects are mixed and conflicting. Nudges range from "Time Out" phone lock boxes to commitment contracts and if-then plans for coping with temptation (Corno et al., 2021). Digital nudges seek to leverage DT through default settings and screen-time tracker apps (like "Moment"), which provide smart feedback on phone use and encourage users to set limits. Due to their emergent nature, evidence of effectiveness is scarce and mixed. Monge-Roffarello and De Russis' (2019) study suggests that while DWB apps may serve to raise awareness, the restrictions imposed are too weak to change DT usage habits. Furthermore, while providing timely feedback (e.g. vibration) may shorten the duration of screen-time episodes, frequency may remain unaffected (Purohit et al., 2023). Finally, experiments show that reducing screen time may not necessarily increase WB (Zimmermann & Sobolev, 2023) and may even reduce it through FOMO (fear-of-missing-out).

These initiatives are mainly negative interventions which seek to mitigate DT harm by limiting exposure. This is problematic for several reasons. Firstly, it is impractical given the digital–offline "*hybrid reality*" inhabited by today's adolescents (Granic et al., 2020, p. 196). Secondly, it suggests that heavy users who want to cut down merely need to exercise self-control despite evidence to the contrary relating to other behaviours. For users with high digital literacy, it is also potentially infantilising and agency threatening. Finally, the positive and negative outcomes of DT are intertwined. (Vanden Abeele, 2021).

To date, positive interventions which seek to actively foster positive DT–WB outcomes have been severely lacking. However, this may be changing. Policy recommendations for maximising the benefits of SMU for young people were recently published in the UK. These include a Social Media Health Alliance, financed by a 0.5% levy on SM companies and tasked with teaching digital coping skills and encouraging reflective attitudes towards DT. Initial experimental evidence suggests that educational initiatives may be effective at reducing problematic SMU (Gui et al., 2023) and that incorporating boosting techniques which teach children how to exploit the positive potential of DT into school curricula warrants exploration (Fasoli, 2021). Another promising development is the emergence of WB theory-led design from within the human–computer interaction community (see Cecchinato et al., 2019's review). Inspired by neuroscience and positive psychology research, positive computing (Calvo & Peters, 2014) seeks to integrate EWB antecedents into all stages of the DT design cycle. Positive technology (Riva et al., 2012) on the other hand seeks to create user experiences which generate positive emotions, support social connections and create self-actualising experiences (such as virtual reality games which engage the user in challenging tasks matched to their skills and resources).

Discussion and call to action

Effective intervention relies on high-quality research. While clear conclusions regarding the DT–WB relationship may elude us, some common threads have emerged. Firstly, the net impact of DTU on WB is probably negative, but negligible. Secondly, usage matters. While moderate and active SMU contributes to positive WB outcomes, the opposite is true for low, high and passive SMU. Thirdly, the dominant implicit assumption that DT affects all users similarly has been disproved (e.g. Beyens et al., 2021). This has important implications for policy design. Blunt one-size-fits-all negative interventions may not be warranted. The future for DT research lies in studying how online–offline interactions between person-, device- and context-specific factors dynamically shape WB (Van den Abeele, 2021). Emerging models like Peters' (2022) METUX model, which links different spheres of user experience to EWB indicators, could prove helpful in this regard.

While much has been achieved, progress remains curtailed by knowledge gaps and methodological limitations. Future research would benefit from the following:

- A more consistent approach to WB conceptualisation and measurement
- A shift in focus away from SMU to other aspects of DT (e.g. artificial intelligence)
- The explicit inclusion of digital WB within emerging WB frameworks and indices
- Methodologically rigorous experimental and longitudinal designs
- State-of-the-art data-capturing tools (e.g. application programming interfaces, or APIs)
- Idiographic studies to uncover psychological mechanisms and individual differences
- Greater focus on examining/disseminating the WB benefits of DT (cf. UNICEF, 2022)

Policy-makers in turn must adopt an evidence-based approach to policy design and implementation. Some recommendations include the following:

- A greater focus on positive interventions which target not just high-risk groups (e.g. children from deprived backgrounds who more likely to be high, passive users and subject to less parental controls), but also groups who stand to benefit substantially from DT such as older adults who may be at risk for social isolation
- More resources for high-quality studies and multidisciplinary think tanks, for example the Designing for Digital Wellbeing research forum and the Digital Futures Commission
- In-situ testing of soft-touch behaviourally informed interventions, for example digital nudges and personalisation, which target specific user groups
- Experimentally testing evidence-based digital boosting programmes
- Facilitating ethical, secure, and transparent de-identified data-sharing between SM corporations and researchers, perhaps through embedded research teams

Like it or loathe it, DT is here to stay. It behoves policy-makers, researchers and DT providers to collaborate to produce actionable insights aimed at facilitating DT users to adapt their online behaviours so as to reap the maximum benefits from DT, whilst mitigating its harms.

References

Anderson, M. (2016). *Parents, teens and digital monitoring*. Retrieved April 12, 2023, from https://policycommons.net/artifacts/618677/parents-teens-and-digital-monitoring/1599662/. CID: 20.500.12592/j3whtn.

Beyens, I., Pouwels, J. L., van Driel, I. I., Keijsers, L., & Valkenburg, P. M. (2021). Social media use and adolescents' well-being: Developing a typology of person-specific effect patterns. *Communication Research*. https://doi.org/10.1177/00936502211038l9

Brooks, S. (2015). Does personal social media usage affect efficiency and well-being? *Computers in Human Behavior*, *46*, 26–37. https://doi.org/10.1016/j.chb.2014.12.053

Büchi, M., Festic, N., & Latzer, M. (2019). Digital overuse and subjective well-being in a digitized society. *Social Media + Society*, *5*(4), 205. https://doi.org/10.1177/2056305119886031

Calvo, R. A., & Peters, D. (2014). *Positive computing: Technology for wellbeing and human potential*. MIT Press.

Cecchinato, M. E., Rooksby, J., Hiniker, A., Munson, S., Lukoff, K., Ciolfi, L., Thieme, A., & Harrison, D. (2019). Designing for digital wellbeing: A research & practice agenda. *Extended Abstracts of the 2019 CHI Conference on Human Factors in Computing Systems*, pp. 1–8. https://doi.org/10.1145/3290607.3298998

Corno, F., De Russis, L., & Monge-Roffarello, A. (2021). From users' intentions to if-then rules in the internet of things. *ACM Transactions on Information Systems (TOIS)*, *39*(4), 1–33. https://doi.org/10.1145/3447264

DataReportal (2022). *Digital 2022 global digital overview*. Retrieved May 1, 2023, from https://datareportal.com/reports/digital-2-22-global-overview-report

Deci, E. L., & Ryan, R. M. (2008). Self-determination theory: A macrotheory of human motivation, development, and health. *Canadian Psychology/Psychologie Canadienne*, *49*(3), 182. https://doi.org/10.1037/a0012801

Diener, E., Lucas, R. E., & Oishi, S. (2018). Advances and open questions in the science of subjective well-being. *Collabra: Psychology*, *4*(1). https://doi.org/10.1525/collabra.115
Dienlin, T., & Johannes, N. (2022). The impact of digital technology use on adolescent well-being. *Dialogues in Clinical Neuroscience*. https://doi.org/10.31887/DCNS.2020.22.2/tdienlin
Donoso, G., Casas, F., Rubio, A., & Céspedes, C. (2021). Mediation of problematic use in the relationship between types of internet use and subjective well-being in schoolchildren. *Frontiers in Psychology*, *12*. https://doi.org/10.3389/fpsyg.2021.641178
Fasoli, M. (2021). The overuse of digital technologies: Human weaknesses, design strategies and ethical concerns. *Philosophy & Technology*, *34*(4), 1409–1427. https://doi.org/10.1007/s13347-021-00463-6
Granic, I., Morita, H., & Scholten, H. (2020). Beyond screen time: Identity development in the digital age. *Psychological Inquiry*, *31*(3), 195–223. https://doi.org/10.1080/1047840X.2020.1820214
Gui, M., Gerosa, T., Argentin, G., & Losi, L. (2023). Mobile media education as a tool to reduce problematic smartphone use: Results of a randomised impact evaluation. *Computers & Education*, *194*. https://doi.org/10.1016/j.compedu.2022.104705
Hancock, J. T., Liu, S. X., Luo, M., & Mieczkowski, H. (2022). Social media and psychological well-being. In *The psychology of technology: Social science research in the age of big data* (pp. 195–238). American Psychological Association.
Horwood, S., & Anglim, J. (2019). Problematic smartphone usage and subjective and psychological well-being. *Computers in Human Behavior*, *97*, 44–50. https://doi.org/10.1016/j.chb.2019.02.028
Huppert, F. A., & So, T. T. (2013). Flourishing across Europe: Application of a new conceptual framework for defining well-being. *Social Indicators Research*, *110*, 837–861. https://doi.org/10.1007/s11205-011-9966-7
Huta, V., & Waterman, A. S. (2014). Eudaimonia and its distinction from hedonia: Developing a classification and terminology for understanding conceptual and operational definitions. *Journal of Happiness Studies*, *15*, 1425–1456. https://doi.org/10.1007/s10902-013-9485-0
Kearns, A., & Whitley, E. (2019). Associations of internet access with social integration, wellbeing and physical activity among adults in deprived communities: Evidence from a household survey. *BMC Public Health*, *19*(1), 1–15. https://doi.org/10.1186/s12889-019-7199-x
Kross, E., Verduyn, P., Sheppes, G., Costello, C. K., Jonides, J., & Ybarra, O. (2021). Social media and well-being: Pitfalls, progress, and next steps. *Trends in Cognitive Sciences*, *25*(1), 55–66. https://doi.org/10.1016/j.tics.2020.10.005
Labban, A., & Bizzi, L. (2022). Are social media good or bad for employees? It depends on when they use them. *Behaviour & Information Technology*, *41*(4), 678–693. https://doi.org/10.1080/0144929X.2020.1830174
Livingstone, S., Carr, J., & Byrne, J. (2015). *One in three: Internet governance and children's rights*. UNICEF Office of Research – Innocenti. www.unicef-irc.org/publications/795-one-in-three-internet-governance-and-childrens-rights.html
Luo, M., & Hancock, J. T. (2020). Self-disclosure and social media: Motivations, mechanisms and psychological well-being. *Current Opinion in Psychology*, *31*, 110–115. https://doi.org/10.1016/j.copsyc.2019.08.019
Martela, F., & Sheldon, K. M. (2019). Clarifying the concept of well-being: Psychological need satisfaction as the common core connecting eudaimonic and subjective well-being. *Review of General Psychology*, *23*(4), 458–474. https://doi.org/10.1177/1089268019880886
Meier, A., & Reinecke, L. (2021). *Social media and mental health: Reviewing effects on eudaimonic well-being*. https://doi.org/10.31234/osf.io/xvts8
Monge-Roffarello, A., & De Russis, L. (2019). The race towards digital wellbeing: Issues and opportunities. *Proceedings of the 2019 CHI Conference on Human Factors in Computing Systems*, 1–14. https://doi.org/10.1145/3290605.3300616

Neuman, S. B. (1988). The displacement effect: Assessing the relation between television viewing and reading performance. *Reading Research Quarterly*, 414–440. https://doi.org/10.2307/747641

Orben, A. (2020). Teenagers, screens and social media: A narrative review of reviews and key studies. *Social Psychiatry and Psychiatric Epidemiology*, *55*(4), 407–414. https://doi.org/10.1007/s00127-019-01825-4

Peters, D. (2022). Wellbeing supportive design–Research-based guidelines for supporting psychological wellbeing in user experience. *International Journal of Human–Computer Interaction*, 1–13. https://doi.org/10.1080/10447318.2022.2089812

Pouwels, J. L., Keijsers, L., & Odgers, C. (2022). Who benefits most from using social media, the socially rich or the socially poor? *Current Opinion in Psychology*, 101351. https://doi.org/10.1016/j.copsyc.2022.101351

Przybylski, A. K., & Weinstein, N. (2017). A large-scale test of the goldilocks hypothesis: Quantifying the relations between digital-screen use and the mental well-being of adolescents. *Psychological Science*, *28*(2), 204–215. https://doi.org/10.1177/0956797616678438

Purohit, A. K., Barev, T. J., Schöbel, S., Janson, A., & Holzer, A. (2023). *Designing for digital wellbeing on a smartphone: Co-creation of digital nudges to mitigate instagram overuse*. https://doi.org/10125/103130

Radtke, T., Apel, T., Schenkel, K., Keller, J., & von Lindern, E. (2022). Digital detox: An effective solution in the smartphone era? A systematic literature review. *Mobile Media & Communication*, *10*(2), 190–215. https://doi.org/10.1177/20501579211028647

Riva, G., Baños, R. M., Botella, C., Wiederhold, B. K., & Gaggioli, A. (2012). Positive technology: Using interactive technologies to promote positive functioning. *Cyberpsychology, Behavior, and Social Networking*, *15*(2), 69–77. https://doi.org/10.1089/cyber.2011.0139

Schønning, V., Hjetland, G. J., Aarø, L. E., & Skogen, J. C. (2020). Social media use and mental health and well-being among adolescents–a scoping review. *Frontiers in Psychology*, *11*, 1949. https://doi.org/10.3389/fpsyg.2020.01949

Steinert, S., & Dennis, M. J. (2022). Emotions and digital well-being: On social media's emotional affordances. *Philosophy & Technology*, *35*(2), 36. https://doi.org/10.1007/s13347-022-00530-6

Stoycheff, E., Liu, J., Wibowo, K. A., & Nanni, D. P. (2017). What have we learned about social media by studying Facebook? A decade in review. *New Media & Society*, *19*(6), 968–980. https://doi.org/10.1177/1461444817695745

Tromholt, M., Lundby, M., Andsbjerg, K., & Wiking, M. (2015). The Facebook experiment: Does social media affect the quality of our lives. *The Happiness Institute*. www.happinessresearchinstitute.com/publications/4579836749

Twenge, J. M., & Martin, G. N. (2020). Gender differences in associations between digital media use and psychological well-being: Evidence from three large datasets. *Journal of Adolescence*, *79*, 91–102. https://doi.org/10.1016/j.adolescence.2019.12.018

Twigg, L., Duncan, C., & Weich, S. (2020). Is social media use associated with children's well-being? Results from the UK household longitudinal study. *Journal of Adolescence*, *80*, 73–83. https://doi.org/10.1016/j.adolescence.2020.02.002

Unicef (2022). Responsible innovation in technology for children. *UNICEF Office of Research*. RITEC_Responsible-Innovation-in-Technology-for-Children-Digital-technology-play-and-child-well-being.pdf (unicef-irc.org)

Valkenburg, P. M. (2022). Social media use and well-being: What we know and what we need to know. *Current Opinion in Psychology*, *45*, 101294. https://doi.org/10.1016/j.copsyc.2021.12.006

Vanden Abeele, M. M. (2021). Digital wellbeing as a dynamic construct. *Communication Theory*, *31*(4), 932–955. https://doi.org/10.1093/ct/qtaa024

Vanden Abeele, M. M., & Nguyen, M. H. (2022). Digital well-being in an age of mobile connectivity: An introduction to the Special Issue. *Mobile Media & Communication*, *10*(2), 174–189. https://doi.org/10.1177/20501579221080899

Verduyn, P., Ybarra, O., Résibois, M., Jonides, J., & Kross, E. (2017). Do social network sites enhance or undermine subjective well-being? A critical review. *Social Issues and Policy Review*, *11*(1), 274–302. https://doi.org/10.1111/sipr.12033

Wadley, G., Smith, W., Koval, P., & Gross, J. J. (2020). Digital emotion regulation. *Current Directions in Psychological Science*, *29*(4), 412–418. https://doi.org/10.1177/0963721420920592

Wang, J. L., Gaskin, J., Rost, D. H., & Gentile, D. A. (2018). The reciprocal relationship between passive Social Networking Site (SNS) usage and users' subjective well-being. *Social Science Computer Review*, *36*(5), 511–522. https://doi.org/10.1177/0894439317721981

Webster, D., Dunne, L., & Hunter, R. (2021). Association between social networks and subjective well-being in adolescents: A systematic review. *Youth & Society*, *53*(2), 175–210.

Zimmermann, L., & Sobolev, M. (2023). Digital strategies for screen time reduction: A randomized field experiment. *Cyberpsychology, Behavior, and Social Networking*, *26*(1), 42–49. https://doi.org/10.1089/cyber.2022.0027

17

ART, CULTURE, AND WELLBEING

Reaping the rewards of creativity

Leonie Baldacchino

Introduction

Art, culture, and creativity (ACC) are sometimes linked to psychopathology, with many famous creatives being associated with mental illness and suicide (Bille et al., 2013). However, much of the literature associating creativity and mental illness relies on anecdotal evidence or suffers other methodological shortcomings (Bille et al., 2013; Ginis et al., 2022). Moreover, there are numerous examples of successful creative individuals, including artists, performers, writers, and poets, reaping the rewards of creativity, and living happy and healthy lives (Gilbert, 2016; Ginis et al., 2022). Using quantitative and qualitative longitudinal data from the daily diaries of 222 employees in seven companies, Amabile et al. (2005) find that famous troubled artists are greatly outnumbered by less well-known individuals whose creativity is catalysed by positive affect. Likewise, in his evidence-based book, Gillam (2018) notes that mood disorders and psychotic illnesses are generally detrimental to creativity.

Though the impact of ACC on wellbeing has not been firmly established and should be interpreted with caution (Silvia & Kaufman, 2010), a growing number of researchers have found that engaging in ACC itself enhances wellbeing. This is the literature that the rest of the chapter examines.

The following definitions are adopted: *art* refers to traditional forms including the performing arts (theatre, opera, dance), visual arts (painting, drawing, sculpture, photography), music and literature, as well as the continuously evolving online, digital, and electronic arts. They encompass artistic activities that are carried out and/or displayed in the public domain, and those that take place within people's homes and communities as a product of everyday human creativity. *Culture* refers to a social context in which the arts are embedded and enacted. This includes theatres, concert

DOI: 10.4324/9781003382447-19

halls, museums, and galleries. *Creativity* refers to the generation of ideas that are new and valuable (Amabile et al., 1996), considered crucial for becoming a successful artist (Frey, 2019). It is a skill that everyone possesses, albeit to varying degrees, ranging from the 'little-c' (everyday creativity) to the 'Big-C' (eminent creativity) (Kaufman & Beghetto, 2009). *Mental illness* encompasses a range of conditions that are characterised by changes in thinking, affect, and/or behaviour, which generally cause distress and hinder daily functioning (Waldock, 2015). *Wellbeing* is taken to refer to subjective psychological wellbeing, that is how satisfied one *feels (affect)* and how one evaluates life. Due to space limitations, physiological (or physical) wellbeing is not discussed in this chapter.

ACC may be categorised into active engagement (participation, production, etc.) and passive engagement (attendance, viewing, etc.) (Wang et al., 2020). A further distinction could be between those who perform/produce art for public consumption and those who do so in private or as a hobby. The former are generally regarded as *artists* (although this is perhaps the most debatable definition in this chapter), as are those who have a principal occupation in the arts (Steiner & Schneider, 2013), those who are self-proclaimed, and those for whom artistic creation is central to their life (Briguglio et al., 2020). A further type of engagement entails supporting the arts in some way, such as by volunteering or funding cultural events, but less is known about how this impacts wellbeing. This latter type of engagement is therefore not discussed in this chapter.

Literature on art, culture, and wellbeing

ACC encompass a wide range of activities that are enjoyable, uplifting, and enriching. They enable individuals to feel good (McDonnell, 2014) and are considered to be among the most rewarding activities that one can engage in (Layard & De Neve, 2023). As McDonnell (2014) posits, even simple creative activities, such as writing, drawing, singing, or dancing, often generate positive affect, fostering a sense of accomplishment and personal satisfaction.

Empirical studies have indicated that both active and passive ACC engagements are associated with higher wellbeing and lower distress, although the effects of active engagement tend to be stronger. Briguglio et al. (2020) analysed cross-sectional data derived from 1,125 interviews conducted for the Malta Cultural Participation Survey (NSO, 2017), and found that while both audiences and participants reported higher levels of life satisfaction than the culturally unengaged, the actively engaged enjoyed the greatest wellbeing of all groups, even after controlling for other determinants of wellbeing. Wang et al.'s (2020) analysis of longitudinal survey data from 23,660 participants of the UK Understanding Society Study similarly found that regular participation in the arts and attending cultural events was associated with reduced mental distress and increased life satisfaction, and that active involvement was linked to improved mental health functioning. The reasons for these effects are varied and interrelated.

For example, creative arts programmes may enable at-risk individuals to satisfy basic needs. Ferrell et al. (2023) conducted a survey among 42 marginalised young people in a youth theatre programme in England, followed by in-depth qualitative interviews with a subset of three survey participants, their parents, and teachers, and found that theatre participation was associated with wellbeing through the satisfaction of basic needs, including autonomy, empowerment, relatedness, and competence. McDonnell (2014) carried out a 14-month ethnographic study in a mental health day centre in Ireland and found that the daily creative activities held at the centre provided service users with somewhere to go and something to do, along with consistent and dependable social assistance.

Other ways in which ACC enhance wellbeing is via self-expression, self-disclosure, and distraction. In their qualitative study with ten eminent Australian female visual artists, Ginis et al. (2022) found that producing art is a way of expressing thoughts and feelings, or revealing hidden traumas, allowing individuals to process suffering and come to terms with it. Such catharsis provides emotional release and respite, which results in reduced stress and an enhanced sense of wellbeing. Some of the artists interviewed even found comfort in transforming pain into works of art. Creative activities involve more than simple recall and expression; they also involve actively engaging with thoughts and experiences, which in turn facilitates their evolution and reinterpretation (Forgeard et al., 2014). Nainis et al. (2006) conducted a quasi-experimental design among 50 adult cancer patients in northwestern United States to examine the effect of a one-hour art therapy session on their symptoms and found that ACC serve to distract their mind from troubles and pain, thereby enhancing wellbeing by reducing stress and suffering.

ACC may further contribute to wellbeing by providing opportunities for learning and skill development, and by enhancing self-esteem and self-efficacy. For example, marginalised young people interviewed by Ferrell et al. (2023) in their UK-based study reported that when they perform on stage, in front of an audience who can appreciate the show and their effort, they experience feelings of self-worth, accomplishment, and empowerment. Boutry's (2017) qualitative study found that a community college creativity programme helped develop a positive self-image among traditionally underserved and challenged students which in turn enabled them to visualise and explore future possibilities and aspirations. According to Hughes and Wilson (2017), this is in itself a basic act of creativity.

ACC are also associated with wellbeing via the state of flow. This refers to a complete immersion or absorption in an activity, or 'being in the zone', which often leads to feelings of happiness and fulfilment (Csikszentmihalyi, 1997). Flow and its wellbeing outcomes may be experienced in many activities that are absorbing and that improve with effort and time, such as work, science, sports, and the arts. However, Csikszentmihalyi (1997) considered creativity to be at the heart of the flow and wellbeing experience, because discovering and creating new things generates happy feelings. This notion has been supported by various authors including Ginis et al. (2022) in their study of eminent female artists in Australia, who found that creative pursuits such as painting, sculpture, and photography foster a sense of absorption and deep engagement with the task (i.e. flow), which in turn promote wellbeing and autonomy.

There appears to be diversity in the degree of impact of ACC. Researchers have analysed panel data to examine the impact of socio-demographic variables on the relationship between ACC and wellbeing, with findings strongly indicating that disadvantaged groups such as low-income families and single-person households in Korea (Lee & Heo, 2021), those living in deprived areas in the UK (Mak et al., 2021), and persons with disability in Germany (Pagán, 2015) have the potential to derive greater benefits from ACC than others. Yet high-income households and multi-person families tend to engage in ACC more frequently and more broadly. This is likely due to the high entrance fees of mainstream ACC and the lower opportunity cost of alternative activities (Frey, 2019), and implies that ACC are less accessible to minorities and disadvantaged groups. The APPGAHW (2017) in fact identifies a lack of diversity in the creative industries in the UK. Employment in the creative industries also lacks diversity (APPG, 2017).

Finally, despite the 'anguished artist' stereotype, empirical research reviewed by Frey (2019) indicates that artists report higher levels of happiness and life satisfaction than non-artists of similar demographics. This is supported by Briguglio et al.'s (2020) analysis of the Malta Cultural Participation Survey (NSO, 2017) data, who found wellbeing to be higher among actively employed artists. This, of course, does not imply that wellbeing is high among all artists, as the nature of professional creative work could be very demanding and stressful (Frey, 2019; Ginis et al., 2022). Yet such work can be highly satisfying as it entails creative processes that are characterised by novelty and variety, and which generally takes the form of autonomous and self-determined self-employment (Frey, 2019; Steiner & Schneider, 2013). In accordance with this, Bille et al.'s (2013) study of artists in 49 countries found that they appreciate the possibility to take initiative in their work and the inherent interest of their job and that they exhibit significantly higher job satisfaction than nonartists.

Evidence of interventions

Several studies have provided evidence on the effectiveness of ACC interventions on wellbeing of individuals of all ages, from schoolchildren to senior citizens. Some studies contain real-world ACC interventions whose impact is assessed, while others consist of trials or experiments in which research participants engage in ACC activities and their outcomes are compared to those of a control group.

The UK's *Creative Partnerships* (CP) programme (2002–2011), which involved over 5,000 schools, 90,000 teachers, and over one million young people who worked with approximately 6,500 arts organisations, evaluated CP with respect to a variety of dimensions including wellbeing. According to Thomson et al.'s (2018) review of the CP research archive, one of the reported outcomes of CP was that schools were happier, livelier, and generally better places with higher teaching morale and freedom to innovate.

Cohen (2006) found that an intervention group, comprising elderly individuals who were engaged in intensive participatory art programmes in Washington, United States, fared significantly better than the unengaged control group after one and two years. Notably, the intervention group reported improved health, fewer medical visits, and decreased medication usage, more positive responses in mental health measures, and generally higher levels of activity.

Bell and Robbins (2007) conducted a randomised, controlled trial with 50 adults in Pennsylvania, United States, to compare the effects of producing versus viewing art on reductions in stress and elevations in mood. Their participants were randomly divided into two groups – one group was given drawing/painting materials and asked to produce (draw/paint) a picture of their choice, while the other group were given prints of famous paintings and asked to view and sort them as they deemed fit. The findings revealed significantly larger drops in negative mood and anxiety among participants engaged in art production, compared to those in the art-viewing control group.

Sandmire et al. (2012) investigated the impact of ACC on the mental wellbeing of 57 undergraduate students in the northeastern United States, who were randomly assigned to either an art-making test group or a no-activity control group one week before their final exams. Artistic tasks included painting, colouring mandalas, making collages, still life drawing, and clay modelling. Findings revealed that the control group experienced a significant decrease in anxiety after their artistic activities, while no change was observed in the control group. These results indicate that a brief session of art making can alleviate anxiety levels.

Boutry (2017) implemented a creativity programme at a community college for underserved, challenged students in California, United States, and evaluated it by means of self-assessment reports from programme participants. She reports overwhelmingly positive feedback, with students revealing wellbeing benefits such as improved self-image, self-esteem, and pride in their accomplishments. Boutry concludes that creativity equips students with enhanced capabilities to navigate life challenges, which encourage students to tap into their creative capacities.

Finally, it is worth noting that there are many examples of inclusive ACC interventions whose impacts have not been documented. Examples from Malta are the specialised movement classes for individuals living with Parkinson's and their caregivers (Step up for Parkinson's, n.d.), dance classes for persons living with dementia and their carers (Malta Dementia Society, 2024), and arts training and performances for adults with intellectual disabilities (Opening Doors Association, n.d.).

Discussion and actionable points

Before concluding with a few points for action, it is worth noting that intervention studies are sometimes criticised as the mere act of observing participants may alter outcomes including affect and wellbeing (Muldoon & Zoller, 2020). Moreover, as discussed at the outset, a reverse causality may also exist, that is happy people are more likely to become artists and to visit art activities and cultural events, because they are more curious and open to experiences. This may be the case, but such a reverse effect does not appear to be dominant (Frey, 2019). It is also worth acknowledging that art and culture could have negative effects on bystanders such as residents who suffer negative consequences. For example, cultural events that entail public gatherings, such as outdoor concerts and music festivals, are often criticised for leaving various undesirable consequences including noise, litter, and traffic congestion (Frey, 2019).

On the basis of the literature reviewed in this chapter, the following are recommended actions for the enhancement of wellbeing via ACC:

- Active engagement can generate higher effects than passive engagement, suggesting room for intervention. Opportunities should be provided for learning, participation, and performance. Existing social venues and communities, such as educational institutions, religious establishments, and family centres, could be leveraged for greater cost-effectiveness. Investment is needed to educate people about the positive effects of ACC and to promote cultural events, while mitigating their possible negative impacts on the broader community.
- While everyone benefits from ACC, this is more beneficial yet less accessible to minorities and disadvantaged groups. An explanation for this is the possibility that minorities have their own art forms that were not measured or considered in research, such as church music and singing. However, it is also likely that they do not have the money, time, and energy to engage in costly mainstream ACC. Interventions may therefore be needed to promote active ACC engagement generally, as well as to level the playing field among different strata of society, for instance through subsidies.
- Despite the potential benefits of ACC occupations, employment in creative industries lacks diversity. To address this, policy-makers could draw inspiration from the OECD's (2015–2023) inclusive entrepreneurship book series and initiatives, which aim at increasing self-employment opportunities for underrepresented and disadvantaged groups.
- More scientific research on the effects of ACC on wellbeing is needed to better understand the mechanisms underlying this relationship. Formal evaluations of arts-based interventions are also required to inform future policy-making. Rigorous research and evaluation require funding, which could come from government programmes and other sources, such as philanthropists and social innovators.

References

All-Party Parliamentary Group on Arts, Health and Wellbeing (2017). Inquiry report: Creative health: The arts for health and wellbeing (2nd ed.). *All-Party Parliamentary Group*. https://ncch.org.uk/uploads/Creative_Health_Inquiry_Report_2017_-_Second_Edition.pdf

Amabile, T. M., Barsade, S. G., Mueller, J. S., & Staw, B. M. (2005). Affect and creativity at work. *Administrative Science Quarterly*, *50*(3), 367–403. https://doi.org/10.2189/asqu.2005.50.3.367

Amabile, T. M., Conti, R., Coon, H., Lazenby, J., & Herron, M. (1996). Assessing the work environment for creativity. *Academy of Management Journal*, *39*(5), 1154–1184. https://doi.org/10.5465/256995

Bell, C. E., & Robbins, S. J. (2007). Effect of art production on negative mood: A randomized, controlled trial. *Art Therapy*, *24*(2), 71–75. https://doi.org/10.1080/07421656.2007.10129589

Bille, T., Fjællegaard, C. B., Frey, B. S., & Steiner, L. (2013). Happiness in the arts – International evidence on artists' job satisfaction. *Economics Letters*, *121*(1), 15–18. https://doi.org/10.1016/j.econlet.2013.06.016

Boutry, K. (2017). "Creativity takes courage": The link between creativity programs and student well-being in the urban community college. In F. K. Reisman (Ed.), *Creativity, innovation and wellbeing: Proceedings of international conference on knowledge, innovation and enterprise*. KIE Conference Publications. https://kiecon.org/wp-content/uploads/2020/07/Creativity-Innovation-Wellbeing.pdf

Briguglio, M., Camilleri, G., & Vella, M. (2020). Artists, audiences & wellbeing: An economic analysis. *International Journal of Wellbeing*, *10*(4). https://doi.org/10.5502/ijw.v10i4.1205

Cohen, G. (2006). Research on creativity and aging: The positive impact of the arts on health and illness. *Generations*, *30*(1), 7–15.

Csikszentmihalyi, M. (1997). Happiness and creativity. *The Futurist*, *31*(5), S8–S12.

Ferrell, A., Levstek, M., & Banerjee, R. (2023). "We have a voice: We exist": Value of basic needs satisfaction for well-being and goal development in inclusive theater spaces for young people. *The Journal of Creative Behavior*, *57*(4), 1–16. https://doi.org/10.1002/jocb.608

Forgeard, M. C., Mecklenburg, A. C., Lacasse, J. J., & Jayawickreme, E. (2014). Bringing the whole universe to order: Creativity, healing, and posttraumatic growth. In J. C. Kaufman (Ed.), *Creativity and mental illness* (pp. 321–342). Cambridge University Press. https://doi.org/10.1017/CBO9781139128902.021

Frey, B. S. (2019). *The economics of art and culture*. Springer International Publishing. https://doi.org/10.1007/978-3-030-15748-7

Gilbert, E. (2016). *Big magic: Creative living beyond fear*. Penguin.

Gillam, T. (2018). *Creativity, wellbeing and mental health practice*. Palgrave Pivot Cham. https://doi.org/10.1007/978-3-319-74884-9

Ginis, K., Stewart, S. E., & Kronborg, L. (2022). Inter-relationships between artistic creativity and mental and physical illness in eminent female visual artists: A qualitative exploration. *The Journal of Creative Behavior*, *56*(3), 414–431. https://doi.org/10.1002/jocb.537

Hughes, G., & Wilson, C. (2017). From transcendence to general maintenance: Exploring the creativity and wellbeing dynamic in higher education. In F. K. Reisman (Ed.), *Creativity, innovation and wellbeing: Proceedings of international conference on knowledge, innovation and enterprise*. KIE Conference Publications. https://kiecon.org/wp-content/uploads/2020/07/Creativity-Innovation-Wellbeing.pdf

Kaufman, J. C., & Beghetto, R. A. (2009). Beyond big and little: The four c model of creativity. *Review of General Psychology*, *13*(1), 1–12. https://doi.org/10.1037/a0013688

Layard, R., & De Neve, J. E. (2023). *Wellbeing*. Cambridge University Press. https://doi.org/10.1017/9781009298957

Lee, H., & Heo, S. (2021). Arts and cultural activities and happiness: Evidence from Korea. *Applied Research in Quality of Life*, *16*, 1637–1651. https://doi.org/10.1007/s11482-020-09833-2

Mak, H. W., Coulter, R., & Fancourt, D. (2021). Associations between community cultural engagement and life satisfaction, mental distress and mental health functioning using data from the UK Household Longitudinal Study (UKHLS): Are associations moderated by area deprivation? *BMJ Open*, *11*(9), e045512. https://doi.org/10.1136/bmjopen-2020-045512

Malta Dementia Society (2024). *DancingtoDementia*. https://maltadementiasociety.org.mt/dancing-to-dementia/

McDonnell, R. (2014). *Creativity and social support in mental health: Service users' perspectives*. Palgrave Macmillan London. https://doi.org/10.1057/9781137345486

Muldoon, J., & Zoller, Y. (2020). Contested paths: A meta-analytic review of the Hawthorne studies literature. In K. Bruce (Ed.). *Handbook of research on management and organizational history* (pp. 56–79). https://doi.org/10.4337/9781788118491.00010.

Nainis, N., Paice, J. A., Ratner, J., Wirth, J. H., Lai, J., & Shott, S. (2006). Relieving symptoms in cancer: Innovative use of art therapy. *Journal of Pain and Symptom Management*, *31*(2), 162–169. https://doi.org/10.1016/j.jpainsymman.2005.07.006

National Statistics Office (NSO) (2017). *Culture participation survey 2016*. National Statistics Office.

OECD/European Commission (2015–2023). *The missing entrepreneurs: Policies for inclusive entrepreneurship and self-employment*. OECD Publishing. https://doi.org/10.1787/43c2f41c-en

Opening Doors Association (n.d.). *Welcome to opening doors*. https://openingdoors.org.mt/

Pagán, R. (2015). How do leisure activities impact on life satisfaction? Evidence for German people with disabilities. *Applied Research in Quality of Life*, *10*, 557–572. https://doi.org/10.1007/s11482-014-9333-3

Sandmire, D. A., Gorham, S. R., Rankin, N. E., & Grimm, D. R. (2012). The influence of art making on anxiety: A pilot study. *Art Therapy*, *29*(2), 68–73. https://doi.org/10.1080/07421656.2012.683748

Silvia, P. J., & Kaufman, J. C. (2010). Creativity and mental illness. In J. C. Kaufman & R. J. Sternberg (Eds.), *The Cambridge handbook of creativity*. Cambridge University Press. https://doi.org/10.1017/CBO9780511763205

Steiner, L., & Schneider, L. (2013). The happy artist: An empirical application of the work-preference model. *Journal of Cultural Economics*, *37*, 225–246. https://doi.org/10.1007/s10824-012-9179-1

Step up for Parkinson's (n.d.). *Step up for Parkinson's*. https://stepupforparkinsons.com/

Thomson, P., Coles, R., & Hallewell, M. (2018). What did creative partnerships achieve? A review of the Creative Partnerships (CP) research archive. In K. Snepvangers, P. Thomson, & A. Harris (Eds.), *Creativity policy, partnerships and practice in education: Creativity, education and the arts*. Palgrave Macmillan. https://doi.org/10.1007/978-3-319-96725-7_2

Waldock, H. (2015). Understanding mental illness. In P. Callaghan & C. Gamble (Eds.), *Oxford handbook of mental health nursing*. Oxford University Press. https://doi.org/10.1093/med/9780198703853.001.0001

Wang, S., Mak, H. W., & Fancourt, D. (2020). Arts, mental distress, mental health functioning & life satisfaction: Fixed-effects analyses of a nationally-representative panel study. *BMC Public Health*, *20*, 1–9. https://doi.org/10.1186/s12889-019-8109-y

PART III

Wellbeing

Evidence from countries

18

WELLBEING AND POLICY IN BHUTAN

Kehinde Balogun and Kariuki Weru

Overview

Bhutan is a Democratic Constitutional Monarchy (Dorji, 2020) with diverse ethnicities comprising about 0.7 million people, which has globally spearheaded a wellbeing-based development framework. The concept of Gross National Happiness (GNH) was introduced in 1979 (Meier & Chakrabarti, 2016) and subsequently declared as a superior policy directive to Gross Domestic Product (Verma, 2022). Its novelty paved the way for the 2011 United Nations (UN) resolution 65/309 on Happiness, and its efficacy as a new global economic paradigm was discussed on the sidelines of the UN General Assembly in April 2012. In 2013, the UN recognized March 20 as the International Day of Happiness, inspired by GNH's emphasis on happiness and collective wellbeing, moving away from the monetization at the heart of the GDP-driven global development model (Verma, 2022).

Happiness has long been at the forefront of policy in the Kingdom of Bhutan. This dates back to the country's unification in 1729, when the legal code stated that the central function of the government is to provide enabling conditions for its citizens to achieve happiness (Masaki & Tshering, 2021; Meier & Chakrabarti, 2016; Ura et al., 2012, p. 111). The concept of happiness in Bhutan differs significantly from the hedonistic and individualistic understanding that fuels the current economic and developmental trajectories (Verma, 2022; Levenson et al., 2004). For Bhutan, happiness is endogenous and directly linked to social responsibility (Verma, 2022). This form of happiness takes center stage in the holistic development of the wellbeing of individuals (Meier & Chakrabarti, 2016) and it acknowledges the interconnected nature of all lives (Richardson, 2023). The GNH policy emerged from the integration of Buddhist philosophy, local Indigenous development approaches, and the translation of research into policies and practices

DOI: 10.4324/9781003382447-21

(Richardson, 2023). The resultant merging of external and internal ideas (Richardson, 2023) makes it distinct from other wellbeing approaches, as noted by Sithey et al. (2018). This is because the GNH policy prioritizes the tripartite interconnected spheres of (1) preserving the environment, (2) promoting collective wellbeing, and (3) the pursuit of individual happiness. In wellbeing science, this is referred to as relational wellbeing, where the individual, societal, and environmental spheres are interdependent and mutually supportive in achieving holistic wellbeing (Balogun et al., 2023).

From this perspective, the principles of sufficiency (or contentment) and balance guide the harmonious interdependence of the individual and the collective on nature to concurrently meet spiritual and material needs. By emphasizing the importance of spiritual development to address "inner" or cultural poverty, which involves a deficit in fundamental human values and compassion, encompassing negative emotions and their impacts (Singye, 2014), GNH provides a comprehensive governance framework with happiness and wellbeing as the ultimate goals and outcomes of all growth efforts. This chapter illustrates how GNH policy strives to create the necessary conditions for happiness by addressing both internal factors (such as perceptions and values) and external challenges (including social inequality and biodiversity loss) through various government policies (Richardson, 2023). We present GNH as a holistic wellbeing initiative at a national level, while exploring its effectiveness and governance. Furthermore, we highlight GNH's knowledge gaps on mental health and offer areas of further research and public dialogues on wellbeing and sustainable development at global level.

Wellbeing initiatives in Bhutan

The GNH framework can broadly be described as aiming toward the harmonious balance of human happiness within the bounds of localized sustainability by enhancing wellbeing in the economic, social, environmental, and cultural dimensions of Bhutanese society. GNH policy formation is institutionalized through both the GNH *Index* (GNHI) and the GNH *Commission* (*GNHC*), in which the former is a measurement tool that appraises the happiness of the population, while the latter is a multilayered governance framework that monitors and evaluates policies based on GNH philosophy (Masaki & Tshering, 2021). GNH differs from other wellbeing initiatives because it equally balances the four pillars of (1) sustainable socioeconomic development, (2) preservation and promotion of culture, (3) environmental conservation, and (4) good governance (Richardson, 2023; Dorji, 2020). From these pillars emerge nine policy domains: living standards, education, health, cultural diversity and resilience, community vitality, time use, psychological wellbeing, ecological diversity, and good governance. This forms the basis of the GNHI, thereby constituting the yardstick of progress used by the GNHC. As a framework that seeks the public good, GNH requires responsibility shared across government, individuals, communities, and businesses to achieve positive results both over time and across different regions (Balasubramanian & Cashin, 2019; Ura et al., 2012, pp. 113 & 143).

In 2008 Bhutan created its first GNHI (Sithey et al., 2018) and in 2010 it introduced the revised GNHI and policy screening tool. The GNH *policy screening tool* allows for a systematic assessment of policies across the GNH domains (Sithey et al., 2018) and to prompt public deliberation, policy design, and resource allocation (Ura et al., 2012, p. 113). The GNHI on the other hand draws from a holistic and intentional vision of development (Ura et al., 2012, p. 113) consisting of 33 total indicators with 124 variables, each with their own indicator weights and considered equally important for achieving happiness (Balasubramanian & Cashin, 2019; Sithey et al., 2018). The selection of indicators was informed by participatory consultations based on the GNH pilot *surveys* conducted in 2006 and 2008 involving decision-makers, government agencies, autonomous bodies, and academics (Sithey et al., 2018). The GNH survey is a tool developed by the Centre of Bhutan Studies to measure happiness across GNH domains (Meier & Chakrabarti, 2016). It allows survey enumerators to engage with respondents, ensuring a thorough understanding of their perspectives and insights (Ura et al., 2012, p. 114) in order to rank their level of satisfaction on a scale from deeply unsatisfied to incredibly satisfied (Meier & Chakrabarti, 2016). As such, the data from GNH surveys can be compared longitudinally or be granularly disaggregated, by identifying (un)happy people by subgroups of districts, demographics, or particular indicators (Ura et al., 2012, p. 140). In so doing, the GNHI is a dynamic tool that captures the holistic experience of individuals and shows the diverse faces of happiness across time.

The GNHI was developed using the robust Alkire Foster methods for measuring concepts such as poverty or inequality, but tailored to Bhutan's needs to identify people either as happy or not yet happy by considering the "*sufficiencies*" that they enjoy (Ura et al., 2012, p. 130). The GNHI's sufficiency threshold indicates how much a person needs to enjoy sufficiency in all 33 indicators of the GNHI and how a particular respondent enjoys or lacks sufficiency in each indicator (Ura et al., 2012, p. 128). Measuring sufficiency thresholds determines the ratio of people who are either extensively or deeply happy (enjoy sufficiency) versus those who are not yet happy (lacking sufficiency) (Ura et al., 2012, p. 128). To date, three surveys in 2010, 2015, and 2022 followed the same 66% sufficient happiness threshold; that is an individual is considered happy if they met two-thirds of the variables and indicators stipulated by the GNHI.

For GNH policy creation and integration, the GNHC is the responsible body for the inclusion of GNH into all levels of governmental functions and policies across administrative and judicial districts, as well as locally at the level of residential blocks (gewogs) (Sithey et al., 2018). According to Balasubramanian and Cashin (2019), the GNHC implements such policy through a 5-Year Plan (FYP) with a results-based approach to assess each sector's performance across the four pillars of GNH. Sithey et al. (2018) noted that this requires individual government agencies to submit concept notes for review and consideration by the Council of Cabinet

Ministers. The initial screening of the concept note is done by the GNHC secretary to ensure its adherence to the GNH framework, by using the GNH policy screening tools and GNH indicators as reference points (Balasubramanian & Cashin, 2019). Thereafter, the GNHC, a 15-member committee with representatives from ministries to industries gives a score of 1 to 4 for 22 variables (Balasubramanian & Cashin, 2019; Sithey et al., 2018). The minimum score for proceeding to the policy approval process is 66 points and policies scoring less are rejected or require adjustments (Sithey et al., 2018). If successful, the concept notes proceed to the Cabinet for approval (Balasubramanian & Cashin, 2019). Upon approval, the planning, monitoring, and evaluation of the projects and policies occur continuously throughout their lifecycle (Balasubramanian & Cashin, 2019) and are spearheaded by the GNHC. As such, public surveys inform the GNHI, which then shapes GNH policy through the policy screening tool to allow for evidence-based decision-making for effective implementation.

Evidence of effectiveness of existing wellbeing initiatives

The overall effectiveness of GNH policy can best be shown through the holistic logic of relational wellbeing, a dynamic and interdependent tripartite relationship between the environment, society, and individuals (Balogun et al., 2023). On the individual level, according to Ura et al. (2023, pp. 61–62), the proportion of individuals reporting happiness from 2010 to 2022 increased by 7.2%—from 40.9% in 2010 to 48.1% in 2022. The proportion of those categorized as "not yet happy" had negligibly increased, from 56.6% in 2015 to 57.9% in 2022. This shows the effectiveness of the survey in measuring happiness and its utility for time-based comparison, both of which consequently provide a feedback loop to enable specific corrective policy measures.

On the societal level, the national GNHI rating rose from 0.743 in 2010 to 0.756 and 0.781 in 2015 and 2022, respectively (Ura et al., 2023, p. 5). Balasubramanian and Cashin (2019) noted that this achievement was a consequence of the focus on poverty reduction during the 2008–2013 Five Year Plan, aligned with GNH principles. For example, from 2000 to 2010, GNH-inspired development approaches shifted resources to local districts and communities, thereby enhancing localized capacity, accountability, communication, and coordination. Over this period, GNH-based policies played a vital role in achieving economic growth, environmental legislation, biodiversity action plans, enhanced credit access for entrepreneurs, and sustainable industrial development. As a result, Bhutan averaged around 6% real GDP growth between 2010 and 2017, positioning it as one of the fastest growing low-income countries (Balasubramanian & Cashin, 2019).

Although GDP is widely associated with people's wellbeing, it is limited in this measurement, as it does not capture environmental damage to produce goods and services, nor does it consider the distribution of wealth among citizens. Studies have shown that higher levels of GDP and income do not correlate with happiness in the long run, namely the Easterlin Paradox. This has also been observed in Bhutan, where substantial GDP growth has also remarkably contributed to poverty decline since 2007 (Balasubramanian & Cashin, 2019), leading to improvements in material wellbeing, including increased income, better housing, and enhanced healthcare (Centre for Bhutan Studies & GNH Research, 2016, p. 6). However, several psychological wellbeing indicators have significantly regressed (Centre for Bhutan Studies & GNH Research, 2016, p. 7). A recent study notes that while individuals in lower- and middle-income brackets exhibit a heightened vulnerability to suicidal thoughts, individuals in the middle-income category demonstrated a reduced propensity for suicide attempts compared to their high-income counterparts (Dendup et al., 2020).

Bhutan's modernization efforts have inadvertently created some counterintuitive trends. For example, van Norren (2023) highlighted that the modifications made to educational criteria and curricula by the GNHC have created a scenario in which individuals who have undergone the latest school curricula hold an advantage in parliamentary elections (van Norren, 2023). Additionally, despite many youths passing national secondary examinations, only approximately half of these students can secure admission to national higher education institutions (Lester et al., 2020). Furthermore, youth in urban areas are often unable to secure employment, and those who recently migrated to the capital are frequently unable to cope with the demands of modernity, with many subsequently abusing substances (Grimmond et al., 2019). The substance abuse alongside food insecurity, stressful life events, academic pressures, physical and sexual violence, as well as loneliness and despair have been reported to contribute to suicidal ideation and attempts in Bhutan (Dendup et al., 2020; Dema et al., 2019). These studies show that women, and girls in particular, have a heightened vulnerability to both suicidal ideation and attempts as compared to their male counterparts (Dema et al., 2019).

The 2022 GNH report acknowledges and expresses concerns about both the heightened prevalence of unhealthy lifestyles—such as obesity—and the decline in mental health indicators (Ura et al., 2023, p. 74). For the latter, suicide ranks among the primary causes of mortality rates in Bhutan, representing an intricate interplay of personal, socio-economic, psychological, cultural, biological, and environmental factors (Dema et al., 2019). Given Bhutan's emphasis on non-economic measures to alleviate inner poverty through psychosocial wellbeing indicators, there is a need to better understand and address this phenomenon. However, preventive measures such as awareness-raising activities in schools and religious institutions, training of health workers as first responders, the establishment of a 24-hour crisis support hotline, and a national suicide registry are being implemented (Dendup et al., 2020).

Another outcome of GNH is environmental sustainability, rooted in the Buddhist principle of seeking harmony and balance with all living beings. Before GNH's inception, Bhutan's people valued their natural environment and acknowledged it as part of their own national identity (Thinley & Hartz-Karp, 2019). This led to

Bhutan's policy-makers and population advancing this inherent inclination towards the continued preservation of the environment by translating it into their development agenda. As a result, despite its accelerating modernization and development from the early 1960s to the late 2010s, Bhutan's forest cover increased by 8%. To this end, Bhutan remains one of the few carbon-negative nations and has pledged to remain at most carbon neutral in the future (Thinley & Hartz-Karp, 2019).

Discussion and conclusion

This chapter discussed the GNH philosophy, its framework, index, survey, and policy screening tools, all of which were created to ensure happiness for Bhutan's population. It presented GNH as a national governance framework that considers GDP as one of the tools for achieving holistic wellbeing. By conducting a deeper exploration of the Buddhist and Indigenous thoughts that informed the GNH, this chapter underscores how a relational approach has shaped economic development and policy frameworks. Overall, GNH's focus on promoting happiness has resulted in policy reforms within a dynamic and inclusive form of governance. It achieved this by successfully harmonizing local belief systems with international best practices to simultaneously achieve economic growth and environmental sustainability. However, a key finding of this chapter is the concerning trend of unhealthy lifestyles and the decline in the mental health of Bhutanese citizens. In this regard, the chapter highlights knowledge and policy gaps in the interplay of socioeconomic status and mental health challenges that lead to high rates of suicide. Given GNH's focus on non-economic measures of wellbeing, we suggest key action points later, both for and beyond Bhutan.

Actionable points

GNH as an alternative development paradigm highlights two important lessons: (1) the benefit of aligning development policies with locally shared identities and values and (2) establishing inclusive governance mechanisms that involve early consultation with diverse stakeholders to frame national wellbeing policies. However, wellbeing practitioners and policy-makers need to be sensitive to underlying inequality patterns and process unique to different contexts in adapting GNH to other localities and following the following recommendations:

- *Greater investment in Indigenous Knowledge* is needed due to its emphasis on spiritual and inner growth for intellectual diversity in understanding how psychosocial deficiencies link to various socioeconomic contexts. This should focus on the youth with an intersectionality approach, given that on a global scale, suicide ranks as the third leading cause of death for females and fourth for males among young people aged 15 to 29 years (World Health Organization, 2021).

- *Prioritizing non-economic wellbeing measures*, like a shared environmental identity, has enhanced GNH's success. However, limiting people to a single identity within national boundaries that exclude global influences, through access to the Internet for example, can hinder their capabilities (Sen, 2014). Given that the GNH agenda closely aligns with international development goals (Yangka et al., 2018), further research is needed to explore the impact of a rapidly changing global culture on individual identities and their wellbeing.
- GNH's approach to development requires *an ontological understanding of the interdependence of human wellbeing and environmental sustainability*. While there has been an increase in the calls for wellbeing-centered economies, Balogun et al. (2023) underscore that there is a need to realize that the current economic paradigm—centered around autonomous individuals and hypercompetition—is in itself a *belief* that undermines the essential relationships essential for human growth and development. The disregard of this growth and development from a young age can impede an individual's ability to achieve happiness and harmony with nature (Singye, 2014). Thus, we call for global research and public deliberation on the role of belief systems on human development to generate insights that can support the reorientation of institutions and policies toward sustainability and wellbeing.

References

Balasubramanian & Cashin (2019). *Gross national happiness and macroeconomic indicators in the kingdom of Bhutan*. s.l.: International Monetary Fund Working Papers.

Balogun, K., Weru, K., & Shen, X. (2023). Freedom from want: A critical reflection in the face of the anthropocene. *Journal of Human Development and Capabilities*, *24*(2), 274–283. https://doi.org/10.1080/19452829.2022.2161493

Centre for Bhutan Studies & GNH Research (2016). *A compass towards a just and harmonious society*. Thimphu: Centre for Bhutan Studies & GNH Research.

Dema, T., Tripathy, J. P., Thinley, S., Rani, M., Dhendup, T., Laxmeshwar, C., Tenzin, K., Gurung, M. S., Tshering, T., Subba, D. K., Penjore, T., & Lhazeen, K. (2019, December 2). Suicidal ideation and attempt among school going adolescents in Bhutan – a secondary analysis of a global school-based student health survey in Bhutan 2016. *BMC Public Health*, *19*(1), 1605. https://doi.org/10.1186/s12889-019-7791-0.

Dendup, T., Zhao, Y., Dorji, T., & Phuntsho, S. (2020, January 30). *Risk factors associated with suicidal ideation and suicide attempts in Bhutan: An analysis of the 2014 Bhutan STEPS Survey data. PLoS One*, *15*(1), e0225888. https://doi.org/10.1371/journal.pone.0225888

Dorji, T. (2020, December 22). The gross national happiness framework and the health system response to the COVID-19 pandemic in Bhutan. *American Journal of Tropical Medicine and Hygiene*, *104*(2), 441–445.

Grimmond, J. K., Kornhaber, R., Visentin, D., & Cleary, M. (2019). A qualitative systematic review of experiences and perceptions of youth suicide. *PLoS One*, *14*(6).

Lester, S. V., Sacra, M. M., Durham, J. C., & Nirola, D. K. (2020). Youth and young adult suicide in Bhutan: A stress and resilience approach. *International Journal for the Advancement of Counseling*, *42*, 132–146.

Levenson et al. (2004). *Happiness in the midst of change: A human development approach to studying GNH in the context of economic development* (pp. 450–460). Centre for Bhutan Studies.

Masaki, K., & Tshering, J. (2021). Exploring the origins of Bhutan's gross national happiness. *Journal of South Asian Development*, *16*(2), 273–292.
Meier, B. M., & Chakrabarti, A. (2016). The paradox of happiness: Health and human rights in the kingdom of Bhutan. *Health Human Rights*, *18*(1), 193–208.
Richardson, J. (2023). How does Gross National Happiness offer an integrated perspective linked with health, economics, and nature? *Journal of Ayurveda and Integrative Medicine*, *14*(1).
Sen, A. (2014). Justice and identity. *Economics and Philosophy*, *30*, 1–10.
Singye, N. (2014). Role of teachers in alleviation cultural poverty: GNH begin in the classroom. *Journal of the Open University of Japan*, *31*, 47–54.
Sithey, G., Li, M., & Thow, A. M. (2018). Strengthening non-communicable disease policy with lessons from Bhutan: Linking gross national happiness and health policy action. *Journal of Public Health Policy*, *39*, 327–342. https://doi.org/10.1057/s41271-018-0135-y
Thinley, J. Y., & Hartz-Karp, J. (2019). National progress, sustainability and higher goals: The case of Bhutan's gross national happiness. *Sustainable Earth*, *2*(11).
Ura, K., Alkire, S., Wangdi, K., & Zangmo, T. (2023). *GNH 2022*. Centre for Bhutan and GNH Studies.
Ura, K., Alkire, S., & Zangmo, T. (2012). *Case study: Bhutan: Gross national happiness and the GNH index*. s.n.
van Norren, D. E. (2023). Gross national happiness in Bhutan: Is Buddhist constitutionalism legitimate in the age of secularism? A post-colonial view. *Religions*, *14*(72).
Verma, R. (2022). Bhutan's gross national happiness: A development alternative at the interface of anthropology. *General Anthropology*, *29*(2), 3–6.
World Health Organization (2021). *Suicide worldwide in 2019: Global health estimates*. s.n.
Yangka, D., Newman, P., Rauland, V., & Devereux, P. (2018). Sustainability in an emerging nation: The Bhutan case study. *Sustainability*, *10*(5), 1622.

19

WELLBEING AND POLICY IN NEW ZEALAND

From a wellbeing framework to a government-wide approach

Dan Weijers

Overview

In recent years, New Zealand has fundamentally reframed the policy-making process into a wellbeing approach (Weijers & Morrison, 2018). The reframing is multifaceted, including new guiding concepts and models, new methods of policy creation and analysis, new laws, and new reporting infrastructure. Since 2011, the Treasury has explicitly understood its goal of achieving higher living standards for New Zealanders in terms of how to achieve wellbeing for all New Zealanders, now and in the future (Treasury, 2011). After this, the Treasury published a series of guides, tools, and models and encouraged their use across the public sector (Treasury, 2021a). Led by the Treasury, policy-makers in New Zealand tend to work with a pluralistic view of wellbeing that is influenced by Utilitarianism, Amartya Sen's capabilities approach, and Māori and Pasifika notions of what is important in life (Hughes, 2021). In practice, this means considering how policies might impact the wellbeing-related domains in the Living Standards Framework (LSF), a conceptual model of the stocks and flows of the determinants of wellbeing, and He Ara Waiora, a conceptual model of the ends and means of wellbeing from the perspective of New Zealand's indigenous Māori people (Treasury, 2021b).

New Zealand ranks 13th on the Human Development Index (HDI) for 2021 with a score of 0.937, behind Switzerland (1st, 0.962) but above the United States (21st, 0.921) (HDR, 2023). New Zealand's HDI rose rapidly from 1990 to 2005 (0.806 to 0.912) and has risen more slowly since then. Based on data from 2022, New Zealand was ranked 27th (78.43) on the United Nations Sustainable Development Goals (SDGs), well behind Finland (1st, 86.76) but, again, above the United States (39th, 75.91) (SDR, 2023). New Zealand made slow progress on the SDGs from 2000 to 2020 (74.38 to 76.78) but is now progressing faster (SDR, 2023). It is

DOI: 10.4324/9781003382447-22

one of only a few countries to have achieved the gender equity goal. The OECD's (2020a) Better Life Index ranks New Zealand 12th overall (Norway is 1st and the United States is 8th). New Zealand ranks highly in many domains, especially civic engagement (3rd) and health (4th), and only compares unfavourably in work–life balance and safety (the latter mainly due to domestic violence and perceptions of public unsafety). New Zealand's performance on the OECD's headline wellbeing indicators and inequality of wellbeing has remained relatively steady since 2010 (OECD, 2020b, pp. 36, 39). The 2023 World Happiness Report (based on 2020–2023 data) ranks New Zealand as 10th (7.123) on average life evaluation, better than the much wealthier United States (15th, 6.894), but worse than Finland (1st, 7.804) (Helliwell et al., 2023).

Internal wellbeing research reveals similar results to many other colonial nations, including problems with inequality in most domains. This is especially so for indigenous Māori (and some immigrant communities) (McLeod, 2018), which is only partially explained by their younger demographic (Reid & Evans, 2022). Objective and subjective indicators show Māori lagging behind in several important wellbeing domains, including income, health, and housing, with only very gradual improvements over time (Reid & Evans, 2022). Trends of note over the past decade include high and improving employment rates and air quality, high and worsening mental health issues among young people, and declining school attendance and achievement in poorer areas (Hughes et al., 2022). In terms of subjective life evaluations, the research shows that mental health (Crichton & Nguyen, 2022), positive experiences, and satisfaction with household income (Jarden et al., 2022) are important predictors of satisfaction with life.

Wellbeing initiatives in the country – a brief chronology

In 2011, the Treasury reinterpreted its mission from improving living standards (narrowly construed) to improving wellbeing (broadly construed). Inspired by the Stiglitz, Sen, and Fitoussi report (2009) and Sen's (1993) capabilities approach, Treasury staff devised the LSF, which incorporated a wide range of long-term and immediate contributors to wellbeing (Treasury, 2011). This conceptual model of the stocks and flows of contributors to wellbeing was led entirely by the public sector but was not directly requested or funded by the government at the time. Without direct governmental support, the Treasury worked on a (now-defunct) LSF Tool designed to help policymakers operationalize the LSF in their day-to-day work (Karacaoglu, 2012). The Tool substantially narrowed the broad range of stocks and flows in the LSF down to five: economic growth, reducing macroeconomic vulnerability, sustainability for the future, growing social capital, and increasing equity (Karacaoglu, 2012, p. 1). A series of articles developed conceptual depth, guidance, and suitable indicators for each of the five priority areas over the next few years (2012–2015) (Treasury, 2021a).

In 2018, Jacinda Ardern became Prime Minister and announced a wellbeing focus for her new coalition government. New laws changed the way the budget and wellbeing reporting would work. The Treasury was tasked with creating the infrastructure for annual wellbeing budgets and to prepare for regular wellbeing reporting. Statistics New Zealand was tasked with discovering what matters to New Zealanders, how data could be collected to monitor those things, and to work with the Treasury to ensure sufficient data collection to make the various wellbeing-related instruments viable. A major wellbeing and public policy conference brought together international academic and public sector wellbeing experts with a range of policy-makers to help reframe policy-making in New Zealand to a wellbeing approach (Weijers & Morrison, 2018).

Based on the Conference of European Statisticians' recommendations on measuring sustainable development (UNECE, 2013), Statistics New Zealand consulted widely to devise a suite of indicators (Indicators Aotearoa New Zealand) that would help fulfil New Zealand's reporting obligations to the United Nations, help operationalize the Treasury's LSF, provide data for the various governmental and non-governmental agencies working toward sustainable wellbeing, and enable reporting on what matters to most New Zealanders (StatsNZ, no date). The consultation process included multi-modal public consultation, especially with indigenous Māori (StatsNZ, 2019). The project identified over 100 indicators that provided near complete coverage of the SDGs, the various domains of the LSF and Treasury's other wellbeing instruments.

Inspired by the OECD's Better Life initiative (and in order to align the LSF with its new reporting obligations to the OECD), the Treasury updated the LSF, including subjective wellbeing as a domain for the first time (Treasury, 2018). It also released articles on Māori (O'Connell et al., 2018), Pasifika, and Asian (Yong, 2018) perspectives on wellbeing, which were meant to complement the 2018 LSF. In 2018, the Treasury launched the LSF Dashboard, an interactive public portal for wellbeing data (Treasury, 2023a). The LSF Dashboard continues to be upgraded as data for new indicators become available. It now covers over 100 indicators and is updated twice a year (Treasury, 2023a).

New Zealand's (and the world's) first official annual Wellbeing Budget was delivered in 2019. Much like ordinary budgets, the Wellbeing Budget set out where the government would spend tax revenue and explain why certain areas were prioritized. A new budget process required public agencies to collaborate on cross-agency funding bids that had to discuss the projected impacts on all of the domains of the LSF (Treasury, 2019).

In 2020, some of these initiatives were encoded in law: The 2020 amendments to the 1989 Financial Reporting Act required annual Wellbeing Budgets and a Wellbeing Report at least every 4 years. The amendments required the Treasury to produce the Wellbeing Reports, which would have to discuss the state of wellbeing in New Zealand, trends over time, and risks and resources relevant to the future state of wellbeing (Treasury, 2022).

The Treasury evolved the LSF again in 2021. The 2021 LSF added an institutional level to the model, with domains such as "Families" and "Markets." It also included domains to reflect New Zealand's indigenous Māori people's conceptions of wellbeing, such as "Whānau, hapū and iwi," a domain that includes connections with kin and culture (Treasury, 2021c).

The Treasury now advocates for *wellbeing* Cost Benefit Analysis of policy proposals and encourages policy-makers to use its custom-made CBAx tool (Treasury, 2023b). First launched in 2015 (Jensen & Thompson (2020), the 2022 version of CBAx includes all the LSF domains and considers current and future effects as well as risks and resilience (Treasury, 2023b). CBAx can convert many indicators into monetary values and some indictors into non-monetary wellbeing values, including subjective wellbeing (Treasury, 2023c).

In 2022, The Treasury published the first Wellbeing Report, a summary of the state of wellbeing in New Zealand, trends over time, and risks and resources relevant to the future state of wellbeing (Treasury, 2022). The Wellbeing Report was accompanied by 12 background reports that focused on specific areas of concern, such as equality, social cohesion, and Māori and Pasifika peoples' wellbeing (Treasury, 2023d).

Discussion

In New Zealand, progress on the wellbeing approach to public policy greatly accelerated when the 2018 government actively supported a shift to this approach. By assigning agencies to lead specific wellbeing initiatives with short deadlines, and legally enforcing new requirements on them, the government drove rapid and widespread change. By requiring cross-agency collaboration, the government also encouraged and enabled more holistic and robust policy proposals (Treasury, 2019). Furthermore, by requiring that policy proposals comment on all the wellbeing domains, more of what is important to New Zealanders will likely be factored into policy-making.

Wellbeing approaches to public policy could easily falter if policy-makers and the public do not accept the idea. Some policy-makers within the Treasury were adversarial to the wellbeing approach because they saw it as setting values, rather than just advising on efficiency and effectiveness (Weijers & Mukherjee, 2016). Public sector workers can be suspicious of subjective measures of wellbeing: economists may question the validity of the measures, and social workers may worry about them being used to mollify the underprivileged and excuse not giving them more resources or respect.

Achieving widespread public license for the wellbeing approach may also require a more involved and democratic process. The public is not familiar with the various aspects of the wellbeing approach and the wellbeing frameworks, the LSF and He Ara Waiora, have not explicitly been agreed to by the public. Indeed, general public and cross-sector public service discussion of these issues could be encouraged before wellbeing initiatives begin. It could be explained that not adopting a wellbeing approach is also setting values by endorsing the status quo, focusing on the traditional economic indicators that are now widely viewed as being insufficient measures of all that should matter (Stiglitz et al., 2009). It could also be pointed out that subjective measures of wellbeing can predict important events that traditional economic indicators miss, such as the political unrest of the so-called 'Arab Spring' (Arampatzi et al., 2018).

The snapshot of New Zealand's wellbeing paints a rosy picture. However, this is not true for all New Zealanders. If wellbeing data are only ever presented as averages, then the public may lose interest, thinking New Zealand's wellbeing is stable and at an acceptable level. By always reporting on vulnerable populations and the lower quartiles or quintiles of the general population, the areas that most need policy intervention should be clear. Reducing inequality in a range of wellbeing outcomes may also be a good strategy for improving overall wellbeing, as discussed in the 2020 World Happiness Report (Helliwell et al., 2020). In addition to the LSF, New Zealand has wellbeing frameworks for specific populations, such as Māori and children (Hughes, 2021). Providing insight into all important subgroups usually requires specific measures and data collection initiatives. Guidance is also required for when to use which framework, and how to deal with conflicting analyses between frameworks. In New Zealand, policy proposals have had to indicate wellbeing impacts for all of the domains of the LSF since 2019 and He Ara Waiora (the Māori-specific wellbeing framework) since 2021 in a side-by-side manner (Treasury, 2023e).

As mentioned earlier, the Treasury's mission is to improve the lives of all New Zealanders, including future New Zealanders. The current wellbeing initiatives in New Zealand have been criticized for not doing enough for *future* New Zealanders by downplaying the importance of environmental contributors to wellbeing (PCE, 2021). One important issue is the use of the official 5% or the alternative 2% discount rates in CBAx. An analysis of CBAx concluded that using the lower discount rate would have made very little difference to the final outputs (Jensen & Thompson, 2020). However, the huge impact of current extreme weather events suggests that the discount rate should be revisited and potentially disastrous and irreversible events, such as climate disaster or ecosystem failure, should be included in the analyses.

The wellbeing approach outlined here has made the wellbeing of New Zealanders more transparent to anyone inclined to investigate. This means that governments cannot easily hide setbacks to the nation's wellbeing or inequalities in domains of wellbeing between various subgroups. This transparency promotes the democratic process in New Zealand because citizens, researchers, journalists, and various organizations can question why the government is not prioritizing areas that, as measured by wellbeing outcomes, appear to be in greater need of assistance. This increased transparency is magnified by the requirement for policy proposals to indicate the likely effects on all domains of the LSF. Especially when combined with CBAx, this documents the wellbeing priorities of policy-makers, including making it clear what domains might worsen in order to improve other domains. Taken together, these wellbeing initiatives should improve democratic processes in New Zealand.

Given the difficulty of increasing all wellbeing domains at once on a limited budget, successive wellbeing budgets have been setting specific wellbeing indicator targets (and more recently just targeting indicators or domains for improvement), to focus on areas in which the policy can make the most positive difference in New Zealanders' lives (Treasury, 2019). Appropriately (based on relative need), the target areas in the first Wellbeing Budget included youth mental health, child poverty and abuse, and Māori language preservation (Treasury, 2019), among more traditional policy goals. Focusing on mental health has been identified as a cost-effective win-win because it benefits both psychological wellbeing and the economy (e.g., Layard & Clark, 2014; Peasgood et al., 2019). Focusing on *youth* mental health may be even more cost effective due to preventative benefits over the life course and the increase of mental distress in youth since 2016 (especially in 2021) (MSD, 2022, p. 28): Around 28% of high-schoolers experienced levels of psychological distress that put them at risk of serious mental illness. The wellbeing reporting in 2022 highlighted this problem. Identifying and publicising policy-apt problems is an important success criterion for the wellbeing approach.

Action points

The following suggestions are targeted at the New Zealand context, but all countries could benefit from adopting these action points (with slight changes to fit their local context).

- Take the environment seriously: The Parliamentary Commissioner for the Environment should work with the Treasury to ensure policy-making and analysis better account for future people and the possibility of environmental disasters.
- Fix data gaps: Statistics New Zealand and other government agencies should continue to investigate ways to plug data gaps in Indicators Aotearoa and the Living Standards Dashboard. The government should set up a specific fund for research that can help fill in the values in CBAx in all of the domains of the LSF and Te Ara Waiora.
- Consider reporting frequency and usefulness: The Wellbeing Report should be published every year and should include a reflection on previous reports analysis of wellbeing risks and resiliency.
- Provide ongoing training and connection for policy-makers and analysts: Many policy-makers and analysts are still learning how to use the wellbeing tools effectively. General wellbeing and specific wellbeing tool training should continue to run for all policy groups. Selective secondments and dedicated nodes of individuals or small teams should facilitate the knowledge sharing required for all policy teams to estimate a broad range of wellbeing effects.

- Set up one-off or rolling citizens assemblies on wellbeing: A stratified sample of the country (that made sure to represent all minority groups) could be paid to learn about and evaluate the wellbeing approach and especially the wellbeing frameworks and policy analysis tools.
- Support wellbeing initiatives at all levels of government: The main lesson for other countries to learn from New Zealand is to provide support and direction from the highest levels of government. Encoding the key elements of a wellbeing approach in law encourages quick development and longevity.

References

Arampatzi, E., Burger, M., Ianchovichina, E., Röhricht, T., & Veenhoven, R. (2018). Unhappy development: Dissatisfaction with life on the eve of the Arab Spring. *Review of Income and Wealth*, *64*, S80–S113. https://doi.org/10.1111/roiw.12388

Crichton, S., & Nguyen, H. (2022). *Wellbeing in Aotearoa New Zealand: A population segmentation analysis*. The New Zealand Treasury. Retrieved June 30, 2023, from www.treasury.govt.nz/sites/default/files/2022-10/bp-population-segmentation-analysis.pdf

HDR (2023). Human Development Index (HDI). *UNDP Human Development Reports*. Retrieved, June 30, 2023, from https://hdr.undp.org/data-center/human-development-index#/indicies/HDI

Helliwell, J. F., Huang, H., Norton, M., Goff, L., & Wang, S. (2023). World happiness, trust and social connections in times of crisis. In *World happiness report 2023* (11th ed., Chapter 2). Sustainable Development Solutions Network.

Helliwell, J. F., Huang, H., Wang, S., & Norton, M. (2020). Social environments for world happiness. In *World happiness report 2020* (8th ed., Chapter 2, pp. 13–45). Sustainable Development Solutions Network.

Hughes, T. (2021). Towards a living standards framework for all Aotearoa: Culture, children and wellbeing. *The New Zealand Treasury Discussion Paper*, (DP 21/01). Retrieved June 30, 2023, from www.treasury.govt.nz/publications/dp/dp-21-01

Hughes, T., Cardona, D., & Armstrong, C. (2022). *Trends in wellbeing in Aotearoa New Zealand: 2000–2020*. The New Zealand Treasury: Wellington. Retrieved June 30, 2023, from www.treasury.govt.nz/sites/default/files/2022-04/bp-trends-wellbeing-aotearoa-new-zealand-2000-2020.pdf

Jarden, R. J., Joshanloo, M., Weijers, D., Sandham, M., & Jarden, A. J. (2022). Predictors of life satisfaction in New Zealand: Analysis of a national dataset. *International Journal of Environmental Research and Public Health*, *19*(9), 5612. https://doi.org/10.3390/ijerph19095612

Jensen, K., & Thompson, C. (2020). Valuing impacts: The contribution of CBAx to improved policy practices. *Policy Quarterly*, *16*(1), 67–76. https://doi.org/10.26686/pq.v16i1.6357

Karacaoglu, G. (2012, June 13–15). Improving the living standards of New Zealanders: Moving from a framework to implementation. *International Wellbeing and Public Policy Conference*, Wellington. Retrieved June 30, 2023, from www.treasury.govt.nz/sites/default/files/2012-06/sp-livingstandards-paper.pdf

Layard, R., & Clark, D. M. (2014). *Thrive: The power of evidence-based psychological therapies*. Penguin UK.

McLeod, K. (2018). Our people: Multidimensional wellbeing in New Zealand. *The Treasury*. Retrieved June 30, 2023, from https://www.treasury.govt.nz/sites/default/files/2018-11/ap18-04.pdf

MSD (2022). What about me? The national youth health and wellbeing survey 2021. *Ministry of Social Development*. Retrieved June 30, 2023, from www.msd.govt.nz/documents/about-msd-and-our-work/publications-resources/consultations/youth-health-

and-wellbeing-survey-results/the-national-youth-health-and-wellbeing-survey-2021-overview-report-september-2022.pdf

O'Connell, E., Greenway, T., Moeke, T., & McMeeking, S. (2018). He Ara Waiora/A pathway towards wellbeing. *The New Zealand Treasury Discussion Paper*, (DP 18/11). Retrieved June 30, 2023, from www.treasury.govt.nz/sites/default/files/2018-09/dp18-11.pdf

OECD (2020a). *OECD better life index*. OECD Publishing. Retrieved June 30, 2023, from www.oecdbetterlifeindex.org/

OECD (2020b). *How's life? 2020: Measuring well-being*. OECD Publishing. https://doi.org/10.1787/9870c393-en

PCE (2021). *Wellbeing budgets and the environment: A promised land?* Parliamentary Commissioner for the Environment: Wellington. Retrieved June 30, 2023, from https://pce.parliament.nz/media/lxgb4pt5/wellbeing-budgets-and-the-environment-report-pdf-225mb.pdf

Peasgood, T., Foster, D., & Dolan, P. (2019). Priority setting in healthcare through the lens of happiness. In Global Council for Happiness and Wellbeing (Ed.), *Global happiness and wellbeing policy report 2019* (Chapter 3, pp. 26–51). Sustainable Development Solutions Network.

Reid, C., & Evans, P. (2022). *Trends in Māori wellbeing*. The New Zealand Treasury: Wellington. Retrieved June 30, 2023, from www.treasury.govt.nz/sites/default/files/2022-12/ap22-02.pdf

SDR (2023). Sustainable development report 2023 rankings. *Sustainable Development Solutions Network*. Retrieved June 30, 2023, from https://dashboards.sdgindex.org/rankings

Sen, A. (1993). Capability and wellbeing. In M. Nussbaum & A. Sen (Eds.), *The quality of life*. Clarendon Press. https://doi.org/10.1093/0198287976.003.0003

StatsNZ (2019). Indicators Aotearoa New Zealand – Ngā Tūtohu Aotearoa: Key findings from consultation and engagement. *Statistics New Zealand*. Retrieved June 30, 2023, from www.stats.govt.nz/assets/Uploads/Indicators-Aotearoa-New-Zealand-Nga-Tutohu-Aotearoa-Key-findings-from-consultation-and-engagement/Downloads/indicators-aotearoa-new-zealand-nga-tutohu-aotearoa-key-findings-from-consultation-and-engagement.pdf

StatsNZ (n.d.). About Ngā Tūtohu Aotearoa – Indicators Aotearoa New Zealand. *Statistics New Zealand*. Retrieved June 30, 2023, from https://statisticsnz.shinyapps.io/wellbeingindicators/_w_52b24671/?page=about&subpage=main

Stiglitz, J. E., Sen, A., & Fitoussi, J. P. (Eds.) (2009). *Report by the commission on the measurement of economic performance and social progress*. Commission on the Measurement of Economic Performance and Social Progress.

Treasury (2011). *Working towards higher living standards for New Zealanders*. The New Zealand Treasury: Wellington. Retrieved June 30, 2023, from www.treasury.govt.nz/publications/research-policy/tp/higherlivingstandards

Treasury (2018). *Our people our country our future living standards framework: Background and future work*. The New Zealand Treasury: Wellington. Retrieved June 30, 2023, from www.treasury.govt.nz/sites/default/files/2018-12/lsf-background-future-work.pdf

Treasury (2019). *The wellbeing budget 2019*. The New Zealand Treasury: Wellington. Retrieved June 30, 2023, from www.treasury.govt.nz/sites/default/files/2019-06/b19-wellbeing-budget.pdf

Treasury (2021a). *History of the LSF*. The New Zealand Treasury: Wellington. Retrieved June 30, 2023, from www.treasury.govt.nz/information-and-services/nz-economy/higher-living-standards/history-lsf

Treasury (2021b). *He Ara Waiora*. The New Zealand Treasury: Wellington. Retrieved June 30, 2023, from www.treasury.govt.nz/information-and-services/nz-economy/higher-living-standards/he-ara-waiora

Treasury (2021c). *The Living Standards Framework (LSF) 2021*. The New Zealand Treasury: Wellington. Retrieved June 30, 2023, from www.treasury.govt.nz/sites/default/files/2021-10/tp-living-standards-framework-2021.pdf

Treasury (2022). *Wellbeing reports*. The New Zealand Treasury. Retrieved June 30, 2023, from www.treasury.govt.nz/publications/strategies-and-plans/wellbeing-report

Treasury (2023a). *Measuring wellbeing: The LSF dashboard*. The New Zealand Treasury: Wellington. Retrieved June 30, 2023 from www.treasury.govt.nz/information-and-services/nz-economy/higher-living-standards/measuring-wellbeing-lsf-dashboard

Treasury (2023b). *A wellbeing approach to cost benefit analysis*. The New Zealand Treasury: Wellington. Retrieved June 30, 2023, from www.treasury.govt.nz/information-and-services/nz-economy/higher-living-standards/our-living-standards-framework/wellbeing-approach-cost-benefit-analysis

Treasury (2023c). *The treasury's CBAx tool*. The New Zealand Treasury: Wellington. Retrieved June 30, 2023, from www.treasury.govt.nz/information-and-services/state-sector-leadership/investment-management/plan-investment-choices/cost-benefit-analysis-including-public-sector-discount-rates/treasurys-cbax-tool

Treasury (2023d). *Te Tai Waiora: Wellbeing in Aotearoa New Zealand 2022*. The New Zealand Treasury: Wellington. Retrieved June 30, 2023, from www.treasury.govt.nz/sites/default/files/2022-11/te-tai-waiora-2022.pdf

Treasury (2023e). *Using the LSF and He Ara Waiora*. The New Zealand Treasury: Wellington. Retrieved June 30, 2023, from www.treasury.govt.nz/information-and-services/nz-economy/higher-living-standards/using-lsf-and-he-ara-waiora

UNECE (2013). Conference of European Statisticians recommendations on measuring sustainable development. *United Nations Economic Commission for Europe*. Retrieved June 30, 2023, from https://unece.org/statistics/publications/conference-european-statisticians-recommendations-measuring-sustainable

Weijers, D., & Morrison, P. S. (2018). Wellbeing and public policy: Can New Zealand be a leading light for the wellbeing approach? *Policy Quarterly*, *14*(4), 3–12.

Weijers, D., & Mukherjee, U. (2016). *Living standards, well-being, and public policy*. The New Zealand Treasury: Wellington, NZ. Retrieved June 30, 2023, from www.treasury.govt.nz/government/longterm/fiscalposition/2016/ltfs-16-bg-lswpp.pdf

Yong, S. (2018). An Asian perspective and the New Zealand treasury living standards framework. *The New Zealand Treasury Discussion Paper*, (DP 18/10). Retrieved June 30, 2023 from www.treasury.govt.nz/sites/default/files/2018-09/dp18-10.pdf

20

WELLBEING AND POLICY IN FINLAND

The economy-of-wellbeing approach

Riikka Pellikka and Heli Hätönen

Introduction

Finland can be seen as an international leader in wellbeing and sustainability with good outcomes for the economy, the planet and the people in a wide range of wellbeing aspects. The 2023 World Happiness Report ranks Finland as first in terms of wellbeing in the world, a position it has held for six years running (Helliwell et al., 2023). While the high life evaluations that Finns report are attributed to a wide range of factors, from environmental quality to social trust, a prioritisation of wellbeing in both civil society discourse and policy-making for over a decade in Finland has played a key role. In what follows, we will provide some further background to the current state of wellbeing in Finland before offering an overview of the economy-of-wellbeing approach (EoW), which underpins Finland's success, and the National Action Plan for the Economy of Wellbeing, which embeds this approach within national policy strategy, as well as detailing some of the policy insight that have emerged from adopting a EoW lens in Finland. We will conclude by outlining future directions and identifying some actionable points to take forward.

Wellbeing in Finland

In addition to topping the rankings of the World Happiness Report, Finland performs well in other indices that focus on key determinants of how well people feel. For example, Finland ranks 11th on the Human Development Index for 2021 with a score of 0.94, behind Switzerland (1St) and Sweden (7th) (HDR, 2023), and was ranked first in 2022 on the United Nations Sustainable Development Goals (SDGs), Sweden being second and Denmark third (SDR, 2023).

DOI: 10.4324/9781003382447-23

Despite these positive relative rankings, analyses from the OECD and other bodies have highlighted several challenges to sustaining the high levels of wellbeing in Finland (Fleischer & Stokenberga, 2023). These include skill shortages and mismatches, ensuring that the necessary transition to the green economy is inclusive, inequalities in wellbeing and other important factors like discrimination, poverty, violence and many health problems, debt accumulation and housing affordability and increasing trends in obesity and mental health issues.

These challenges need to be tackled in order for all groups to enjoy the quality of life and contribute to society, the economy and the green transition (Finnish Institute for Health and Welfare and Government Agency Kela, 2023). These issues emphasise the need for strong leadership and cross-governmental cooperation when systematically monitoring, identifying and addressing trade-offs and synergies across different policy sectors with a view to safeguarding and promoting wellbeing.

A brief overview of the history of the economy-of-wellbeing approach in Finland

Finnish civil society actors launched the concept of EoW back in 2012 (Särkelä et al., 2014). In the beginning, the concept was aligned with the idea of social sustainability and represented communities and societies existing and thriving in an equal, fair and healthy way. Nowadays in Finland, EoW is more often understood as a decision-making approach aimed at achieving a better balance between the economic, social and ecological dimensions of sustainable development. Under the EoW approach, the economy and economic policies should serve the wellbeing of people, communities, societies and nature in a fair and sustainable manner. More broadly, it is also understood as a policy orientation that puts the people and the planet and their wellbeing at the center of all policy and decision-making. In Finland, EoW can be seen as a continuation to the concept of 'Health in all policies' that was coined in the late 1990s – an approach which systematically took into account health implications of all decisions, sought synergies and avoided harmful health impacts (Leppo et al., 2013). However, EoW is a broader concept in that it stresses not just the health but the wellbeing of humans and in addition to nature as being central to decision-making processes.

The work that the civil society actors started back in 2012 continued during Prime Minister Juha Sipilä's (of the Finnish Centre Party) government term (2015–2019) and as part of Finland's Presidency of the Council of the EU fall 2019. The EoW initiative created a basis for further work on the concept in Europe, calling on the European Commission and the Member States to integrate a cross-sectoral EoW perspective into all policy areas of the EU and the Member States (General Secretariat of the Council, 2019). This process benefited from a valuable piece of background analysis by the OECD, commissioned by Finland (Martin, 2019). The work then continued during Prime Minister Sanna Marin's (of the Finnish Social Democratic Party) term (2019–2023).

Prime Minister Petteri Orpo's (of the National Coalition Party) Government Programme (2023–2027) states that the Government will prepare an operating model that measures overall sustainability alongside GDP, that is wellbeing, economic viability and the state of the environment. Alongside and in cooperation, the work on implementation of the EoW approach continues in accordance with Finland's National Action Plan recommendations (see section "The national action plan for the economy of wellbeing").

The national action plan for the economy of wellbeing

A National Action Plan for the Economy of Wellbeing was developed to integrate the EoW approach into knowledge-based decision-making. The plan was launched in March 2023 and its overarching aim is that by 2025 the EoW approach is part of the national, regional and local decision-making. In order to develop the plan, the Ministry of Social Affairs and Health convened the high-level National Steering Group on EoW to prepare the National Action Plan. The Ministry also engaged a wide network of domestic experts in a participatory process. Participants from the Prime Minister's Office, the Ministry of Finance, Ministry of Employment and Economy, Ministry of Environment, the Ministry of Education and Culture and Ministry of Justice all contributed (Ministry of Social Affairs and Health, 2023b).

The resulting Action Plan for EoW includes five recommendations to promote the wellbeing economy in Finland:

1 **Prepare a steering model for EoW and incorporate it into Government steering.** This includes, for example, defining a framework for evaluating social sustainability and creating structures of expert advice such as an independent expert forum or scientific panel on social sustainability.
2 **Further integrate the monitoring of wellbeing into central government, regional and municipal decision-making.** The Ministry of Social Affairs and Health is working closely with the Prime Minister's Office to develop a cross-governmental sustainability review. Its purpose is to combine different sustainable development models (such as the EoW, green transition, planetary health) to produce regular and broad-based assessments of the different dimensions of sustainability. This review is both present and future focused. Its key aims are to enhance society's capacity for extensive sustainable change and to create capabilities for sustainable action during new crises that have not yet been identified.
3 **Develop impact assessments and strengthen competence.** This includes, for example, piloting impact assessments from the perspective of EoW in legislative projects/reforms, strengthening impact assessment competence and resources in ministries.
4 **Influence at an EU-level.** The aim of these efforts is to encourage the Commission's new work programme and the preparation of the Council's strategic programme to take into account and strengthen EoW principles and to support

the implementation of the Social Pillar and the UN 2030 Agenda. This includes developing reliable and internationally commensurate indicators for measuring and monitoring human wellbeing in the Union and linking the EoW thinking to other relevant programmes such as the EU's Mental Health and Healthier Together initiatives (Ministry of Social Affairs and Health, 2023a).

5 **Strengthen the participation of civil society and generate dialogue with the private sector.** This involves ensuring inclusive communication and interaction as part of the development of tools for EoW, developing the knowledge base describing civil society activities and the effectiveness of activities, integrating it into the knowledge base of EoW and exploring different models for strengthening cooperation and dialogue with the private sector (Ministry of Justice, 2023).

Overall, the Action Plan aims to establish EoW as a central part of the government processes and policies. In order to mainstream the EoW approach, structures that support its realisation and incentives for changing practices need to be identified. Moreover, municipalities and regions have an important role in implementing EoW in practice. Designated parties, 'owners', are needed to support the implementation and ensure that cross-administrative work makes headway. Finally, co-agreed approaches and metrics adopted by different branches of government to monitor and evaluate changes in perceived wellbeing at individual, organisational and population levels are required.

Applying an EoW lens to existing policy approaches and domains

EoW aims to incorporate wellbeing into knowledge-based decision-making in order to enhance economic, ecological and social sustainability. We now describe some examples of how an EoW lens can inform policy practice.

Knowledge of impacts is a key part of the policy decision-making process. However, historically, a key challenge has been the balanced review of the evidence on economic and wellbeing impacts of different policy options. The Sola 2.0 calculation tool was developed to serve the wellbeing cost assessment needs of municipalities and social and healthcare services. The tool has 23 indicators of social quality divided into four dimensions: social inclusion, socio-economic security, social empowerment and social integrity; each main indicator has between 20 and 50 partial effects to value the cost and the savings potential of the indicator. The partial effects are based on studies that provide information on the impact and cost of the main indicators at the individual and community levels. For example, in the city of Kuopio, the Sola tool has been used to demonstrate both the costs of significant psychological load and the savings brought by the movement of children and young people.

Cultural wellbeing activities refer to art- and culture-based activities or services that aim to promote the wellbeing of an individual or communities. There are currently a wide variety of narrow approaches to valuing cultural wellbeing activities, for example economic support model, cultural prescription and service counselling. The EoW approach helps to identify the economic and wellbeing benefits related to the cultural activities and arts and provide supporting evidence of their value. While we still need further evidence on the economic and wellbeing impacts of cultural wellbeing activities efforts are ongoing to harmonise practices.

In the development of EoW a key focus has been striking a balance between the wellbeing of people and the planet. Social and healthcare consumes large amounts of energy and materials and its operation generates both direct and indirect emissions. The ethos of social and healthcare is based on the protection of human wellbeing and health. However, as highlighted by the EoW approach, the climate and environmental impacts produced by social care and healthcare are at odds with this ethos. More information is needed on how to enact mitigation measures while simultaneously ensuring the quality of health and social care (Pulkki et al., 2023).

The development of economy of wellbeing in Finland – looking forward

Sustainable thinking has been promoted in Finland by several ministries and institutions under different names, such as the sustainable transition, green transition, wellbeing economy, sustainable development and planetary health and wellbeing. Further integration and streamlining is needed. In the spring of 2023, three round tables were held together with government officers and the research sector to reach a common understanding of the different concepts in use. The small group from different ministries finalised the list of recommendations to the Head of Cabinets of the Ministries for the next Government Programme.

According to the group, first, the government programme should have only a few key goals and a shared mission for sustainability. Second, the key activities of the government should include sustainability assessment and monitoring. Third, monitoring should be strengthened. Fourth, social sustainability should have a clear definition and the knowledge base around it should be strengthened. Fifth, good governance and performance management should support sustainable thinking (Head of Cabinets meeting, 2023).

First, these recommendations are being taken forward by two key two initiatives. The Prime Minister's Office is preparing a social sustainability assessment that will provide an annual review on sustainability and possible developments to support government decision-making. (Furman, 2023) Second, the Finnish Institute for Health and Welfare is preparing the proposal for a wellbeing economy framework including a steering model and indicator set (Finnish Institute for Health and Welfare, 2022). This work will support the Prime Minister's Office sustainability assessment.

When promoting the EoW approach in Prime Minister Marin's government term, it was sometimes difficult to motivate the need for the Economy of Wellbeing as there were many elements already in the government programme that supported ecological and social sustainability. Additionally, during the Covid-19 pandemic, the government made notable investments in social sustainability. The Prime Minister Orpo's Government Programme emphasises that a sustainable economy is the foundation for prosperity. Effective welfare policy measures can strengthen the sustainability of the economy. In this the recommendations and goals of the National Action Plan for the Economy of Wellbeing can be a useful tool (Programme of Prime Minister Sanna Marin's Government, 2019, December 10).

Actionable points

Based on the experiences embedding the EoW approach into Finnish policy-making and practice, we wish to highlight the following recommendations:

- Both centralised and decentralised policies to promote sustainable wellbeing should be identified and valued.
- The public sector should strive for and measure wellbeing, long-time economic sustainability and system resilience. To achieve this, it is important for the public sector to have a constant dialogue with civil society. As OECD recommends, Finland should open up the development of policy alternatives connected with future challenges by systemically involving citizens and other stakeholders in future-oriented policy creation (OECD, 2022).
- A system change in the decision-making process should be independent from the composition of the government. Frameworks that are used in government's decision-making processes ought to be apolitical. The politicians set the values but the decision-making processes stay the same. This goal requires persistence from the government officers, the toleration of uncertainty and dialogue with the whole of society.
- When building the decision-making model, framework and indicator set for EoW or/and sustainable future, every country has to follow its own path depending on the national characteristics. However, the principle stays the same, balancing different aspects of sustainability in the decision-making process for the benefit of present and future generations.

References

Finnish Institute for Health and Welfare (2022). *Building a knowledge-based wellbeing economy in Finland*. Retrieved August 5, 2023, from https://thl.fi/documents/10531/10313388/THL_Hanke-esite_Building_a_knowledge-based_saavutettava.pdf/62cfe30d-df57-e3c9-93f5-e3ace6c9d1cb?t=1687932151700

Finnish Institute for Health and Welfare and Government Agency Kela (2023). *Väestön terveys- ja hyvinvointikatsaus 2023: tavoitteena sosiaalisesti kestävä Suomi*. Retrieved August 3, 2023, from https://urn.fi/URN:ISBN:978-952-408-072-9

Fleischer, L., & Stokenberga, L. (2023). *Well-being in Finland: Bringing together people, economy and planet*. OECD Papers on Well-being and Inequalities, No. 14. OECD Publishing. https://doi.org/10.1787/ecf06a58-en

Furman, E. (2023). *Government of Finland 's cross-ministerial sustainability thinking process*. Retrieved August 15, 2023, from https://kestavakehitys.fi/en/materials

General Secretariat of the Council (2019). *The economy of wellbeing council conclusions*. Retrieved August 3, 2023, from https://data.consilium.europa.eu/doc/document/ST-13432-2019-INIT/en/pdf

HDR (2023). Human Development Index (HDI). *UNDP Human Development Reports*. Retrieved October 20, 2023, from https://hdr.undp.org/data-center/human-development-index#/indicies/HDI

Head of Cabinets meeting (2023). Esittelymuistio kestävyyysajattelu KP kokous 13032023. *Finnish Government Document Management VAHVA*.

Helliwell, J. F., Layard, R., Sachs, J. D., Aknin, L. B., De Neve, J.-E., & Wang, S. (Eds.) (2023). *World happiness report 2023* (11th ed.). Sustainable Development Solutions Network. Retrieved November 6, 2023, from https://worldhappiness.report/ed/2023/

Leppo, K., Ollila, E., Peña, S., Wismar, M., & Cook, S. (Eds.) (2013). *Health in all policies seizing opportunities, implementing policies*. Retrieved September 3, from https://julkaisut.valtioneuvosto.fi/bitstream/handle/10024/69920/URN_ISBN_978-952-00-3407-8.pdf?sequence=1&isAllowed=y

Martin, N. (2019). The economy of wellbeing, creating opportunities for people's wellbeing and economic growth. *SDD Working Paper No. 102*, OECD. Retrieved August 3, 2023, from https://one.oecd.org/document/SDD/DOC(2019)2/En/pdf

Ministry of Justice (2023). *Advisory board on civil society policy (KANE)*. Retrieved November 8, 2023, from https://oikeusministerio.fi/en/advisory-board-on-civil-society-policy

Ministry of Social Affairs and Health (2023a). Priorities for promoting the economy of Wellbeing (EoW). *Discussion Paper*. Retrieved September 5, 2023, from https://stm.fi/en/finland-is-proactive-in-promoting-the-economy-of-wellbeing

Ministry of Social Affairs and Health (2023b). Suomen kansallinen hyvinvointitalouden toimintaohjelma 2023–2025. *Sosiaali- ja terveysministeriön julkaisuja 2022:2012*. Retrieved August 3, 2023, from http://urn.fi/URN:ISBN:978-952-00-6875-2

OECD (2022). *Anticipatory innovation governance model in Finland: Towards a new way of governing*. OECD Public Governance Reviews, OECD Publishing. https://doi.org/10.1787/a31e7a9a-en

OECD. *Measuring well-being and progress: Well-being research*. Retrieved August 3, 2023, from www.oecd.org/wise/measuring-well-being-and-progress.htm

Programme of Prime Minister Petteri Orpo's Government (2023, June 20). *A strong and committed Finland – The Government's vision*. Retrieved August 3. 2023, from http://urn.fi/URN:ISBN:978-952-383-818-5

Programme of Prime Minister Sanna Marin's Government (2019, December 10). *Inclusive and competent Finland – A socially, economically and ecologically sustainable society*. Retrieved August 3, 2023, from http://urn.fi/URN:ISBN:978-952-287-808-3

Pulkki, J., Wulff, P., Iivonen, S., Alanko, L., Alhola, K., Frilander, O., Hiilamo, H., Meriläinen, P., Nissinen, A., Savolainen, H., Suomalainen, E., & Setälä, L. (2023). Ecologically sustainable social and health care. *Debriefing of the National Goal and Steering Mechanisms*. Retrieved September 12, from https://julkaisut.valtioneuvosto.fi/bitstream/handle/10024/165113/VNTEAS_2023_49.pdf

SDR (2023). Sustainable development report 2023 rankings. *Sustainable Development Solutions Network*. Retrieved October 20, 2023, from https://dashboards.sdgindex.org/rankings

Särkelä, R., Siltaniemi, A., Rouvinen-Wilenius, P., Parviainen, H., & Ahola, E. (2014). *Hyvinvointitalous. SOSTE Suomen sosiaali ja terveys ry*. Retrieved August 3, from www.soste.fi/wp-content/uploads/2018/11/hyvinvointitalous_final.pdf

21

WELLBEING AND POLICY IN THE UNITED ARAB EMIRATES

Strategic directions and lessons learned

Ahmad Samarji and Amal AlBlooshi

Introduction

In the UAE, promoting wellbeing is a top policy priority. This is reflected in the country's national vision, strategies, processes, and practices. The UAE approaches wellbeing from a holistic lens, which considers individual, communal, and national wellbeing. Several strategic objectives and directions, in addition to numerous initiatives, have been devised and are being implemented to deliver wellbeing at these different levels. This chapter outlines the Emirati's unique approach to wellbeing, happiness, and quality of life, detailing the UAE's efforts to transform wellbeing into a culture that is nourished across every domain and aspect of the Emirati's lives.

Wellbeing in the UAE

In the UAE, the wellbeing and happiness of all Emirati residents (nationals and ex-pats) have been among the top priorities since the establishment of the Union between all the emirates in 1971. From the beginning the founding fathers set happiness as a "national culture and way of life" (National Program for Happiness and Wellbeing, 2022a, p. 7). The quote from the late Sheikh Zayed bin Sultan Al Nahyan – "My wealth is the happiness of my people" (WAM, 2021) – reflects the UAE's leadership commitment to fostering happiness and wellbeing. Indeed, the rationale behind establishing the "Union" of all seven emirates was advancing the quality of life and wellbeing of all Emiratis, where prior to 1971 each emirate possessed its own passport and flag, and mobility across the emirates was a very demanding process (Etihad Museum, n.d.).

DOI: 10.4324/9781003382447-24

Within the UAE, wellbeing is not seen as the sole responsibility of one party but the result of a well-coordinated approach and integrated efforts amongst all stakeholders to build a wellbeing culture which facilitates a "holistic and balanced state for living the best life" (National Program for Happiness & Wellbeing, 2022b, p. 8).

Over the past decade, the UAE has been at the forefront of embedding wellbeing into policy and creating initiatives and programs that focus on the happiness and wellbeing of its citizens and residents. In February 2016, the UAE Government created the post of "Minister of State for Happiness" to achieve a happier society by harmonizing all government plans, programmes, and policies (The Official Portal of the UAE Government, 2016), "creating genuine and authentic happiness" for all (Ribeiro et al., 2020, p. 226). Soon after establishing the Ministry, His Highness Sheikh Mohammed bin Rashid Al Maktoum, Vice-President and Prime Minister of the UAE and Ruler of Dubai, asserted that "happiness and positivity in the UAE are a lifestyle, a government commitment and a spirit uniting the UAE community" (Media Center, UAE Cabinet, 2016).

On March 20, 2016, Sheikh Mohammed approved the "National Programme for Happiness", which has served as the "National Charter for Happiness" (The Official Portal of the UAE Government, 2016). His Highness also approved several initiatives that aim to create happy and productive work environments at federal government offices. Subsequently, the UAE Cabinet endorsed several initiatives and projects, including (Media Center, UAE Cabinet, 2016) the following:

- Appointing chief executive officers for happiness and positivity across all governmental entities,
- Creating happiness and positivity councils in all governmental entities,
- Allocating hours for the happiness programmes and assigning activities to promote a happy and positive work environment,
- Transforming "Customer Service Centres" to "Customer Happiness Centres", optimizing customers' happiness and satisfaction, and
- Setting indicators, collecting data, and preparing annual reports to measure happiness and wellbeing levels across all sectors.

In March 2017, in collaboration with the "National Programme for Happiness and Wellbeing", the UAE University established the Emirates Center for Happiness Research, the first of its kind in the UAE and the Middle East (WAM, 2017). The center aims to contribute to governmental efforts on happiness and wellbeing by carrying out research studies related to the science of happiness and measuring happiness indices (WAM, 2017).

Informed by its 2021 vision and 2071 centennial plan, in 2022 the UAE Government adopted "The National Strategy for Wellbeing 2031", which aims to position the UAE as a world leader in the field of "quality of life" (The Official Portal of the UAE Government, 2022). The strategy is designed to engage all the UAE sectors in enhancing wellbeing across 3 framework levels, 14 dimensions, 9 strategic objectives, 41 strategic directions, and 90 supporting initiatives (National Program for Happiness and Wellbeing, 2022a).

This strong commitment from the UAE Government toward advancing the wellbeing, happiness, and quality of life of all Emirati residents is reflected in the latest global reports and indicators for happiness and quality of life. For instance, the "World Happiness Report 2023" ranks the UAE as 26th globally and first within the Arab world for average life evaluation (Helliwell et al., 2023). Additionally, the 2022 IMD World Talent Ranking criterion "Quality of Life" ranks the UAE 11th globally (out of 63 countries) (IMD World Competitiveness Center, 2022).

Wellbeing, strategies, policies, and initiatives in the UAE

To generate further insights into wellbeing strategies, policies, and initiatives in the UAE, we carry out a mixed-method study, combining policy document analysis and semi-structured interviews. The policy document analysis generated insights into the value-based intent (Busher, 2006; Stone, 2012) in the "National Wellbeing Strategy 2031", how the strategy was constructed, and the way it is being implemented to achieve its purposes (Cardno, 2018). We also carried out semi-structured interviews with key executive personnel in the UAE government to gain in-depth insights into the belief system underpinning the strategy and the lessons learned and best practices acquired from an Emirati policy-making lens.

Data analysis

We carried out policy document analysis of the UAE National Wellbeing Strategy 2031. The analysis follows the conceptual framework by Taylor et al. (1997) and subsequently developed by Cardno (2018), where three subconstructs (context, content, and consequences) and nine associated areas of inquiry were explored. The result of the analysis is detailed in Table 21.1.

The policy document analysis indicates that the strategy has been designed in a structured manner based on a three-level national wellbeing framework: "Flourishing Country," "Connected Communities," and "Thriving Citizens." The strategy is dynamic in nature and involves both:

- A top–down approach: the strategy was designed based on a set of principles that reflects the vision and stance of the UAE leadership.
- A bottom–up approach: the implementation of the strategy is heavily shaped by numerous wellbeing initiatives and programs, and the effectiveness of their implementation is assessed through data collected from the national wellbeing questionnaire and the national wellbeing index pillars and sub-pillars.

TABLE 21.1 Policy document analysis for the UAE National Wellbeing Strategy 2031

Subconstructs	*Areas of Inquiry*
Context	Purpose • Institutionalizes wellbeing • Establishes a new guiding philosophy in government work Drivers • Supports the realization of the UAE Vision 2021, making the UAE amongst the best countries in the world • Builds the foundation for achieving the UAE Centennial Plan 2071, making the UAE the best country in the world by its centennial in 2071 through a future-focused government, excellent education, diversified knowledge economy, and a happy and cohesive society Values • Emphasizes the happiness of the Emirati nation as a top priority • Stresses mutual and shared responsibility, where UAE's long-term prosperity and advancement are achieved through joined efforts to design a clear vision and constructively aligned plans to attain happiness and enhance wellbeing
Content	Structure • Starts with the design principles, establishing the context • Progresses to a three-level national wellbeing framework • Details the dimensions, strategic objectives, strategic directions, and supporting initiatives related to the framework Component elements • Emerges from a three-level national wellbeing framework • Exemplifies the framework with 14 dimensions • Drives the framework with nine objectives • Guides the implementation of the framework through 41 strategic directions • Achieves the desired outcome through 90 supporting initiatives Emphasized initiatives, procedures, and best practices • Enables the strategy through an operating model that integrates wellbeing across the core operations, procedures, and practices of governmental work Intended overall impact • Promotes and prompts the wellbeing of society through a holistic, carefully planned, structured, sustainable, and data-driven strategy that is implemented through a set of processes, practices, initiatives, and approaches
Consequences	Monitoring of implementation • Measures and monitors the current level of wellbeing at personal, local, and governmental levels through the national wellbeing index pillars and sub-pillars Review and reflection processes • Reviews current approaches, initiatives, and practices informed by data collected through the "National Wellbeing Questionnaire"

Additionally, the analysis of the strategy reveals the following:

- Constructive alignment across its levels, dimensions, strategic objectives, strategic directions, supporting initiatives, and strategy enablers to attain happiness and enhance wellbeing in a holistic and sustainable manner.
- A multi-dimensional approach that maps physical activity, physical health, mental health, communal health and contributions, cultural dimensions, and national advancement as contributors to wellbeing.
- A focus on behavioral change to positively transform practices, and lifestyles toward a healthy and happy life.

Semi-structured interviews

We carried out semi-structured interviews with five executive personnel from various government departments. Participants were selected based on their expertise and leadership of the wellbeing and happiness portfolios within their departments. To maintain participants' anonymity, the five participants are referred to with alpha-numeric codes: P1, P2, P3, P4, and P5. Participants' answers to the research questions were coded and analyzed using thematic coding (Miles et al., 2018). Table 21.2 details the main questions posed during the semi-structured interviews.

When answering the first question about their perceptions of wellbeing from a policy-making lens, participants' answers converged toward perceiving wellbeing as the top priority that resides at the core of all governmental strategies, policies, plans, processes, and practices. For instance, P1 asserted: "I perceive wellbeing, happiness, and quality of life as key indicators of the success of our policymaking." Likewise, P3 argues that wellbeing is at the heart of UAE policies due to its "profound impact on the overall growth and development of our nation." Subsequently, P4 emphasized that wellbeing is not only "one of the main governmental mandates but the most important one."

The second theme that emerged from participants' responses was wellbeing as a multidimensional construct which therefore necessitates a multidimensional approach to UAE policies and practices. This is evident from the following quote.

> *It includes factors such as access to healthcare, food, and clean water, as well as social support and a sense of purpose. From a policymaking perspective,*

TABLE 21.2 Set of major questions articulated during the semi-structured interviews

Q1	How do you perceive wellbeing from a policy-making lens?
Q2	From a UAE perspective, what are some of the lessons learned and success stories achieved about wellbeing and happiness that you believe would inform wellbeing strategies and practices of policy-makers at an international scale?
Q3	Thinking about the "National Wellbeing Strategy 2031," could you please elaborate on the nature of this strategy in terms of structure, impact, and continuous improvement?

> *policies that promote access to healthcare, education, and social services can help improve the wellbeing of all.*
>
> *(P2)*

> *We need to ensure that our policies address the full spectrum of human needs – from basic necessities like food, water, and shelter to more holistic requirements such as mental health, emotional wellbeing, and spiritual fulfillment. Policymaking should prioritize the creation of a sustainable environment that enables individuals to lead fulfilling lives and realize their full potential. High quality of life for the people of the UAE means access to excellent healthcare, education, infrastructure, public services, and opportunities for personal and professional growth.*
>
> *(P1)*

Such an "interplay between wellbeing, happiness, and quality of life" (P2) is central across "real and digital environments . . . [ensuring] that UAE citizens and residents lead fulfilling, happy, and productive lives" (P3).

In response to the question about lessons learned and success stories achieved about the Emirati wellbeing experience, participants' answers revealed a set of national and international initiatives and exemplars. When it comes to national initiatives, P1, P2, and P5 assert that two of the major success stories that have transformed wellbeing from being a personal matter to becoming a matter of public policy in the UAE were the establishment of the "Ministry of Happiness and Wellbeing" and subsequently the "National Program for Happiness & Wellbeing." The program is responsible not only for "developing policies and initiatives to improve the quality of life for UAE residents" (P2) but also for "setting national wellbeing indicators to monitor progress and guide policymaking" (P1). Additionally, several national councils have been established to collect data, input, and feedback from "multiple perspectives, such as the Wellbeing Council, the Digital Wellbeing Council, and the Private Sector Wellbeing Council" (P3). These bodies together "inform the design and implementation of policies and initiatives" (P3).

These initiatives led to the collection of longitudinal, cross-sectional, and real-time data to assess the implementation of the various wellbeing procedures and practices and evaluate the wellbeing and happiness of UAE citizens, residents, and visitors. For instance, the "National Wellbeing Survey," which runs every 2 years, provides invaluable longitudinal data to measure the wellbeing of community members in the UAE as outlined by the "National Wellbeing Strategy 2031" (P1, P4, and P5). Additionally, regular cross-sectional surveys are conducted to assess the wellbeing indicators in the UAE. In terms of real-time data, "Happiness Meter" is an initiative that makes Dubai the first city in the world to interactively measure happiness and satisfaction levels of citizens, residents, and visitors (P1 and P3). These meters are "available in taxis, buses, hotels, and clinics, allowing citizens, residents, and visitors to share their feelings and experiences, providing valuable feedback on what can be improved" (P3). This "real-time data helps the government become more responsive and efficient in addressing issues promptly, creating a happier environment for everyone" (P3). All these initiatives are designed and facilitated using advanced technologies, including AI, which provide optimal avenues to measure, monitor, and improve wellbeing and happiness levels (P1 and P3).

Beyond the UAE's border, the UAE Government actively contributes to global efforts to prioritize wellbeing and create positive outcomes for the global community. This contribution is reflected by several international initiatives, such as the Global Dialogue for Happiness and Wellbeing, the Global Happiness Council, and the Global Happiness Coalition (P1 and P3). Such initiatives have been either founded or strongly supported by the UAE Government. These international platforms "provide opportunities for policymakers and experts from around the world to share successful experiences and tools to boost happiness and wellbeing across all communities" (P3).

Finally, when asked to elaborate on the nature of the "National Wellbeing Strategy 2031" in terms of structure, impact, and continuous improvement, participants' responses converged into the one theme: The strategy is dynamic, adaptive, and evolving in nature, where it guides and informs wellbeing practices, processes, and initiatives and at the same time is informed by them. In this context, P1 commented: "In its design phase, the National Wellbeing Strategy 2031 was informed by extensive consultations with various stakeholders across the country, including individuals, community organizations, and private sector entities. This collaborative approach ensured that the strategy reflected the needs and aspirations of the people, as well as the broader social, economic, and environmental realities of the UAE." After its launch, "the strategy has undergone continuous evaluation and improvement through ongoing feedback and engagement from stakeholders" (P1), where it is "designed to be regularly reviewed and updated based on new data and insights" (P2). "This allows policymakers to identify emerging trends and issues and make adjustments to their policies and initiatives, as needed" (P2).

The strategy guides wellbeing practices in several key areas, including education, health, environment, economy, and social cohesion (P1, P2, P3, and P5). In doing so, the strategy "recognizes that wellbeing is not a static concept but rather a dynamic one that is shaped by a range of factors" (P2). Additionally, the "establishment of enablers such as the UAE Wellbeing Observatory and the Community Design for Wellbeing Centers demonstrates the commitment of the UAE government to track and monitor the progress of wellbeing initiatives and provide support and resources to both government officials and community members" (P3).

Such a dynamic approach enables the strategy to adapt to changing circumstances and challenges while also fostering a culture of innovation and creativity in wellbeing practices and initiatives, where the strategy:

- "Learns from and adapts to the experiences and outcomes of wellbeing initiatives, scaling up successful practices to ensure broader impact and reach" (P1),

- "Facilitates continuous learning, innovation, and improvement, while also ensuring that policymaking is grounded in the needs and aspirations of the people" (P3), and
- "Emphasizes the importance of evidence-based policymaking, ongoing dialogue, and collaboration between the government, private sector, and the public, making the strategy relevant and effective in addressing the changing needs of the society" (P3).

Actionable points derived from the UAE experience

Promoting and advancing wellbeing is now a culture in the UAE that resides at the core of all governmental strategies, policies, and practices and actively involves the private sector and the general public. This culture is integrated across various sectors, reflecting a multidimensional approach to wellbeing in the UAE. The results of policy document analysis and semi-structured interviews carried out in this work highlight some key lessons for UAE and beyond. They emphasize the importance of the following.

Find a critical balance between top–down and bottom–up approaches

From a top–down perspective, the UAE's strategy was designed on a set of principles that reflects the vision and stance of the UAE leadership on wellbeing as being a top priority and a culture that needs to be integrated across all sectors and avenues of life in the UAE. From a bottom–up perspective, the strategy emerged from extensive consultations with various stakeholders, reflecting the needs and aspirations of the people, as well as the broader social, economic, and environmental realities of the UAE.

Ensure constructive alignment

Wellbeing is a multidimensional construct and wellbeing in the UAE is shaped by many different areas of policy. The various elements and constituents of the strategy are constructively aligned to promote overall wellbeing in the UAE.

Adopt an adaptive approach

The UAE's wellbeing strategy is regularly reviewed and updated, informed by new data and insights, enabling policy-makers to identify emerging trends and issues and proactively make the required reviews and adjustments.

Be data driven

Emirati practices rely on longitudinal, cross-sectional, and real-time data to provide a holistic assessment of wellbeing and its drivers. This is facilitated through the adoption of advanced technologies, including AI and various digital tools and ensures that policy decisions are shaped by up-to-date empirical evidence.

Engage globally

The Emirati investment in wellbeing is not limited to local initiatives but extends to international initiatives and programs that have been founded or strongly supported by the UAE Government, reflecting the UAE's commitment to contributing to a global policy discourse on this fundamental topic.

These lessons have the potential to inform public policy in the field of wellbeing at a regional and global level. Additionally, the chapter adds to the developing literature about wellbeing in the Arab world and invites further research on this topic to respond to the implications of future changes, challenges, and realities.

Acknowledgment

The authors would like to show their heartfelt gratitude to Her Excellency Hessa bint Essa Buhumaid for her support throughout the journey of producing this chapter.

References

Busher, H. (2006). *Understanding educational leadership: People, power and culture*. Open University Press.
Cardno, C. (2018). Policy document analysis: A practical educational leadership tool and a qualitative research method. *Kuram ve Uygulamada Eğitim Yönetimi*, *24*(4), 623–640. https://doi.org/10.14527/kuey.2018.016
Etihad Museum (n.d.). *The establishment of the union*. Etihad Museum.
Helliwell, J. F., Huang, H., Norton, M., Goff, L., & Wang, S. (2023). World happiness, trust and social connections in times of crisis. In *World Happiness Report 2023* (11th ed., Chapter 2). Sustainable Development Solutions Network.
IMD World Competitiveness Center (2022, December). *IMD world talent ranking 2022*. IMD World Competitiveness Center. https://imd.cld.bz/IMD-World-Talent-Ranking-2022
Media Center, UAE Cabinet (2016). *News*. Retrieved January 9, 2023, from https://uaecabinet.ae/en/details/news/mohammed-bin-rashid-happiness-positivity-are-lifestyle-government-commitment-and-a-spirit-uniting-uae-community
Miles, M. B., Huberman, A. M., & Saldaña, J. (2018). *Qualitative data analysis: A methods sourcebook*. Sage publications.
National Program for Happiness and Wellbeing (2022a). *UAE national wellbeing strategy 2031*. National Wellbeing Observatory. www.hw.gov.ae/en/download/uae-national-wellbeing-strategy-2031
National Program for Happiness & Wellbeing (2022b). *UAE national wellbeing report 2022*. National Wellbeing Observatory.
The Official Portal of the UAE Government (2016). *Happiness: National programme for happiness and wellbeing*. The Official Portal of the UAE Government. https://u.ae/en/about-the-uae/the-uae-government/government-of-future/happiness
The Official Portal of the UAE Government (2022, November 24). *National strategy for wellbeing 2031*. The Official Portal of the UAE Government. https://u.ae/en/about-the-uae/strategies-initiatives-and-awards/strategies-plans-and-visions/social-affairs/national-strategy-for-wellbeing-2031

Ribeiro, D., Costa, A. P., & Remondes, J. (2020). Government communication – the Dubai and United Arab Emirates Ministry of Happiness: The objective of the creation of the Ministry of Happiness – content analysis. In *Computer supported qualitative research: New trends on qualitative research (WCQR2019) 4* (pp. 226–238). Springer International Publishing. https://doi.org/10.1007/978-3-030-31787-4_19

Stone, D. (2012). *Policy paradox: The art of political decision making*. Norton & Company.

Taylor, S., Rizvi, F., Lingard, B., & Henry, M. (1997). *Education policy and the politics of change*. Routledge. https://doi.org/10.4324/9780203349533

WAM (2017, March 23). *UAEU opens country's first Emirates Centre for Happiness Research*. Wam. https://wam.ae/en/details/1395302604703

WAM (The Emirates News Agency) (2021, April 6). *Abdullah bin Zayed statement on the occasion of the 43rd anniversary of UAE National Day, 1st Add*. WAM. Retrieved January 9, 2023, from http://wam.ae/en/details/1395273298225

22

WELLBEING AND POLICY IN CANADA

Progress towards measurement and practice

Chris P. Barrington-Leigh

Overview

Recently, the Canadian federal government has embraced a quality-of-life framework which privileges subjective measures such as life satisfaction as an "umbrella measure" to inform policy priority setting and decision-making. Accordingly, this chapter focuses on subjective life evaluations as a measure of wellbeing, and begins with an account of the history of life satisfaction in Canada, using available data from prominent surveys followed by a description of the recent history of approaches to conceptualizing and measuring wellbeing in Canada.

How's life in Canada?

Canada has measured life satisfaction (LS), and some other measures of subjective wellbeing, since 1985 (Barrington-Leigh, 2013) in its General Social Survey (GSS), since 2005 in the Canadian Community Health Survey, and most recently in the Canadian Social Survey (CSS).[1] Figure 22.1 displays trends in average life evaluations from the Gallup World Poll as well as the CSS. Importantly, these surveys *exclude* residents of First Nations reserves and some other Aboriginal settlements, and the GSS and CSS further exclude Canada's three Territories – the Yukon, Northwest Territories, and Nunavut.

Together, data from all four surveys are consistent with an ongoing decrease in average reported wellbeing over the past decade. Because life satisfaction can be affected by so many different things, it is difficult to explain changes in the average or even differences across geographies or groups. A further challenge facing all national statistical agencies is the decline in response rates to social surveys. In Canada, for instance, the fraction of Canadians willing to respond to the GSS has been declining from a stable 80%, prior to 2000, down to near or below half in

DOI: 10.4324/9781003382447-25

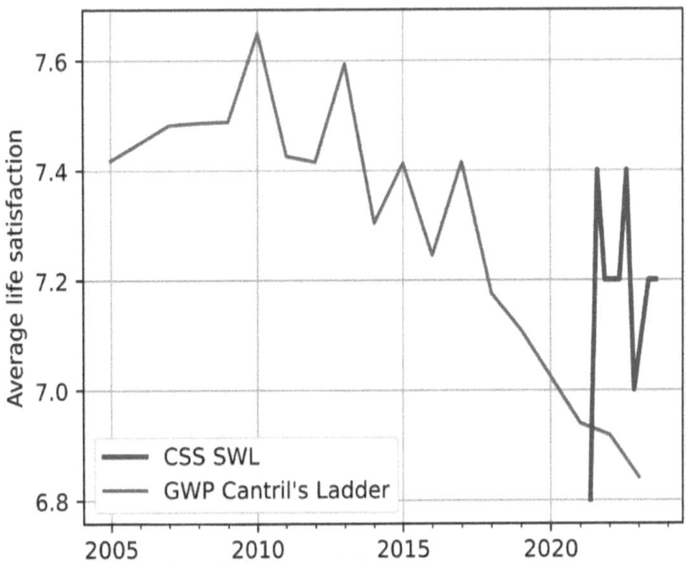

FIGURE 22.1 Life satisfaction in Canada from Statistics Canada's GSS, and another life evaluation question (Cantril's Ladder) from the Gallup World Poll.

recent years. While some social statistics can increasingly be derived from administrative data, for subjective variables there is no alternative to a survey.

Despite the challenges, numerous studies using Canadian data have shed light on the determinants of wellbeing, and a public dataset exists of local-level LS averages, with possibly globally unmatched geographic resolution (Helliwell et al., 2019). A number of other specialized Statistics Canada surveys have posed the LS question, along with domain-specific satisfaction questions and other important measures of wellbeing. The GSS especially has been useful for quantifying social dimensions of Canadians' lives, such as trust, social identity, and social interactions, which are known to be important determinants of LS. The recent quarterly CSS includes a number of such factors, including a sense of meaning and purpose, self-rated mental health, future outlook, loneliness, having someone to count on, a sense of belonging to a local community, and a measure of difficulty meeting household financial needs. In contrast to the UK's ONS4 "dimensions" of wellbeing, the CSS relies on LS and a sense of meaning and purpose as the only overarching indicators of wellbeing. In this approach, the aim is to track important determinants of wellbeing, rather than multiple dimensions of wellbeing.

Wellbeing initiatives in Canada

As in other countries, there is a long history in Canada of striving to define comprehensive and appropriate measures of social progress. Often these have been branded using the language of "wellbeing" or "quality of life" (QoL). The value of having such a cross-cutting index or measure of success includes being able to evaluate the success of government programs in a consistent and holistic way, as well as communicating and gauging an overall objective for society or for jurisdictions within the country.

For instance, in 1999 the annual report of the Treasury Board of Canada announced a new effort to link societal indicators into "a more comprehensive performance framework to help provide a broader context both for measuring performance and developing policy" (Treasury Board of Canada Secretariat, 1999). This led to a substantial report in 2000 on defining, measuring, and reporting on QoL with a vision for a comprehensive federal performance measurement and reporting process (Treasury Board of Canada Secretariat, 2000). The Treasury Board's *Quality of Life Indicators* was developed and published annually between 2004 and 2010 – and then it was dropped.

Another federal government agency, the Human Resources and Skills Development Canada, developed its own indicators of *Well-being in Canada*, measured and reported between 2009 and 2014 – and then they were dropped. Meanwhile, Indigenous Services Canada defined the "Community Well-Being index" using four domains – education, labour force activity, income, and housing – in 2004 and reported it for census years up until 2016 (O'Sullivan, 2011). In 2017, Veterans Affairs Canada defined *A Veteran Well-being Surveillance Framework*, which is still in use in 2025.

This account of federal government initiatives suggests that reaching consensus on a universal wellbeing evaluation framework is likely to remain difficult, and faces both conceptual and political challenges. Indeed, it may be that the more any definition of wellbeing, or framework for measuring it, becomes prominent in a government's policy platform or accountability framework, the more it risks being considered a partisan brand when the government changes.

The quality-of-life framework

In April 2021, in accordance with a series of mandate letters from the Prime Minister in 2019, and in conjunction with the Federal Budget release, Canada's Department of Finance (2021) published its work on a new quality-of-life strategy. This conceptual framework and measurement strategy is intended to guide evidence-based budgeting and decision-making at the federal level, and to strengthen integration and coordination between existing policy commitment frameworks.

Some distinguishing features of Canada's framework are that (1) subjective wellbeing – and specifically life satisfaction – stands as a *headline indicator* outside and above the five quality of life *domains*, which are called Prosperity, Health, Society, Environment, and Good Governance; (2) questions of long-run sustainability and questions of poverty, equity, and distributions are handled by overarching lenses, rather than reduced to a set of scalar indicators within any domain;

and (3) the quantitative indicators used to track each domain are considered "evergreen", that is always provisional and subject to supplanting or supplementing as better data become available (Sanmartin et al., 2021).

These features are farsighted, facilitate use in policy of academic evidence on life satisfaction, and have already inspired a similar framework in Australia (Treasury, 2023).

In January 2022, Statistics Canada (2022) published an ambitious and remarkable manifesto entitled "The System of National Quality-of-Life Statistics: Future Directions". It lays out the intent to build a knowledge base within Statistics Canada that can support wellbeing decision-making based on characteristics at the individual level and on the latest data. This "what works" and "what is likely to work best" knowledge will eventually be available to individual citizens, as well as informing social interventions, service provision, and government budgeting through simulation and prediction of full distributional outcomes. According to the Future Directions document (Statistics Canada, 2022, p. 4), the system will lead to

> major improvements in the operation of labour markets, health, learning and other social dimensions of life in Canada, both on average and for all population groups – and direct benefits to individuals as they make big decisions in the social, health and labour domains of life.

This vision, somewhat of a holy grail of social sciences, is clearly a long-run objective. The 2022 paper outlines the state the system could have achieved by 2027–2032, but explicitly admits that human capacity at Statistics Canada may be a limiting factor.

The Canadian Index of Wellbeing

The Canadian Index of Wellbeing (CIW) was developed by the Atkinson Charitable Foundation between 1999 and 2011, and consists of 64 indicators, largely available from Statistics Canada, organized into eight domains and further aggregated into a single index. It was intended to provide a lens for decision-making, and a complement to the policy focus on economic growth. The most recent CIW report is from 2016, with data up to 2014, and in addition to an account of the trends in the index, it features proposals for a universal basic income, national education strategy, and a more upstream approach to health.

The (eponymous) organization behind the CIW has also partnered with several Canadian communities to field social surveys of its own design. Such local surveys may in some cases be large enough to glean some useful data and inference, or they may act more to raise awareness of modern measures of wellbeing and as seeds of changing the conversation about policy-making. The largest case is that of Engage Nova Scotia, an organization which has used a province-wide CIW-based wellbeing survey as part of its mission to build awareness, relationships, and new policy priorities for wellbeing at all levels across the province.

Indigenous wellbeing

An important question for any effort to promote wellbeing measurement standards or wellbeing knowledge mobilization for policy in Canada is how to represent Indigenous peoples' perspectives on wellbeing. This might mean recognizing distinct approaches, or it could mean incorporating Indigenous knowledge about wellbeing into a country-wide framework, as has happened to some extent in New Zealand.

The current status of the federal quality-of-life framework does not yet reflect the distinctiveness of Indigenous knowledge. On the other hand, the situation in Canada is entirely different from countries like New Zealand, where one ethnic group, the Maori, make up the vast majority of the Indigenous population, and 17% of the country's overall population. In Canada the situation is much more fractured. Inuit, Métis, and over 50 distinct First Nations may have different concepts around wellbeing and, as importantly, different political and legal relationships to Canada. First Nations also differ in their proclivities to participate in frameworks or programs originating in the federal government or from "Western" academic thinking more generally. This latter outcome arises both from a history of betrayal and from a historical Western focus on overly narrow economic outcomes as proxies of wellbeing, which lies in contrast to most Indigenous conceptions of wellbeing.

This is in spite of a similarity which may be noticed between Indigenous descriptions of wellbeing and the type of social- and place-based connectedness which looms large in the academic literature on life satisfaction. That is, while some Western academics, NGOs, and governments bundle objective measures of environmental service sufficiency and long-run sustainability together with human outcomes under a "wellbeing" banner, many Indigenous frameworks and empirical evidence from the life satisfaction approach emphasize instead relationships between people and environment. For instance, the Chair of the Métis Data Governance Committee in British Columbia writes that "health and wellness is rooted in community, culture, self-determination, language, spirituality, and *connection to the land*" (Métis Nation and BC Ministry of Health, 2022).

There are many Inuit, Métis, and First Nation projects which define wellbeing, often described as "health and wellness", and which propose corresponding policy frameworks (First Nations Health Authority Nation and BC Ministry of Health, 2021; Podlasly et al., 2020). For instance, the Thunderbird Partnership Foundation (e.g. 2015, 2020) has developed wellbeing frameworks and, with various partners, released a series of guides for policy implementation (Thunderbird Partnership Foundation, 2018a, 2018b). The Nisga'a Lisims Government in northern British Columbia has developed its own quality-of-life strategy (2013), framework

(2014), and repeated community survey (2018–), the latter to gauge "how well a person is living their daily life". An important intent of this effort is to be able to track and evaluate the impacts of the Nisga'a Final Agreement, an early example of a "modern treaty" for Indigenous land claims in Canada (Bouchard et al., 2021). As well as proposing a 22-indicator health and wellness framework, a report from First Nations Health Authority and BC Ministry of Health (2021) suggests seven priority actions for policy to nourish the First Nations roots of wellness. Bouchard et al. (2021) review the shortcomings of previous central government efforts at measuring Indigenous wellbeing in Canada and emphasize the importance of collaborative and Indigenous-led initiatives to articulate wellbeing concepts and policy frameworks.

The First Nations Information Governance Centre (FNIGC) helps to coordinate these diverse efforts. It considers the choice of what to measure, and the ownership, control, access, and possession of data, to be fundamental to address the long-term wellbeing of First Peoples. The FNIGC coordinates a First Nations Regional Health Survey, and corresponding Regional Social Survey among regional governance organizations across Canada.

Canadian Wellbeing Knowledges Network

Through a series of private meetings and public conferences, a network of practitioners and policy-makers interested in "wellbeing budgeting" has formed into the Canadian Wellbeing Knowledges Network (CWKN). The CWKN has organized a series of reflections and strategy discussions, surveyed the existing wellbeing policy initiatives across Canada, and organized a two-day meeting in Ottawa, called "Wellbeing Ahead!", which was attended by a federal cabinet minister and President of the Treasury Board, a federal senator, Canada's Chief Statistician, as well as many Network members. The CWKN is still at an embryonic stage with respect to its ambition to provide capacity-building support for all levels of government and organizations working to inform policy with evidence on wellbeing.

Evidence of effectiveness of existing wellbeing initiatives

The life satisfaction approach offers a disciplined way to draw a line between evidence and policy advice, while this may be harder with looser definitions. For instance, in the CIW report mentioned earlier, no clear connection is made between the proposed policies and the evidence from the index. Instead, 18 experts (not named in the report) were consulted for their opinions on "innovative and integrated policy directions" which would enhance the wellbeing of all Canadians. In other frameworks in which sustainability and social justice are bundled together, "wellbeing" risks becoming a largely rhetorical device to provide moral weight or attention for one's policy platform (Barrington-Leigh & Escande, 2018).

While it is hard to find evidence of direct influence of the CIW on national policies, the CIW's community wellbeing surveys have helped to change the conversation in local jurisdictions and regions, including the Yukon and Nova Scotia. These are the necessary steps in a long process of changing expectations from the bottom up.

Similarly, when asking whether the federal QoL framework has led to different decisions or allocations of public resources than would have happened without it, evidence is scant. Recent federal budgets have labelled funding programs according to which QoL Framework domains relate to anticipated program outcomes. This kind of labeling could occur as a hollow, retrospective exercise, or it could already reflect a growing practice of upstream thinking about wellbeing outcomes and cross-department benefits and synergies when costs are conceived. Either way, the ambitions of the federal initiative are far-reaching, and involve a long-term plan to build a knowledge base about the determinants of wellbeing at individual and group levels (Statistics Canada, 2022) suitable for informing a wide variety of decisions. Helliwell et al. (2022) review some early successes in applying a life satisfaction approach to program evaluation and to prospective cost-effectiveness estimates within the Canadian government.

Engage Nova Scotia and its flagship program, the Nova Scotia Quality of Life Initiative, is growing in influence and reach by leveraging its wellbeing survey data and interactive online tools to explore wellbeing across the province. Its latest annual report mentions that it is now working with over 20 government departments and agencies on bringing their quality-of-life evidence and approach to policy discussions and priorities.

Key lessons learned to date

Due to the large number of governments and Indigenous governance structures in Canada, it is never possible to feel that everyone implicated by a discussion of "wellbeing in Canada" is represented at the table. This cannot therefore be a prerequisite for pursuing the mission of empowering organizations and governments to bring evidence on wellbeing to policy and practice. In the early experience of the CWKN, merely acting as a meeting point for people with similar needs or with complementary experience is a step towards better policy.

The CWKN has not prescribed a particular conceptual or measurement approach to wellbeing, and its membership holds diverse views about wellbeing. Nevertheless, much of the support cited for the idea that wellbeing evidence could inform policy tends to be from the literature on life satisfaction – presumably due to its conceptual clarity. There is a balance, then, in disciplining the banner of "wellbeing policy" so as not to include arbitrary, wellbeing-branded policy platforms, while at the same time attracting diverse contributions to knowledge about wellbeing.

One of the challenges faced by municipalities in Canada interested in adopting a wellbeing policy orientation is the cost of "reinventing the wheel," that is formulating a local social survey or devising a wellbeing policy framework. A sensible but not inevitable solution is for top–down initiatives, for instance at the Federal government level, to make their work easy to adapt or adopt by other stakeholders. Instantiating wellbeing frameworks and approaches with external partners may also be one key way to ensure their longevity beyond electoral cycles.

Ultimately, the aim for wellbeing policy advocates is to change expectations, public discourse, and accountability around policy in order that the outcomes that matter are the transparent objectives of policy. These expectations are bottom–up changes, which is why a broad base of local wellbeing definition and measurement, community surveys and reflections, and local-government buy-in are critical aspects of wellbeing policy-making for Canada.

Actionable points

- Place a transparent, overarching indicator of wellbeing at the top of any evaluation framework, to allow for communication and synergies across government departments and programs.
- Measuring social capital and trust as part of any policy program evaluation facilitates fuller evaluation of the monetary value of social impacts.
- Especially in diverse cultural contexts, community support for wellbeing policy frameworks is best achieved through bottom–up processes to define wellbeing.

Note

1 This is an abridged and adapted version of a longer working paper by the same author.

References

Barrington-Leigh, C. P. (June 2013). The Québec convergence and Canadian life satisfaction 1985–2008. *Canadian Public Policy*, *39*(2), 193–219. https://doi.org/10.3138/CPP.39.2.193

Barrington-Leigh, C. P., & Escande, A. (2018, February). Measuring progress and wellbeing: A comparative review of indicators. *Social Indicators Research*, *135*(3), 893–925. ISSN: 1573-0921. https://doi.org/10.1007/s11205-016-1505-0

Bouchard, K. et al. (2021). Measuring what counts to advance indigenous self-determination: A case study of the Nisga'a Lisims government's quality of life framework and survey. *International Journal of Community Well-Being*, *4*(3), 415–441.

Department of Finance (2021, April). *Measuring what matters: Toward a quality of life strategy for Canada*. Government of Canada.

First Nations Health Authority and BC Ministry of Health (2021). *First nations population health and wellness agenda*. https://www.fnha.ca/Documents/FNHA-PHO-First-Nations-Population-Health-and-Wellness-Agenda.pdf

Helliwell, J. F., Shiplett, H., & Barrington-Leigh, C. P. (2019). How happy are your neighbours? Variation in life satisfaction among 1200 Canadian neighbourhoods and communities. *PLoS One*, *14*(1). https://doi.org/10.1371/journal.pone.0210091

Helliwell, J. F. et al. (2022). Building an epidemiology of happiness. In A. Hayden, C. Gaudet, & J. Wilson (Eds.), *Towards sustainable well-being: Moving beyond GDP in Canada and the World*. University of Toronto Press. Chapter 11.

Métis Nation and BC Ministry of Health (2022). *Taanishi Kiiya? Miiyayow Métis Saantii Pi Miyooayaan Didaan BC (How are you? Improving Métis health and wellness in BC), Métis Public Health Surveillance Program – Baseline Report, 2021*. https://www2.gov.bc.ca/assets/gov/health/about-bc-s-health-care-system/office-of-the-provincial-health-officer/reports-publications/annual-reports/pho_metis_report_2021c_f3.pdf

O'Sullivan, E. (2011). *The Community Well-Being index (CWB): Measuring well-being in first nations and non-aboriginal communities, 1981–2006*. English. Tech. rep. Aboriginal Affairs and Northern Development Canada, pp. 1–19.

Podlasly, M. et al. (2020, November). *Centering first nations concepts of wellbeing: Toward a GDP-alternative index in British Columbia*. Tech. rep. British Columbia Assembly of First Nations.

Sanmartin, C. et al. (2021, July). *Moving forward on well-being (quality of life) measures in Canada*. Government of Canada.

Statistics Canada (2022, January). *The system of national quality-of-life statistics: Future directions*. https://www150.statcan.gc.ca/n1/pub/11-633-x/11-633-x2021006-eng.htm

Thunderbird Partnership Foundation (2015). *First nations mental wellness continuum framework*. https://thunderbirdpf.org/wp-content/uploads/2015/01/24-14-1273-FN-Mental-Wellness-Framework-EN05_low.pdf

Thunderbird Partnership Foundation (2018a). *Land for healing: Developing a first nations land-based service delivery model*. 22361. https://thunderbirdpf.org/wp-content/uploads/2018/07/Thunderbirdpf-LandforHealing-Document-SQ.pdf

Thunderbird Partnership Foundation (2018b). *The first nations mental wellness continuum framework: A guide to implementation*. 22361. https://thunderbirdpf.org/wp-content/uploads/2018/11/FNMWC_implementation_guide.pdf

Thunderbird Partnership Foundation (2020). *Indigenous wellness framework reference guide*. National Native Addictions Partnership Foundation. www.thunderbirdpf.org/IWF.

Treasury (July 2023). *Measuring what matters: Australia's first wellbeing framework*. Commonwealth of Australia.

Treasury Board of Canada Secretariat (1999). *Managing for results*. Tech. rep. Government of Canada.

Treasury Board of Canada Secretariat (2000). *Quality of life – a concept paper: Defining, measuring and reporting quality of life for Canadians*. Tech. rep. Government of Canada.

23

WELLBEING AND POLICY IN AUSTRALIA

Michelle Baddeley

Introduction

Australia has a rosy macroeconomic record: it currently holds the global record for avoiding recession – its last was in 1992 and it defied pessimistic predictions of a COVID-induced recession in 2021–22, experiencing just a mild downturn and returning to pre-pandemic levels of growth by mid-2021 (OECD, 2021). It also ranks highly internationally in terms of many indicators of overall wellbeing and human development. Yet recent statistics from the OECD *How's Life* wellbeing report tell a different story and highlight a mixed pattern of performance in Australia's wellbeing record (OECD, 2020), in contradistinction with its strong record in terms of GDP growth.

In exploring the complex and multi-faceted dimensions of Australian wellbeing, this chapter begins with an overview of Australia's wellbeing landscape as measured by the OECD's wellbeing statistics. It will then analyse some of the political and policy-making pressures associated with Australia's federal system of government and associated constitutional constraints. It will also set out some of Australia's specific wellbeing policy challenges for its marginalised groups – including Aboriginal and Torres Strait Islanders (ATSIs), refugees and newly arrived migrants and others facing economic and financial disadvantage and deprivation.

Australia's wellbeing record

Australia has a reputation for being a relatively prosperous country, both in terms of its economic performance and in terms of its standard of living – a performance which has been attributed to a range of factors, including its diversified (albeit commodity-focused) economic structure (McLean, 2016). Yet, according to the *World Happiness Report 2023*, it is ranked 12th in the world for average life evaluations,

DOI: 10.4324/9781003382447-26

and 22nd in the world in terms of its "happiness gap" between the top and bottom halves of its population (Helliwell et al., 2023). In unpacking the reasons for this gap, statistics from the OECD's *How's Life Report* illuminate some of the areas in which Australian wellbeing is faltering – focusing specifically on indicators of prosperity; subjective wellbeing measures; youth employment and gender pay gaps; health versus suicide rates and social connectedness versus social fragmentation.[1]

Prosperity versus subjective wellbeing

The OECD data show that Australia is highly ranked in terms of household incomes and earnings, as illustrated in Figure 23.1. This is juxtaposed against

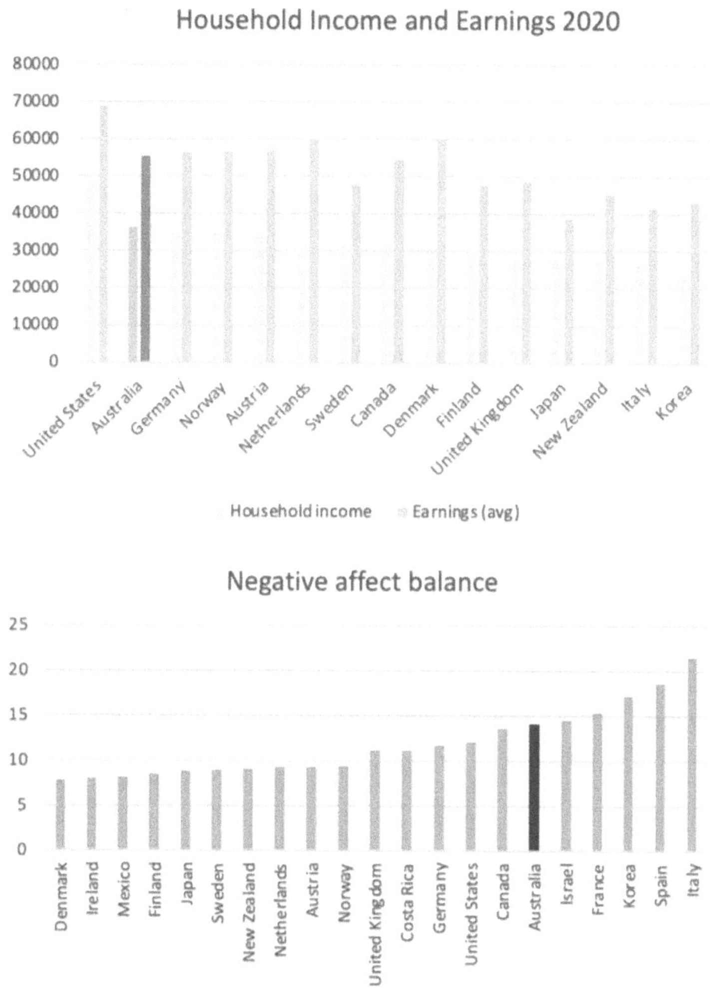

FIGURE 23.1 Income and affect.

subjective wellbeing measures. Life satisfaction statistics are patchy across the OECD. This measure captures self-reported life satisfaction, and 2020 is the most recent OECD data for Australia. Comparisons are difficult because there is very limited data from other countries. Comparing Australia with the highest and lowest scorers, Australia scores 7.2 versus 8 in Canada and 5.83 in Japan. Cross-country comparisons are better enabled by the richer data on negative affect balance, and this reveals that, notwithstanding Australia's strong record in terms of overall prosperity, it is lagging behind in terms of negative affect balance – see Figure 23.1 – second panel.

Employment and gender pay gaps

Employment is strongly correlated with wellbeing and, in common with other OECD nations, Australia does well in terms of its employment rate – it had a comparatively high employment rate of 77.8% in comparison with the best performer – Sweden, which had an employment rate of 84.5% in 2020. But, drilling down from this macroeconomic picture, there are divergences in terms of youth employment – Australia's proportion of 'Youth Not in Employment, Education or Training' (NEETs) is relatively small, but its gender pay gap is relatively large – see Figure 23.2.

Health: life expectancy versus suicide rates

The OECD health indicators show a similar disconnect – whilst Australia's overall life expectancy is strong, looking at health indicators correlated with wellbeing specifically, that is the suicide rate, Australia does not perform so well (see Figure 23.3).

Social connectedness versus social fragmentation

Social indicators of wellbeing, including social connectedness versus feeling safe, are also mixed for Australia. It is one of the lowest-ranked countries on 'feeling safe at night' – prima facie, a surprising result given Australia's generally low crime rate (see Figure 23.4).

But Australia's low ranking here might reflect the inclusion of accidents and natural disasters, following the OECD definition: 'Safety is about freedom from harm, whether that harm comes in the form of crime, conflict, violence, terrorism, oppression, accidents or natural disasters.' This might explain the faltering recent performance, given that the 2019–2020 period coincided with extreme bushfires in Australia's most populous states.

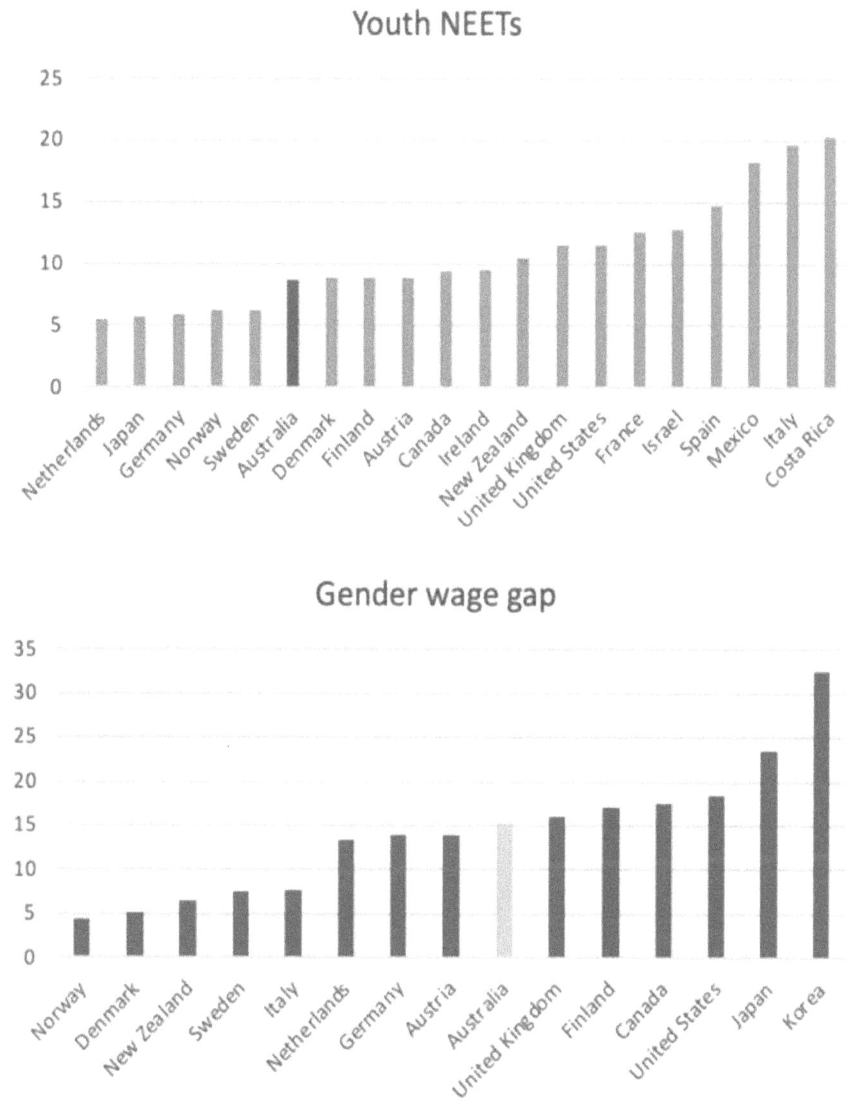

FIGURE 23.2 Employment and gender pay gaps.

Australia's wellbeing policy challenges

A disconnect between monetary measures of macroeconomic performance and indicators of wellbeing is not necessarily surprising, for any country, and it is well established that GDP is very limited as an accurate measure of wellbeing (Stiglitz

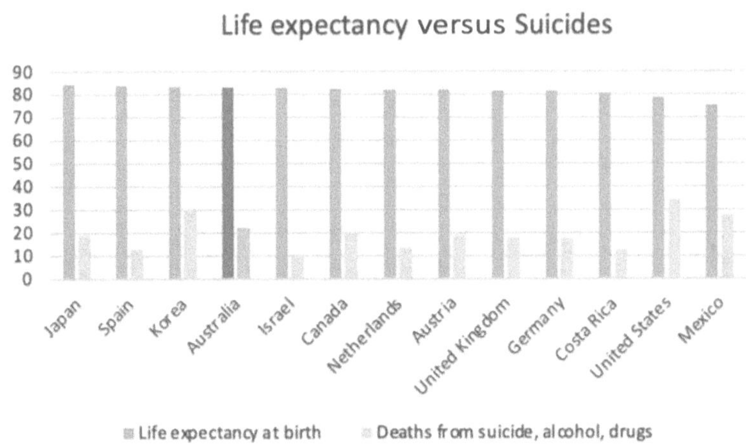

FIGURE 23.3 Life expectancy versus suicide rates.

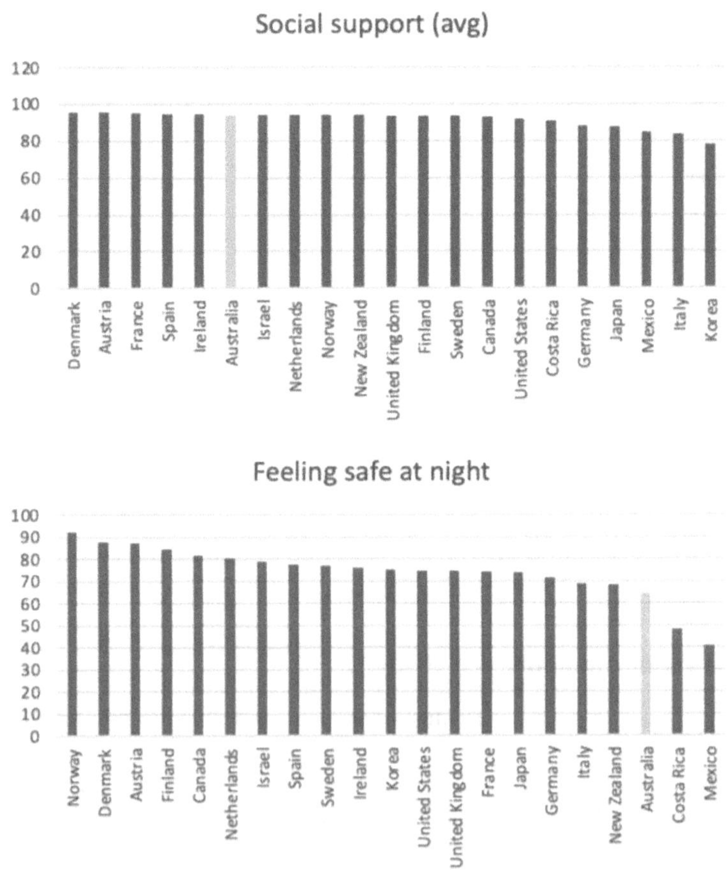

FIGURE 23.4 Social support and feeling safe.

et al., 2009). But perhaps it is more surprising to see such a stark mismatch in Australia – an affluent and thriving democracy with good public services and in which levels of public trust and civic engagement are reputedly high.

Disadvantaged groups

The disconnect between the OECD objective and subjective wellbeing statistics and the broader indirect measures of Australia's macroeconomic performance can be explained by the fact that Australia's healthy 'macro' statistics conceal enduring inequalities in terms of wellbeing, prosperity and freedom across Australia's population. Whilst most Australians would have a broadly positive experience in terms of what their country has to offer, especially if they live in urban centres, Australia does confront serious challenges in terms of the wellbeing, prosperity and freedom of key marginalised groups – most starkly the experiences of ATSI communities facing deeply entrenched health and wellbeing inequalities. Experiences of poverty and deprivation within ATSI communities are on par with the experiences of those in some of the world's poorest nations, as highlighted in Royal Commission reports in 1991 and 2017 (Royal Commission, 1991, 2017).

Other groups suffering severe disadvantage include refugees and newly arrived migrants, and people living with a disability or in aged care – the latter as exposed in the Royal Commission's (2021) report. Severe wellbeing shortfalls also exist for those facing significant financial disadvantage – including those adversely affected by COVID or by the current cost-of-living crisis and also those who were struggling financially pre-COVID. Many of these groups have not been well served by the exercise of the Federal government's executive power. Most recently, the Robodebt Royal Commission exposed 'malfeasance in public office', committed via the previous Federal government's 'robodebt' scheme for welfare debt assessment and recovery: egregiously over-simplified computerised algorithms were used incorrectly to identify and target welfare recipients for repayment of welfare debts which they did not owe – with severe impacts on their mental health and wellbeing (Royal Commission, 2023; O'Donovan, 2023).

Geographical challenges and environmental threats

Wellbeing outcomes are also constrained by the vastness of the Australian continent, creating specific issues for the wellbeing of those living in rural and regional areas – especially for those without easy and reliable access to healthcare and other services. Relatedly, specific wellbeing challenges have emerged for Australians with limited access to infrastructure, including transport systems. The extremes of Australia's environment and its vulnerability to the exigencies of climate change – as illustrated spectacularly during the 2019–20 Australian 'Black Summer' Bushfires and various floods from 2022 onward – all have had significant, deleterious impacts on Australians' wellbeing – and the frequency of these types of natural disasters is likely to increase with climate change. Furthermore, though in common with the rest of the world, Australia's wellbeing outcomes have been severely compromised by the pressures imposed by the COVID pandemic and recent geopolitical tensions - to which Australia is especially vulnerable given its dependences on both the USA and China.

Wellbeing disadvantage from macroeconomic policy

At a macroeconomic scale, inflation is contributing to deteriorations in wellbeing – both because of inflation's direct effects in eroding real incomes and because of indirect effects from inflation in response to monetary policy tightening: the rapid rises in borrowing costs, mortgage stress and rising rental costs are all having disproportionately negative impacts on the already disadvantaged sectors of Australia's population. Furthermore, if rising interest rates fail to bite into inflation over the short term, then Australia's central bank – the Reserve Bank of Australia (RBA) – has indicated that it will target unemployment rates in its bid to reduce inflation. Ironically, increasing the proportion of people out of job is an outcome which the RBA will actively aim to achieve if inflation stays away from the 2–3% target band (Richardson, 2019).

Institutional barriers to wellbeing policy-making

As highlighted here, Australia's wellbeing experiences are complex and diverse and, in navigating the headwinds, Australia's legal and political institutions are associated with some unique policy constraints, and these can prevent a quick and flexible response to wellbeing challenges. These wellbeing policy challenges are magnified by the complexities associated with Australia's federal system of government.

Constitutional challenges

An additional problem for the evolution of Australia's wellbeing policies is that Australia's Constitution imposes additional constraints and rigidities. Australia's Federal government oversees policy for the Australia 'Commonwealth' as a whole, whilst the States and Territories retain a broad range of policy-making powers – leading to problems either when policies get lost in the lacunae between Federal and State policy-making powers or when policies cannot be nimbly adapted to exogenous shocks – as exemplified by the policy confusions surrounding Australia's response to the COVID-19 pandemic.

Principles enabling oversight of administrative decision-making by executive government are well established, and accountability mechanisms are extensive – exemplified by the inquiries conducted via Australia's Royal Commissions – including on a range of issues relevant to some of the wellbeing pressures as outlined here: for example Royal Commissions around injustices affecting ATSI communities, welfare recipients and those in aged care (Royal Commission, 1991, 2017, 2019, 2021, 2023). In developing good wellbeing policies, inquiries are not always effective in practice. Public inquiries are dependent on political support (Donson & O'Donovan, 2021). Without this support, there will be a limit in the extent to which public inquiries can make much of a difference to wellbeing policies 'on the ground'.

Ultimately, the powers of Australia's executive government are constrained by the Australian Constitution – which is designed to ensure that government operates according to principles of democratic accountability, and representative, responsible government – enabled by 'parliamentary vibrancy' (O'Donovan, 2023). Specifically, the ambit of federal executive power is constrained by Australia's Constitution and the legislative 'heads of power' under which the Federal (national) government can exercise its executive power on behalf of Australia's 'Commonwealth'. Section 51 of the Australian Constitution limits this exercise of federal executive power to very specific spheres. Insofar as wellbeing is largely equated with health, the Constitution does not vest any specific legislative power for the Federal Parliament in this field; the State and Territory governments have primary responsibility for health. Other heads of power which might be leveraged to sustain wellbeing policies are limited – though heads of power associated with census and statistics and social security could potentially be leveraged.

In addition, the rigidity of Australia's Constitution is an all but insurmountable obstacle: Section 128 of the Constitution stipulates that any constitutional change requires a national referendum delivering a vote not just of the majority of voters but also of majorities within a majority of States. One illustration of the rigidities imposed by Australia's Constitution was the failure of the Voice Referendum in October 2023. This referendum was about constitutionally enshrining an Indigenous Voice to Parliament and was advocated as part of the Uluru Statement from the Heart (2017) – as a means for Indigenous communities to have more say in the formulation of government policies to address entrenched Indigenous disadvantages and wide gaps in terms of wellbeing and prosperity relative to other Australians. Approximately 60% of Australian voters voted against this change – potentially setting back initiatives to improve Indigenous wellbeing for many years to come.

Perhaps reflecting this hurdle imposed by Australia's constitutionally driven federal system, key wellbeing policy initiatives *have* been spearheaded by many State and Territory governments – for example the New South Wales state government Economic Stewardship Framework and outcome budgeting approach, and Victoria's wellbeing plan (Mental Health Commission of NSW, 2017; Victoria State Government, 2019). Until recently, these policy initiatives have not been coordinated or rolled out on a national scale by the Federal government. Thus, Australia's wellbeing policies have been piece-meal, a situation which might change with the introduction of the Federal government's Wellbeing Framework (Australian Government, 2023).

Future directions for Australia's wellbeing policies

Notwithstanding the wellbeing policy constraints outlined here, the potential for Australia to develop strong and effective wellbeing policies for the long term is relatively good. Australia has a relatively robust democracy and a highly educated population. Australia is resource rich, technologically capable, and well placed to deal with the energy crisis. *Actionable points* for wellbeing policy in Australia include the following:

- Harness the depth of Indigenous ecological knowledge to effectively and comprehensively manage environmental/ecological challenges.
- Focus on geographical and climate-based advantages by investing in renewable technologies to limit the impacts of environmental degradation on the quality of life.
- Further develop and implement the Australian Wellbeing Framework that was introduced by the Federal government (Australian Government, 2023) and continue policy dialogue via established systems for open and transparent public inquiries by the Royal Commissions.
- Enact the recommendations for the overhaul of monetary policy from a recent Reserve Bank review (de Brouwer et al., 2023), which might lead to a better approach to monetary policy which is not so disadvantageous to those suffering from disproportionate wellbeing challenges because they are at the bottom of the income and wealth scales.
- Finally, build on these initiatives, implement successful wellbeing policies that leverage Australia's unique characteristics and natural advantages and prioritise policies to promote wellbeing amongst disadvantaged groups.

Note

1 The analysis focuses mostly on pre-pandemic data given that patterns are likely to be disrupted by different countries' responses in terms of lockdowns.

References

Australian Government (2023). *Measuring what matters: Australia's first wellbeing framework*. The Australian Treasury. https://treasury.gov.au/

de Brouwer, G., Fry-McKibbin, R., & Wilkins, C. (2023). *An RBA fit for the future*. Commonwealth of Australia.

Donson, F., & O'Donovan, D. (2021). Public inquiries and administrative justice. In M. Hertogh, R. Kirkham, R. Thomas, & J. Tomlinson (Eds.), *The Oxford handbook of administrative justice* (pp. 137–155). Oxford University Press.

Helliwell, J. F., Layard, R., Sachs, J. D., De Neve, J.-E., Aknin, L. B., & Wang, S. (2023). *World happiness report 2023*. Sustainable Development Solutions Network.

McLean, I. W. (2016). *Why Australia prospered: The shifting sources of economic growth*. Princeton University Press.
Mental Health Commission of NSW (2017). *Principles for action for thriving individuals, families, workplaces and communities*. Mental Health Commission of NSW.
O'Donovan, D. (2023, 7 July). Victims now know they were right about robodebt all along: Let the royal commission change the way we talk about welfare. *The Conversation*. https://theconversation.com/
Organisation for Economic Cooperation and Development (2020). *How's life 2020: Measuring wellbeing*. OECD Publishing.
Organisation for Economic Cooperation and Development (2021). *OECD economic surveys: Australia*. OECD Publishing.
Richardson, D. (2019). *Tolerate unemployment but blame the unemployed: The contradictions of NAIRU policy-making in Australia*. The Australia Institute.
Royal Commission (1991). *Report of the royal commission into aboriginal deaths in custody*. Commonwealth of Australia.
Royal Commission (2017). *Report of the royal commission into the protection and detention of children in the northern territory*. Commonwealth of Australia.
Royal Commission (2019). *Misconduct in the banking, superannuation and financial services industry royal commission*. Commonwealth of Australia.
Royal Commission (2021). *Report of the royal commission into aged care quality and safety royal commission*. Commonwealth of Australia.
Royal Commission (2023). *Report of the royal commission into the robodebt scheme*. Commonwealth of Australia.
Stiglitz, J., Sen, A., & Fitoussi, J.-P. (2009). *Mismeasuring our lives: Why GDP doesn't add up*. Report of the International Commission on the Measurement of Economic Performance and Social Progress, New Press.
Uluru Statement from the Heart (2017, 26 May). *National constitutional convention, Uluru, Uluru-Kata Tjuta National Park, NT Australia*. https://ulurustatement.org/the-statement/view-the-statement
Victoria State Government (2019). *Victorian public health and wellbeing plan 2019–2023, State of Victoria*. www.health.vic.gov.au.

24

WELLBEING AND POLICY IN THE UNITED KINGDOM

Joanne Smithson

Introduction

Since the early 2010s, the UK has been a forerunner in measuring and embedding subjective wellbeing into policy-making. This chapter begins with a review of how wellbeing is defined and measured in the UK and presents a summary of current performance. The next section details milestones in the journey to embed wellbeing into UK policy. The development of a UK wellbeing framework is discussed alongside advances in methodologies to value and monetise changes in wellbeing. A summary of wellbeing policy-making in the UK nations follows, and the section ends with a narrative on the creation of the What Works Centre for Wellbeing. The third section reviews what is known about 'what works' to improve wellbeing at an individual and a community level. Examples of wellbeing policy-making at different spatial geographies are also described. The fourth section presents priority areas for wellbeing policy and hallmarks for coherent wellbeing policy-making. The chapter concludes with reflections for research and practice.

Monitoring wellbeing in the UK

The UK was one of the first nations in the world to routinely measure personal subjective wellbeing as part of its national statistics. Wellbeing in the UK is defined as

> How we are doing, as individuals, as a community and as a nation. And how sustainable this is for the future.
>
> *(ONS, 2018a)*

DOI: 10.4324/9781003382447-27

Measurement of wellbeing in the UK is anchored by *four personal subjective wellbeing measures*, which ask people directly, on an 11-point scale, how they feel about their own lives and experiences (ONS, 2018b).

On a scale of 0 to 10, where 0 is "not at all" and 10 is "completely":

- Overall, how satisfied are you with your life nowadays?
- Overall, to what extent do you feel that the things you do in your life are worthwhile?
- Overall, how happy did you feel yesterday?

On a scale where 0 is "not at all anxious" and 10 is "completely anxious":

- Overall, how anxious did you feel yesterday?

Today, these measures are included in a wide range of national surveys covering community life, ageing, living costs, crime, housing, sport and engagement with the natural environment. They are asked of families, armed forces, students and civil service employees (ONS, 2018a). The measures also headline the national framework for voluntary reporting on workplace wellbeing (Department for Work and Pensions and Department of Health and Social Care, 2018).

Levels of personal wellbeing of adults in the UK have improved since the measures were introduced in 2011 (ONS, 2023). There was a sharp reversal of this trend during the global COVID-19 pandemic, but rates have partially recovered in recent years. Children's subjective wellbeing appears to have bounced back from its lowest point during the pandemic in 2020. In contrast, and concerningly, there has been a slow but statistically significant decline in the average happiness of 10- to 15-year-olds with their lives in the last ten years. Post-pandemic, there has also been an increase in probable mental health conditions among 17- to 19-year-olds from one in six in 2021 to one in four in 2022 (Department for Education, 2023).

Embedding wellbeing in UK policy

An evidence-informed movement has swept wellbeing into the UK policy landscape as a relevant, credible and measurable way to connect policy goals with policy outcomes in a way that matters to people's lives. This movement has affected how wellbeing is measured and monitored and how it is appraised and valued in policy-making. Today, UK wellbeing data and evidence are robust, comparable and being used with confidence across a wide range of policy areas. Figure 24.1 shows key milestones in UK wellbeing policy development this century. Milestones in bold are discussed in more detail later in this chapter. Although focused solely on UK events, it is important to recognise the significant global wellbeing activity that shaped these milestones, for example, the annual World Happiness Reports

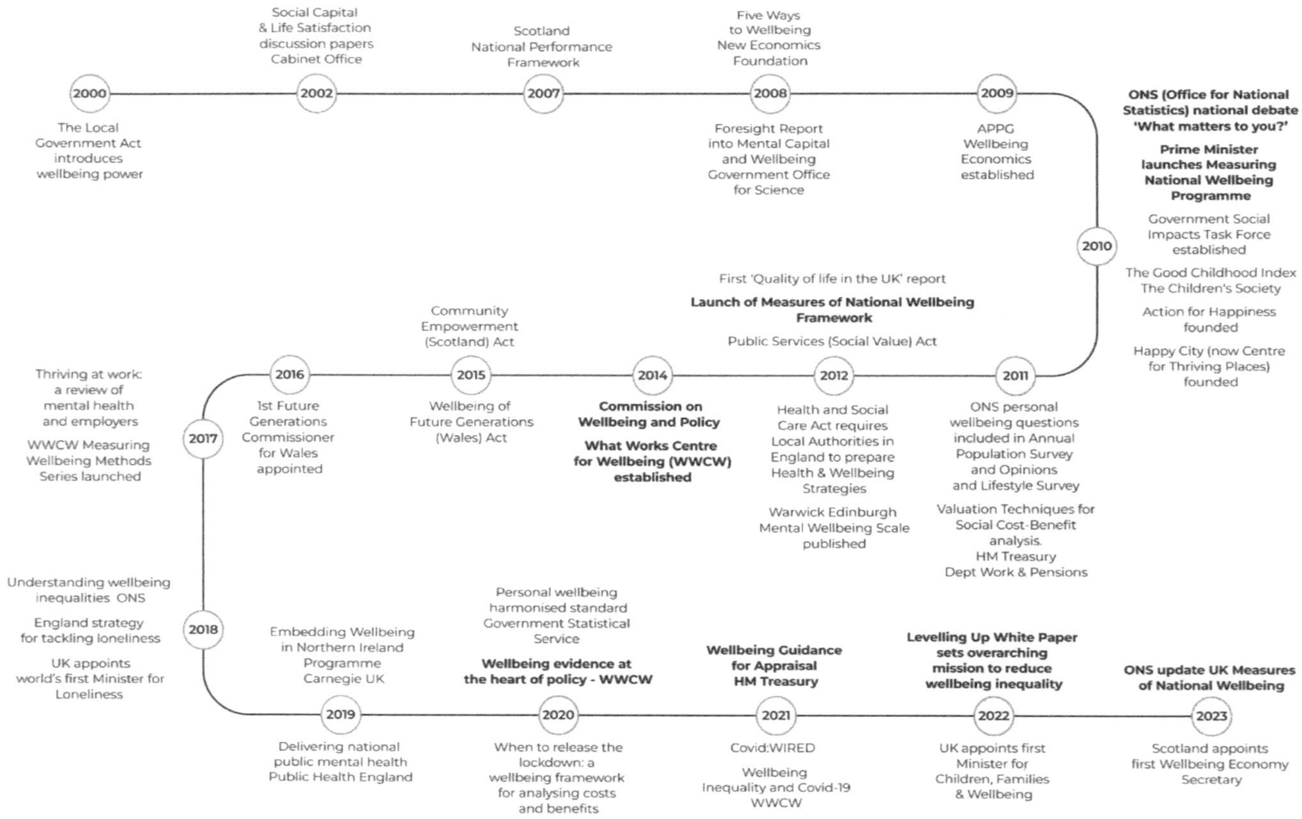

FIGURE 24.1 Wellbeing policy development in the UK from 2000.

Source: What Works Centre for Wellbeing (2023, p. 15).

and international 'beyond GDP' policy-making: all underpinned by an increasingly mature field of interdisciplinary quality of life research.

A UK framework for wellbeing

The UK's commitment to delivering policies that maximise wellbeing is longstanding. In 2006, when shaping the Conservative policies that would ultimately bring his party to power, David Cameron used a series of speeches to discuss 'the things that matter most in people's lives. Working life. Family life. And what we might describe as community life – neighbours, surroundings, local institutions' (The Guardian, 2006). In 2010, tasked by the Prime Minister, the Office for National Statistics (ONS) began the development of a *National Wellbeing Programme*. At its launch, the National Statistician, Dame Jil Matheson emphasised the desire for a more complete set of national accounts, moving beyond GDP:

> We must measure what matters – the key elements of national well-being. We want to develop measures based on what people tell us matters most.
>
> *(The National Archive, Office for National Statistics, 2010)*

The ONS approach to developing a measurement framework built on the OECD's research (Hall et al., 2010) combines a conceptual and consultative approach:

- reviewing the literature on definitions of wellbeing;
- examining existing frameworks;
- building on the findings of the national debate (The National Archives, 2011).

First published in 2012, the *Measures of National Wellbeing Framework* had 44 indicators across ten domains: health, personal wellbeing, our relationships, what we do, personal finance, the economy, education and skills, natural environment, where we live and governance. Reviewed and updated in 2023, the new *Measures of National Wellbeing Framework* retained the original ten domains and included an additional 22 indicators further strengthening inequality data and reflecting more diverse life experiences (ONS, 2023). Many of the new indicators filled identified conceptual gaps including hope, fairness, satisfaction with social relationships, community integration and satisfaction with time use.

The 2022 *Levelling Up the United Kingdom* white paper set an overarching ambition to improve wellbeing in every area of the UK (as measured by life satisfaction) and close the gap between top-performing places and other areas by 2030. Mean life satisfaction data were presented for every local authority highlighting regional disparities. A figure showing determinants of life satisfaction was included to illustrate potential policy approaches (HM Government, 2022, pp. 25–26).

> Levelling up means giving everyone the opportunity to flourish. It means people everywhere living longer and more fulfilling lives, and benefitting from sustained rises in living standards and well-being.
>
> (HM Government, 2022, p. xii)

Creating cost-effective policy with a wellbeing lens

In parallel to deepening our understanding of measuring how the UK is doing, significant progress has been made in quantifying wellbeing benefits. The *HM Treasury Green Book* is the UK government's manual on how to appraise and evaluate policies and projects. Introduced in the 1970s, wellbeing benefits were explored in terms of social and/or public value. Valuation techniques for social cost–benefit analysis were published in 2011 (Fujiwara & Campbell, 2011), and the 2018 update to the *Green Book* explicitly named 'wellbeing' as an aim of policy appraisal. The 2021 *Wellbeing Supplementary Guidance* went further, detailing how wellbeing evidence can inform the strategic stages of policy-making. It also provides guidance for analysts on how wellbeing impacts can be assessed, and in some cases where evidence allows, monetised and included in cost–benefit analysis (HM Treasury, 2021).

The UK 'what works' centre for wellbeing

> 'What works?' is a disarmingly simple question. Answering it is improving services and the lives of millions day in, day out.
>
> Dr David Halpern, What Works National Adviser.
> (What Works Network, 2018, p. 4)

The 'What Works' Network was established by the UK Treasury in 2013 to ensure that UK government spending and practice in public services was informed by the best available evidence. The 2014 *UK Commission for Wellbeing and Policy*, chaired by Lord Gus O'Donnell, brought together leading global wellbeing researchers. Their report proved persuasive, and with support from 13 government organizations including Public Health England and the Economic & Social Research Council, the *What Works Centre for Wellbeing* was established. The Centre worked closely with partners to answer key questions on what works to improve wellbeing and identify gaps in the research to be filled. The Centre, which closed in 2024, worked across five priority areas: national wellbeing, methods and measures; wellbeing during working age; place and community; and loneliness and connection. Their evidence is still being widely used by governments, businesses, academics, professional bodies and civil society groups and organizations.

Wellbeing: reviewing the evidence of what works

This section reviews key findings of what is known to improve wellbeing at an individual and a community level. It also explores how areas of the UK have used these insights to inform wellbeing policy development at different spatial levels. An example of hyper-local activity in Euston in the London Borough of Camden is presented.

What works to improve individual wellbeing

The What Works Centre for Wellbeing reviewed data from longitudinal and intervention studies that used life satisfaction (Blodgett et al., 2024), the wider ONS4 measures (Peto et al., 2020) and the Warwick Edinburgh Mental Wellbeing Scales as outcome metrics (Blodgett et al., 2022). Evidence of effectiveness was found for the following:

- Emotional skills development, including for under 18s, the National Citizens Services and Healthy Minds Curriculum;
- Psychological therapies;
- Emotion-based activities including mindfulness and gratitude;
- Physical activity and healthier lifestyles;
- Social prescribing;
- Housing/neighbourhood energy efficiency;
- Volunteering;
- Financial wellbeing advice and support.

Many of the interventions were aimed at one or more specific demographic groups and were delivered across UK regions.

What works to improve social capital

Building on the strong evidence in support of the positive links between social capital and wellbeing, a systematic review of *community infrastructure* (place and space) to boost social relations and community wellbeing found strong evidence for community hubs and community development, improving social relations, individual and community wellbeing (Bagnall et al., 2023). Many interventions reviewed brought about both positive and negative impacts on wellbeing: for instance, local events can improve community wellbeing for many but have a detrimental impact on those they exclude.

A review of *volunteering* evidence (Stuart et al., 2020) found the following:

- Volunteering is associated with enhanced wellbeing;
- Older people, the unemployed and those who already have chronic ill-health and low wellbeing gain more from volunteering than others;

- Volunteering can have a buffering role for those going through life transitions, such as retirement or bereavement;
- Groups with the most to gain from volunteering face barriers to getting involved. Ill health and disability are particular barriers for low-income groups;
- The intensity and demands of some volunteer roles may have a negative effect. The way volunteers are involved and engaged can enhance or hinder the positive wellbeing effects of volunteering.

A review of *community agency, control and power* and their effects on community wellbeing (Charlesworth & Hashmi, 2023) identified four moderating elements:

- Opportunities for community connections;
- Ability to make decisions;
- Availability and size of funding;
- Maturity of community agency, including existing relationships.

The body of evidence for some areas of wellbeing policy-making is still emergent and may require stronger foundations before effectiveness can be established. For example, when the Centre first reviewed the evidence to find out what interventions worked to alleviate *loneliness* in 2018, it was not possible to establish 'what worked' as studies used a broad range of measures (objective social isolation, social connections generally and feeling lonely) in ways that were not comparable. This led to the following:

- a conceptual review of loneliness to understand the different aspects of social connection;
- harmonised recommended measures of loneliness;
- a guide to measuring loneliness for practitioners.

Five years on, the evidence had matured to the point a rapid systematic review of intervention effectiveness was possible. MacIntyre and Musella (2023) identified successful interventions involved:

- Structured therapeutic support and approaches to develop emotional and social skills;
- Social support that develops social skills through targeted relationship-building skills and discussion-based activities;
- Art and dance activities delivered in community-based settings; and
- A range of social interaction-based activities, including facilitated animal/robot interactions, food delivery and social and health promotion activities.

Almost all of these interventions targeted specific age groups or vulnerable populations.

Wellbeing policy-making in practice

UK wellbeing policy-making takes many forms at the sub-national level: from high-level strategic frameworks led by directly elected mayors, typified by London's Wellbeing and Sustainability measure (Greater London Authority, 2023) and the North of Tyne Wellbeing Framework (The North of Tyne Combined Authority Inclusive Economy Board, 2022), to smaller area plans to maximise wellbeing exemplified in the collaboration between Babergh & Mid Suffolk District Councils' joint Wellbeing Strategy (Babergh & Mid Suffolk District Councils, 2021). Some areas have used a population health approach, for example, the NHS Greater Manchester Integrated Care's Measuring Mental Wellbeing report (Greater Manchester Integrated Care, 2023). The example presented from Camden, London, illustrates how the ONS's national, conceptual and consultative approach to wellbeing framework development can be deployed at a local level.

A WELLBEING INDEX FOR THE LONDON BOROUGH OF CAMDEN

In 2019, Camden Council set out to develop a wellbeing index for the borough, to gain a deeper understanding of how residents were doing (Shinwell & Murphy, 2022). They aimed to bring together data in a structured way to inform decision-making processes, understand impact and help partners in the borough to do the same. They started with a hyper-local project in Euston, testing both their methodology and implementation approach, before extending it out to the whole borough. The Good Life Euston project worked with residents to define what was important for their wellbeing, and what prosperity meant to them. A group of local residents were trained as citizen social scientists, and together they developed a conceptual model comprising six domains, essential for a 'good life' and an overarching principle of 'systemic equity'. Their model was accompanied by a set of metrics, and a household survey was carried out to provide data. The collection of this rich data aims to inform decision-making in Camden, specifically in the areas of measuring the social value of procurement and directing investment.

Key lessons

Policy-making to maximise wellbeing

Looking to the future, reviewing the priorities established by the 2014 Commission for Wellbeing & Policy against the current wellbeing evidence base, the What Works Centre for Wellbeing identified five WISER priority areas:

Work: support stable employment, low unemployment and roles optimised to deliver high job quality.

Income: balanced, stable economic growth, safety netting for effects of debt and insecurity, investment in health and welfare systems, choice and free time for leisure, arts and education.

Society and governance: acknowledge dignity, agency and control, devolve power and control, encourage meaningful citizen-led action and participation, increase trust in our collective institutions and reduce corruption; reduce bureaucracy and provide better feedback loops for services; improve legal and justice systems especially for children and families.

Emotional mental health: treat mental ill-health as professionally as physical ill-health, support parents in their parenting, their relationships and mother's mental health; build social and emotional skills in schools and at work.

Relationships and communities: promote volunteering, giving and place-based arts and culture. Develop opportunities for building meaningful social connections and space to have time alone. Create a built environment that is sociable and connected to accessible green and blue spaces, which allow for shorter, better commutes, with reduced environmental stressors of noise and air pollution.

(What Works Centre for Wellbeing, 2020, pp. 72–73)

Actionable points

As described here, the *what* of policy-making is important, but *how* policy is designed and implemented is also crucial for its success. Analysis of Health & Wellbeing Strategies in England identified six hallmarks that, when used strategically, provide a coherent framework for wellbeing policy-making (Smithson, 2022a). They reflect actionable points that others can take forward:

1. Adopt an inclusive understanding and definition of wellbeing.
2. Make improving wellbeing and reducing inequity concurrent policy goals.
3. a) Draw on evidence of wellbeing need.
   b) Draw on evidence of 'what works' to improve wellbeing.
4. Prioritise Work, Income, Society and governance, Emotional mental health, Relationships and communities (WISER) areas.
5. Apply comprehensive performance measures.
6. Deploy appropriate implementation strategies to get 'what works' into practice.

The accompanying wellbeing policy maturity model provides a tool for policy-makers to self-assess emergent wellbeing policy and/or review established approaches to maximise wellbeing impact and reduce wellbeing inequalities (Smithson, 2022b).

Concluding reflections

At the start of 2020, before the global pandemic had taken hold and current cost of living pressures threatened to put core tenets of wellbeing – food, housing and security – out of reach for an ever-increasing number of individuals, Professor Sir Michael Marmot issued a challenge to UK policy-makers calling for a reordering of national priorities:

> Making wellbeing rather than straightforward economic performance the central goal of policy will create a better society with better health and greater health equity.
>
> *(Marmot et al., 2020. The Marmot Review ten years on, p. 150)*

This chapter has highlighted the huge strides that have been made in UK wellbeing policy in recent years and the ever-maturing evidence base available to inform our decision-making. It has shown how wellbeing frameworks can be developed and tailored at national and local levels and reviewed evidence of 'what works' for both individual and community wellbeing. Despite changes in government administrations and leadership, improving people's lives, particularly for those with the lowest wellbeing, remains firmly in the mainstream political discourse. The 2021 Autumn Spending Review highlighted life satisfaction disparities as an economic indicator for the first time alongside pay and productivity. In autumn 2022 the ONS began producing national wellbeing measures alongside GDP in routine quarterly reporting. In summer 2024 new Prime Minister, Sir Keir Starmer, set out his intention to introduce a Children's Wellbeing Bill to put children and their wellbeing at the centre of the education and children's social care systems, and make changes so they are safe, healthy, happy and treated fairly.

To build on this progress, continued investment in wellbeing research and knowledge mobilisation is essential: conceptual clarity, harmonisation of metrics, building capability and opportunity to design and deliver robust evaluation are unlikely to happen without it. There is no single UK government department or research funder that 'owns' wellbeing. To continue to build this learning system for wellbeing, we all as individuals and organisations have our part to play: across sectors, professions, disciplines and geographies. Sharing openly, and with humility what works, and what doesn't, for who and in what context is needed now, more than ever.

References

Babergh & Mid Suffolk District Councils (2021). *Wellbeing strategy 2021–2027*. www.midsuffolk.gov.uk/assets/Communities/Health-and-Wellbeing/Wellbeing-Strategy-2021-27-with-covers.pdf

Bagnall, A. M., Southby, K., Jones, R., Pennington, A., South, J., & Corcoran, R. (2023). *Systematic review of community infrastructure (place and space) to boost social relations and community wellbeing: Five-year refresh*. What Works Centre for Wellbeing. https://whatworkswellbeing.org/resources/systematic-review-of-community-infrastructure-place-and-space-to-boost-social-relations-and-community-wellbeing-five-year-refresh/

Blodgett, J., Kaushal, A., & Harkness, F. (2022). *Rapid review of wellbeing evaluation research using the Warwick-Edinburgh Mental Well-Being Scales (WEMWBS)*. Kohlrabi Consulting & What Works Centre for Wellbeing. https://whatworkswellbeing.org/resources/rapid-review-of-wellbeing-evaluation-research-using-the-wemwbs-scales/

Blodgett, J., Tiley, K., Kim, E., & Harkness, F. (2024). *What works to improve life satisfaction in intervention and observational research?* What Works Centre for Wellbeing. https://whatworkswellbeing.org/resources/what-works-to-improve-life-satisfaction-in-intervention-and-observational-research/

Charlesworth, L., & Hashmi, I. (2023). *Rapid review of community agency and control, as final outcomes, or enablers of place-based interventions to improve community wellbeing*. New Local & What Works Centre for Wellbeing. https://whatworkswellbeing.org/resources/rapid-review-of-community-agency-and-control/

Department for Education (2023). *State of the nation 2022: Children and young people's wellbeing*. www.gov.uk/government/collections/state-of-the-nation-reports-children-and-young-peoples-wellbeing

Department for Work and Pensions and Department of Health and Social Care (2018). *Voluntary reporting on disability, mental health and wellbeing*. www.gov.uk/government/publications/voluntary-reporting-on-disability-mental-health-and-wellbeing

Fujiwara, D., & Campbell, R. (2011). *Valuation techniques for social cost-benefit analysis: Stated preference, revealed preference and subjective well-being approaches: A discussion of the current issues*. HM Treasury.

Greater London Authority (2023). *London's wellbeing and sustainability measure*. www.london.gov.uk/talk-london/wellbeing-and-sustainability-measure-london

Greater Manchester Integrated Care (2023). *Measuring mental wellbeing in Greater Manchester*. https://gmintegratedcare.org.uk/wp-content/uploads/2023/04/measuring-mental-wellbeing-in-greater-manchester-report-2023.pdf

The Guardian (2006, May 22). *David Cameron's speech to Google Zeitgeist Europe 2006*. www.theguardian.com/politics/2006/may/22/conservatives.davidcameron

Hall, J., Giovannini, E., Morrone, A., & Ranuzzi, G. (2010). A framework to measure the progress of societies. *OECD Statistics Working Papers, No. 2010/05*, OECD. https://doi.org/10.1787/5km4k7mnrkzw-en

HM Government (2022). *Levelling up the United Kingdom*. www.gov.uk/government/publications/levelling-up-the-united-kingdom

HM Treasury (2021). *Green book supplementary guidance: Wellbeing*. www.gov.uk/government/publications/green-book-supplementary-guidance-wellbeing

MacIntyre, H., & Musella, M. (2023). *Tackling loneliness interventions: Insights on the current landscape, evidence and evaluation practice*. Campaign to End Loneliness & What Works Centre for Wellbeing. https://whatworkswellbeing.org/resources/tackling-loneliness-interventions/

Marmot, M., Allen, J., Boyce, T., Goldblatt, P., & Morrison, J. (2020). *Health equity in England: The Marmot review 10 years on*. Institute of Health Equity.

The National Archives (2010). *Office for national statistics: National Well-being Measuring What Matters*. https://webarchive.nationalarchives.gov.uk/ukgwa/20160105160711/www.ons.gov.uk/ons/guide-method/user-guidance/well-being/index.html

The National Archives (2011, August 25). *Measuring what matters: National Statistician's Reflections on the National Debate on Measuring National Well-being*. https://webarchive.nationalarchives.gov.uk/ukgwa/20110825121803/www.statistics.gov.uk/cci/article.asp?id=2718

The North of Tyne Combined Authority Inclusive Economy Board (2022). *Wellbeing framework for the North of Tyne*. www.northoftyne-ca.gov.uk/projects/roundtable-on-wellbeing/

ONS (2018a, September 26). *Surveys using our four personal well-being questions*. www.ons.gov.uk/peoplepopulationandcommunity/wellbeing/methodologies/surveysusingthe4officefornationalstatisticspersonalwellbeingquestions

ONS (2018b, September 26). *Personal well-being user guidance*. www.ons.gov.uk/peoplepopulationandcommunity/wellbeing/methodologies/personalwellbeingsurveyuserguide

ONS (2023). *UK measures of national well-being: Review and latest insights*. www.ons.gov.uk/releases/ukmeasuresofnationalwellbeingreviewandlatestinsights

Peto, L., Pittam, G., & Musella, M. (2020). *What works to improve wellbeing across different interventions: Looking at ONS personal wellbeing findings in impact evaluations*. What Works Centre for Wellbeing. https://whatworkswellbeing.org/resources/ons-personal-wellbeing-findings-in-impact-evaluations/

Shinwell, M., & Murphy, D. (2022). *Understanding wellbeing in a local area*. What Works Centre for Wellbeing. https://whatworkswellbeing.org/practice-examples/understanding-wellbeing-in-a-local-area/

Smithson, J. (2022a). *Learning from research and practice: Local government policy making to maximise wellbeing*. What Works Centre for Wellbeing. https://whatworkswellbeing.org/resources/local-government-policy-making-to-maximise-wellbeing/

Smithson, J. (2022b). *Maturity model for wellbeing policy making*. What Works Centre for Wellbeing. https://whatworkswellbeing.org/wp-content/uploads/2022/09/Maturity-model-for-wellbeing-policy-making.pdf

Stuart, J., Kamerāde, D., Connolly, S., Ellis Paine, A., Nichols, G., & Grotz, J. (2020). *The impacts of volunteering on the subjective wellbeing of volunteers: A rapid evidence assessment*. Spirit of 2012 & What Works Centre for Wellbeing. https://whatworkswellbeing.org/projects/volunteer-wellbeing/

What Works Centre for Wellbeing (2020). *Wellbeing evidence at the heart of policy*. https://whatworkswellbeing.org/resources/wellbeing-evidence-at-the-heart-of-policy/

What Works Centre for Wellbeing (2023). *Our strategy*. https://whatworkswellbeing.org/wp-content/uploads/2023/11/What-Works-Wellbeing-Strategy-version-Oct-2023.pdf

What Works Network (2018). *The what works network five years on*. https://assets.publishing.service.gov.uk/government/uploads/system/uploads/attachment_data/file/677478/6.4154_What_works_report_Final.pdf

25

WELLBEING AND POLICY IN JAPAN

Toshiaki Hiromitsu, Eriko Teramura, and Ryusuke Oishi

Overview

After World War II, Japan focused on economic recovery, prioritizing an increase in citizens' income level. In 1960, the Ikeda Cabinet adopted the National Income Doubling Plan, with the goal to double the national income by achieving an average annual growth rate of 7.2% of real Gross National Product (real GNP) in ten years (from 1961 to 1970). In addition to this pro-growth policy, the Japanese government was concerned with assessing these aspects of the quality of life that cannot be fully understood by examining income alone. To do so, the government has been conducting an annual survey of life satisfaction through the Life in Nations since 1958. Due to increasing concerns in the 1970s regarding the negative aspects of rapid economic growth such as pollution and population concentration, in 1974, the government developed multidimensional indicators to assess quality of life called the Social Indicators. The indicators were primarily composed of nonpecuniary elements covering ten areas including health, quality of employment and work life, as well as leisure. Four generations of indicators were developed, leading up to the Life Reform Indicators in the 2000s (Japan Cabinet Office, 2010; Shiraishi & Shiraishi, 2010).

Comprehensive measurement of wellbeing and its application to Japan's policies started in the 2010s. The Japan Cabinet Office initiated the Study Group on Happiness in 2010 and published *Measuring National Wellbeing – Proposed Wellbeing Indicators* (The Commission on Measuring Wellbeing, 2011). This report proposed the development of the subjective wellbeing (SWB) indicator, which included socioeconomic conditions, health, and social relationships as three pillars, with sustainability as the cross-cutting foundation. This governmental effort was driven by increasing global awareness of the concept of citizens'

DOI: 10.4324/9781003382447-28

wellbeing, a transition to lower economic and population growth that Japan experienced ahead of other advanced countries, and the Great East Japan Earthquake in March 2011. In 2017, the Japan Cabinet decided to "conduct research for the creation of a dashboard of indicators representing people's happiness, utility, richness of society and quality of life" (Japan Cabinet Office, 2017). Referencing the 2011 proposal, the Japan Cabinet Office conducted a four-stage review (Japan Cabinet Office, 2019a, 2019b, 2020a, 2020b), and implemented the Survey on Satisfaction and Quality of Life in 2019. In congruence with the 2018 Cabinet decision, the government also initiated institutional arrangements for integrating the SWB indicator into policies. A liaison meeting spanning relevant ministries and agencies was conducted in 2021, and introduction of the key performance indicators related to wellbeing into various government basic plans was initiated (Japan Cabinet Office, 2021a).

Outside of the government, the Broadcasting Culture Research Institute has conducted surveys on life satisfaction in Japan since 1973 (Nippon Hoso Kyokai (NHK) Broadcasting Culture Research Institute, 2019). In addition, Osaka University has been conducting longitudinal panel surveys since 2003 to track both the individuals' satisfaction and objective information such as income (Institute of Social and Economic Research, Osaka University, 2015). The combined research findings were published in the 2010 book *Happiness in Japan* (Ohtake et al., 2010). This propelled wellbeing as a popular research topic in Japan (e.g. Tanaka, 2014; Oshio, 2014). The interest in wellbeing spilled over from academics to the private sector with private organizations starting to independently conduct surveys and analyses (Nomura Research Institute, 2021, 2023).

As an Asian country, Japan provides an excellent opportunity to consider wellbeing from a different cultural context than that in Europe and the United States. Japan has long been recognized as an economically advanced country and compared with Western countries. Moreover, Japan offers a reference point for other Asian countries that seek to develop such initiatives. As Japan experienced rapid economic growth, it offered a case study for the Easterlin Paradox (Easterlin, 1973), which asserted that SWB does not proportionally improve with income (Veenhoven, 1993; Easterlin, 1995; Stevenson & Wolfers, 2008). Japan's pursuit of economic growth as the main objective is now a part of the nation's history. As Japan has surpassed other countries in terms of population aging and decline and social changes in family formation, it offers valuable examples for other rapidly aging countries. As we show, Japanese citizens' lack of social connections and freedom in life choices render SWB relative to income to be lower than that in other countries.

The remainder of this chapter is organized as follows. In the second section, we discuss Japan's wellbeing initiatives, focusing on the efforts of the Japan Cabinet Office. Specifically, we provide an overview of SWB in Japan based on microdata that are obtained from the Cabinet Office. In the third section, we focus on relevant policy responses to survey findings and perform international comparisons between Japan and other countries. In the fourth section, we detail the key lessons in wellbeing in Japan and examine the transferability of interventions to other countries. Finally, in the fifth section, we conclude by outlining actionable implications for future research and policy-making.

Wellbeing initiatives in Japan

As mentioned earlier, the Japanese government promoted a variety of initiatives related to citizens' wellbeing and quality of life with the central initiative being led by the Japan Cabinet Office. We outline the results of the Satisfaction and Quality of Life Survey and provide an overview of the SWB in Japan based on data obtained from the Cabinet Office. The Satisfaction and Quality of Life Survey was initiated in 2019, conducting surveys over a 5-year period until 2022 (Japan Cabinet Office, 2023a). The survey was developed based on the Better Life Index and Wellbeing framework of the Organization for Economic Cooperation and Development (OECD). This survey comprehensively assesses wellbeing from subjective and objective perspectives using satisfaction across 13 specific domains and domain-specific questions.[1] The survey is conducted online with 10,000 respondents. According to the survey, overall average comprehensive life satisfaction has fluctuated between 5.62 and 5.69, with scores ranging between 5 and 8. Women reported higher satisfaction than men. The highest satisfaction is found in the elderly population (65–89 years old), followed by the young (15–39 years old) and middle-aged (40–64 years) groups. Some of these relationships exhibit gender differences; for instance, educational level and educational environment positively and significantly affect SWB only for men (Japan Cabinet Office, 2023a).

To further investigate the characteristics of SWB in Japan we obtained survey microdata from the Japan Cabinet Office. It should be noted that the 2019 and 2020 data were collected from different respondents, while starting from 2021 onward the same respondents were followed. For the purposes of analysis we used the pooled data from the sample that responded to three survey waves (2019–20, 2021, and 2022) with a sample size of 9,207.

Since many Japanese policies are designed based on life stages determined by age, we start by discussing overall SWB by age group (Figure 25.1). Average life satisfaction exhibits a U-shaped pattern, with higher satisfaction in youth, a decrease in middle age, and an increase in old age. Considering the public policy goal of mitigating inequality, variations in satisfaction are a significant concern. Compared with the middle-aged period, when individuals generally face life challenges, dissatisfaction tends to decrease for older age groups, particularly those aged 70 and above.[2,3] The average life satisfaction for men and women in these age groups were 5.55 and 5.78.

SWB has generally been found to have a positive relationship with economic prosperity (e.g., Stevenson & Wolfers, 2013). Consistent with that, household income and assets exhibited strong positive correlation with individuals' life

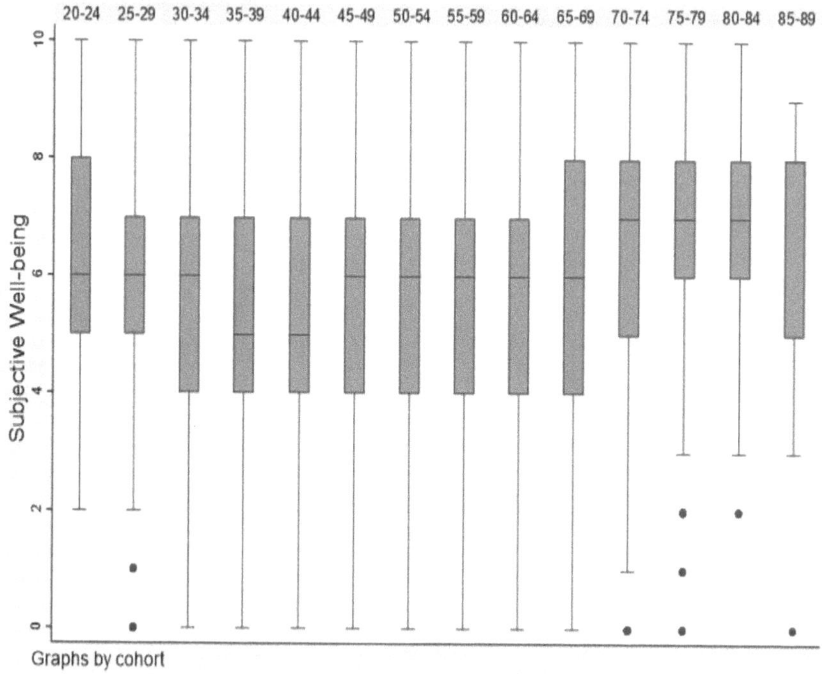

FIGURE 25.1 Age (5-year cohort) and overall SWB.

Source: Japan Cabinet Office Survey on Quality of Life.

satisfaction. Although income tends to be lower in the elderly years, high satisfaction levels among the elderly is supported by substantial assets gained over a lifetime. While we observe significant variations in asset ownership among the elderly, reflecting different life trajectories, variations in SWB are relatively minimal. The latter can be attributed to the income security of public pensions, which reduces income variability among the elderly and affordable healthcare services that are tailored to Japan's elderly population.

Evidence of the effectiveness of Japan's current wellbeing initiatives

In this section, we focus on the related policy responses by the Japanese government and consider international comparisons. According to the World Happiness Report 2024 (WHR, Helliwell et al., 2024) ranking, Japan is ranked 51st, which is a relatively low position. When comparing Japan with top-ranked Finland in the WHR, Japan scores high in per capita GDP and healthy life expectancy, but

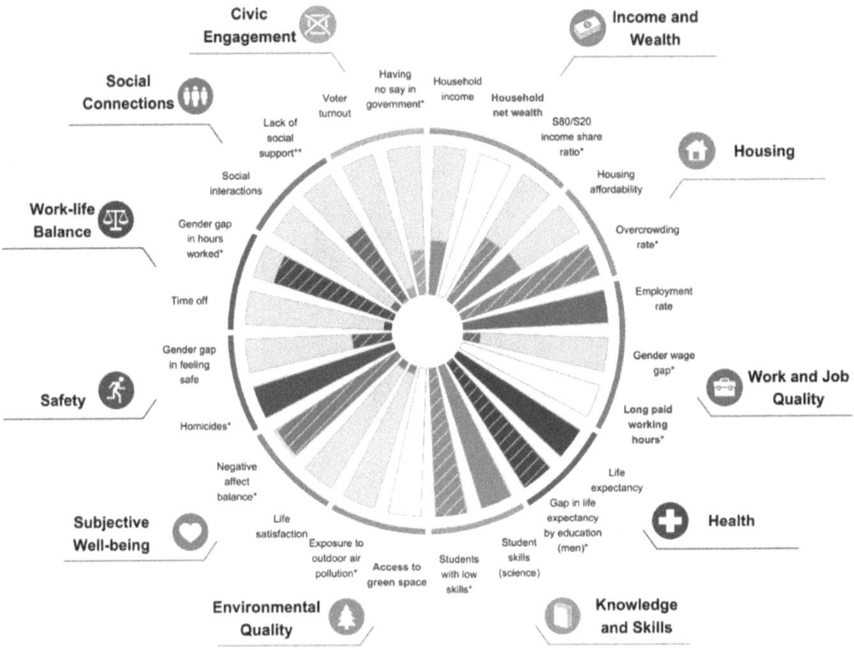

FIGURE 25.2 Japan's current wellbeing.

Source: OECD (2024).

its scores are low in generosity, perceived corruption, and freedom to make life choices.[4]

The international positioning of Japan's SWB indicators in 2022 based on OECD (2024) data (Figure 25.2) clearly illustrates Japan's areas of strengths and weaknesses. Longer bars always indicate higher wellbeing, whereas shorter bars always indicate worse wellbeing, including for negative indicators, marked with an asterisk * (OECD, 2024). Japan excels in areas related to economic and lifestyle factors such as knowledge and skills (students skills in science), work and job quality (employment rate), health (life expectancy), and safety (homicide rate). Conversely, Japan performs poorly in areas related to qualitative wellbeing and quality of life, such as housing (overcrowding rate) and SWB (negative affect balance) and health (gap in life expectancy by education for men). Moreover, Japan's scores are notably low in gender-related aspects of work and social connections. The past trends in Japan's wellbeing for each item (OECD, 2024) reveal that Japan continues to exhibit lower mortality rates compared with other countries. At the same time, Japan continues to face challenges in areas of government net financial assets, endangered species, and gender equality in politics.

Overall, Japan exhibits strengths in areas of longevity, safety, and basic economic and lifestyle factors, and weaknesses in emotional stability, social connections, freedom to make life choices, gender issues, and diversity as compared to other countries.

To improve the freedom to make life choices, Japan's government has been promoting Workstyle Reform policies since 2019 (Workstyle Reform Implementation Council, 2017). Efforts are underway to optimize work–life balance in Japan, including strict regulations on overtime hours to eliminate long working hours. The reforms encourage diverse work-styles, such as prohibiting bans on side jobs that had previously been implemented in many Japanese companies and also promote workplace diversity by encouraging the appointment of female executives and managers. Additionally, Japan's government has implemented specific policies to improve citizens' wellbeing. The "Plan for the Dynamic Engagement of All Citizens" (Japan Cabinet Office, 2016) endeavors to provide support for single-parent households and multi-child households, establish learning opportunities for children facing challenges, and support for women who have temporarily left their jobs to take care of their families to return to the labor force. In 2022, the government launched a new policy with the goal of providing social security for all generations. In addition, one of the nine priority goals of the Moonshot Research and Development System (Japan Cabinet Office, 2023b), which seeks to encourage innovation in advancing SWB, is to "realize a mental richness and dynamic society by increasing mental peace and vitality by 2050" and promote brain research through an ambitious initiative that links wellbeing with science and technology policy.

Key lessons learned to date

In this section we identify the key lessons learned regarding wellbeing in Japan and examine the transferability of interventions to other countries. Economically Japan entered a prolonged period of stagnation following the high economic growth period of the 1970s. During the stagnation period wages did not rise as they did in other countries and there were significant changes in family formation, including a substantial increase in unmarried and childless individuals. Single-person households grew rapidly and Japan experienced an unprecedented aging of the population. Japan's experiences with these demographic changes can serve as a valuable reference for other countries that are anticipating similar demographic shifts. This economic, social, and demographic situation provides a context for considering wellbeing advances in Japan.

As demonstrated by the Japan Cabinet Office's Satisfaction and Quality of Life Survey, wellbeing is related to multiple attributes, including economic prosperity, gender, age, and social connections. At the same time, international comparisons suggest that Japan has weaknesses in social connections and freedom to make life choices, which provides an opportunity for policy improvement. Life satisfaction in Japan is higher among women and the elderly, and their satisfaction levels exhibit relatively low variation, which is a positive sign. Challenges are evident regarding the lower life satisfaction of middle-aged men, who are often engaged in productive work. Thus, it is essential to increase the number of individuals who excel in productive capacity while simultaneously developing a society in which those who are less fortunate in this regard can lead satisfying lives.

The key lessons from Japan's experience for other countries are threefold. First, it underscores the importance of social security systems, such as pensions, in guaranteeing a certain level of income for the elderly population. In an aging society, where the working-age population is smaller than the elderly population, social security systems like public pensions are crucial for mitigating wellbeing disparities among the elderly. Second, it highlights the significance of strategically transitioning from a societal model that prioritizes labor and undervalues connections with others to one that values a balance between work and interpersonal connections. As explained in the second section, interpersonal connections are essential for wellbeing in Japan. Japan's Workstyle Reform policy addresses this concern; however, it has been about 30 years since the transition to lower growth to initiate this endeavor. Third, it outlines the high value of policies that consider diversity within the population. Throughout the periods of economic growth and aging, family sizes in Japan have been shrinking (Ministry of Health, Labor and Welfare, 2023), necessitating policies to address the diminishing role of families in protecting socially vulnerable individuals. These lessons could be particularly valuable for other Asian countries that are transitioning from periods of economic growth that will likely be facing similar challenges to establishing robust social security systems.

Actionable points

In this final section, we present actionable points for further research and policymaking based on our previous discussion.

- Strongly promote the Workstyle Reform and the Plan for Dynamic Engagement of All Citizens initiatives. Workstyle Reform is expected to improve the overall life satisfaction of prime-age men, who generally expressed lower SWB. The Plan of Dynamic Engagement of All Citizens establishes detailed policies that consider heterogeneity within the population.
- Address contemporary challenges that have emerged, particularly in response to the COVID-19 pandemic. The policy initiatives that were developed before the pandemic as well as the response to the new challenges highlighted during the pandemic require separate consideration. The expansion of remote work has the potential to improve life satisfaction by optimizing work–life balance by reducing commuting time. The Japan Cabinet Office's analysis of the 2023 Satisfaction and Quality of Life Survey data revealed that both men and women reported higher satisfaction with ease of child-rearing when remote work was adopted. However, it is essential to consider productivity in addition to SWB when determining the extent to which remote work should be adopted. It is also

crucial to consider broader societal productivity beyond individual productivity. For instance, research in the United States has suggested that the proliferation of remote work has contributed to a loss of training opportunities and higher turnover rates among female and younger employees (Emanuel et al., 2023). Therefore, a comprehensive assessment of various aspects of productivity and additional research on the relationship between remote work and SWB is needed to determine the right balance.

- Consider other measures to improve SWB, such as an adoption of the 4-day workweek, which is gaining momentum in the wake of the COVID-19 pandemic. In 2021, Japan's government endorsed companies' voluntary introduction of the 4-day workweek (Japan Cabinet Office, 2021c). Based on data from Japan and South Korea, Hamermesh and Kawaguchi (2014) found that reduced working hours contribute to increased life satisfaction. However, it is crucial to consider the potential tradeoff between achieving a higher SWB and reduction in macroeconomic activity. For instance, Hayashi and Prescott (2002) presented empirical evidence from Japan that the introduction of the five-day workweek in the 1990s contributed to the stagnation of the Japanese economy. Thus, the consideration of the mandatory implementation of the 4-day workweek warrants a comprehensive analysis of broader societal and economic consequences.

Notes

1 The 13 domains in the survey include (1) Household finances and satisfaction; (2) Employment environment and wages; (3) Housing; (4) Work and life; (5) Health status; (6) Educational level and educational environment; (7) Connection with society; (8) Reliability in politics, administration, and courts; (9) Natural environment; (10) Safety around you; (11) Ease of raising children, (12) Ease of providing care; and (13) Enjoyment and interest of life.

2 Standard deviations peaked at 2.49 for those aged 55–59, 2.45 for those aged 60–64, 2.35 for those aged 65–69, 2.14 for those aged 70–74, and 1.93 for those aged 75–79.

3 Although the dispersion rises between the ages of 85 and 90, a sample size limitation of this age group ($n = 29$) makes meaningful interpretation difficult.

4 The score on life evaluation for Finland, ranking first, is 7.741, while for Japan, ranking 51st, it is 6.060.

References

The Commission on Measuring Wellbeing (2011, December 5). *Measuring national wellbeing-proposed wellbeing indicators*. https://www5.cao.go.jp/keizai2/koufukudo/pdf/koufukudosian_english.pdf

Easterlin, R. A. (1973). Does money buy happiness? *The Public Interest*, *30*, 3–10.

Easterlin, R. A. (1995). Will raising the incomes of all increase the happiness of all? *Journal of Economic Behavior and Organization*, *27*(1), 35–47.

Emanuel, N., Harrington, E., & Pallais, A. (2023). The power of proximity to coworkers: Training for tomorrow or productivity today? *Harvard University, Working Paper*.

Hamermesh, D., & Kawaguchi, D. (2014). Does labor legislation benefit workers? Wellbeing after an hours reduction. *NBER Working Paper* 20398.

Hayashi, F., & Prescott, E. (2002). The 1990s in Japan: A lost decade. *Review of Economic Dynamics*, *5*, 206–235.

Helliwell, J. F., Layard, R., Sachs, J. D., De Neve, J. E., Aknin, L. B., & Wang, S. (Eds.) (2024). *World happiness report 2024*. Sustainable Development Solutions Network.

Institute of Social and Economic Research, Osaka University (2015). *Japan household panel survey on consumer preferences and satisfaction (JHPS-CPS)*. https://www.iser.osaka-u.ac.jp/survey_data/panelsummary.html [In Japanese].

Japan Cabinet Office (1960). *National income doubling plan*. https://www.archives.go.jp/ayumi/kobetsu/s35_1960_03.html

Japan Cabinet Office (2010, December 22). *Indication efforts in Japan. 1st study group on happiness (reference 9)*. https://www5.cao.go.jp/keizai2/koufukudo/shiryou/1shiryou/9.pdf

Japan Cabinet Office (2016, June 2). *Japan's plan for dynamic engagement of all citizens (excerption)*. https://www.mhlw.go.jp/file/05-Shingikai-12601000-Seisakutoukatsukan-Sanjikanshitsu_Shakaihoshoutantou/0000127481.pdf

Japan Cabinet Office (2017, June 9). *Basic policy for economic and fiscal management and reform 2017*. https://www5.cao.go.jp/keizai-shimon/kaigi/cabinet/honebuto/2017/2017_basicpolicies_ja.pdf

Japan Cabinet Office (2018, June 15). *Basic policies for economic and fiscal management and reform 2018*. https://www5.cao.go.jp/keizai-shimon/kaigi/cabinet/honebuto/2018/2018_basicpolicies_ja.pdf

Japan Cabinet Office (2019a, May 24). *First report on the survey on satisfaction and quality of life*. https://www5.cao.go.jp/keizai2/wellbeing/manzoku/pdf/report01.pdf

Japan Cabinet Office (2019b, July 30). *Second report on the survey on satisfaction and quality of life*. https://www5.cao.go.jp/keizai2/wellbeing/manzoku/pdf/report02.pdf

Japan Cabinet Office (2020a, April 3). *Third report on the survey on satisfaction and quality of life*. https://www5.cao.go.jp/keizai2/wellbeing/manzoku/pdf/report03.pdf

Japan Cabinet Office (2020b, September 11). *Fourth report on the survey on satisfaction and quality of life*. https://www5.cao.go.jp/keizai2/wellbeing/manzoku/pdf/report04.pdf

Japan Cabinet Office (2021a, July 30). *Related ministries and agencies liaison conference on wellbeing*. https://www5.cao.go.jp/keizai2/wellbeing/action/20210730/shiryou1.pdf

Japan Cabinet Office (2021b, September 1). *Survey report on satisfaction and quality of life 2021 ~Trends in wellbeing in Japan*. https://www5.cao.go.jp/keizai2/wellbeing/manzoku/pdf/report05.pdf

Japan Cabinet Office (2021c). *Basic policies for economic and fiscal management and reform 2021 (basic policies)*. https://www5.cao.go.jp/keizai-shimon/kaigi/cabinet/honebuto/2021/2021_basicpolicies_ja.pdf

Japan Cabinet Office (2022, July 29). *Survey report on satisfaction and quality of life 2022*. Trends in wellbeing in Japan. https://www5.cao.go.jp/keizai2/wellbeing/manzoku/pdf/report06.pdf

Japan Cabinet Office (2023a). *Survey report on satisfaction and quality of Life 2023*. Trends in wellbeing in Japan. https://www5.cao.go.jp/keizai2/wellbeing/manzoku/pdf/report07.pdf

Japan Cabinet Office (2023b). *Moonshot goals, moonshot research and development program*. https://www8.cao.go.jp/cstp/english/moonshot/target_en.html

Ministry of Health, Labor and Welfare (2023, July 4). *Overview of the 2022 basic survey on national living*. https://www.mhlw.go.jp/toukei/saikin/hw/k-tyosa/k-tyosa22/dl/14.pdf

NHK Broadcasting Culture Research Institute (2019). *Summary of the 10th "Japanese Attitudes" survey results*. https://www.nhk.or.jp/bunken/research/yoron/pdf/20190107_1.pdf

Nomura Research Institute (2021, November, 19). *9th "10,000 Consumer Survey" conducted*. https://www.nri.com/jp/news/newsrelease/files/900036839.pdf

Nomura Research Institute (2023, April 4). *GDP+i: New economic indicator proposal for the digital age*. https://www.nri.com/content/900032103.pdf

OECD (Organization for Economic Co-operation and Development) (2024, November 5). *How's life in Japan? OECD better life initiative.* https://www.oecd.org/en/publications/how-s-life-2024-country-notes_2603b12c-en/japan_8aa72c34-en.html

Ohtake, F., Shiraishi, S., & Tsutsui, Y. (2010). *Japan's happiness: Inequality, labor, and family.* Nippon Hyoronsha.

Oshio, T. (2014). *How to determine happiness: Economics of subjective welfare.* Nihon Keizai Shimbun Publishing.

Shiraishi, K., & Shiraishi, S. (2010). Current status and challenges of the economics of happiness. In F. Ohtake, S. Shiraishi, & Y. Tsutsui (Eds.), *Happiness in Japan: Inequality, labor, and family.* Nippon Hyoronsha.

Stevenson, B., & Wolfers, J. (2008). Economic growth and subjective wellbeing: Reassessing the Easterlin Paradox. *Brookings Papers on Economic Activity, 2008*(1), 1–87.

Stevenson, B., & Wolfers, J. (2013). Subjective well-being and income: Is there any evidence of satiation? *American Economic Review, 103*(3), 598–604.

Tanaka, Y. (2014). Reconsidering "happiness". *Planning and Administration, 37*(2), 3–4.

Veenhoven, R. (1993). *Happiness in nations: Subjective appreciation of life in 56 nations, 1946–1992.* RS Publishing, Erasmus University Rotterdam.

Workstyle Reform Implementation Council (2017, March 28). *Workstyle reform.* https://www.kantei.go.jp/jp/headline/pdf/20170328/05.pdf

26

WELLBEING AND POLICY IN MALTA

Doing well; feeling good?

Marie Briguglio

Introduction

At the time of writing, Malta, a small Mediterranean island, had been an independent country for a mere 60 years, and a member state of the European Union (EU) for 20 of them. Since independence, its population has almost doubled,[1] as life expectancy rose and net outward migration was replaced by high net inward flows. The economy, previously dependent on British naval forces, transitioned to manufacturing and then to service provision, enjoying negligible unemployment and a high degree of openness (Briguglio, 2022). Real GDP grew at an average rate of 6% per year since 1964 (Central Bank of Malta, n.d.). Society, formerly mainly Roman Catholic and organised around traditional family structures, experienced higher education levels, broader civil liberties, secularism and multiculturalism (Gellel et al., 2021). The role of government transitioned from protectionism and production of goods and services, to managing an expansive welfare system, including free healthcare and education. Meanwhile, the pressures of soaring population density, tourism, construction and motorization, all on a mere 316 km^2 area, brought forward environmental challenges like urbanisation, noise, air pollution and waste (Briguglio, 2022). Notwithstanding its (very) small size and inherent vulnerabilities (Moncada et al., 2018), Malta has found itself ranked among the top 12% of the countries of the world on the Human Development Index – rising from 0.730 in 1990 to 0.915 in 2022 (UNDP, n.d.).

Wellbeing in Malta

Malta is *doing well* overall, but assessing wellbeing also requires an understanding as to whether people are *feeling good* (Ryan & Deci, 2001). The longest series of data available for Subjective Wellbeing (SWB) in Malta is that gathered by Gallup

DOI: 10.4324/9781003382447-29

and reported in the World Happiness Report (WHR). In its three-year rolling average of life evaluation across the world, Malta consistently emerges in the top fourth of the 164 countries (or so) surveyed (Helliwell et al., 2023; Briguglio et al., 2024). The EU Quality of Life Dashboard reports that Malta's average exceeds the EU's on life evaluation (Eurostat, n.d.). Yet Eurostat data also reveals that people in Malta feel nervous more often than the average European and feel less satisfied with their leisure time (Briguglio, 2022b). By global comparisons, Maltese people also show low frequencies of enjoyment and high frequencies of negative affect (Zammit, 2022). Indeed, in the last Gallup emotions survey, 64% of the Maltese reported experiencing a lot of worry – in contrast with the 42% world average (Gallup, 2023; Briguglio et al., 2024). Distinctions between eudaimonic and hedonic wellbeing also play out regionally in Malta. For instance, people on the more rural, and far less densely populated sister island (Gozo) tend to experience lower levels of nervousness although they also have lower levels of life satisfaction (Briguglio, 2022b).

A review of Malta's performance on various indicators yields more nuanced information on the conditions of life that may impact SWB in Malta. By Eurostat's Sustainable Development Goal indicators, Malta reports strong performance on material and health aspects, employment and adult learning outcomes, but weaker outcomes on obesity, science, research and development, environment, corruption perceptions, work accidents/deaths and inequality (Lafortune et al., 2024). On the SDSN's EU Sustainable Development Goals Index, Malta's score is 65.88 (lower than the EU's 72.02); while Malta performs better than the EU average on matters like severe material deprivation and at-risk of poverty rates, it faces challenges with obesity, fatal accident rates at work, some aspects of environmental management and expenditure on research and development (SDSN, 2024). On the EU's quality of Life Dashboard (Eurostat, n.d.) Malta outperforms the EU average on material living conditions, housing and safety and social interaction but returns weaker results on time-use and education (Briguglio et al., 2024). The WHR also ranks Malta highly on all determinants of life evaluation except corruption perceptions (Helliwell et al., 2023; Briguglio et al., 2024). A study employing the OECD's Better Life Index indicators to Malta also draws attention to long hours of work, low school-leaving age/educational attainment, poor environmental quality, rising inequality and obesity (Justice and Peace Commission, 2020). Meanwhile, children in Malta rank in the bottom third for all wellbeing domains for children in rich countries (mental wellbeing, physical health and skills), displaying high rates of obesity and being the least likely to agree that there are enough places to play (Gromada et al., 2020). This brisk review offers some insights as to the conditions of life that merit attention in Malta, including environmental quality/engagement, safe working conditions/time use, corruption perceptions, rapid population growth rising inequality, schools and obesity.

Academic research in Malta has also produced evidence on the links between conditions of life and SWB. Much of this research has been conducted in the last 10 years employing cross-sectoral micro-data in a multivariate models where self-assessed life-satisfaction or happiness is the outcome variable (e.g. Vella, 2017; Briguglio et al., 2020), with some employing panel data (e.g. Debono, 2020; Briguglio et al., 2021) and others adopting a qualitative approach (e.g. Sammut et al., 2019; Satariano, 2019; Briguglio, 2015b). The findings that emerge broadly conform to those in other Western, Educated, Industrialised, Rich and Democratic countries: SWB in Malta is lower among those in poor health, those experiencing material deprivation/unemployment/low income, with limited social interaction and lack of participation in creative activities, sport, religious/spiritual activity, environmental engagement or voluntary work. Low government trust and (higher) political participation are also associated with lower SWB in Malta. Children from lower income households and a migrant background being are more likely to report lower levels of wellbeing (Cefai et al., 2024).

Policy and interventions for wellbeing

Successive governments in Malta have articulated visions that go beyond GDP growth and sought to implement these, to different degrees of success, through a variety of institutions and interventions. Various editions of strategies for sustainable development, policies for social cohesion, land-use planning policies, a dense body of environmental legislation (mostly acquired in the process of EU accession), as well numerous sectoral strategies (e.g. health, sport, ageing, youth, disability, children, culture) have set goals that can generally be expected to enhance wellbeing. But the notion of "wellbeing" as a policy outcome of interest (in place of, say, "prosperity", or "sustainable development") seems to be gaining traction. For instance, the 2020 environmental vision for Malta entitled "Wellbeing First" (Environment and Resource Authority, 2020) includes strategic goals for livable towns and villages. The new Social Vision for Malta 2035 was crafted "with the ultimate objective being to improve social wellbeing and provide a better quality of life to citizens" (Ministry for Social Policy and Children's Rights, 2022, p. 9). The National Strategic Policy for Active Ageing 2023–2030 aims to protect the human rights of older people through actions in three key areas including healthy ageing – where mental wellbeing is one of the priorities (Government of Malta, 2022). The suggestions to enhance wellbeing in the newly minted draft National Strategy for Non-Communicable Diseases echo the issues outlined earlier and advocate for better work–life balance, reducing and dealing with life stressors, addressing excessive social media in young children and adolescents, enhancing mental health literacy, focused interventions among vulnerable and minority groups and the role of schools and digital apps for wellbeing (Government of Malta, 2024). Even Malta's 2021 Smart Specialisation strategy features "Health and Wellbeing" as one of six areas of focus (The Malta Council for Science & Technology, 2021).

Within the public sector, one entity which has taken it upon itself to champion the cause of wellbeing is the Malta Foundation for the Wellbeing of Society (MFWS, 2024). Founded in 2014 by the then President of the Republic (H.E.

Marie Louise Coleiro Preca, formerly the Minister for the Family and Social Solidarity), the Foundation first formed part of the President's own portfolio and subsequently transitioned to the portfolio of the Ministry of Finance. Against a backdrop of "marked differences in the quality of life and wellbeing enjoyed by the members of society in Malta. . . . reflected in inequitable access to physical and mental health, income and employment, family and social interactions, knowledge and information technology, levels of education and skills, freedom of expression and engagement, leisure, environmental quality, and open spaces", the Foundation set out "to narrow the gaps in these inequalities, by promoting wellbeing for all" (MFWS, 2024). The profile of the Foundation was bolstered not only by that of its Chairperson, but also by the consultative Council of Governors, which included the Speaker of the House of Representatives, representatives from the Government and the Opposition, as well as representatives from the Ministry of Finance, the Voluntary Sector, the Public Sector, Local Councils and the University of Malta (UM). The Foundation forged further alliances and partnerships with a range of NGOs, government agencies and local councils through Memoranda of Understanding and focused on activities in the domain of advocacy, creating safe spaces for dialogue, training, developing toolkits and providing technical assistance (MFWS, 2024).

Of particular relevance to this chapter is the Foundation's portfolio of work focused on developing mechanisms to measure wellbeing and promote evidence-based wellbeing interventions in Malta. Within one year of its establishment, in 2015, the Foundation had held its first National Conference on Wellbeing fielding the prospect of "a wellbeing framework for Malta" (Briguglio, 2015). Community meetings took place through the Community Forum[2] which organised various mobile pop-up events (The President's Foundation for the Wellbeing of Society, 2016). In such events, participants were asked to reflect on a typical day in their lives and to share insights as to what makes them feel happy or unhappy. Responses frequently centered around family and social interaction, the environment and health but also yielded insights on day-to-day issues which are frequently ignored by international metrics (e.g. time spent in traffic, noise, litter). The hallmark of these fora was that they were held in the community spaces (e.g. public gardens, shopping mall, in a pedestrian space in the capital city, in a village square, at a day care centre for the elderly), thereby making it possible to gather the views of people who would not ordinarily be present in more formal consultation processes. These events were also often accompanied by street games, performances, singing and other socially interactive experiences. They eventually evolved into an outreach initiative – Vanni Fil-Komunita' – a van equipped with a stage and various audio-visual and interactive tools visiting different localities in Malta and Gozo to listen and interact with diverse communities (The President's Foundation for the Wellbeing of Society, 2019).

In 2020, the Foundation signed an agreement with UM to launch the "Wellbeing INDEX project" (the name INDEX representing its scope, namely Indicators, Networking, Data, Exploration, and eXchange) (Wellbeing INDEX, n.d.).[3] The aim of the project was to pave the way for wellbeing statistics beyond traditional economic measures of progress, and to seed research on the wellbeing with a view to guiding policies (Coleiro Preca, 2021). An Advisory Board (with representatives from the National Statistics Office, the World Bank Group, the New Economics Foundation, the London School of Economics and the European Commission) offered strategic guidance and a number of academics (including economists, psychologists and data-scientists) worked alongside officials at the MFWS and the National Statistics Office (NSO) for the duration of the project (Wellbeing INDEX, n.d.). Data on SWB, using indicators in Wellbeing Module of the European Union Survey on Income and Living Conditions (EU-SILC), drawn from a representative sample of some 10,000 individuals, began to be annually collected by the NSO (NSO, n.d.) and to be made available online in an interactive dashboard (Wellbeing INDEX, n.d.). Here, users could examine evaluative and affective wellbeing variables and their relationship with living conditions and diverse demographics. The website also started to serve as a one-stop shop for headline data and links to global indicators relevant to wellbeing in Malta. Research on the state of the art of wellbeing policy-making, on the determinants of wellbeing in Malta and on the wellbeing of children and young people was underway at the time of writing this chapter. The project also sought to bring wellbeing on the national agenda through active stakeholder engagement exercises, participation in policy debates, the creation of a network of wellbeing researchers in Malta and through educational print and bi-lingual audio-visual materials (in Maltese and English). Finally, with an eye on impact, the project presented annual updates on wellbeing in Malta at Parliament on the International Day of Happiness, March 20 (Parliament of Malta, 2020), receiving considerable media coverage (Wellbeing INDEX, n.d.).

Discussion and actionable points

While readily available data on SWB and its correlates offer valuable insights to policy-makers in Malta, there are some notable gaps. For instance, some segments of society are insufficiently represented in official statistics (e.g. institutionalised people, migrants, children); statistics available from global metrics are not always available in micro-data format and not always capable of disaggregation and some phenomena which appear relevant to people are insufficiently captured by official statistics. Furthermore, wellbeing policy is still at its infancy in Malta and there is considerable potential for programmes and budgets (at EU, national and local levels) to be assessed for their wellbeing impact, both *ex ante* and *ex post* (Briguglio, 2024). Given the increased emphasis on wellbeing measurement and policy at both the EU level (European Commission, 2023) and the UN level (UNECE, 2023), it is likely that these issues will acquire increased importance in Malta's policy-making agenda. In late 2023, Malta also announced its intention to join the OECD (Ellul, 2023), potentially paving the way for its participation in a multidimensional, internationally comparable wellbeing index as part of the Better Life Index initiative.

On the basis of this review, the following reflections emerge that may serve as actionable points in other contexts:

- Understanding wellbeing in a country requires an examination of life conditions as well as insights on how people themselves evaluate their lives and day-to-day feelings (subjective wellbeing). While there are linkages, doing well on the former does not automatically translate to doing well on the latter.
- In the absence of a bespoke framework and wellbeing data collection, existing data (gathered by national and international organisations) can yield useful insights on wellbeing. This may be particularly useful for small states like Malta, where the per capita cost of data collection is high. Scarce resources may then be dedicated to adding wellbeing modules to existing surveys and collecting data on underrepresented people and issues.
- Collaborations between the public sector and academic/research institutions offer a win–win solution – generating evidence for policy-makers and enhancing impact for research work.
- Having a champion for wellbeing and integrating wellbeing in the various sectoral policies can help overcome inertia to place wellbeing on the national agenda.
- Wellbeing matters attract media attention. Focusing communications on the International Day of Happiness can reap the benefit of international momentum on the topic.

Notes

1 As of 2024, conservatively estimated to be around 535,000.zam
2 Chaired by the present author.
3 The present author serves as the principal investigator for the project.

References

Briguglio, M. (2015). Towards research on wellbeing in Malta. In *The determinants of wellbeing: Insight from research and implications for Malta.* First National Conference on Wellbeing (pp. 52–67). The President's Foundation for the Wellbeing of Society & the University of Malta Department of Economics. Retrieved May 1, 2024, from www.um.edu.mt/library/oar/bitstream/123456789/25734/4/Towards_research_on_wellbeing_in_Malta_2015.pdf

Briguglio, M. (2022a). Economics and the Maltese economy. In E. Galea Curmi & S. Vella (Eds.), *Social policy in Malta: An introduction*. Midsea Books Ltd.

Briguglio, M. (2022b, August 19). Why do we feel so bad? *Times of Malta*. Retrieved May 1, 2024, from https://timesofmalta.com/articles/view/feel-bad-marie-briguglio.974954

Briguglio, M. (2024, March 24). "Well-being" – where's the evidence? *Times of Malta*. Retrieved May 1, 2024, from www.timesofmalta.com/article/wellbeing-evidence.1086919

Briguglio, M., Camilleri, C., Camilleri Fenech, M., Mangion, N., Spiteri, J., & Spiteri, G. W. (2024). *Policy brief: Wellbeing in Malta – insights from global indicators*. Retrieved May 1, 2024, from https://wellbeingindex.mt/wp/wp-content/uploads/2024/05/PB-INDICATORS.pdf

Briguglio, M., Camilleri, G., & Vella, M. (2020). Artists, audiences and wellbeing: An economic analysis. *International Journal of Wellbeing, 10*(3), 20–34. https://orcid.org/0000-0003-4018-795X
Briguglio, M., Caruana, M., & Debono, N. (2021). Wellbeing disparities during the COVID-19 outbreak: Evidence from Malta. *Traumatology, 27*(4), 388–398. https://doi.org/10.1037/trm0000323
Cefai, C., Spiteri, R., Galea, N., & Briguglio, M. (2024). *The wellbeing of children and young people in Malta: The Malta Wellbeing INDEX project*. University of Malta & The Malta Foundation for the Wellbeing of Society.
Central Bank of Malta (n.d.). *Economic analysis and research*. Retrieved February 28, 2025, from https://www.centralbankmalta.org/en/economics
Coleiro Preca, M. (2021, July 2). Let's talk about well-being. *Times of Malta*. Retrieved May 1, 2024, from https://timesofmalta.com/article/lets-talk-about-well-being-marie-louise-coleiro-preca.883528
Debono, N. (2020). The determinants of wellbeing during a time of economic growth: The case of selected European Union member states. *Mediterranean Journal of Social Sciences, 11*(4), 49–60. https://doi.org/10.36941/mjss-2020-0040
Ellul, D. (2023, November 14). Malta to apply for OECD membership in coming months. *Times of Malta*. Retrieved May 1, 2024, from https://timesofmalta.com/article/malta-apply-oecd-membership-coming-months.1067418
Environment and Resources Authority (2020). *Wellbeing first – a vision for Malta's environment: National strategy for the environment for 2050*. Ministry for the Environment, Climate Change and Planning. Retrieved May 1, 2024, from https://era.org.mt/wp-content/uploads/2020/12/NSE-Wellbeing-First-Vision-Final.pdf
European Commission (2023). *Strategic foresight report 2023*. European Commission. Retrieved May 1, 2024, from https://commission.europa.eu/document/download/ca1c61b7-e413-4877-970b-8ef619fc6b6c_en?filename=SFR-23-beautified-version_en_0.pdf
Eurostat (n.d.). *Quality of life*. Retrieved May 1, 2024, from https://ec.europa.eu/eurostat/cache/infographs/qol/index_en.html
Gallup (2023). *Gallup's latest global emotions report* [webpage]. Retrieved May 1, 2024, from www.gallup.com/analytics/349280/gallup-global-emotions-report.aspx
Gellel, A. M., Arvanitidou, Z., & Rossi, C. (2021). Religious diversity and the secularization process in Malta: A reflection through the experiences of health, social work and education professionals. In A. Unser (Ed.), *Religion, citizenship and democracy* (pp. 175–197). Springer. https://doi.org/10.1007/978-3-030-83277-3_10
Government of Malta, Ministry for Active Aging (2022). *National strategic policy for active ageing 2023–2030*. Retrieved July 1, 2024, from https://activeageing.gov.mt/wp-content/uploads/2023/04/NSPActiveAgeing2023-30.pdf
Government of Malta, Ministry for Health and Active Ageing (2024). *The 2025–2035 non-communicable diseases prevention framework: Policy framework for the prevention of non-communicable diseases and the promotion of wellbeing consultation document*. Retrieved July 1, 2024, from https://health.gov.mt/wp-content/uploads/2024/06/Non-Communicable-Diseases_Prevention_Framework_2024_Public_Consultation_Document.pdf
Gromada, A., Rees, G., & Chzhen, Y. (2020). Worlds of influence: Understanding what shapes child well-being in rich countries. *Innocenti Report Card*, no. 16, UNICEF Office of Research – Innocenti, Florence. www.unicef-irc.org/publications/1140-worlds-of-influence-understanding-what-shapes-child-well-being-in-rich-countries.html
Helliwell, J. F., Layard, R., Sachs, J. D., Aknin, L. B., De Neve, J.-E., & Wang, S. (Eds.) (2023). *World happiness report 2023* (11th ed.). Sustainable Development Solutions Network. Retrieved May 1, 2024, from https://worldhappiness.report/ed/2023/
Justice and Peace Commission Malta (2020). *Beyond GDP*. Commission of Justice and Peace, with EY and Seed. Retrieved May 1, 2024, from https://gp.knisja.mt/wp-content/uploads/2022/03/BEYOND-GDP-REPORT-2020-3.pdf

Lafortune, G., Fuller, G., Kloke-Lesch, A., Koundouri, P., & Riccaboni, A. (2024). *European elections, Europe's future and the SDGs: Europe sustainable development report 2023/24*. SDSN and SDSN Europe and Dublin University Press. Retrieved May 1, 2024, from https://doi.org/10.25546/104407

The Malta Council for Science and Technology (2021). *Malta's national research and innovation strategic plan 2021–2027*. MCST, with the Ministry for Equality, Research & Innovation. Retrieved May 1, 2024, from https://mcst.gov.mt/wp-content/uploads/2022/01/RIS3-Strategy-2020-2027.pdf

Malta Foundation for the Wellbeing of Society (MFWS) (2024). *Resources*. Retrieved May 1, 2024, from https://mfws.org.mt/

Ministry for Social Policy and Children's Rights (2022). *A social vision for Malta 2035*. Retrieved May 1, 2024, from https://familja.gov.mt/wp-content/uploads/2023/04/Social-Vision-for-Malta-2035-Policy-Document-EN.pdf

Moncada, S., Spiteri, J., & Briguglio, M. (2018). Environmental economics: Special considerations for small states. In L. Briguglio (Ed.), *Handbook of small states: Economic, social and environmental issues*. Routledge. www.um.edu.mt/library/oar//handle/123456789/25604

National Statistics Office (NSO) (n.d.). *Statistics on income and living conditions*. NSO Malta. Retrieved May 1, 2024, from https://nso.gov.mt/themes_sources___met/statistics-on-income-and-living-conditions/

Organisation for Economic Co-operation and Development (n.d.). *Measuring wellbeing and progress: Wellbeing research*. Retrieved May 1, 2024, from www.oecd.org/statistics/measuring-wellbeing-and-progress.htm

Parliament of Malta (2020). *Launch of wellbeing index a win for society*. The Malta Foundation for the Wellbeing of Society & University of Malta. Retrieved May 1, 2024, from https://parlament.mt/media/109825/the-malta-wellbeing-index-press-release.pdf

The President's Foundation for the Wellbeing of Society (2016). *Annual report – 2014/2015*. Malta Foundation for the Wellbeing of Society. Retrieved May 1, 2024, from https://mfws.org.mt/wp-content/uploads/2022/09/Annual-Report-2014-2015.pdf

The President's Foundation for the Wellbeing of Society (2019). *Annual report – 2017/2018*. Malta Foundation for the Wellbeing of Society. https://mfws.org.mt/wp-content/uploads/2022/09/Annual-Report-2017-2018.pdf

Ryan, R. M., & Deci, E. L. (2001). On happiness and human potentials: A review of research on hedonic and eudaimonic well-being. *Annual Review of Psychology*, *52*, 141–166. https://doi.org/10.1146/annurev.psych.52.1.141

Sammut Scerri, C., Grech Lanfranco, I., & Abela, A. (2019). Family wellbeing. In S. Vella, R. Falzon, & A. Azzopardi (Eds.), *Perspectives on wellbeing* (pp. 63–78). Koninklijke Brill NV.

Satariano, B. (2019). Blue therapeutic spaces on islands: Coastal landscapes and their impact on the health and wellbeing of people in Malta. *Island Studies Journal*, *14*(2), 245–260. https://doi.org/10.24043/isj.100

Sustainable Development Solutions Network (SDSN) (2024). *Sustainable development report 2023/2024*. Retrieved July 1, 2024, from https://dashboards.sdgindex.org/explorer

UNECE (2023). In-depth review of measurement of current well-being: Outcomes of the Recent in-depth reviews carried out by the bureau of the conference of European statisticians. *Conference of European Statisticians Seventy-First Plenary Session*, Israel. Retrieved May 1, 2024, from https://unece.org/statistics/documents/2023/05/working-documents/depth-review-measurement-current-well-being-prepared

United National Development Programme (n.d.). *Human Development Index (HDI)*. Human Development Reports. Retrieved May 1, 2024, from http://hdr.undp.org/en/content/human-development-index-hdi

Vella, S. (2017). *Does trust in government influence wellbeing in Malta?* [Bachelor dissertation, University of Malta]. Open Access Repository. www.um.edu.mt/library/oar/handle/123456789/55696

Wellbeing INDEX – Wellbeing in Malta (n.d.). www.wellbeingindex.mt

Zammit, M. (2022, August 25). Why are the Maltese so angry and anxious? *Times of Malta*. Retrieved May 1, 2024, from https://timesofmalta.com/article/maltese-angry-anxious.975512

APPENDIX

Evidence for Action

Income (Kudrna, 2025)

Evidence	*Action*
Higher income is usually thought to translate into higher subjective wellbeing, but the link between the two is complex. For individuals, life satisfaction increases with income, but it does so at diminishing rates. There is also evidence of satiation and turning points at the higher end of the income distribution, with some studies finding that higher income is associated with no better or worse subjective wellbeing. At the community and national levels, increases in Gross Domestic Product do not consistently lead to higher life satisfaction over time. Potential explanations include adaptation, social comparison, and loss aversion.	1. Among low-income people, improve wellbeing by raising incomes. In such cases, complement cash transfers with efforts to address stigma and trust, considering individual differences and community contexts. 2. When assessing the costs and benefits of income interventions, use subjective wellbeing valuation approaches to assess social value – higher income does not necessarily lead to higher wellbeing. 3. Undertake further research to understand how income redistribution initiatives are shaped by system-level implementation contexts.

Work (Kirienko, Laffan, Giurge, 2025)

Evidence	*Action*
Understanding wellbeing at work is critical for optimizing outcomes for both employees and employers. Employee wellbeing influences organizational goals like productivity, performance, and retention. Work–life balance, working arrangements, relationship with manager, social relationships, and job fit are all drivers that affect subjective wellbeing at work. Interventions aimed at improving workplace wellbeing are typically implemented at the organizational level and not through public policy.	1. Collect subjective wellbeing and objective wellbeing indicators regularly from all staff and analyze data and identify areas for improvement in organizations. 2. Develop policies that support work–life balance, flexible working arrangements, social connection, and job fit. 3. Enhance collaboration between practitioners and academics to develop evidence-based interventions and measure their impact.

Health (Czap, H. & Briguglio, 2025)

Evidence	*Action*
Health indicators are a ubiquitous feature of objective measures of wellbeing. Good health and health interventions typically lead to better subjective wellbeing, but there are disparities in these outcomes depending on the type of health issue, how health is measured, the type of intervention, and the demographic targeted.	1. Use impact assessments to measure the effects of interventions not just on health but also separately on wellbeing throughout the treatment. 2. Promote interventions for wellbeing, noting that subjective wellbeing responds more strongly to mental health than physical health. 3. Tailor interventions to the context and individual needs.

Family (Xia, 2025)

Evidence	*Action*
Family wellbeing is an essential aspect of individual wellbeing and an indicator of development and societal wellbeing. It merits holistic evaluation beyond the sum of individuals' wellbeing. The Hong Kong Family Wellbeing Index is a culturally specific framework providing a comprehensive measurement that can be used to assess family wellbeing within a region.	1. Conceptualize family wellbeing in the local sociocultural context. 2. Embed family wellbeing measurement when assessing the effectiveness of family policies and social services. 3. Undertake international comparisons to identify the universal and context-specific dimensions of family wellbeing.

Altruism (Preston & Nichols, 2024)

Evidence	*Action*
Altruism has long-term benefits, such as propagating one's genes, increasing cooperation, and improving societal wellbeing, which offset the immediate costs of the decision to help. Prosociality feels good and improves wellbeing; conversely, wellbeing feels good and promotes prosociality.	1. Highlight unfairness and inequality and the associated suffering and ensure that those in need become part of an interconnected group. 2. Highlight what we gain from altruistic actions, such as the positive feelings from helping others and receiving gratitude and reciprocation, in policy framing and appeals for action. 3. Press politicians into action by tying votes to policies that promote altruism.

Aging (Górny & Hajder, 2024)

Evidence	*Action*
While older individuals generally report higher life satisfaction than those in middle age, aspects of aging pose substantial challenges to wellbeing. The key determinants of seniors' wellbeing span diverse domains, encompassing social relationships, financial situations, and personal characteristics. Social connectedness and psychological resilience emerge as crucial protective factors, while loneliness and involuntary retirement pose significant risks. Besides traditional interventions, positive psychology practices and positive technology interventions offer promising supports.	1. Support initiatives that can help foster social connectedness and mitigate loneliness, the risks of lower-than-expected income, and involuntary retirement among the elderly. 2. Consider how positive psychology practices aimed at building psychological resilience and promoting positive emotions can be integrated into the existing services delivered for seniors, as well as whether new services could be offered. 3. Support the development and testing of positive technology interventions that span domains from entertainment to social connection and which can improve both health and wellbeing.

Gender (Kalsi & Mavisakalyan, 2025)

Evidence	*Action*
Under the influence of gendered norms, the experiences of men and women may differ at key stages of the life course, with respective implications for wellbeing. Transitions related to employment, parenthood, and retirement often serve as critical junctures where gendered dynamics shape distinct wellbeing outcomes.	1. Promote policy interventions that break down gendered norms and breadwinner ideologies. 2. Enact evidence-based parental leave and retirement policies that are equitably designed to enhance wellbeing in both men and women. 3. Implement organizational policies around pay equity, recruitment, and retention as well as other policies, such as parental leave, family and caregiving, and elimination of sex-based harassment.

Education (Kristoffersen, Dockery & Li, 2025)

Evidence	*Action*
Most of the research on education and wellbeing is correlational, with scarce reliable causal evidence. There is a positive association between education and objective quality-of-life measures at the individual and societal levels. However, the association is nuanced: investing in education is costly and is subject to diminishing returns; education changes not only our objective circumstances but also our subjective evaluations of these circumstances.	1. Distinguish between objective circumstances of life and their subjective evaluations by people. 2. Recognize that there is a high opportunity cost of leisure and that 'time-poverty' can occur during active working years. 3. Be careful not to overestimate the consequences of the pursuit of additional education for individuals and societies.

Housing (Briguglio, Cassar & Gravino, 2025)

Evidence	*Action*
Housing provides the context for several of the factors that determine subjective wellbeing: family life, social interaction, work and lifestyle choices, as well as environmental quality. Housing tenure and improved housing and neighborhood quality are positively linked to wellbeing, while financial burden may have a negative impact. While effects of housing interventions on wellbeing are generally positive, the results are not unequivocal and are context dependent.	1. Feature housing and neighborhood policies and wellbeing impact assessments in the public sector agenda, given that they can directly boost or suppress key determinants of wellbeing. 2. Involve the targeted population in the design and implementation of housing and neighborhood interventions for wellbeing. 3. Invest in research on the wellbeing effects of housing and neighborhood interventions in diverse contexts, also examining interaction effects (e.g., income, age, gender).

Environment (Laffan, Czap H. & Czap, N., 2025)

Evidence	*Action*
Air and water pollution, excessive noise, and the absence of green spaces lead to poor physical and mental health, reduced productivity, and lower subjective wellbeing. Interventions can improve wellbeing directly through environmental quality and indirectly by signaling government action and transparency. Pro-environmental behaviors, especially those that are more visible and involve socializing, are also associated with higher subjective wellbeing. Nature connectedness, pro-environmental attitudes, and identity are also linked to higher wellbeing.	1. Combat environmental injustice, given that disadvantaged communities have fewer resources to improve environmental quality yet would benefit the most from it. 2. Communicate good environmental conditions clearly and highlight the work done to improve these, emphasizing the wellbeing benefits of pro-environmental action, rather than presenting it as a sacrifice. 3. Develop evidence-based guidance for interventions to treat eco-anxiety.

Crime (Krulichová, 2025)

Evidence	*Action*
While the direct relationship between subjective wellbeing and individual victimization proves to be rather weak, the effect of fear of crime and perceived unsafety on subjective wellbeing is consistent and likely mediates the victimization–subjective wellbeing link. At a country level, neither low crime rates nor repressive criminal policies necessarily translate into higher subjective wellbeing. Conversely, trust in the police and legal system appears to be a crucial factor in enhancing subjective wellbeing.	1. Enhance security, improve the quality of the built environment, boost cooperation between the police and community members, and encourage community engagement and volunteerism. 2. Reduce social and economic vulnerability (e.g., social safety net, quality healthcare and education, and job opportunities) and foster social capital and trust in institutions by promoting governmental transparency and accountability as well as impartial law enforcement and justice systems. 3. Refrain from repressive interventions and anti-crime measures leading to higher imprisonment rates but focus on rehabilitation, community-based initiatives, and restorative justice.

Democracy (Stutzer, Jansen & Schib, 2025)

Evidence	*Action*
The pursuit of happiness is often closely linked to the idea of a constitution by the people and for the people.	1. Gather additional evidence on which form of democracy is the best for people across a wide range of contexts.
State institutions affect individual lives and wellbeing mainly through outcome utility and procedural utility: individuals derive wellbeing not only from the results of democratic processes but also from participating in them, which enhances their sense of self-worth.	2. Investigate further the effect of proportional representation, direct democratic participation, and decentralized decision-making powers in federal systems on wellbeing. 3. Explore additional institutional features that enable inclusion and representation of broad segments of the population that have the potential to improve wellbeing.

Migration (Hendriks, 2025)

Evidence	*Action*
Migration shows a marginal overall impact on the subjective wellbeing of the hosting population, while migrants tend to experience increased subjective wellbeing that diminishes over time.	1. Implement interventions that facilitate migrants' acculturation into society (while allowing them to maintain their heritage culture) and that reduce anti-immigrant sentiments by improving social cohesion between immigrants and natives.
Migrants' subjective wellbeing is contingent upon factors such as social connections, antidiscrimination measures, and cultural engagement initiatives.	2. Improve cooperation between policy makers and researchers to test the effectiveness of various migration and integration interventions. 3. Reduce outmigration, particularly a 'happiness drain' in developing countries, by improving not only the objective wellbeing of citizens but also their subjective wellbeing.

Religion and spirituality (García-Muñoz & Neuman, 2025)

Evidence	*Action*
Religious and spiritual interventions include: mindfulness, meditation, yoga, mantra repetition; programs targeting trust, resilience, patience, altruism, forgiveness, active listening, supportive presence; and engaging in prayer or reading sacred texts. Such interventions consistently generate positive results on wellbeing, especially when combined. They are particularly powerful among participants with mental and physical problems. These practices can decrease stress and pressure; improve mood; and provide a sense of meaning, purpose, or hope.	1. Train professionals in the healthcare sector to sensitively address and accommodate patients' spiritual and religious needs and practices. 2. Design and offer spiritual-religious interventions for interested patients and employees having stressful occupations, especially where connection, belonging, and social interaction are missing. 3. Design educational programs and awareness campaigns for a more inclusive and tolerant society and to reduce discrimination based on religious/spiritual beliefs.

Technology (Pelly, 2025)

Evidence	*Action*
Digital technology (DT) affords numerous educational, social, and entertainment benefits, but it is often blamed for contributing to negative health outcomes such as depression, anxiety, and addiction. The negative impact of digital technology on wellbeing is likely to be negligible but usage dependent. Initiatives would benefit from the recognition of individual differences and from a greater focus on interventions aimed at harnessing digital technology for wellbeing.	1. Focus on positive interventions targeting not just high-risk groups (e.g., children from deprived backgrounds) but also groups who stand to benefit substantially from DT such as older adults at risk for social isolation. 2. Invest in high-quality studies and multidisciplinary think tanks; test soft-touch behaviorally informed interventions and boosting programs, which target specific user groups. 3. Facilitate ethical, secure, and transparent de-identified data-sharing between corporations and researchers, perhaps through embedded research teams.

Art and Culture (Baldacchino, 2025)

Evidence	*Action*
Engagement in art, culture, and creativity improves wellbeing through enhanced enjoyment, social connectedness and support, distraction from suffering, self-expression, skills development, self-esteem, self-efficacy, and states of flow. Both active and passive engagements are positively associated with wellbeing, but the benefits of the former tend to be stronger. Engagement seems to be more beneficial yet less accessible to disadvantaged groups.	1. Promote active engagement in art, culture, and creativity with an emphasis on learning, participation, and performance. 2. Increase access to art, culture, and creativity among minorities and disadvantaged groups by subsidizing it. 3. Increase self-employment opportunities for artists from the underrepresented and disadvantaged groups.

Bhutan (Balogun & Weru, 2025)

Evidence	*Action*
In Bhutan, happiness has been a longstanding focal point in policy-making. Bhutan's Gross National Happiness policy has oriented its economic and governance structures to increase people's multidimensional wellbeing, while concurrently ensuring environmental sustainability. Given the rising number of mental health challenges in Bhutan and globally, it is recommended to focus on measuring and tracking inner and cultural poverty along with income poverty.	1. Utilize indigenous knowledge with its emphasis on spiritual and inner growth for intellectual diversity to understand how psychosocial deficiencies link to various socioeconomic contexts. This is especially relevant when it comes to the high youth suicide and suicide ideation rates. 2. Prioritize noneconomic wellbeing measures like shared environmental identity. 3. Shift away from the current economic paradigm centered around autonomous individuals and hyper-competition toward communities, institutions, and policies promoting sustainability and wellbeing.

New Zealand (Weijers, 2025)

Evidence	*Action*
New Zealand often ranks in or near the top 10 nations on international wellbeing metrics and is regarded as one of the leaders in wellbeing policy. In 2011, it adopted the Living Standards Framework, a new model of wellbeing for policy-making. Since 2018, New Zealand has employed a wellbeing approach to the national budget and reporting processes, much of which are codified into new laws. Key innovations include an interactive dashboard of wellbeing data and a wellbeing cost–benefit analysis tool.	1. Conduct wellbeing cost–benefit analysis when designing policies, aiming to reduce inequality in wellbeing outcomes. 2. Share wellbeing knowledge and train policymakers; report frequently on wellbeing; and analyze wellbeing risks, resilience, and inequalities experienced by vulnerable populations. 3. Set up citizen assemblies for wellbeing using a stratified sample representing all minority groups.

Finland (Pellikka & Hätönen, 2025)

Evidence	*Action*
Finland has a long tradition of promoting sustainability and wellbeing. The National Action Plan for the Economy of Wellbeing was developed to integrate this approach into knowledge-based decision-making. Even though Finland ranks well on many indexes, there are still challenges to sustain the high levels of wellbeing for the present and future generations. There is a need for strong leadership and cross-governmental cooperation as well as apolitical frameworks that are independent of the composition of the current administration.	1. Implement both centralized and decentralized policies to promote sustainable wellbeing, involving citizens and other stakeholders in future-oriented policy development. 2. Measure wellbeing, long-time economic sustainability, and system resilience. 3. Establish a decision-making process which is independent of the composition of the government, whereby politicians set the values.

United Arab Emirates (Samarji & AlBlooshi, 2025)

Evidence	*Action*
In the UAE, wellbeing is not only a top policy priority but also a culture that is integrated across all sectors and domains. The UAE National Wellbeing Strategy 2031 represents a dynamic, adaptive, evidence-based strategy with a balance between top-down and bottom-up approaches.	1. Find a balance between top-down (vision and set of principles), bottom-up (broad consultation with stakeholders), and adaptive approaches with regular reviews of wellbeing strategy and its proactive adjustment and updating. 2. Ensure constructive alignment, acknowledging that wellbeing is a multidimensional construct, using data-driven holistic assessment and employing longitudinal, cross-sectional, and real-time data. 3. Engage globally and contribute to international wellbeing initiatives.

Canada (Barrington-Leigh, 2025)

Evidence	*Action*
Canada was an early adopter of subjective wellbeing and measures of social connection in its mainline surveys and has begun integrating the Quality of Life framework in the federal government. However, due to its federal structure, large size, and diverse Indigenous cultures and knowledge systems, it is a challenging context for coalescing on standardized measures and approaches to wellbeing. While there is plenty of evidence of the effectiveness of policies targeting determinants of wellbeing, there is relatively little evidence about the effectiveness of a wellbeing orientation to policy, overall.	1. Place a transparent, overarching indicator of wellbeing at the top of any evaluation framework to allow for communication and synergies across government departments and programs. 2. Measure social capital and trust as part of any policy program evaluation to evaluate the monetary value of social impacts. 3. Achieve community support for wellbeing policy frameworks through bottom-up processes to define wellbeing, especially in diverse cultural contexts.

Australia (Baddeley, 2025)

Evidence	*Action*
Australia has a high standard of living, but significant happiness and wellbeing gaps, with challenges disproportionately experienced by vulnerable and disadvantaged groups.	1. Harness indigenous ecological knowledge to manage environmental challenges and invest in renewable technologies to limit the impacts of environmental degradation on the quality of life.
The main obstacles are the constitutional constraints and federal system, limiting federal executive power and impeding coordinated responses to wellbeing challenges.	2. Implement a wellbeing framework and policy dialogue via established systems for open and transparent public inquiries.
However, Australia's robust democracy, educated population, and resource-rich status provide a solid foundation to address wellbeing disparities through initiatives like the Australian Wellbeing Framework.	3. Leverage a country's unique characteristics and natural advantages and prioritize policies which improve wellbeing among disadvantaged groups when implementing policies.

United Kingdom (Smithson, 2025)

Evidence	*Action*
Wellbeing in the UK is how we are doing as individuals, communities and nations and how sustainable this is for the future.	1. Consider the improvement of wellbeing and reduction of inequity as concurrent policy goals, adopting an inclusive understanding and definition of wellbeing.
The UK Measures of National Wellbeing framework has 10 topic areas including personal wellbeing, relationships, health, and governance.	2. Use evidence to determine both needs and to assess 'what works' and utilize comprehensive performance measures.
In 2021, HM Treasury introduced guidance for incorporating wellbeing evidence into policy-making, including how to assess and monetize wellbeing impacts.	3. Maximize wellbeing by prioritizing policy areas of work, income, society and governance, emotional mental health, relationships and communities.

Japan (Hiromitsu, Teramura & Oishi, 2025)

Evidence	*Action*
In Japan, the systematic measurement of wellbeing started in the 2010s, which led to the development of the Satisfaction and Quality of Life Survey in 2019. This survey assesses wellbeing using satisfaction across 13 domains. Japan exhibits strengths in the areas such as longevity, safety, and basic economic and lifestyle factors, while experiencing weaknesses in emotional stability, social connections, freedom to make life choices, gender issues, and diversity.	1. Promote the dynamic engagement of citizens, taking into account heterogeneity within the population. 2. Evaluate the expansion of remote work, which has the potential to improve life satisfaction by optimizing work–life balance and reducing commuting time, taking into account productivity in addition to subjective wellbeing. 3. Consider an adoption of the four-day work week, while also evaluating the trade-off between achieving a higher subjective wellbeing and broader societal and economic consequences.

Malta (Briguglio, 2025)

Evidence	*Action*
Malta went through a rapid development over its 60 years of independence and now ranks among the world's top performers on the Human Development Index. However, 'doing well' by traditional metrics does not always translate into people 'feeling good,' as revealed by global measures of subjective wellbeing and more recent data collection at the national level. Specifically for Malta, some aspects that merit attention include environmental quality/engagement, working conditions/time use, corruption perceptions, rising inequality, schools, and obesity.	1. Include subjective wellbeing modules in the existing official surveys and use wellbeing data collected by international organizations to understand wellbeing trends in the country. 2. Establish collaborations between the public sector and research institutions to enhance the impact of research and generate evidence for policy-making. 3. Place wellbeing on the national agenda by establishing a national champion, integrating wellbeing into sectoral policies, harnessing international momentum, and attracting media attention (e.g., focusing communications around the International Day of Happiness).

INDEX

Note: Page numbers in *italics* indicate a figure, and page numbers in **bold** indicate a table on the corresponding page. Page numbers followed by "n" with numbers refer to notes.

FSC
www.fsc.org
MIX
Papier | Fördert gute Waldnutzung
FSC® C083411

Kolibri 360 GmbH
Ferdinand-Jühlke-Straße 7
99095 Erfurt, Deutschland
produktsicherheit@kolibri360.de